PUBLIC RECREATION ADMINISTRATION

PUBLIC RECREATION ADMINISTRATION

Jesse A. Reynolds
Formerly Director of Recreation and Parks Department
City of Richmond, Virginia

Marion N. Hormachea
Virginia Commonwealth University

RESTON PUBLISHING COMPANY, INC.
Reston, Virginia
A Prentice-Hall Company

Library of Congress Cataloging in Publication Data

Reynolds, Jesse A
Public recreation administration.

Includes bibliographies and index.
1. Recreation and state—United States. 2. Recreation—Administration. 3. Parks—Management.
I. Hormachea, Marion N., joint author. II. Title.
GV53.R48 658′.91′7900973 76-5841
ISBN 0-87909-662-4

Reston Publishing Company, Inc.
A Prentice-Hall Company
Reston, Virginia 22090

10 9 8 7 6 5 4 3 2 1

Printed in the United States of America.

Contents

APPENDICES

Preface

This book is based on the practical experiences of a public recreation executive and a recreation educator with the objective of portraying just how public recreation administration functions. It concerns relationships among people, background information, and who and what are involved in the various elements of management. It is designed as a basic text for college courses in administration as well as a guide for the recreation executive, supervisor, staff member, and board member, and gives practical working knowledge and capability in recreation management.

It includes administrative goal setting, objectives, guidelines, observations, successful practices, related examples, possible solutions to problems, and a reservoir of knowledge on which to draw when the individual comes face to face with decision-making situations. It emphasizes involvement of citizens and others affected by management decisions, new ideas, and the many changes taking place in our society. Although the material, to limit volume, is focused primarily on local government, the same general management principles apply to private and semi-private agencies and units of all levels of government. The ultimate objectives are (1) to provide students, recreation professionals, and management personnel with a useful basic foundation of information, resource material, and decision-making capabilities, and (2) to help the individual to be reasonably informed, competent, comfortable, confident, and understanding of the gamut of administrative processes, responsibilities, opportunities, and personal involvements in his or her particular position on the job.

Part I deals with administration foundations such as the overview of recreation and public administration; legal aspects; the general scope of public recreation administration; organization; concepts; elements of the administrative process; agency purposes, objectives, policies, procedures; other administrative guidelines; and municipal, county, regional, state, and federal relationships.

Part II deals with management responsibilities and coordination of resources through staffing, developing, supervising, financing, budgeting, planning, programming, equipping, and human relations.

The main source of information was the authors' actual experience in the various fields of recreation services (private, semi-private, higher education, and all levels of government), supplemented by inspection, observation, problem solving, review of annual reports and other printed material, and discussion with hundreds of informed citizens, practitioners, technicians, professional staff, recreation educators, and participants related to each field of service. The second source resulted from the authors' close association with professional groups, committee work, teaching, research for information from technical and professional sources, professional conferences, workshops, training institutes, and the strong desire of the authors to be where the action was and to research and foster new ideas and improved professional services.

While it is not possible to acknowledge all sources of expert help and information, we especially recognize our professional colleagues, recreation educators, associates, and friends who shared their needs, information, ideas, experiences, problems, and successful practices; Muriel Clarke Reynolds, who did the typing, retyping, and filing; pioneers in recreation, our early instructors and later authors of books from which we have taught—George Hjelte, George D. Butler, Lynn S. Rodney, and Arthur T. Noren; our many staff members and professional associates; national, state, regional, county, and municipal officers (information, reports, resource materials, interviews); The National Recreation and Park Association; the International City Management Association, and various state recreation and park societies. We acknowledge especially James T. Williams, Henry M. Jarvis, Frank M. Mattone, Robert L. Martin, and Philip Leveque for their assistance in the specialized fields of accounting and office management, planning, law, personnel, and finance.

Jesse A. Reynolds
Marion N. Hormachea

PART I

Administrative Foundations

CHAPTER 1

Overview of Recreation and Public Administration

"Recreation" is an important element in the lives of most people but the term "Recreation" has different meanings to different people under different circumstances. Therefore, like many aspects in the broad field of recreation, there is no simple definition that has the same meaning for everyone. People tend to think of "recreation" in terms of their own associations and experiences. All have their points. For instance, the hardworking businessman may think of recreation in terms of getting away from the strains of the day by using commercial recreation activities. The outdoorsman tends to think in terms of hunting, fishing, camping, outdoor life and the pleasures of nature; the athlete, of sports and physical improvement; the educator, of training; the social worker and the medical practitioner in terms of rehabilitation and therapy. Private agencies tend to think in terms of character building, correction and training; the professional recreationist in terms of fun, growth and development—what the activity may do constructively for the individual, group, and community. All of these interpretations have special significance in their respective settings. They are in line with the purposes of recreation and tend to identify a particular concept of service. The executive needs to understand all of the different points of view.

There are negative elements, too, that identify with the word "recreation." It might be interesting to deal with them, but since recreation has gained acceptance principally on its identity with positive benefits to the individual and society, we recommend the positive approach.

Definition of Recreation in a Public Setting

Recreation programs and services are so broad and variable that a meaningful definition for recreation needs also to be broad and inclusive. Public recreation agencies offer a variety of programs and services that must be considered in the definition.

In the pioneer days of recreation, when public recreation was largely confined to the large cities and public parks, there were almost as many definitions as there were career recreation people. There was more of a tendency, then, to use recreation activities as a means of correcting or alleviating individual and community ills. Words like "wholesome" and "constructive" were often, therefore, injected into the definition of recreation.

During the depression years when masses of people could find no work, definitions began to associate recreation as a complement to work such as "Recreation is refreshment of one's strength and spirits after work." [1] This concept has carried forward and applies very well to many situations today. There are, however, retirees, senior citizens, the ill and handicapped, and others in our society who are not working, and recreation can no longer be considered solely as a complement to work but must also be thought of as a way of life.

Unemployment today has a different connotation than it had during the depression. Since then, social security benefits, pension payments for retirees, unemployment compensation, welfare payments, surplus food programs, food stamps and other assistance for those not working have developed and expanded. Most people now have some cash income even if they are not working. Time devoted to leisure has increased relative to that devoted to work during the past generation. Meyer and Brightbill state: "recreation is activity engaged in during leisure and primarily motivated by the satisfaction derived from it." [2]

In recent years the many ways of defining recreation have come closer together and now almost all definitions by professionals emphasize that recreation is an activity engaged in voluntarily during free time and motivated by the satisfaction it gives to the participant. Management may emphasize the *goal-oriented* aspects of recreation. The concept of recreation as perceived by management, therefore, often influences supervisory and management staff in decision making and program planning for the respective agency.

THE GROWING IMPORTANCE OF PUBLIC RECREATION

In strictly rural and sparsely populated areas recreation is liable to be centered around the individual, family, and church and is dependent upon one's own private resources. There is little free time, but plenty of open space and interesting challenges of nature, and public recreation is of less concer machinery, methods, and transportation im- prove le can do more work in less time, rural unem- ploy people move to cities to find work. There they find abor saving devices, shorter working hours, earlier ret vay of life in some ways, but some problems, too, sı disadvantaged people, unemployment, lack of open ime and delinquency. Youngsters and adults with time more prone to get into trouble. These situations affect create the need for outlets for free time and recreation nd, consequently, the need for space, facilities, budget, d administration.

ion methods, procedures, and opportunities, under good can overcome an individual's weaknesses and strengthen his ts through participation. Recreation, therefore, not only pro- vid asure, relaxation, growth and development but also is an important therapeutic factor in rehabilitation, convalescence, re-direction of behavior or interests, and correction. It is, also, a good investment for government to provide planned recreation services in the various settings because of their aid in preventing or solving people problems.

The past two decades have witnessed an unprecedented expansion of recreational services. Especially significant have been the expansion of parks and usable open space, the extension of supervised recreation to seven days a week and the broadening of programs to special groups such as the handicapped, and supervised recreation in convalescent and correctional institutions. There has been a significant increase in the number of county recreation departments and programs have expanded at a surprising rate.

RECREATION AS A FUNCTION OF GOVERNMENT

At the turn of the century, before the impact of the automobile, government, particularly local government, was relatively simple. The basic government functions were the provision of protective services and collection of taxes. Many of the other services we have today were originally provided by private agencies, churches, and philanthropists. The next decade marked the founding of several privately supported national agencies and service organizations of a recreational nature such as Y.W.C.A., 1906 (the Y.M.C.A. had been established in America in 1851); Boys Clubs of America, 1906; 4-H Club, 1907; Boy Scouts of America, 1910; Camp Fire Girls, 1910; and Girl Scouts, 1912.[3]

Justification for Public Recreation

The surplus time that comes with growth of industrialization and improvement in living creates problems that cannot be handled by the individual family, church and private resources. When surplus time becomes a serious community problem, it then becomes a justifiable problem for government.

Most cities and urban populations have not planned for today's recreation needs. Private recreation agencies often cannot expand because of high land values, construction costs and taxes. Many neighborhoods have no private agencies although occupied by low-income families in need of recreational facilities. The only way, therefore, to acquire sufficient space may be for government to use its powers of eminent domain. Only government can afford to provide the variety of facilities necessary for a comprehensive recreation program.

BRIEF HISTORY OF MUNICIPAL RECREATION

The Court House Squares were among the first visible public areas for free public use. One of the first park areas was the Boston Common established by the Colonies in 1634.[4] The success in use of outdoor gymnasia between 1820 and 1840 at several schools and colleges focused attention on physical education and gymnastic programs in educational institutions.[5] By 1860 games and sports had become an essential activity at schools and colleges. The interest carried over to the organization of sporting clubs. At mid-century, several cities took positive action in establishment of public parks. For instance, in 1851, the city of Richmond, Virginia, acquired with public funds land for park purposes and established three parks in different areas of the city.[6] In 1853, New York City acquired the first large park, 843 acres of land which is now Central Park; Fairmont Park in Philadelphia was acquired in 1867, and Franklin Park in Boston in 1883.[7] Other cities followed suit in the acquisition of park lands but for many years municipal parks were used mainly for rest, meditation, and passive recreation. In 1872, Congress established the first national park in western Wyoming known as Yellowstone National Park.[8]

In 1881, a Division of Forestry was established in the U.S. Department of Agriculture. This has become the U.S. Forest Service and is now one of the principal providers of recreation opportunities. Niagara Falls, New York, was set aside as a public reservation in 1885 and Fort Mackinac was given to Michigan as the first of that state's recreational areas. Also, in 1885 New York State instituted the first comprehensive forestry administration act in America.[9] It began acquisition of the Adirondack and Catskill areas for forest and recreation preserves which led other states to begin acquiring land for recreation purposes. The New England Association of Park Superintendents, forerunner of the America Institute of Park Executives, was established in 1898.[10]

The Beginning of Public Recreation

One of the first events which initiated the recreation movement occurred in 1885. It was the establishment in Boston of the sand gardens, the outdoor play center for children, which consisted mainly of a large, privately supervised sand pile. For this reason, Boston is credited by professionals as being the birthplace of public recreation. In the 1890's several cities set up park boards and commissions.[11] In 1892, after a study of needs, Boston passed enabling legislation and set up a unified metropolitan park commission, the first in the United States, which has been used as a model by other cities.[12] In 1895 Essex County, New Jersey, established the first county park system.[13] In 1901 several playgrounds were operated by the Boston School Committee, thereby extending recreation administration to the schools.[14] In 1904, Los Angeles appointed a board of playground commissioners which created a separate playground function of government.[15] In 1905, Chicago used a highly publicized and successful $5,000,000 bond issue to develop and open ten recreation parks for family use.[16] This added impetus to the spread of the recreation movement westward. Chicago was credited by professionals with setting a new standard in park recreation development and expanding the recreation programs from mainly sports to the arts and indoor activities. The parks contained a variety of athletic facilities usable the year round, including field houses with a gymnasium, showers, dressing rooms, assembly hall and club rooms.

Many cities had not planned for recreation areas and, like the situation today, the public economy did not favor acquisitions of improved land and razing of buildings on them for recreation purposes. Localities looked, therefore, to the use of parks, schools and open spaces for the development of the new recreational services. This led to several states passing enabling legislation to permit the use of school facilities—playgrounds, pools, gymnasia, auditoriums, special activities rooms, classrooms—for community recreation purposes when they were not in use for school purposes.

Leadership and Training

There were no trained experts in the new recreation movement; therefore, there was quite a demand for advice and assistance from those with recreation experience. In April 1906, the Playground Association of America, a non-profit private service organization, was founded.[17] This proved to be one of the most significant developments for park and recreation administration. It soon provided competent and dedicated national leadership, field and research workers, and served as a pool and clearing house for information. It also conducted national conventions, published technical books, established standards, made surveys, provided personnel services, trained leaders and administrators, and advised communities about their recreation problems free or at nominal cost. The name was broadened in 1911 to "Playground and Recreation Association of America." In 1966, it merged with several professional recreation organizations and became the "National Recreation and Park Association" which is the umbrella organization for the several national professional and lay organizations in the recreation field.

In 1911, courses in recreation activities were conducted at Chicago Training School for Playground Workers and, in 1912, The New York School of Forestry at Syracuse University was the first college to present a definite program for the training of professionals for parks administration and city forestry.[18] In 1915, New Jersey was the first state to enact the modern type of legislation which, in one law, provides every municipality in the state with general powers to conduct a broad recreation program under any organization of the local government which the municipality may consider most effective or desirable.[19] In 1916, the National Park Service was established.[20] The National Conference of State Parks was established in 1921[21] to assist in state park administrative problems. The concept of parks changed to include active recreational activities. From 1926 to 1935, the National Recreation School was conducted by the National Recreation Association to provide graduate training in parks and recreation administration for about 35 enrollees each year or a total of about 300 men and women graduates.

A recreation and municipal forestry major was established in the Department of Forestry, Michigan State University, in 1935. A full program of recreation education at the undergraduate and graduate levels was established at New York University in 1936.[22]

The Federal Emergency Programs

Beginning in the mid 1930's, the Work Projects Administration (WPA), the National Youth Administration (NYA), and the Civilian Conservation

Corps (CCC) provided two types of recreation-related assistance: (1) jobs for unemployed persons and (2) development of recreation areas and facilities. Most cities expanded their recreation programs and facilities with these relief funds and many villages, towns, and counties with the help of lay leadership and "in kind" contributions provided their citizens supervised recreation programs for the first time. Under these programs, leaders, volunteers, supervisors, and administrators were trained, extensive recreation research was done, and an abundance of recreation information was prepared and distributed. These were the forerunners of many of the fine recreation programs and facilities in the United States today.

Additional Professional Recreation Organizations

The American Camping Association was organized in 1924.[23] It publishes the monthly *Camping Magazine* and provides for camping interests.

In 1937, the American Association for Health, Physical Education, and Recreation (AAHPER) was founded as a branch of the National Education Association.[24] It has been effective in extending recreation in the public schools.

State recreation societies were organized, beginning in the 1930's, and in October 1938, the Society of Recreation Workers of America (later, [1946] the American Recreation Society and [1966] the American Park and Recreation Society) was organized.[25] It was the major professional organization for recreation personnel and executives at the national level. Membership was provided for special interest sections such as Hospital, Armed Forces, Industrial, Rural, and State.

Other Important Events

North Carolina established the first State Recreation Commission in March, 1945.[26] It was not only instrumental in establishing recreation departments at the local level but also cooperated with other states and localities in initiating public recreation and park programs.

Park management and recreation administration were included in college curricula in the 1950's. Graduates were employed in administrative positions in small communities.

The American Recreation Society adopted a model plan for the registration of professional recreation personnel, including executives in 1954,[27] and this has been used as a minimum standard for the profession generally. It was distributed to all ARS members in the ARS publication, the *Quarterly Bulletin,* July 1955.

In 1962, the establishment of the Bureau of Outdoor Recreation in the Department of Interior provided a broader recreation service at the federal level.

Developments Following World War II

Federal funds were made available for the acquisition and development of open space through the Department of Housing and Urban Development (HUD) grant-in-aid programs and the Land and Water Conservation Fund of the Department of the Interior. The Economic Opportunity Act, which provided jobs for young men, was helpful, as were the federal revenue sharing allotments provided to local governments for recreation and other services.

Living memorials of a recreation nature, such as parks, athletic fields, swimming pools, and recreation buildings, were established in many communities in memory of those who served their country.

Information, facilities and programs for older adults developed rapidly after 1950. States and localities organized commissions and staffs to assist in providing for the needs, including recreation, of the older citizen. New emphasis was also placed on the involvement of youth in the planning, coordinating, development and operation of recreation programs, facilities and services for youth.

There was a rapid increase in the number of colleges and universities which established curricula in recreation. Community colleges also included recreation courses in their curricula.

The development of theme parks such as "The Safari Country" in Kings Dominion (1974) near Richmond, Virginia, and "The Old Country" in Busch Gardens (1975) near Williamsburg, Virginia, even though privately owned, have attracted 15,000–20,000 visitors a weekend, and may indicate a trend which may serve to supplement the activities of the public parks.

RECENT CHANGES AFFECTING THE ROLE OF PUBLIC RECREATION

The growth of all phases of the recreation movement has been phenomenal since the end of World War II. In addition to state parks, forests and game and wildlife programs, states have added or enlarged their planning, coordination, promotion and consultation activities and have appropriated funds for the acquisition, development and protection of recreation areas, scenic rivers, open spaces, beaches and flood plains. Many have added recreation staff to provide recreation services within the state institutions.

States have made recreation and park surveys and prepared long range plans, both at the state level and at that of their political subdivisions, and have gone a long way towards implementing the plans. State grant programs and agencies for administering state and federal grant monies have been established.

Changing Times and Values

In the 1960's and early 1970's communities experienced many changes which affected values in general and the attitude of the public towards recreation. The change which has created the most far reaching results has been the development of federal grant programs and the surrender of state and local controls under federal pressure. This has produced new guidelines, standards, program emphasis, social and political values, and a tendency towards uniformity of guidelines under federal supervision. Local and state governments, short of new sources of local revenue, have tended to be dependent on the federal government for funds and this has, in turn, resulted in greatly increased federal control, often politically oriented. Many local programs were developed with federal funding in accord with federal requirements rather than local priorities. There were workable local program plans, including open space plans, new zoning codes, building codes, plumbing codes, electrical codes, flood control projects, flood plain zoning, open space programs, reduction and elimination of overhead power lines in parks, urban renewal and urban redevelopment and model cities programs. Emphasis was on aesthetics, community development, conservation, antipollution, and programs for the disadvantaged and minority groups.

Some parks became a focal point for protests, demonstrations, controversies, and resistance to police as a result of resentment against the draft, the Vietnam War, busing, and other controversial issues of the time.

In physical developments, there were multiple-use buildings, innovations in playgrounds, the conversion of streets in downtown sections to park-like malls, emphasis on bicycle paths and routes, scenic river plans to protect streams for recreation, scenic or open space easements to protect views without having to acquire the land.

Programs for special groups were developed, including those for the mentally and physically handicapped, senior citizens, and youth. Recent developments have added new challenges for the recreation specialist and executive.

Changes Within Urban Areas

1. *Populations needing extra services* have concentrated in cities where service and facilities such as those dealing with health, welfare, recreation and public transportation are more readily available to

them. This is especially true of the older adults, the disadvantaged, and the handicapped. There has been a corresponding increase in the cost of these services.

2. *The flight of the more affluent to the suburbs* has put pressure on counties to establish county recreation services and has drained off support and many good lay leaders from municipal programs.
3. *Inflation* has caused great increases in the recreation budget without a corresponding increase in services. In fact, in the late sixties and early seventies some cities curtailed their recreation staffs and programs to balance city expenses with available funds.
4. *Increased recreation needs* in built-up areas, particularly in central multiple family areas, the scarcity and fantastic rise in the cost of suitable land, and competition for land in general became a major problem for recreation agencies.
5. *More leisure time* available for all as a result of the shorter work week, longer vacations, and early retirement has brought about an increased demand for recreation services.
6. *Demands for higher standards, variety, and quality of programs* are being voiced by the public, emphasizing the need to achieve perfection in recreation programs and services. Some cities have emphasized "culture" in the naming of their recreation agency, using names such as "Department of Culture and Recreation", which may include the public library, performing arts, and human services.
7. *The urbanization of rural areas near adjoining cities* has made open land in and immediately adjoining cities almost non-existent.
8. *The growth of private recreation* has included the development of two types of private recreation service: (1) that provided by subdividers and apartment house complexes; and (2) the membership recreation association which provides indoor and outdoor facilities for the family and may include golf, tennis, basketball, swimming pool, club rooms, meeting rooms, meals and refreshments. The apartment recreation complex may also involve payment of dues and management by the occupants.
9. *The mobile population* has crowded into preferred recreation facilities, creating problems of maintenance and supervision. Families from outlying areas often find their recreation at municipal facilities. The city taxpayers insist on first use of facilities and this creates strong feelings on both sides. Some jurisdictions charge fees, or higher fees, for non-resident enrollees and others try to give residents priority scheduling, but no completely satisfactory method has been found to handle non-resident participation except where admissions and fees are charged.

10. *Federal and state grant-in-aid programs* have brought about many changes in the park and recreation field. They made it possible for government agencies at all levels: (1) to initiate and expand public park and recreation programs; (2) to acquire and develop land for park and recreation purposes; (3) to preserve open space and natural areas; and (4) to make it possible for smaller communities and towns to establish a public recreation and park service.
11. *Recreation is called on to do many jobs,* which go beyond the normal public recreation program of the past, such as: (a) to provide temporary housing and recreation services during mass evacuations and emergencies; (b) to provide counteracting activities to "cool" the population against violence and riots; (c) to provide activities that appeal to school drop-outs, work drop-outs, non-conformists, and others with unoccupied time, to try to direct their interest to more positive activities; (d) to sponsor state and federally funded projects for the disadvantaged and poor, including free lunches, youth employment, and educational trips.

Outdoor Recreation

In recent years there has been a "back to nature" movement in recreation activities. Outdoor recreation has been expanded at all levels.

Facilities have included new and enlarged parks, particularly at state and local levels. The transfer of government land and federal funds for open space acquisition and development have helped communities with their land problems. Localities have passed flood plain zoning which has restricted construction on areas subject to destructive flooding, and made much needed space available for outdoor recreation.

GENERAL SCOPE OF PUBLIC RECREATION ADMINISTRATION

The previous paragraphs have outlined important events leading to the development of public recreation administration. It is well now to review briefly the present scope of public recreation administration. At each level and sub-level of government, administration of public recreation may be involved in several ways.

Public Recreation Administration at the Local Level

Local public recreation administration includes municipal, county, borough, special district, township, village (town), or any subdivisions, thereof. Local government, being closest to the people it serves, is called on to provide a wide variety of recreation facilities, programs, and services for the people residing within its jurisdiction. The distinguishing feature of the role of local government is the direct face-to-face leadership which it provides. Services are focused on the interests of the people they serve, primarily those living within the boundaries of the jurisdiction. A wide variety of administrative units may occur:

1. Public park and/or recreation agencies having general facilities such as indoor and outdoor recreation centers; special facilities such as marinas, golf courses, and amphitheatres; and special programs for senior citizens, youth, the handicapped, and others.
2. Independent public recreation facilities and programs such as arenas, botanical gardens, coliseums, libraries, museums, stadiums, aquariums, zoos, and others.
3. Public recreation programs managed as secondary functions by agencies primarily concerned with activities such as public works, schools and public housing.
4. District or regional operations in which two or more public jurisdictions participate in a cooperative joint program under a single administration, such as the Upper Valley Regional Park Authority, Harrisonburg, Virginia.
5. Local units of federal or state recreation agencies, such as park and forest areas, and camp sites.

Public Recreation Administration at the State Level

Public recreation at the state level includes:

1. State parks and forests and their sub-divisions including beaches, museums, camping areas, and other special recreation facilities;
2. State recreation commissions or other recreation advisory services agencies;
3. Professional training in colleges and universities and outreach programs;
4. Recreation in institutions such as hospitals, confinement and rehabilitation facilities;
5. Special commissions such as those for youth or older citizens, or the Commissions of Outdoor Recreation which administer federal and state recreation grant programs such as Land and Water Conservation Funds, and Fish and Game; and

6. Others, such as historic and prehistoric sites, scenic and natural areas, and winter sports facilities.

Public Recreation Administration at the National Level

The Recreation and Park Yearbook 1966 prepared and published by the National Recreation Association [28] lists 72 agencies of the federal government including 3 presidential committees, 9 departments and their 49 agencies and programs, and 11 independent agencies or commissions that provide recreation and related services. Several of the agencies have regional and state units and special programs. Federal agencies, therefore, have a widespread involvement in public recreation administration at national, state, and local levels, especially those involved in natural resources and grants-in-aid programs. For instance, the federal government has a rule of not permitting property acquired for parks or recreation purposes with the use of federal funds to be used for other purposes without federal approval as specified in Section 5 of the "Land and Water Conservation Act of 1965" which provides:

> No property acquired or developed with assistance under this section shall, without the approval of the Secretary, be converted to other than public outdoor recreation uses. The Secretary shall approve such conversion only if he finds it to be in accord with the then existing comprehensive statewide outdoor recreation plan and only upon such conditions as he deems necessary to assure the substitution of other recreation properties of at least equal fair market value and of reasonably equivalent usefulness and location.

Questions for Discussion

1. What is the purpose of public recreation?
2. How would you define the term "recreation"?
3. Why has recreation grown in importance in recent years?
4. How would you determine the scope of services in planning a local public recreation agency?
5. What have been the significant influences in the development of public recreation?
6. How has the role of public recreation changed in recent years?
7. What influence does the state have on local recreation operations? The federal government?
8. What do you consider is the present role of public recreation? Of private agency recreation?

9. Historically, how do public recreation agencies relate to private recreation agencies? To commercial recreation?

Short Problems

1. In a community of your choice, study and outline the changes within the past decade that have affected public recreation.
2. List and describe briefly the factors that influence the administration of a public recreation agency.

References

1. *Webster's Elementary Dictionary,* rev. ed., 1941, s.v. "Recreation".
2. Harold D. Meyer and Charles K. Brightbill, *Recreation Administration* (Englewood Cliffs, N.J.: Prentice-Hall, Inc., 1956), p. 1.
3. Charles E. Doell and Gerald B. Fitzgerald, *A Brief History of Parks and Recreation in the United States* (Chicago: The Athletic Institute, 1954), p. 118.
4. *Ibid,* p. 56.
5. *Ibid,* p. 58.
6. Council Minutes, Richmond, Va., 1851.
7. Doell and Fitzgerald, *A Brief History,* p. 58.
8. *Ibid,* p. 33.
9. Alfred B. LaGasse and Walter L. Cook, *History of Parks and Recreation,* Management Aids, Bulletin No. 56 (Arlington, Va.: National Recreation and Park Association, Reprinted 1974), pp. 14-15.
10. *Ibid,* p. 16.
11. Doell and Fitzgerald, *A Brief History,* p. 58.
12. *Ibid,* p. 33.
13. *Ibid,* p. 58.
14. *Ibid,* p. 70.
15. *Ibid,* p. 71.
16. *Ibid,* p. 70.
17. *Ibid,* p. 100.
18. LaGasse and Cook, *History of Parks,* pp. 20-21.
19. *Municipal Recreation Administration,* 3rd ed. (Chicago, The International City Manager's Association, 1948), pp. 292-93.
20. LaGasse and Cook, *History of Parks,* p. 21.

21. *Ibid,* p. 22.
22. *Ibid,* pp. 25-26.
23. Doell and Fitzgerald, *A Brief History,* p. 97.
24. LaGasse and Cook, *History of Parks,* p. 25.
25. *The American Recreation Society—Its Early Years 1937-1952* (Washington, D.C.: The American Recreation Society, 1953).
26. North Carolina Senate Bill No. 140, An Act to Create a State Recreation Commission (1945).
27. *Quarterly Bulletin* (The American Recreation Society, July 1955).
28. *Recreation and Park Yearbook 1966* (Washington, D.C.: National Recreation and Park Association, 1967).

Selected Readings

Brightbill, Charles K., *Man and Leisure: A Philosophy of Recreation.* Englewood Cliffs, N.J.: Prentice-Hall, Inc., 1971.

Corbin, H. Dan, and William J. Tait, *Education For Leisure,* pp. 3-46. Englewood Cliffs, N.J.: Prentice-Hall, Inc., 1973.

Doell, Charles E., and Gerald B. Fitzgerald, *A Brief History of Parks and Recreation in the United States.* Chicago: Athletic Institute, 1954.

Dulles, Foster Rhea, *A History of Recreation: America Learns to Play* (2nd ed.) New York: Appleton-Century-Crofts, 1966.

Fitch, Edwin M., and John E. Shankin, *The Bureau of Outdoor Recreation,* pp. 3-78. New York: Praeger Publishers, 1970.

Heady, Ferrel, *Public Administration: A Comparative Perspective.* Englewood Cliffs, N.J.: Prentice-Hall, Inc., 1966.

Hjelte, George, and Jay S. Shivers, *Public Administration of Recreational Services,* pp. 3-26. Philadelphia: Lea and Febiger, 1972.

Hormachea, Marion N., and Carroll R. Hormachea, *Recreation in Modern Society.* Boston: Holbrook Press, Inc., 1972.

Kando, Thomas M., *Leisure and Popular Culture in Transition.* St. Louis: The C.V. Mosby Company, 1975.

Kraus, Richard G., and Joseph E. Curtis, *Creative Administration in Recreation and Parks,* pp. 1-15. St. Louis: The C.V. Mosby Company, 1973.

Lutzin, Sidney G., and Edward H. Storey, *Managing Municipal Leisure Services,* pp. 14-38. Washington, D.C.: International City Management Association, 1973.

Rodney, Lynn S., *Administration of Public Recreation,* pp. 3-25. New York: The Ronald Press, 1964.

CHAPTER 2

Introduction to Administration

Administration deals with management of people and also involves the management of other resources—money, materials, equipment, tools, information, land, and structures. Therefore, *administration* may be defined as the process of organizing and managing people and other resources to accomplish a predetermined purpose. Stated plainly, the purpose of administration is to get a job done as efficiently, effectively, and economically as possible.

The scope, concepts, and nature of public recreation services usually are established in a general way by legislative action when the charter or other action which establishes the recreation agency and grants it certain authority and responsibilities is approved.

CONCEPTS AND MEANINGS

Public recreation administration functions have not only increased in scope but also have changed in character in recent years. Modern methods have made community services increasingly more technical and less intelligible to the public. As a result, there is dependence on specialized services which have added complications to administration. Values, methods of dealing with people, motivations, standards, and ways of life are being changed with emphasis being placed on quality of performance, preservation of nature, ecology, and preservation of our natural resources.

Growth of Management

Basically, the functions of management involve the direction of the very important elements of the administrative process. Changing social conditions, the growth of big business, big government, and big labor, as well as the increasing complexity of life all have a decided impact upon various fields of service. As a result, not only do these fields change to survive, but also new fields develop as dynamic forces. Such is the case in the emergence of management in the twentieth century; important not only as a separate entity, but also as one exerting a great influence on how other professional fields conduct their basic activities.

Relationship Of Administration And Management

While there is a tendency to consider "administration" and "management" as synonymous terms, we will consider them separately in attempting to clarify the concepts. According to Tead, administration is the comprehensive effort to direct and guide human resources towards specific ends in order to achieve certain desired and defined objectives.[1] There are numerous other definitions of administration advanced by countless authors, but each states or implies similar elements. Rodney sums this up by saying, "administration is the process that mobilizes an organization's resources, human and material, to attain predetermined goals. Thus the goals must be chartered and a direction given." [2]

If we accept the premise that it is the purpose of administration to set the goals of the organization, then it is logical to consider that management's purpose is to work towards the achievement of these goals. Management, then, can be considered as dealing with the coordination and direction of the organization's efforts to achieve those predetermined goals which are set by the administration.

Who Are the Administrators and the Managers

Pursuing this philosophy, we may view persons and their roles and functions in an organization in the following manner. Depending upon the type of organization (i.e., industry, educational institution, municipal, or county department of recreation and parks), the terminology used to designate those performing managerial functions may vary.

Level	Examples and Functions
Policy making	Elected members of a city council or county board of supervisors; policy making recreation boards and commissions (public, private, or voluntary agencies); owners of a company (private industry).

	Determine *what* will be done and the purpose (mission) of agency.
Administration	City or county managers; directors of departments of recreation and parks; directors of other municipal or county departments; bureau chiefs of large departments. Referred to also as "top level management." Carry out (execute) policy set by the policy makers. Also advise boards on policy matters and have wide latitude and authority in implementing policy and determining *how* it will be done.
Managers	Divisional or bureau chiefs; district or program superintendents. Referred to as "middle management." Managers implement policy established at higher levels.
	Supervisors. Referred to sometimes as "bottom management." Implement policy through working with level below and appraising and improving services provided.
Providers of Service	Program (leadership or instructional) personnel at both professional and technical levels; clerical staff; park and facility maintenance personnel. Referred to as "non-managers." Render direct service to public or function as specialists.

In writing about managers as a classification of personnel, Massie and Douglas refer to managers as "persons who get things done through others . . ." This very simple and broad statement includes all kinds of managers—the president of U.S. Steel, a day care center director, or the administrator of an educational institution.[3] They go on to point out that managers have one thing in common—subordinates who work under them. However, the term "manager" refers to a very diversified population.[4]

Elements of the Administrative Process

The management responsibility is to take a group of individuals, with and without technical training, and to mold them into a performing organization that will attain established objectives efficiently. This may involve one or more of eight elements of the administrative process. The first seven are described by Gulick and Urwick as planning, organizing, directing, staffing, coordinating, reporting, budgeting.[5] Rodney includes evaluating.[6] Researching is growing in importance and soon may be classified as an element.

1. *Planning* is assembling information, examining the needs, facts, resources and alternatives; looking ahead, setting objectives, and determining a course of action. Recreation needs are constantly changing and planning, therefore, is a continuous process. To plan is to explore alternative courses of action, to visualize their consequences, and to evaluate all aspects in determining the best use of resources. Everyone involved, including the public, when possible, takes part in the planning.
2. *Organizing* is the mobilizing and grouping of resources into functional units, assigning responsibilities, and delegating authority commensurate with responsibilities to perform certain assignments.
3. *Directing* comprises decision making, selecting objectives, implementing plans, giving instruction and assignments, controlling, and leading the organization and focusing all of its resources to achieve the desired objectives.
4. *Staffing* is selecting, assigning, developing, and motivating human resources to perform the functions of the agency.
5. *Coordinating* is bringing together for unified action various resources needed to achieve an objective.
6. *Reporting* is assembling, reviewing, and presenting information in usable form.
7. *Budgeting* is planning for the fiscal needs of the organization and controlling monetary resources.
8. *Evaluating* is the process of comparing, appraising or measuring the relative worth of a project, program, or other item against standards of perfection, including the achievement of goals or objectives. It is closely associated with planning, research and directing.

These elements are the basic components used in planning this book and will be discussed in detail in later chapters.

MANAGEMENT BY OBJECTIVES

Certain management techniques have been established to increase motivation, based on evidence that some appraisal and motivational programs ensure good results. One such program is Management by Objectives

(MBO), which was first developed for private industry. The first use of the concept and term "Management by Objectives" was made by Peter Drucker in 1954.[7] Odiorne describes Management by Objectives as, "a process whereby the superior and the subordinate managers of an organization jointly identify its common goals, define each individual's major areas of responsibility in terms of results expected of him and use these measures as guides for operating the unit and assessing the contribution of each of its members." [8]

Mali defines Managing by Objectives as "a strategy of planning and getting results in the direction that management wishes and needs to take while meeting the goals and satisfactions of its participants. In its simplest form, it is blending individual plans and needs of managers towards a large-scale accomplishment within a specific period of time." [9]

There is nothing in the concept of MBO that differs from or negates other management principles such as planning, organizing, coordinating, etc. Rather it is an intrinsic part of all of them. There will be, of course, different procedures in implementing MBO within different settings such as public agencies, business, industry, and educational institutions, due to the number of variables involved. Basically, MBO involves setting priorities and allocating resources for both long and short term goals and objectives and communicating this information throughout the organization, both up and down the organizational ladder.

As we consider MBO further, it becomes apparent that this managerial technique works on two major levels. One level refers to MBO for an entire complex or system of operations. The other involves the individual himself and plans for his growth and development, and through this, his contribution to the total effort of the system of which he is a part.

Examples of the first level would be MBO for an entire city, county, recreation and parks system, industry, or educational institution. The other, or personal, level would be exemplified by a supervisor and employee in any of the afore-mentioned settings planning together and mutually establishing and agreeing upon specific items of performance and their completion times for the employee. This mutual approach to establishing goals for the individual constitutes the behavioral approach to job evaluation. After a specified period of time the supervisor and employee appraise the progress made towards the objectives which they established. In *Fundamentals of Management* the extensive works of several authors writing on MBO are synthesized as follows:

1. Superiors and subordinates meet and discuss goals (results) for the subordinates which are in line with the overall organizational goals.
2. The superior and subordinate jointly establish attainable goals for the subordinate.

3. The superior and subordinate meet again after the initial goals are established and evaluate the subordinate's performance in terms of the goals. The essential feature is that the *feedback* on performance is provided the subordinate. The subordinate knows where he stands with regard to his contribution to his organizational unit and the firm.[10]

Four basic ingredients of any MBO plan, according to Mali, are: (1) objectives; (2) time strategy; (3) total management; and (4) individual motivation.[11]

The *objectives* of a recreation and parks department may be to increase program participation, to develop new programs, to improve facility maintenance and attractiveness, to improve cost accounting methods, and to effect better citizen relations programs. Objectives for the individual could be to improve leadership techniques, to complete a directed reading program, to reduce absenteeism or tardiness, to develop more cooperative employee and community relationships and to develop specific new programs.

Time strategy refers to the coordination of human and material resources to achieve the objectives within designated time frames and involves the coordination and timing of the overall agency efforts as well as those of each bureau, division, location, and individual.

Total management involves the coordination of efforts and input from each manager (supervisor, superintendent, bureau chief, and director) towards the common goal.

Finally, *individual motivation* deals with the participation of each individual in the setting of objectives for his agency and himself and the working towards mutual goals.

Differentiating Among Purposes, Goals, and Objectives

Many people experience difficulty in differentiating among purposes, goals, and objectives as they apply to administration and management. Indeed, some agencies implementing MBO for the first time find that they spend considerable time in clarifying and separating these terms before they can proceed with the formulation of specific objectives. It would be helpful, therefore, to refer to Rodney's definitions and manner of relating these terms. He says, "it is obvious that the effectiveness of a recreation system is judged by how well objectives are attained, and if administration is the directing force that propels the organization towards them, a clear understanding of terms is necessary."[12]

Rodney goes on to define "purpose" as the ultimate or long range goal to be achieved, this term being synonymous with "goal," "end," or "aim." In many agencies this is referred to as "purposing" and relates to *why* the agency exists—what is its reason for being.

"Objectives," however, are viewed by Rodney as *attainable ends* which are more immediately visible.[13] These objectives, of course, are met through programs which are aimed at their achievement. Schematically we could view it this way:

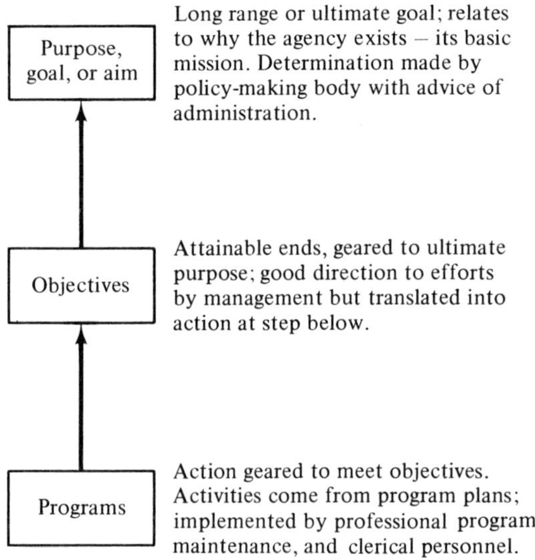

Purposes (or goals) being long range and idealistic are somewhat remote and, perhaps, never fully attainable. However, specifically stated objectives are attainable within certain planned time frames (six months, one year, three years, five years, etc.) and give direction to behavior and effort. Each of these objectives will have a program plan of activities, detailing how they will be met, the time schedule for doing this, and a cost analysis. Based on this information, available resources then can be allocated.

MBO is a way of showing what is expected and of measuring what actually is achieved. It sometimes is referred to as "Management by Results," whereas managing by handling problems as they arise is called "Management by Crisis." MBO is based on the premise that everyone in the organization knows not only the purpose (goal) and the specific objectives to be achieved (results) but also the time frames for accomplishing these. In other words, each person has had a voice in determining where he is going and when he will arrive at his destination. Objectives

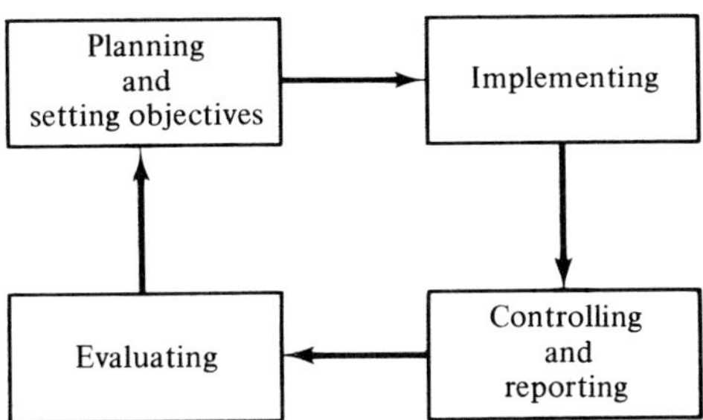

can range from very broad ones which will require considerable time to accomplish, to more immediate and specific day to day objectives that can be met in a short time. MBO develops a more methodical approach to planning, integrating the long range purpose or goal with more immediate objectives, and emphasizing individual and group efficiency. In a large department of recreation and parks where there are various bureaus, divisions, and special staff services, there must be, of course, a hierarchy of objectives. The city, county, or agency will have certain broad objectives; each department will have more specific objectives. The various bureaus and their numerous divisions will have objectives and, finally, each position will have assigned objectives.

To assess effectiveness, there must be provisions for periodic appraisal of the functioning of the organization's various units, as well as evaluation of the performance of each employee. It is only through continuous study followed by objective appraisal that improvement of the individual and, through him, improvement of the organization and its services can occur.

The problems of initiating MBO in public agencies are different from those of private industry for which MBO was first designed. There are three problem areas, according to Brady: (1) defining objectives; (2) measuring benefits; and (3) the operating cycle.[14] For example, private industry is profit-motivated, whereas the objectives of a large city and its recreation department are diverse and not as quickly and easily defined and pin-pointed. The measurement of benefits is difficult for the public sector, whereas private industry can easily determine profits. In terms of the operating cycle, the annual budgets of government agencies make long range plans somewhat uncertain.

While there are problems involved in implementing MBO in recreation agencies, the assets of this management system outweigh the difficulties. The advantages lie primarily in the fact that the recreator is forced to plan, to define objectives clearly and to organize programs consistent with these objectives. This motivates the manager and his or her staff.

DEPARTMENT OF RECREATION AND PARKS
MBO

Staff: | *Bureau:*__________

*Division:*__________

Period: from______to______ *Section:*__________

	Objectives	Starting date	Activities planned to meet objectives	Finish date	Achieved efforts/results	Man days	Estimated cost
1			*1* *2* *3* *4*				
2			*1* *2* *3* *4*				
3			*1* *2* *3* *4*				
4			*1* *2* *3* *4*				
5			*1* *2* *3* *4*				

FIGURE 2-1.

Because staff members at all levels have contributed to the determination of the organization's objectives and the target dates for meeting them, a sense of pride in achievement is fostered. While increased paperwork will result, the designing of standardized forms such as those presently used for other types of reporting can simplify this task. See Fig. 2-1.

MAKE-UP OF THE PUBLIC SECTOR

The government is composed of three distinct branches: (1) The legislative which enacts laws and makes policies, including those bearing on fiscal matters such as setting tax rates, fees, and charges, makes appropriations and budget allocations, and makes contracts or other legal commitments on behalf of the citizens; (2) The judicial which is responsible for administering justice; and (3) The executive (management) which puts into practice and implements the laws and carries out the services and work programs of government. Although there is no direct administrative relationship among the three branches, it is important that there be a close cooperative interrelationship among them if the most effective results are to be achieved. For instance, the executive branch should consult with the judicial branch on legal matters and make recommendations to the legislative body concerning technical and good operational matters. The system breaks down and loses effectiveness when members of the legislative branch or the judicial branch attempt to influence or direct the administration of any program or service of the executive branch or vice versa. This book, of course, is concerned mainly with matters pertaining to the executive branch but includes discussions of pertinent relationships with the legislative and judicial branches when they concern operational matters.

Public Recreation Administration

The administration of public recreation is a little more involved than the administration of most public services. Its activities involve directly or indirectly the total community and many of its organizations because recreation deals with an everyday need for all people. It works best when citizens are involved with planning, decision making, and delivery of services. It relates to: (1) Planning, communicating, regulating, and directing individuals and groups that use agency services; (2) Consulting and planning with parents and community and group leaders; (3) Planning, coordinating, and cooperating with community agencies, news media, institutions, and other government agencies; (4) Evaluating and reporting to the administration or policy board and the public in general. In varying degrees, the recreation executive and staff serve as leaders and tend to mobilize, coordinate, and guide the total recreation resources of the community to accomplish community recreation objectives. The public agency makes a major contribution to the total accomplishment.

The public recreation agency is in a position of community leadership and is expected to practice in all its dealings the good qualities of leadership and effective human relations. It is not expected to use its authority in any way to manage and control recreation activities beyond the specific jurisdictions of the agency.

Administration is more than knowledge; it is skill, leadership, and good judgement developed through practice and experience in dealing with the intangible qualities of human beings. In recreation, administrative experience is an important factor because it deals with such a variety of people and circumstances. No set of rules or list of successful practices can be applied equally to two different situations with the same results. An effective administrator has a "feel" for what a specific set of circumstances requires. The ability to practice good human relations is a major contributing factor in successful recreation administration.

GENERAL POLICIES AND GUIDELINES

Once the concepts, purposes, objectives, and services to be provided by the agency have been decided, general policies, practices, procedures, rules, and regulations are established to provide direction in their implementation. Policies are necessary as guides in decision making to keep efforts channeled in the direction of goals and to prevent resources from being diverted to other uses, which is a constant danger in recreation with its many facets of interest.

A *policy* is a course of action. It is particularly important in conserving staff time, providing maximum use of resources and guiding relationships. Administrative policies, such as purpose, budget, salaries, and charges are determined by the legislative board and can be changed only by that board. Management policies, such as program, safety, scheduling, and staff management may be determined and modified by the executive so long as they conform to and are consistent with administrative purposes and policies.

Conserving Staff Time

A public agency has many legitimate calls for use of staff time for purposes neither included in objectives nor in the budget. This has led, in some instances, to work weeks of as many as 50 to 60 hours for conscientious workers who voluntarily choose to use some of their own time to try to accomplish requests for service by the public. A sound administrative policy helps to alleviate that kind of situation. For example, the objective may be "to provide trained and experienced supervision at each recreation location." The budget makes proper provision for this but people sometimes request leadership for such items as a picnic in the park, a program at the church, or help in installing swings at a private agency, and so on. These are worthy requests for the good of the total community recreation program, but the performance budget provides that every person work for 8 hours a day (40 hours a week) in conducting programs which the policy board has approved in the budget. Other services must be on staff time or substituted for normal authorized assignments. Differences will show up in cost accounting records. If a service is performed for one group or individual, it should be performed for all on the same basis. Likewise, a policy must apply equally to all under the same circumstances. A policy (not a rule, not a law) is thoughtfully prepared and checked out with staff and board. An example is to "provide leadership at public places (or legally rented places) open to the general public." This does not completely limit requests accepted but it reduces them considerably, identifies the course of action for staff, and gives direction because it limits operations to public places.

Maximum Use of Resources

The public tends to think government has unlimited resources. Expenditures, of course, are usually limited by law to the amount of income a government has and the proportion of that income which has been allocated in the budget by the legislative body for use of the agency. There are many justifiable requests from citizens for services not included in the budget. In an inflating economy, the budget may fall short of providing funds for normal needs rather than providing a surplus for performing special requests. In any event, policies are needed to safeguard authorized uses of budget allocations. For instance, the objective may be to provide "a balanced recreation program for all ages." This is very broad and more than the budget provides. A policy sets the course of action, therefore, by stating: "all adult groups above 18 years of age shall be self-sustaining."

Guiding Relationships

In recreation, or any other successful operation, human relationships often determine success or failure. A major element of recreation is good human relations. Laws, rules, and procedures help but policies, sometimes called "practices," are used as much as anything to direct courses of action in human relations. Every function of management involves policies concerning human relations. Policies have the effect of law, but they usually carry no penalty in themselves (violations may cause disciplinary action) and they can be adjusted or refined from time to time as conditions change.

Some Suggested Policies

Agency policies may be divided into two types: those concerning staff matters and agency operations, and those dealing with general matters for users and outside relationships. Examples of these are:

1. *Agency operations*
   - *a.* Every effort will be made to allow vacations when requested by staff. Staff are expected to take vacations each year.
   - *b.* The agency encourages staff training and self-development.
   - *c.* The agency will cooperate in sharing expenses for training appropriate to the job or to advancement.

   d. The agency will provide transportation for staff whose assignments require travel.
   e. Opportunities will be provided to everyone alike.

2. *General*
   a. The public and participants will be involved in planning and the decision-making process at every opportunity.
   b. Private organizations are welcome to use agency facilities when they are not being used for agency-sponsored programs.
   c. The agency will attempt to avoid competition with and duplication of facilities and programs of private and semi-private agencies.
   d. The agency will encourage activities such as tournaments and conventions that will assist the economy and avoid as much as possible competition with private enterprise.
   e. Public facilities and programs are not available for commercial activities.
   f. The agency encourages self-directed recreation activities.

A suggested general management policy is: *Do not permit a temporary gain to conflict with a long range objective.*

Procedures

Procedures, also called methods, are guidelines which refer to the manner in which actions are performed. They may be simple or may list the steps to be followed to perform a duty or to achieve an objective. They are usually concerned with *how* to do something or how an authority wants something done. Generally, in recreation, the executive and administrative staff determine management and operational procedures and supervisory and field staff determine program procedures. For example, the procedure to obtain use of a picnic shelter in the park may be: "Contact central office. Request date. Give beginning and ending time, number expected, name, address, and phone number of person responsible. A permit will be mailed with copies to parkkeeper and to file. Parkkeeper checks on the scheduled day to see if all is well." A form with adequate copies, often of different colors for easy identification, is used to conserve time and provide identical information for those involved.

RULES AND REGULATIONS

Rules and regulations of conduct are specific and essential means by which staff and people who use the public facilities may be managed. Authority for making rules is usually provided by the charter. Rules have the effect of law. Some localities require that the legislative body adopt rules which affect the public. Others provide the administrator or executive with the authority to make rules but request that a copy of any rule concerning regulation of the public be recorded with the clerk of the legislative body, which gives it the status of law.

The majority of rules for the regulation of conduct within an agency, together with procedures, are often made by other bodies such as personnel, finance, health, budget, chief administrator, and legislative body. The recreation executive has the responsibility for enforcing all these rules plus a few of his own which mainly apply to safety of people, protection of property, and the mechanics of operating the agency programs. Positive phrases should be used in framing rules. Negatively stated rules tell what not to do rather than what is acceptable.

The Administrative Manual

Most agencies prepare administrative manuals of some kind which are comprehensive guides for the use of staff members. In smaller localities, rules of all the government agencies may be compiled in a single manual. In larger localities, each agency or program unit may prepare a separate manual of rules, procedures, policies, and other guidelines to fit their specific needs.

INFLUENCES ON PUBLIC ADMINISTRATION

Public services, particularly local public services, are very susceptible to local influences. The federal government decision makers are located mainly in the Capitol, far removed from most people except for contacts by letter, telegram, telephone, and an occasional visit. The state officials are closer to the people they serve and are more susceptible to their needs and interests. The local official generally lives and works in the same community he serves. He comes in regular contact with all segments of the local population and is expected to be responsive to their needs and concerns. Often the local official gets the blame for the actions of all levels of government because he is the only government official most people can reach conveniently. In recent years, especially, government at all levels has tried to involve citizens in various phases of decision making: studies, planning, policy making, and programming.

Communities are experiencing constant changes. Growth and movement of population, congestion, crime, drugs, violence, traffic and transportation problems, pollution, social changes, unbalanced ecology, lack of space, and more free time are all problems too great for private resources to handle. Therefore, government must assume the responsibilities and adjust to need for changes. It must be sensitive to needs—all needs.

Politics

The political structure, philosophy and composition of the society play major roles in determining the direction public services take.[15] It is impossible to know the feelings of all segments of our complex society. The politician, therefore, relies greatly upon acquaintances, news media, representatives of organizations, letters and communications, public hearings, advice of the administrator, and personal judgement in making decisions. He has influence in determining policies, making appointments to boards, selecting the chief public administrator, and may use influence in making appointments to key positions. In some instances campaign workers are promised public jobs in appreciation for their efforts in the campaign. These "patronage appointments" are practiced more often in states and communities where the balance of power is close in the two party system and the administrative control changes from time to time from one party to the other or to independent candidates. In some instances, the political appointment holds the top executive position which is the one replaced with the change of parties but usually in these instances, there is an assistant (a career technician, professional, or expert) who is not replaced and who adds stability and continuity to administration. More and more, merit systems (civil service type systems) and laws are reducing the opportunities for "patronage appointments." One compensating factor in patronage appointments, however, is that a good politician and his appointee want their administration to be a good one and, therefore, one can expect good cooperation. Laws, rules, and procedures should prevent interference at agency and technical levels by pressure groups and politicians. Good democratic practices and management procedures, however, do suggest providing for hearings with policy boards and elected bodies and procedures for appeals.

Jurisdictional Structure

The nature of government organization and jurisdictional boundaries affects the efficiency of administration. The larger and more complex or interdependent the structure is, the more time is lost in administrative ineffectiveness and communication inadequacies. The average person comes in contact occasionally with local or regional units of state agencies. About one in four persons comes in contact with regional, city, county, special-services district, burrough, parish, township, or village units. Each has a form of administration. Each of the larger units has several subunits all of which have a form of administration adapted to its particular needs and may be semi-independent (school board, library). Some people may have government services administered by several government agencies, namely, state, region, county, city, one or more special purpose district services, plus, perhaps, school board, public housing, recreation commission, or library board. One of the confusing problems of public administration is who should provide what or who will give up something in order to provide for simpler, more efficient services with less overlapping and less duplication. The merging of political subdivisions has developed to administer services regional in nature—transportation, planning, water and air pollution, open space and recreation, sewage treatment and solid waste disposal, law enforcement, airports, and health services. The problems are how to get long-established political subdivisions to finance these services and give up jurisdictional authority. Politics, finances, power, laws, and the limitations of human nature are involved.

Tradition and Common Practice in the Community

Changes, under normal circumstances, are made slowly, particularly in public services where decision makers are sensitive to citizen requests, both pro and con. Every public program serves a community interest and has a number of supporters which make a strong case: (1) for continuing a service to them; (2) against making a major change that affects their special interest; (3) against raising taxes; or (4) against reducing the number of public jobs. It is often easier to get a public program started than it is to get it stopped, particularly if it involves major policy changes. Changes are brought about by good administrators who are constantly observing services under their jurisdiction and evaluating them in terms of priority of continuing needs.

Communities have conventional ways of functioning. From among the various forms of government and means of financing their government, they have selected the way that suits them best. Policies, traditions, methods, and procedures have been established and are understood by the public they serve. So long as the masses are reasonably satisfied and costs are in line, it is well to be in harmony with common practices in the community but to be ever alert for the need for change. The good administrator is the leader. He brings about changes when needed. He is also a follower and knows when the organization he serves will accept a change. The administrator has the responsibility of preparing his areas of jurisdiction for a change or of maintaining the status quo, if that is best. Changes are often necessary in our changing society. This is one reason public relations specialists have become so important in administration.

Other influences on public administration are the attitude of the policy board and administrator, the economy and taxes, decision makers who are economy-minded rather than service-minded, long-range cost (maintenance and operations), physical resources, news media, and community reactions and support or lack thereof.

Community Resources

Community and staff involvement are important ingredients of a successful public recreation program. If a community has good community leaders and a training institution for staff, it usually provides both community leadership and recreation leadership.

Numbers and types of industries influence public recreation programs. In some smaller communities with one major industry, the industry may provide the only recreation facilities or it may be the major contributor to the support of a semi-public facility. In recent years, however, industry has tended to use and support public recreation facilities in order that the employee's whole family may feel free to participate in recreation as citizens of the community and not feel restricted or influenced by a company-sponsored facility. Industries do, however, sponsor company employee athletic teams, outings, socials, and entertainment in public programs and facilities very satisfactorily.

Community volunteer resources add quality, supplement professional staff, and give support by serving on boards and committees, sharing their skills and talents in program activities, interpreting community needs to agency staff and interpreting policies, plans, procedures, and programs to the community.

Educational Factors

Training institutions in the area provide leadership, ideas, trained personnel, institutes and in-service training opportunities, part-time leaders, interns, field practice, research, and information which is a major contribution to recreation administration. Communities that do not have a training institution in the area have to compensate for this lack by providing more pre-service and in-service training; individuals in the community who have special skills; greater use of written material and contacts by mail; conventions and visits to sources of information; use of state and federal service agencies and professional organizations. This kind of a situation places different emphasis on the responsibilities of the administration, affects services, and may affect staff organization.

Public recreation programs are generally associated with special facilities; large facilities and services to groups, particularly large groups, are sometimes spoken of as "service to the masses." Although recreation stands for "growth and development," it generally does not have staff trained counselors and resources needed to "tutor" or give basic training to individuals and small groups. The learning and the recreation-type activities the individual experiences in school, therefore, greatly influence his choices and levels of participation in his recreational activities.

Characteristics of Area and Population

The physical characteristics such as mountains, streams, barriers, soil conditions, drainage, water supply, open space, and natural resources of the area influence administration. A village beside a valley stream and highway between two ranges of mountains has lots of space but not the kind that can be used for some kinds of recreation. The program has to be adapted to fit the space. The beautiful stream in the populated area is polluted and, no doubt, subject to flooding. The water, therefore, has restricted uses for recreation but the floodlands have opportunities for area recreation uses, except in times of flooding, but does restrict the building of structures. Administrators, therefore, have to work around the assets and liabilities of physical characteristics.

The make-up of the population, also, affects the type and emphasis of the program. A strictly industrial community will have needs closely related to and influenced by the type and interests of its personnel, probably sports, crafts, and nature-related activities. A college town will be interested in sports, especially if the college has a popular sports program, but it also would extend interests to the performing arts and special features. Nationality groups tend to add folklore and interests related to their heritage. Communities with a large population of older citizens have special programs and sometimes special facilities for older adults. In areas where there is a large population of the poor and disadvantaged, the program and services need to be broad. The public services may provide the only opportunity the large majority has for recreational experiences.

In the average urban area natural neighborhoods develop around interests in common and are of similar economic, social, and cultural standing. Their leisure time interests are similar. It is easier to communicate with them as compared to a mixed neighborhood of like economic status but which has a wide variety of differing backgrounds, leadership, points of view, likes, dislikes and loyalties.

Questions for Discussion

1. How would you define administration? Management?
2. How is administration related to leadership?
3. How is administration related to management?

4. What are the "basic processes of administration"?
5. What are the major influences on public administration?
6. How may administration of public recreation agency differ from administration of other public agencies?
7. How are state recreation services related to local recreation services?
8. How should a public recreation executive relate to nonprofit groups, politicians, semi-public recreation agencies, and special interest recreation groups in the community?
9. Describe "Management by Objectives" and point out its strong points.
10. Why is it important to involve citizens in public recreation administration processes?
11. Differentiate among purpose (aim or goal), objective, and method.

Short Problems

1. In a locality of your choice with a population of 75,000 or more, determine if recreation services by types (public, semi-private, private) are reasonably balanced and adequate for the community. What recommendations for improvements would you make?
2. Prepare recommendations for goals, objectives, and scope of services for a public recreation agency.

References

1. Ordway Tead, *The Art of Administration* (New York: McGraw-Hill Book Company, Inc., 1951), p. 3.
2. Lynn S. Rodney, *Administration of Public Recreation* (New York: The Ronald Press Company, 1964), p. 26.
3. Joseph L. Massie and John Douglas, *Managing: A Contemporary Introduction* (Englewood Cliffs, N.J.: Prentice-Hall, Inc., 1973), p. 5.
4. *Ibid.*, p. 6.
5. Luther Gulick and L. Urwick, editors, *Papers on the Science of Administration* (New York: Institute of Public Administration, 1937).
6. Rodney, *Administration of Public Recreation*, p. 52.

7. John Humble, *How To Manage By Objectives* (New York: AMACOM, 1973), p. 4.
8. George S. Odiorne, *Management By Objectives* (New York: Pittman Publishing Corporation, 1964), pp. 55-56.
9. Paul Mali, *Managing by Objectives* (New York: John Wiley & Sons, Inc., 1972), pp. 1-2.
10. James H. Donnelly, Jr., James L. Gibson, and John M. Ivancevich, *Fundamentals of Management* (Austin, Texas: Business Publications, Inc., 1971), pp. 144-145.
11. Mali, *Managing by Objectives,* p. 2.
12. Rodney, *Administration of Public Recreation,* p. 7.
13. *Ibid.,* p. 8.
14. Rodney H. Brady, "MBO Goes to Work in the Public Sector," *Harvard Business Review* (March-April 1973), 66.
15. George Hjelte and Jay S. Shivers, *Public Administration of Recreational Services* (Philadelphia: Lea and Febiger, 1972), p. 10.

Selected Readings

Albers, Henry H., *Principles of Management: A Modern Approach* (4th ed.), pp. 3-47. New York: John Wiley and Sons, Inc., 1974. *The management problem: past and present.*

Bannon, Joseph L., *Problem Solving in Recreation and Parks.* Englewood Cliffs, N.J.: Prentice-Hall, Inc., 1972.

Bonovetz, James M., ed., *Managing the Modern City.* Washington, D.C.: International City Management Association, 1971.

Kraus, Richard G., and Joseph E. Curtis, *Creative Administration in Recreation and Parks,* pp. 17-55. St. Louis: The C.V. Mosby Company, 1973.

Lutzin, Sidney G., and Edward H. Storey, *Managing in Municipal Leisure Services,* pp. 41-54. Washington, D.C.: International City Management Association, 1973.

Massie, Joseph L., and John Douglas, *Managing: A Contemporary Introduction.* Englewood Cliffs, N.J.: Prentice-Hall, Inc., 1973.

Murphy, James F., John G. Williams, and William E. Niepoth, *Leisure Service Delivery System.* Philadelphia: Lea and Febiger, 1973.

Rodney, Lynn S., *Administration of Public Recreation,* pp. 26-54. New York: The Ronald Press Company, 1964.

Stokes, Paul M., *A Total Systems Approach to Management Control,* pp.

13-57. New York: American Management Association, Inc., 1968. *Management controls, standards, and performance.*

Tead, Ordway, *The Art of Administration.* New York: McGraw-Hill Book Company, Inc., 1951.

Young, Stanley, *Management: A Systems Analysis.* Glenview, Ill.: Scott, Foresman and Company, 1966.

CHAPTER 3

Legal Authority for Public Recreation

Every individual, every group, every agency and organization has certain rights, powers, privileges and authority. Each, also, is subject to certain restrictions—rules, regulations, ethics, standards, procedures, bylaws, codes, laws—to define general conduct and relationships with others and permit freedom of action within the separate jurisdictions. As individuals pass from home, where each has the greatest freedom and authority, to group, agency, school, church, business, community, government and other jurisdictions, they are subject to the rights, privileges and restrictions of others and are expected to honor them if they, in turn, want continued freedom, and wish to enjoy reciprocation and good relationships in their own jurisdictions.

Individuals, groups, and governments that make rules, laws and restrictions also must conform to them. In the United States the Congress is the highest law making authority. It passes laws which apply to everyone.

The states are given their rights, powers, authorities, and privileges by the United States Constitution and federal laws. The state makes laws, which must not conflict with the Constitution and federal laws, which apply to everyone, including visitors, within the respective state and gives rights, powers, authority and privileges to its political subdivisions which, in turn, make laws (ordinances) that apply only locally and assign rights, powers, authority and privilege to its subunits. Subunits usually are given authority to make rules and regulations that apply to functions within the limits of their jurisdictions, but only legislative bodies have the authority to make laws. In order to establish federal, state and local recreation services, therefore, there must be appropriate enabling legislation at each level of government.

FEDERAL CONSTITUTION: FEDERAL LAWS

In recent years, recreation has become a major concern of government at all levels. Almost every major agency of the federal government provides recreation services in some way.[1] States have a growing number of recreation services, the latest of which is the state recreation agency for advisory services. An increasing number of localities have Recreation Departments and sub-agencies such as public housing, institutions, and special facilities that provide recreation services.

Recreation services are ranked with education, health, safety and welfare as essential services of government. One of the problems is to determine which level of government is to provide what services and under what circumstances. Various units of federal, state, and local government may provide services at the local level although the primary operating unit is the county or municipal department.

Federal Authority

George Hjelte and Jay S. Shivers emphasize that initial authority for recreation comes from two basic federal documents. The first is the Declaration of Independence which has the general welfare clause. The second is the United States Constitution which makes the United States a sovereign power not accountable to a higher jurisdiction and gives the separate states, but not the District of Columbia and territories, certain powers, not in conflict with federal powers, to have complete authority over the administration of certain internal affairs of the states. It gives to the states protective power which provides for the general welfare of its people and control of their behavior so long as the states' activities do not conflict with the Constitution and the constitutional rights of the citizens.[2]

In recent years, the federal government, aided by certain liberal decisions of the Supreme Court and Amendments to the Constitution, has assumed more power and given the states less. Federal administrative guidelines handed down to the states, in conjunction with the distribution of federal monies, tended to override state and local authority. The local appeal of grants-in-aid programs has caused state and local agencies to yield some of their rights and privileges to federal control and regulations as opposed to their own. Local jurisdictions, however, administer the programs in their respective localities. Some states and localities have tended to become dependent upon federal assistance and federal sharing of revenues. The federal requirements and minimum guidelines which accompany federal grants are expected to be a continuing way of life.

Generally, as a matter of policy, if not of law, federal and state governments provide services national or state-wide in scope but only support local programs and services within local jurisdictions. These higher echelons of government will provide services directly in emergency situations or when requested by local authorities.

STATE ENABLING LEGISLATION: STATE STATUTES

The U.S. Constitution assigns certain powers to federal government and others to state governments. The state governments, in turn, grant to their political subdivisions certain powers. Since World War II, recreation services provided by state governments have been largely in state parks, and forest, game, and other natural preserves. Scenic rivers, floodlands, marshes and swamps, beaches and other marginal use lands are included in some states. Localities use state and federal parks and other public areas as supplements to local recreation programs.

State Authority

In setting up a recreation service, one of the first items to be considered is the determination of the legal authority that applies to public recreation systems. It is then necessary to make sure the legislation will provide all the desired authority such as that: (1) To acquire, own, develop, operate, and maintain areas and structures for recreation and parks both within and without the jurisdictional boundaries; (2) To organize, conduct, and promote recreation programs for all age groups in various parts of the jurisdiction both indoors and outdoors; and (3) To acquire and use areas and facilities jointly with schools and/or other public agencies when they are not in use for their primary purposes, subject to such reasonable rules and regulations as the school board or other agencies may establish, and provided the using agency shall be responsible for damages or extra expenses as a result of such use.

The activities of public recreation under current conditons may be so vastly different from those at the time legislation was authorized that some amendments to existing state enabling legislation will have to be made or special legislation enacted to permit certain desired services. Most states, however, have already updated their enabling legislation to permit localities to operate comprehensive public recreation services. All states have regulatory and protective laws mainly relating to health, safety and conservation features.

A local unit functions only through authority given to it by the state. This varies from one state to another and even with localities within the same state where authority is granted by special laws or separate charters. Local subdivisions of the state include cities, counties, regional authorities, school districts, special purpose districts, villages and townships.

States generally grant authority to their political subdivisions in four ways: (1) General enabling legislation; (2) Specific purpose laws; (3) Self-government or home rule; and (4) Separate charter.

State Enabling Legislation

Enabling legislation, commonly called "Enabling Act" and sometimes "State Code," is general permissive legislation that authorizes localities to establish recreation services within their jurisdictions. It is permissive, not mandatory, and must be followed by local ordinances or referenda and appropriations for action to be initiated. The first all-inclusive, comprehensive type of recreation enabling act was passed by New Jersey in 1915.[3] The enabling legislation provides the local government with certain powers to authorize a board or agency or means of administering, staffing and financing a recreation service; specify the powers, conditions, and restrictions; authorize the organization and conducting of recreation activities and programs; permit two or more public agencies or jurisdictions to operate recreation programs jointly; and authorize the acquisition, ownership, development, and maintenance of recreation areas and facilities, and the accepting of gifts.

Some enabling legislation authorizes only cities to operate a public recreation system; others provide authorization only to cities above a specified population; but most authorize a full and complete recreation service.

Special Purpose Laws

Special purpose laws authorize a locality to provide a specific recreation function, facility, or activity. The main feature of this procedure is that it applies to a single locality and does not relate to or conflict with authority of any other community. Examples are authority to use a state facility, or to operate a stadium or golf course.

Self Government

Some states provide for self government or home rule which permits cities and counties to prepare, adopt, and amend their local charters. This requires a favorable vote of the people in the respective jurisdictions. Some states restrict this power to a population class or make other restrictions.

The Separate Charter

The local governing body prepares and officially recommends to its representatives in the state legislature the powers and authorities it desires in its local charter. The representatives from the locality, if they agree, sponsor appropriate legislation and guide it through legislative channels for approval. Sometimes the state legislature does not agree with local requests and makes amendments. After the charter has been approved by the state legislature, the local government must operate within the confines of the charter and general laws. Recreation services and authorities may be included in the charter if special provisions are desired. Items not specifically covered in the charter are subject to general laws.

Charters may be general or they may be detailed. General charter provisions usually give the local legislative body authority to determine the kind of organization it desires and how it should be administered.

Regulatory Laws

As the word implies, regulatory laws are those which regulate the standards of health, safety and protection of the public. Health regulations involve sanitation, the purification of swimming pools, cleanliness of food handlers, sanitation of camping operations, and control of insects and rodents. Safety involves law enforcement, traffic and parking control, hunting and fishing regulation, wildlife protection and conservation.

Local Relationships

A local unit of government must first take appropriate legal action within the authority granted to it by the state in order to establish the type of recreation service it wishes to have with the necessary authority and funding capability. The action may be in the form of an ordinance, referendum, charter amendment, or special law depending on the existing enabling legislation, attitude of the legislature, and general laws applicable to the community. The administrative unit may be a commission, separate agency, or a service within an existing agency.

In some localities, particularly those having city or county managers, a citizen advisory board is preferred to the authoritative board or commission. Boards will be more fully discussed in Chapter 5.

District Laws

All states have provisions for the establishment of special districts for special purposes. These were originally conceived to handle special services such as water and sanitary facilities. An example would be an urbanizing section of a county which needs a service but which cannot expect a favorable vote from the unit of which it is a part. A few localities have authorized special districts for recreation and parks, including the right to tax. Those special districts relating to recreation or park services may be referred to by different names in different states depending on how the state legislatures look at the broad field of recreation when considering the initial legislation. Special districts may be set up to administer special or comprehensive recreation services in a portion of a political jurisdiction, the total jurisdiction, or portions of two or more jurisdictions. They are usually autonomous, independent of other local governing entities, and are provided, in effect, with all the powers of any political subdivision of the state. The residents of the locality involved must initiate the request for the establishment of a special district. It may be authorized by the state legislature or county board. It is governed by an elected or appointed board, sometimes separate and sometimes as an additional function of a legislative body.

City-County Relationships

State enabling acts authorize two or more political subdivisions of the state to combine in providing a recreation service under a single authority. The needs, practices, financing, and political climate of political subdivisions are so varied and complex, however, that it is more of an exception than a rule for two separate political jurisdictions to combine for a service under a single administration unless resources obtained from outside, such as state and federal grants, make it expedient to do so.

Traditionally, counties, with their wide open spaces and scattered population, have been thought of as providing agriculture-related services while cities, with their industries, limited space, and dense populations, were thought of as providing services for business, industry and heavy concentrations of people. There were few cities and many counties. There were more county representatives in state legislatures. Since the majority of law-makers were from the counties, many basic state laws and practices were rural oriented. Many city industries provided products for the farmer such as machinery, fertilizer, processed food, clothing, building materials and, therefore, cities had an interest in the rural communities and were sympathetic to their needs. As cities increased in population, their problems and needs for additional services also increased. They were obliged to turn their thoughts to services for people in addition to services for things.

One continuing problem for the cities was lack of space, both for people and industry. They needed to expand their boundaries as well as their tax bases. They needed more space. They could build up, down, or out. They went up a little, mainly in the central business area, but mostly they were forced to go out beyond their existing boundaries. This was the beginning of the end of a long period of free exchange of neighborly deeds. From here on it was mainly business and law and human relations. The cities had to have more space. Counties did not want to give up the business, industry and support of their urbanizing areas near the cities. The suburban people did not want to face higher city taxes, either, "without getting additional services," since they already had the use of city services.

Laws provide some alternate remedial measures but none are completely satisfactory: (1) A city may extend its boundaries by annexing portions of adjoining counties, by court action; (2) Governments of adjacent political units may consolidate; (3) Governments may cooperate by contracting services to each other or by joint operations; and (4) A special purpose district or region may be established. With today's mobility and ease of communication, the extensive nature of today's problems, and the need to reduce taxes and lower costs, the regional or metropolitan type government might serve to alleviate many problems. Each change, however, tends to create new problems. Consolidation would inconvenience some and change their patterns of life; local governments would be eliminated, together with some jobs; and government would be further removed from the people and would tend towards centralization. From a management point of view, regional government has many advantages, but from a political point of view it involves almost insurmountable political problems. In recent years, however, as metropolitan problems have become more acute, competent leadership, with the support of community interests, and aided by good public information programs and convincing lists of expected benefits to the total area, has brought about the consolidation of some political jurisdictions or the formation of a few regional governments and area programs. These have given clear-cut authority to the new governments, reduced duplication and costs, and generally improved efficiency.

Most states follow the usual pattern of counties, cities, towns, townships, and unincorporated areas. The county is the main political subdivision of the state and all other political subdivisions are within the county boundaries. Cities and towns may incorporate and form their own independent governments for most functions but are subject to the applicable laws (including taxation) of the county, state, and federal government. There are instances, e.g., in the Commonwealth (State) of Virginia, and a few cities such as Baltimore and St. Louis, in which cities and counties are completely independent of each other. The changing of political boundary lines would mean, therefore, that one political jurisdiction would have to give up area, tax revenues, votes, and prestige while the other jurisdiction would gain those things. Decisions affecting boundary changes are usually made by referendum except in Virginia where they are made by the courts.[4]

Exploding urban population, lack of space within city boundaries, the automobile and improved thoroughfares, lower taxes, more open space, extension of urban type conveniences and suburban developments have attracted masses of urban families into the rural areas outside city boundaries. They demand the same services that they had in the cities, including recreation services. Many new county recreation agencies are being established to satisfy these needs. Counties are also expected to provide all of the other services available in the cities. The public services of the counties and the cities are, therefore, coming closer together. This makes it even more difficult to expand city boundary lines and emphasizes the importance of area-wide services or regions.

Regional Legislation

If a special district includes two or more jurisdictions it would, in effect, be a region. Obviously, if older cities grow they must have more space. Adjoining counties are growing, too, and many urbanizing counties have many of the same characteristics, needs and functions as cities. Transportation, utilities, economy, resources, employment, recreation and other services are common to the metropolitan area and cannot effectively be isolated in any one political subdivision. District, metropolitan, and regional government; mergers or consolidation of political subdivisions; or business-like cooperation provide opportunities for solution. Some form of regional or metropolitan government or merger may, of necessity, be the next step in urban government.

ORDINANCES: LOCAL LEGISLATION

An ordinance is a rule of authority (law) passed by a local legislative body. In order for a local body to enact local legislation, it must be given authority to do so by the state enabling legislation, charter, or special legislation. In early stages of the playground movement, however, cities authorized recreation programs on the basis of general police powers provided in the state constitutions and general welfare clauses of special legislation. Some localities, in starting playground programs, expanded the powers of park and school boards or followed a liberal interpretation of their authorities. Indiana, in 1859, was the first state to enact legislation to permit community use of schools for recreation.[5] Special purpose laws gave considerable concern because they applied to a specific jurisdiction and usually were restricted to specifically named facilities or functions. Localities inaugurating recreation programs under special laws were very often seriously restricted in their operations until support could be mustered to enact legislation that provided adequate authority to provide comprehensive recreation services under any circumstances.

Beginning with New Jersey in 1915, the separate states updated their enabling legislation for recreation until all states now provide rather comprehensive authority for any locality to administer a rather complete and diversified recreation program.[6]

Preparation of Local Ordinances

In preparing local legislation, it is the responsibility of the chief administrator to deal with the local legislative body and the recreation executive's responsibility to deal with a recreation policy board (or advisory board) and the chief administrator. In inaugurating a plan for the establishment of a recreation agency, the chief administrator or a member of the legislative body would prepare the general proposal in the form of an ordinance for consideration and approval by the local legislative body. Usually, a committee of interested citizens, self-initiated or appointed by the legislative body, would research the situation, report its findings and make recommendations to the chief administrator or legislative body.

After a recreation agency has been established, it is the responsibility of the recreation executive to review all proposed legislation to see that none adversely affects recreation interests or agency operations and to prepare and recommend, with justifications to the chief administrator and/or recreation board, if there is one, matters concerning recreation that require legislative approval. Sometimes, the executive may draft ordinance proposals, but legal and legislative papers are usually prepared by the legal department.

LAWS, RULES AND REGULATIONS

A law is a rule of conduct binding upon members of society usually enacted by a legislative body elected by members of a specified jurisdiction —local, state, or federal. Laws usually impose penalties (fines or confinement) for failure to conform. Rules and regulations are also rules of conduct, with or without penalties, binding upon members, staff and visitors who are involved in specified situations. They are usually made by individuals and groups in authority. Penalties for infractions are usually less severe than for laws and more in the nature of discipline imposed by the individuals or groups who made the rule or regulation, as compared to laws which usually are enforced by others. Makers of good rules, regulations, and laws provide for adequate procedures for appeal to the highest source of authority for those who feel they have been treated unjustly.

In public recreation, the executive will be involved in conforming to federal, state, and local laws, rules, and regulations of agencies at each level. Each of the many agencies and organizations dealt with at the local level will also have rules and regulations.

Making Local Rules and Regulations

The recreation executive may or may not be given authority by charter or legislation to make rules and regulations to control the conduct of the general public. Very often that responsibility is assigned only to the legislative body, but that body may delegate certain authority to the chief administrator or agency executive. Very often, too, rules for the control of the general public, such as parking regulations and various prohibitions, need the force of law and policing to be effective. A rule not enforced equitably is demoralizing and worse than no rule at all.

The recreation executive will be involved in determining procedures both for staff and public. It takes much staff time to enforce rules of conduct for the public. The fewer rules there are, the more staff resources can be directed towards the achievement of objectives. On the other hand, some rules governing conduct are essential to reduce interruptions and provide maximum opportunity for progress towards predetermined goals.

Laws are more difficult to change than rules because they are subject to public hearings, require legislative action and at least a majority vote of the legislative body. Regulations concerning prohibitions and the control of people, therefore, that are constantly subject to challenge by the general public, and rules that need strong support are usually referred to the legislative body for approval. Rules, regulations, and procedures that control internal operations and may change from time to time, or are subject to occasional exceptions, may well remain rules of the department and be enforced, amended, or terminated by it.

Agency rules, in so far as the public is concerned, involve matters of the protection, health, safety, and convenience of the users. An executive cannot know all of the factors that need to be considered in making good rules. It is very desirable, therefore, to review proposals with users, staff and others involved before putting them into effect. It is recommended that rules, regulations, policies, procedures, and other guidelines be reproduced and widely distributed to staff and key people and even be published in newspapers, if practical.

LIABILITY IN PUBLIC RECREATION

The recreation executive has three relationships with legal matters that should be given priority attention: (1) to watch carefully all proposed legislation to see that none affects recreation adversely; (2) to practice "safety first" and see that no conditions develop that would provide legitimate opportunity for claims of liability against staff or agency; and (3) to observe carefully the attitude of the courts and the results of suits or claims involving recreation that are handled by the courts. Decisions of the courts, for or against, have a cumulative influence on future decisions and provide an indication of trends.

Liability, relating to recreation, involves either injury to person or damage to property as a result of negligence, direct or indirect, on the part of the agency or agency personnel.

Personal Involvement in Liability

Liability suits, whether against a public agency or private business, usually include as co-defendants the agency, the chairman of the policy board, chief administrator, the agency head and all individual staff members connected with the situation on the basis that all persons are responsible for their own acts. The agency usually defends the individuals if the alleged incident occurred in the line of duty and was not deliberate and was not the result of criminal action and misconduct on the part of the agency personnel. Some individual staff members carry liability insurance at their own expense and some agencies carry liability insurance for all employees or groups which might be subject to claims of false arrest or similar problems in the line of duty.

All employees, both in the private and public sectors, may be subject to personal damage suits if an injury to person or property occurs while under their supervision if negligence, error, or failure to carry out the responsibilities of their job is claimed against them. There are records of very few instances where claims against individual employees have been upheld in court.

Individuals are very vulnerable to claims in instances where swimmers in a pool are left unattended and someone drowns, or when the individual is told of an unsafe condition and does nothing about it until someone is injured. Every individual should understand the factors involving problems of liability.

Factors Related to Liability

Most claims result from individual neglect, although sometimes a failure of equipment, accidents, normal wear and unobserved weathering, breakage and misuse by participants may be responsible. Successful claims against public recreation agencies in the United States and Canada have been because of "gross negligence" which means someone in the agency knew the situation was wrong or dangerous and failed to take reasonable action to correct it. Agencies, like individuals within them, are considered responsible for acts, actions, and lack of appropriate action. Language and judicial interpretation of the law may vary until tested in court. Minors, especially those under 12 years of age, are said not to be responsible for themselves. Extra care must, therefore, be taken to see that all is right for them. Liability depends on whether or not the individuals concerned, such as protective and investigative officers, have immunity in carrying out their functions; whether neglect can be proven; whether the agency knew of a safety hazard and failed to act appropriately and promptly; whether services are mandatory for the general welfare of all people or if they were permissive functions; or, in instances of fees and charges, whether a profit was intended. Courts have been liberal where service to the public is emphasized. Great emphasis has been placed by the courts on the equal rights of citizens and the emphasis in the Constitution on providing for the health, safety, protection and general welfare of the people. Some courts have taken budgets and tax funds that could have helped numbers of people to pay liability claims.

Immunity and Liability

In recreation services, there is no definite assurance that any function or action is completely immune from liability. Courts in various states have made decisions for and against claims evolving from what looks to the layman like similar incidents. A closer look reveals justification for reasons the executive and recreationist ordinarily may not understand, but should. Recreation is not static; it is subject to changes and many variations. There is a difference in judicial opinion as to where recreation belongs, governmental or proprietary. In some states, it is considered a governmental function and in other states it is considered a proprietary function. Benefits of recreation reach beyond the boundaries of the political subdivisions which provide the service. State statutes are not inclusive and courts have tended to define the law on the principle of equity and justice and what is in the best interest of the general welfare of the public. Recreation of the type provided has been traditionally a public service not generally provided by private enterprise. Basic services of an agency may be considered governmental, but some activities may be considered proprietary. The shifting of the public's attitude and judicial interpretation of the laws affect decisions. How recreation functions are identified in local enabling legislation does not affect immunity. Federal laws and state statutes that affect all the people are, however, important considerations.

It is generally accepted that governmental functions such as law enforcement, fire protection, health, welfare and public education have a high degree of immunity. It is not unusual, however, for governments to carry liability insurance on these functions.

Several current trends with regard to liability may be noted: (1) There is an increased tendency on the part of lawyers and the public to make claims; (2) Courts are less tolerant and more liberal on claims of deliberate neglect, omissions, and improper protection of attractive nuisances; and (3) An attitude that no individual should bear the cost resulting from negligence of others even though, traditionally, the agency may have been classified as having immunity.

Prevention of Liability Claims

The very best protection against liability claims is to perform properly, be knowledgeable about factors leading to claims, and prevent the development of opportunities for legitimate claims. The best prevention is prudent operation. Practice "Safety First." Make each staff member, user, and participant "safety conscious" and alert at all times to detect developing dangerous conditions and safety hazards. Make, widely distribute, and strictly enforce at all times health and safety rules. Promptly correct, guard, or remove from service any item that is defective or not performing properly. *Do not take chances with health and safety matters.*

Common mistakes are overcrowded swimming pools, rooms with inadequate emergency escapes, and delaying repairs to equipment and facilities. Keep abreast of decisions made by courts. Often, legal matters are frustrating to recreationists, but it is helpful to remember that laws are based on the same principles as recreation, namely: "what is fair and reasonable" and "equity and justice for all." The public has a right to expect "fair and reasonable" performance from staff and equipment at all times. The individual and the agency which carry out their functions properly with reasonable competence and integrity may expect to prevent claims of liability and may also expect maximum support should some problem develop over which they have no reasonable control. There should be no laxity even in functions that are considered to have immunity.

Insurance Protection and Security

Some agencies find it advisable to carry insurance. Insurance against litigation and liability is available for individuals at their own cost. Some agencies carry liability and property damage insurance for all functions, others only on selected high risk functions such as firefighting.

It is a standard practice to require contractors and commercial users of public property such as vendors and concessionaires, owners of temporary equipment, and construction contractors to carry a specified amount of liability and property damage insurance and to include the agency as co-insurer. Agencies often require performance bonds.

For the security of the agency, staff members who handle money and stock rooms or authorize expenditures are bonded in an amount equal to the largest amount in possession at any one time. Some governments carry a blanket bond policy that includes every employee for a specified amount.

Definitions of Legal Terms [7]

A few legal terms which recreationists commonly need to know are:

Liability is a state, condition or obligation for which an agency or individual is legally responsible. In recreation, this could apply to performance, conduct, use of equipment, supervision and responsibility for others which may result in injury to person or damage to property and which is subject to court action.

Tort is a wrongful act, injury, or damage (not involving a breach of contract) for which a civil action may be brought.

Governmental functions are those functions required by the state for the good of all people, such as health, education, welfare, police protection. They are said to be mandatory and have a degree of immunity.

Proprietary functions are permissive functions that a government may desire to provide for citizens within its jurisdiction such as airports, stadiums, and auditoriums. They are not required.

Due process is a legal term that refers to the right of the individual to fair and equal treatment.

Referendum is subjecting an issue to the vote of the people for decision.

Feasance refers to the performance of a responsibility or the fulfillment of an obligation.

Nonfeasance is the omission, neglect, or failure to perform a legal duty which may or may not cause injury, or damage to person or property, such as failure to lock the gate on the pool and a child falls in and drowns. It is a reason for liability claims.

Malfeasance is willful performance of a wrongful act or one that a person has agreed not to perform in connection with an official duty such as accepting a "kick back" on a contract purchase.

Misfeasance is performing an official duty in a careless, irresponsible manner that results in injury or damage to property such as sweeping up the glass from a broken window but leaving fragments of glass in the frame. A child later sticks his head out of the open frame and is severely cut with jagged edges of glass remaining in the frame.

Attractive nuisance is any continuing condition, device, structure or situation which is both dangerous and attractive to children, usually under twelve years of age, who are not yet mature enough to realize or foresee dangers and to be completely responsible for themselves. An unfenced sawmill or a deep water pond could be attractive nuisances.

Questions for Discussion

1. What enabling legislation is involved in establishing a public recreation agency? What kinds of enabling legislation are there?
2. What is the difference between an enabling act and an ordinance?
3. What is meant by "home rule"? Regulatory laws?
4. What is the difference between a special purpose law and a district law?
5. What is the role of legislation at the city level? County level? Regional level? State level? Federal level?
6. Explain the differences among laws, rules, regulations and policies.
7. Why is there concern about liability in public recreation?
8. How are employees personally involved in liability?
9. What factors are related to liability?
10. How would you prevent liability claims?
11. What kinds of insurance would you recommend that a recreation agency should carry?
12. What is meant by governmental function? Proprietary function? Attractive nuisance? Malfeasance? Misfeasance? Nonfeasance?

Short Problems

1. Prepare a model ordinance to establish a local recreation agency.
2. Prepare all safety rules for a comprehensive recreation agency.
3. Inspect a city of your choice and list all of the situations that could be sources of liability claims and recommend how each can be eliminated or improved.

References

1. *Recreation and Park Yearbook 1966* (Washington, D.C.: National Recreation and Park Association, 1967), pp. 1–2.

2. George Hjelte and Jay S. Shivers, *Public Administration of Recreational Services* (Philadelphia: Lea and Febiger, 1972), p. 28.
3. Charles E. Doell and Gerald B. Fitzgerald, *A Brief History of Parks and Recreation in The United States* (Chicago: The Athletic Institute, 1954), p. 82.
4. Statement, Assistant City Attorney, Richmond, Va., 1974.
5. Hjelte and Shivers, *Public Administration of Recreational Services,* p. 39.
6. *Municipal Recreation Administration,* 3rd ed. (Chicago: The International City Managers Association, 1948), p. 293.
7. Definitions were designed after consultation with Assistant City Attorney, Richmond, Va., 1974.

Selected Readings

Adrian, Charles R., and C. Press, *Governing Urban America* (3rd ed.). New York: McGraw-Hill Book Company, 1968.

Banfield, Edward C., ed., *Urban Government* (2nd ed.). New York: The Macmillan Company, 1969.

Hjelte, George, and Jay S. Shivers, *Public Administration of Recreational Services,* pp. 27–48. Philadelphia: Lea and Febiger, 1972.

Kraus, Richard G., and Joseph Curtis, *Creative Administration in Recreation and Parks,* pp. 31–46. St. Louis: The C.V. Mosby Company, 1973.

Lorch, Robert S., *Democratic Process and Administrative Law.* Detroit, Mich.: Wayne State University Press, 1969.

Lutzin, Sidney G., and Edward H. Storey, *Managing Municipal Leisure Services,* pp. 68–96. Washington, D.C.: International City Management Association, 1973.

Mathews, N., *Municipal Charters: A Discussion of the Essentials of a City Charter.* College Park, Md.: McGrath Publishing Co., 1969.

Van der Smission, Betty, *Legal Liability of Cities and Schools for Injuries in Recreation and Parks.* Cincinnati: W.H. Anderson Co., 1968.

CHAPTER 4

Organizing the Recreation and Park Agencies

The recreation executive of today is concerned with many and varied ideas about recreation. The opportunities for service are unlimited. They run from services to individuals through services to corporations and government. Recreation seems to be involved in every phase of human activity in some aspect and is an important element in the lives of every individual and family. One of the problems of recreation is the vast scope of its opportunities, making it frustrating sometimes for the recreationist to decide what should have the highest priority, especially when resources are limited. It is easy to take on too much and spread oneself too thin. This should be avoided. Recreationists have commented, "The world is our laboratory; there is no end to our opportunities." This appears justified when one observes the wide variety of uses of recreation and how citizens look to recreation for solutions to individual and community problems in addition to the normal functions of providing for fun, growth, and personal and community development.

The essential elements of a public recreation agency are leadership, areas and facilities, finances, and activities. In order to make these elements function effectively, there must be organization: the bringing together of personnel and other resources to achieve specific objectives. In order to do this, some existing agency of government must assume the responsibility of organizing recreation programs or a new recreation agency must be established to render these services and to provide the greatest opportunities for the least effort. This chapter deals primarily with local organization since most recreation services to the public are at the community level.

ADMINISTRATION OF THE RECREATION FUNCTIONS

The history of recreation administration in most communities is that private committees of interested citizens or community agencies first demonstrate the values of recreation to the community and the local government gradually assumes responsibility. In the early stages of development, there were only schools and a few public parks in the larger cities closely related to the supervised playground movement. Schools had playgrounds and sports facilities, and parks had some equipment areas. But some localities had only schools, health, welfare, libraries, safety and public works departments. Consequently, the responsibility for the growing recreation programs was assigned by the legislative body to various agencies that existed at the time. Some people thought recreation was closely associated with social work so administration of recreation services was assigned to the welfare department. Others were assigned to public works where parks were administered, and recreation needed facilities. Other programs started under independent recreation commissions similar to school boards. About 10 percent had their beginning in and are still administered by school boards in some areas of the nation. Others were operated in cooperation with semi-private local agencies. Many localities set up separate recreation departments which have continued. Cities that had separate park and recreation agencies have, for the most part, combined these into a single park and recreation unit since 1940. Also, during that time, most of the public recreation programs that were administered as a secondary function of other agencies were converted into separate agencies with recreation and parks as the primary function. At the present time, with a few exceptions, public recreation programs are administered by combined recreation and parks agencies, separate agencies, or by schools.[1] Functions are organized into work programs which are usually administered by highly skilled specialists.

DEVELOPING BASIC WORK PROGRAMS

There is no one standard type of work program for management of a public recreation agency. No one dreamed, when supervised play began for children on a public area at the turn of the century, that public recreation would reach the proportion it has today. There were no recreation professionals or national organizations at that time to set standards, promote any one way to administer a public recreation program, or define services. Consequently, the local playground program was assigned as a secondary function to whatever agency had legal authority and was willing to take it. Therefore, recreation services became attached to different departments, and once established many continued as originally structured. The separate recreation agencies that were established in the beginning gave full time, thought, and effort to recreation services as a primary function. That type of organization was generally satisfactory and, therefore, greatly influenced trends, concepts, purposes, and objectives for the development of the separate recreation agency plan of organization.

The work program is a spending unit composed of closely related activities such as playgrounds, special facilities or centers. The work programs in the beginning were mostly *maintenance, playgrounds,* and *sports,* similar to those found in schools. As resources and programs are expanded, other work programs are added, such as arts and crafts, dance, drama, music and rhythm, nature and outings, socials and special events, educational features, community services, and other special categories. The organization, in many instances, is based on some combination of general administration, sports and games, centers and playgrounds, special facilities, special services, special events, youth activities, cultural activities, and maintenance. On the physical side, the work programs include landscaping, planning, major construction, maintenance of structures, and park and playground maintenance. In more recent years, the work programs consist of combinations or consolidations of these items for the smaller departments, or further expansion of them and greater specialization for the larger departments. Some include specialized work programs such as programs for senior citizens, the mentally and physically handicapped, roving counselors, and security personnel. However, there is considerable difference of opinion among recreationists as to whether policing and security work should be performed by the public recreation agency or left to the local and state police. A greater breakdown of the work program is made possible largely by modern data processing methods, and we expect that there will be further refinement in the future.

ORGANIZATIONAL STRUCTURE

The variety of services provided by a local government requires the full time efforts of many individuals having many different kinds of skills and occupations. They require the use of a variety of specialized equipment and the operation and maintenance of a large physical plant seven days a week, sometimes around the clock. The recreation and parks organization generally has a relationship with all the functions of local government and must be designed to fit into the established practices, patterns, resources, and local ways of doing things, in so far as possible, for ease of operation, communications, and teamwork.

Achievement requires an orderly application of the resources available. This may be accomplished through organization, which in government is in two parts: external or general administrative, and internal or departmental, and program.

Administrative Organization

The structures of local government vary with such items as state enabling legislation, general government structure and laws, existing community services, political concepts, adequacy of resources, purposes, work programs, public opinion, and size of the community. Organization is the process by which the resources, responsibilities, and authority essential to the operation of the different work programs and purposes are apportioned. In order for the executive to be accountable for the performance of all organizational components he must be provided with a means of centralized control and clear-cut responsibilities, authority, and support.

The organizational pattern for administering the recreation agency is concerned with legal authority, beginning with the voting electorate and what the people want, how the legislative body, which represents the electorate, provides the resources, decides the best way to provide the services, and designates authority and accountability. The form of the administrative organization and any later amendments are determined by the local legislative body within the authority given it by the state. Some times the legislative body chooses to delegate some of its authority to an independent administrative board or commission.

FORMS OF RECREATION ORGANIZATION

The public recreation organization may be established as a separate agency or as a secondary function of another agency. Whether it is a primary function depends on the character and purpose of the parent agency and local conditions. Those that started under schools and parks tended to stay in combination with them. However, most recreation services that originated in welfare, public works, and similar departments have changed over the years to separate recreation agencies or combined recreation and parks agencies. In recent years, most new recreation services have been established separately or in combination with parks or cultural activities and provide opportunities for the total family.

The addition of many new functions and departments of government since World War II, has crowded top management beyond the point of efficiency. That, plus the acute rise in the cost of government, has started a trend towards reorganization and consolidation of functions and administration. The creation of new crash programs and services for the disadvantaged and minority groups has developed recreation programs under more than one local agency, thus creating some duplication, overlapping of services, and need for coordination and consolidation. Some professional consultants and urban planners have urged the consolidation of recreation, libraries, and similar human services under new departments such as cultural activities and human resources and have suggested assigning administration of parks to the department of public works. Some consideration has also been given to combining the administration of health, welfare and recreation in a super department.

There are several forms of organizational structure, but five are most commonly used, namely: (1) separate recreation department and a separate parks department; (2) an independent recreation and/or park agency under a commission or board; (3) a combined recreation and parks department; (4) recreation directed by parks agency; and (5) recreation directed by public schools.

Separate Recreation Departments

The recreation executive is responsible to the chief administrator. The plan in Fig. 4-1 is typical of this group. Providing recreation activities and program opportunities is the only function of the separate recreation department. It has no direct authoritative relationship with any other agency, either school or parks, although both have a cooperative relationship with recreation. It has equal status with other departments of government. Parks is a separate agency concerned primarily with aesthetics, nature, horticulture, historical sites, monuments, formal gardens, open areas, physical facilities, and landscaping. Recreation, in contrast, is concerned primarily with programs, playgrounds, active use areas, and leadership activities.

The advantages of the single department are better identity and better support. It enables full time to be given to recreation services; usually attracts better and more highly skilled personnel; promotes unification of interests and loyalties and the coordination of activities and use of facilities; and is capable of giving prompt response to citizen requests. It is people oriented and more appealing to volunteers.

The disadvantages, assuming there is also a separate parks agency, are duplication and unnecessary costs, divided authority which is confusing to the public, divergence of philosophies, lack of comprehensive planning, and a tendency to be competitive.

Independent Agency Under a Board

The plan in Fig. 4-2 is typical of the commission or board form of organization. Members are appointed by the legislative body, often supplemented by a member of the school board and a member of the planning

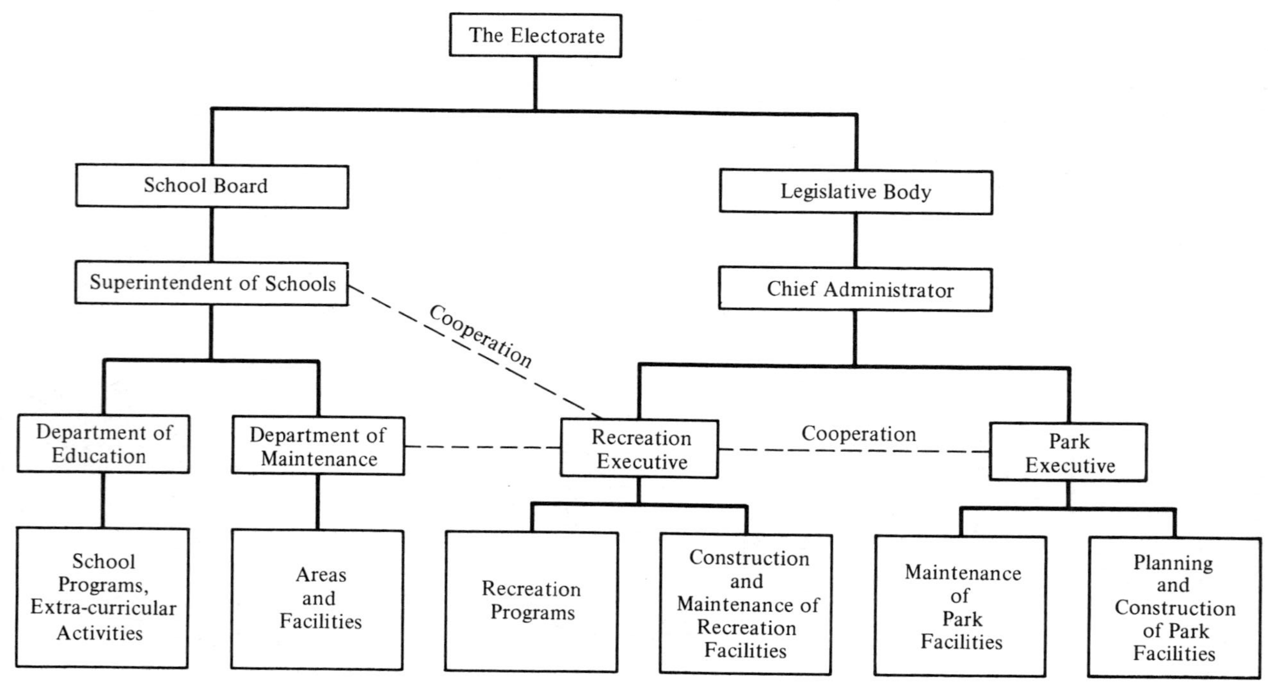

Figure 4-1. Separate recreation department (hypothetical example).

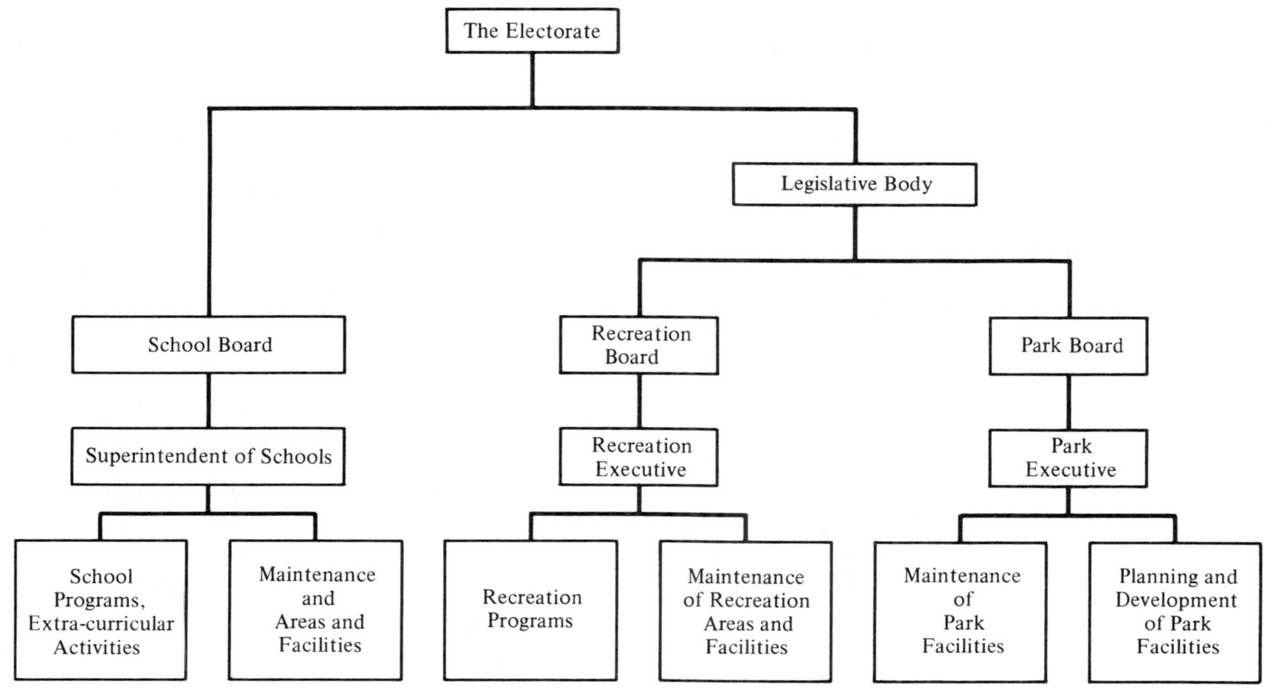

FIGURE 4-2. Independent agency under a board (hypothetical example).

commission. The board, similar to a school board, has full authority over all public recreation services and use of facilities for public recreation purposes wherever they may be. It emphasizes program services and has a minimum of facilities but uses school, parks, and other public properties. It may be financed by the mill tax or by direct appropriation, but the board is independent of political ties. It is administered by a recreation executive employed by and responsible to the board.

A disadvantage is its dependency on other agencies for many physical facilities. It is an independent board and an exception to the usual plan of operational management under a chief administrator. There is a division of authority. The city manager form of government does not look with favor upon independent boards which divide the authority of management. Sometimes the public is confused about who is really responsible for the facilities used for recreation. There is no clear understanding as to what authority belongs to the chief executive and legislative body and what belongs exclusively to the board. Lack of cooperation and even tension often develop between the board and the administrative branch and this can seriously affect recreation administrative processes, budget allocations, coordination, use of general government resources and the amount of support obtained from other department heads. The management process would be slow and unwieldy if all agencies had policy-making boards. The special tax, when used, often does not yield sufficient funds to take care of all the needs.

A Combined Recreation and Parks Agency

This plan, shown in Fig. 4-3, is one of the more popular forms of organization, both for agencies and professional recreation organizations. It combines in a single agency, under a trained and experienced executive, who is titled "director," all of the functions of parks and recreation. All resources are oriented to a single purpose which is providing recreation services. The theory is that both facilities and program are for the use of the people which has highest priority. All parks are for the use of people and some may even have active play areas. Areas are designed for a purpose. Some are for active and some for passive uses. This type of organization results in three main divisions: (1) administrative; (2) recreation (leadership); and (3) parks (areas and facilities), each expert in its respective field and complementary to one another.

The advantages are that all services are under the jurisdiction of a single agency and use, repairs and maintenance can be coordinated with a minimum of effort. There is opportunity for better understanding and joint effort among staff. Facilities are essential to the recreation program and only program can justify facilities; one complements the other and

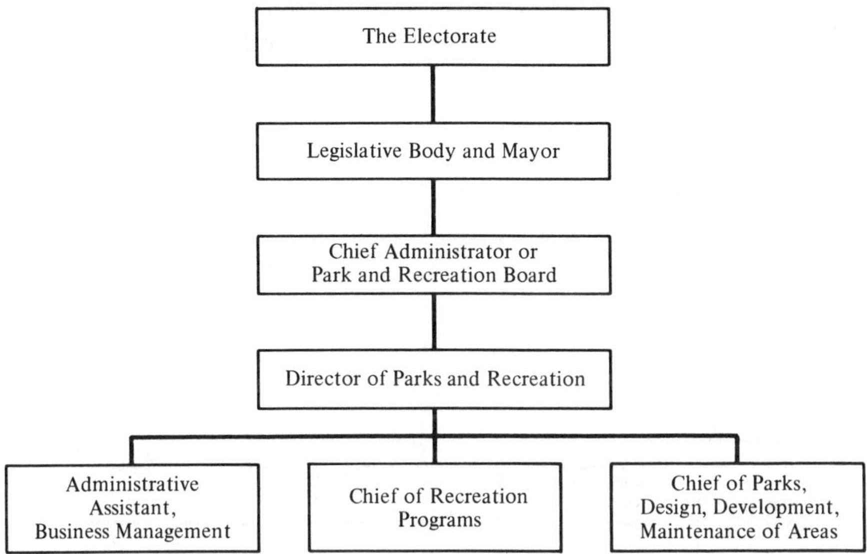

Figure 4-3. Combined recreation and park department (hypothetical example).

both are essential elements of a successful service. All efforts are pointed in the same direction. Duplication and overlapping are reduced along with costs and a more efficient use of skilled personnel is achieved. The form is adaptable to small and large communities and provides for maximum efficiency and economy. Maintenance and landscaping upgrade the recreation areas and add beauty.

The disadvantages are that the executive may not be equally competent or interested in both the parks and recreation phases, but this is not a very strong reason if there is a good administrator. The separate services are not independent but tend to operate independently.

Recreation Directed by Park Agency

The plan shown in Fig. 4-4 is similar to that of the combined recreation and park agency except that recreation is subordinate to the park commission or executive. This form is an outgrowth of a continuing strong parks organization that has adjusted somewhat to the changing times but has maintained its basic structure and identity. It, like the combined agency, is effective in both small and large communities but recreation, like any secondary program, under this plan yields administrative authority and prestige to the primary function of parks. As a result, in some instances, incomplete community recreation services are provided. Other public agencies such as schools, community action programs, and county

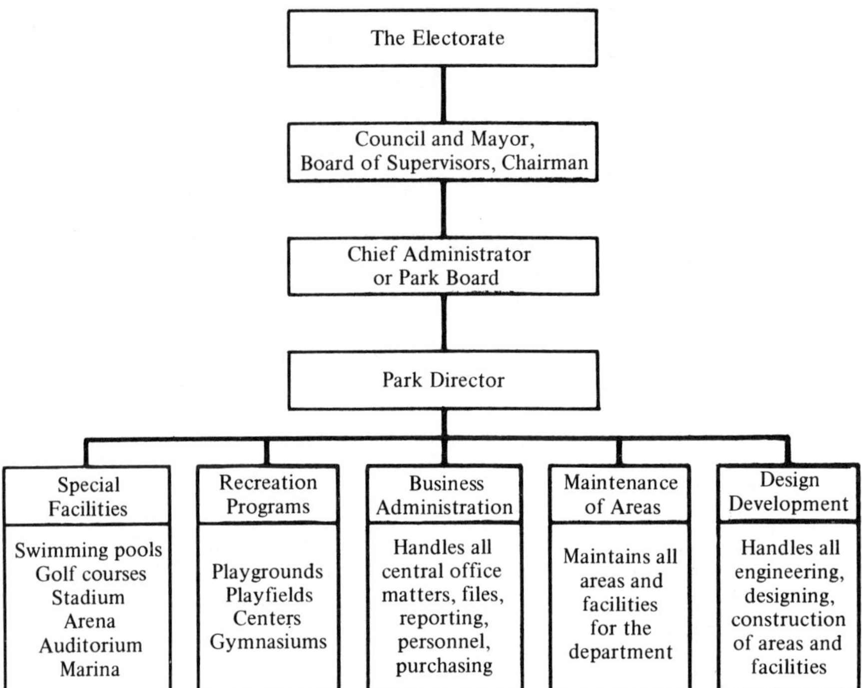

Figure 4-4. Recreation directed by park agency (hypothetical example).

authorities may also independently develop recreation programs in the same area, thus creating duplication of effort and division of authority.

The advantages are that provision is made for a recreation program even though it may be a secondary function. Use of park facilities is stimulated and often improved maintenance is provided.

The disadvantages are that schools and other facilities often are not widely used for recreation, programs are sometimes limited in scope and usually are the first to be curtailed or eliminated when funds are short. Work programs tend to be facility-oriented rather than people-oriented. Sometimes, indoor programs are lacking. Often park personnel do not understand the full values of recreation.

Recreation Directed by School Board

In certain areas of America, such as the Middle Atlantic and Great Lakes States,[2] several public recreation programs are conducted by the public school system, as described in Fig. 4-5. In Milwaukee, Wisconsin, for instance, an assistant superintendent of schools is in charge of public recreation and adult education. Cities which have used this form successfully are White Bear Lake, Minnesota; Salem, Oregon; and Newark, New Jersey. This form is more popular in cities of heavy population concentration and older cities where space is at a premium and recreation needs are great. Many educators in the United States and Canada support this form of organization. Recreationists, however, generally support plans which make recreation a primary function of the agency. Executives who have worked in both systems state the problems of joint use of facilities are the same. The success of any system is affected by what is permitted by law and how well the individuals involved cooperate and use their resources.

Both schools and recreation agencies in recent years have had many challenges that have taxed the resources and ingenuity of each. Naturally, when there are limited resources and problems develop that require full effort, priorities have to be determined. Decision and policy makers are obliged to give the primary function priority attention.

Trends show an increase in the role of schools in providing use of facilities for community purposes,[3] in preparing individuals for leisure time, providing training in recreation skills, re-training adults for a new leisure through adult education, and night schools, but a diminishing role nationally as a primary agency for administering public recreation. Also, in some instances, there is an increasing tendency on the part of public recreation to make its facilities available for school purposes through joint planning and coordination of efforts.

The advantages of a school-administered program are that training for leisure and the provision of opportunities for self expression are under the same jurisdiction. The school facilities may be more completely used and better planned for recreation. More staff resources are available and the programs would have the full backing of the school personnel. On the premise that play is educational, play can be administered by persons skilled in education.

The disadvantages are that the school board is primarily concerned with school age children and is not responsible for the whole family—pre-school, parents, and senior citizen. Schools are designed for the mass education of children and are not adaptable or available for total recreation services. In many communities, school budgets are inadequate for school purposes and recreation programs would provide a further strain. Recreation is a secondary function of schools and experience has shown that secondary functions are the first to be curtailed when budgets are inadequate. School personnel tend to apply to recreation the same philosophy and practices they use in education. Schools are under state influence and, therefore, are not strictly flexible to serve all community recreation needs. The school board, in most instances, is an independent authority

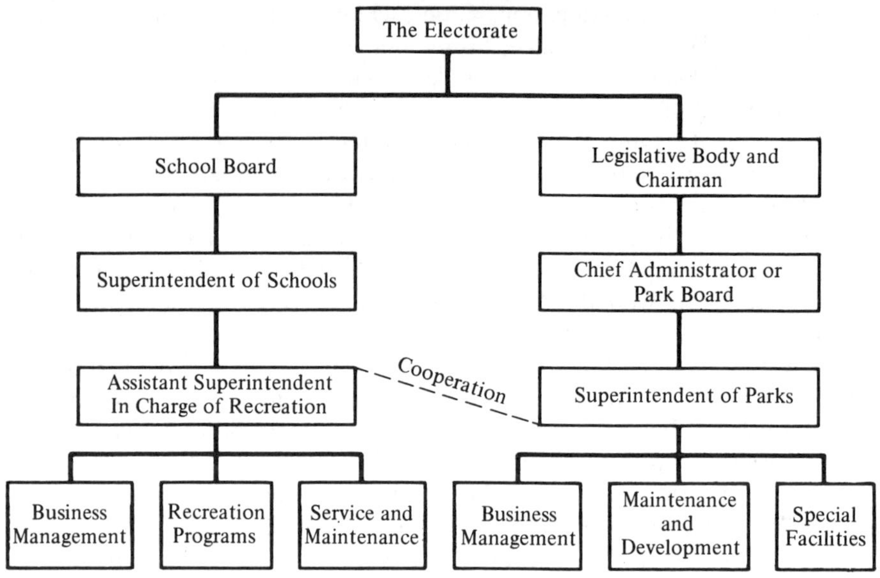

Figure 4-5. Recreation directed by school board (typical example).

and cooperation with other agencies is not assured. The many recreation facilities and opportunities not normally under jurisdiction of schools such as parks, beaches, camping areas, golf courses, zoos, marinas would necessitate another agency to cover them. Relationships with schools are discussed further in Chapter 6.

Miscellaneous Organizational Forms

Various localities throughout the country have different forms of organization to meet local conditions. For example, several cities include in the recreation and/or parks department other functions such as cemeteries and memorial parks, stadiums, auditoriums, marinas, yacht basins, coliseums, arenas, libraries, cultural activities, and symphony orchestras. These services are sometimes added to the organization as separate units. A few agencies may be structured as divisions or bureaus. There are district and county forms that may be different but the same general principles of organization apply.

No matter how the organization is structured, the recreationist's goals and objectives at the program level are the same—to provide services to people. The more direct the lines of communication are, the more effective administration is. It takes time and effort to pass a directive through several levels of supervision. Each time it is relayed, it stands the chance of losing effectiveness or even having someone change its meaning. The organizational structure, therefore, should be as simple as possible.

Considerations in Organization

The efficient achievement of objectives may be accomplished through good organization. Since work can be divided in several ways, the choice and effectiveness of the organization depends greatly upon the skill of management in arranging the work and the motivations. Since decisions are involved, the decision-maker looks for guidelines which, in organization, may be certain principles learned through research and experience. These involve identification of component parts, assignment of duties, defining responsibilities, delegation of authority, coordination of resources, establishment of lines of communication and defining the "chain of command."

Organizational relationships should motivate individual initiative and enhance the quality of service. Ideally, in recreation, the organization should permit flexibility in order to allow individuals to adjust services to meet the requirements of changing interests or needs. The organizational structure should be a means to expedite the work to be performed and should not act as a hindrance.

The organization is built first around goals, objectives and the scope of services to be performed, rather than around personalities, individual attitudes or interests. It must be realized, however, that the organizational structure must take into consideration human relationships, human nature, human traits, and even matters which involve the emotions. The management theory is that the organization is set and the staff should be selected, developed, and adjusted to perform the desired tasks most efficiently. This is good strictly from a management point of view, but in modern times more stress is put on team effort and consideration is given to the component parts, including the subgroups and individuals and their attitudes, interests, loyalties and motivations. Needs, purposes, and personnel change. The organization structure and job assignments will, therefore, change from time to time. One can expect major changes at least every five years.

Modern management control is not directly authority-oriented. It is influenced by union contracts, public opinion, and staff involvement—again a team effort. Direction is accomplished more or less indirectly by a combination of records, psychology, human relations, public relations and influences to which individuals and groups of the organization respond favorably. Force and demand methods are out of style.

Assignments with similar duties and skills should be grouped together under the supervision of a specialist in the respective field of service. Specialization limits the scope of work to closely related elements.

Full effort, thought, skilled personnel and specialized equipment can, therefore, be directed towards a single subject, as compared to a general situation where personnel has to divide its attention among many subjects. For instance, recreation, depending on the size of program and resources, may be organized under the different program categories of sports, arts and crafts, and so forth. Certainly better performance can be expected of an arts and crafts specialist as compared to a general playground worker who instructs in the arts and crafts along with other activities. A suggested rule—*when an assignment utilizes full-time specialized equipment and personnel, specialists rather than generalists should be used.*

The organizational structure should attempt to reduce duplication and overlapping.

Professionalization and over-specialization tend towards isolation in government programs. Loyalty to the group or a cause may sometimes be greater than loyalty to the agency. One of the problems for the recreation executive is how to prevent "separatism" between program personnel and area and facility personnel.

The organizational structure should provide a balance of the program services of an agency and equalize the work loads of the agency staff. For instance, it is not unusual for the executive to be particularly interested in sports and add considerable emphasis to that one phase of program.

When the organization is large enough to divide and keep a full-time staff busy it is well to form districts and decentralize. This saves travel time, puts decision-making closer to the people served, and provides better opportunity for greater community involvement. Organization by districts or geographic areas, particularly in larger jurisdictions, is common but centralization is more generally used in smaller departments until the numbers of staff and operation sites justify at least two districts.

Rules for Organizing

These rules or principles apply particularly to the internal organization of the public recreation agency. They are widely used as guides in the administrative process.

1. Every position in the recreation and park organization plan should have a position card showing clearly defined duties, responsibilities, whom it is responsible to, whom it is responsible for, and the extent of authority. This is covered in the job specification for the position.
2. Every individual should be responsible to only one immediate boss. In other words "a man cannot serve two masters."

3. The need for coordination should be kept to a minimum. Decisions on routine matters should be made within two levels of supervision. Exceptions to rules or changes of policy, of course, will have to be made by the ones who established them.
4. The *span of control* (number of individuals a person supervises directly) should not exceed five immediate subordinates at the administrative level or generally no more than eight at the supervisory or foreman level.
5. Authority and resources should be delegated commensurate with responsibility. Administrative and supervisory personnel must be given sufficient authority to manage effectively all personnel and resources for which they are responsible. The person delegating the authority is, however, in the final analysis, always responsible.
6. Each individual should be placed under a supervisor sufficient in competence to direct his work. This means he should not be less competent than the subordinates he supervises. Persons should not be accountable to, or for, other persons of equal rank.
7. Decisions should be made and problems resolved as near the source of origin as possible. Lines of communications should be through the *chain of command,* which means the lines of administrative responsibility should be vertically from the executive at the apex of the pyramid of authority through channels of middle management and supervision to the individual unit worker at the base of the pyramid.
8. A "line" officer or supervisor should supervise two or more individuals. One over one is confusing and a duplication of responsibility.

INTERNAL ORGANIZATION

Internal organization is the grouping of the functions of the agency into similar specialized units of work, assigning responsibility, delegating authority, arranging relationships and defining lines of authority. The grouping generally includes five basic functions: (1) administrative (business management); (2) programs (recreation); (3) special facilities (golf, camps, zoos); (4) maintenance and development; and (5) design and construction. In larger organizations these functions may be expanded further or organized by areas, districts, or special purpose (single function) such as the swimming program. In public organizations they may be called divisions, bureaus, sections, districts, areas or units. A typical hierarchical triangle is shown in Fig. 4-6 which also shows levels of responsibility and chain of command.

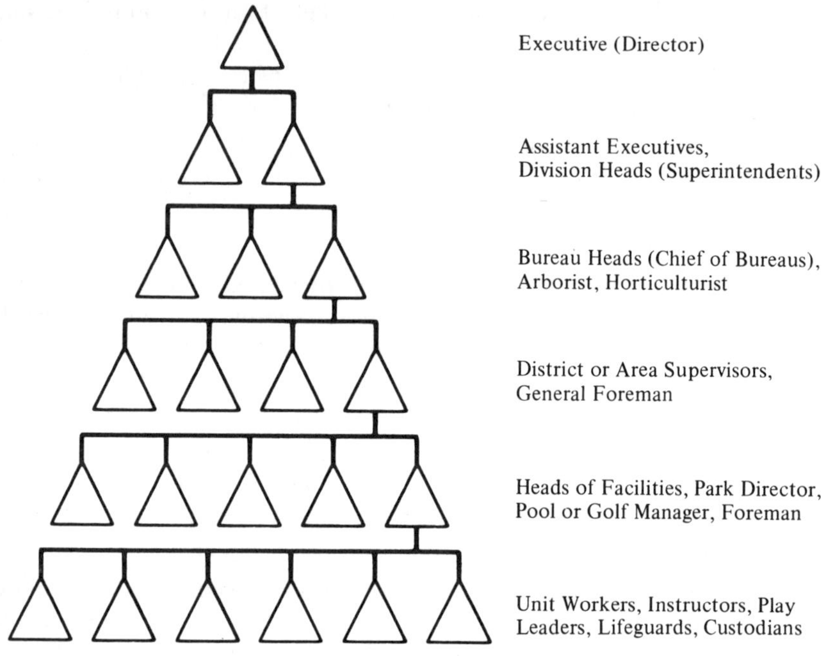

FIGURE 4-6. Hierarchical triangle.

Span of Control

Span of control refers to the number of subordinates for which a supervisor is directly responsible. It includes directly all of the workers on a horizontal level of the hierarchical triangle (organization chart) and indirectly, all workers below the immediate subordinates to the base of the triangle (See Fig. 4-6). The number of persons for which a supervisor may be responsible depends on the following factors:

1. The capacity and skill of the supervisor and methods of operation. Some people work fast and organize their time and resources well, delegating lesser important matters to others and handling only the essentials themselves. Others, require more contacts and details from subordinates and are slower to function.
2. The skill and independence of the employees. Professionals and well-trained employees usually require less time than the untrained and unskilled. A foreman usually spends full-time with laborers while the leader of a professional group may spend only a few minutes a day.
3. The diversity and complexity of the services. The more variable and

changing the duties, the more time they require as compared to repetitive and routine activities, so that fewer persons can be directed effectively.

4. The rate of turnover in personnel. Considerable time may have to be spent in replacement—recruiting, interviewing, orientation and rearranging of work plan.
5. The need for in-service training and re-training.
6. The amount of time superior, peers, and public require. Programs of recreation require considerable administrative, supervisory, and employee time in public involvement.

In a small department, the executive has a dual function as executive and supervisor. He may be responsible for a secretary, a few full-time people and several part-time workers. Often the secretary doubles as an assistant or the executive delegates considerable authority to the full-time workers.

When three or more levels of supervision are involved, communication begins to be a problem. The former friendly, closely knit, well informed, two-level organization becomes a multi-level one with a top, bottom, and one or more middle echelons. Relationships become less personal, and regular, direct communication between top and bottom ceases to exist. Communication often becomes fuzzy and incomplete. Relationships in the organization are mainly within the individual's own unit, with his immediate supervisor, and with the adjoining horizontal units. Loyalties tend to develop in the area of contacts. Additional levels of supervision further complicate communications and administration. No perfect solution for handling communications in a multi-level organization has been devised. The executive and all staff members have to work hard constantly to keep communications open and running smoothly. Communication is one of the major problems in large organizations.

Internal Staff Structure

Although the forms of organization of the managing authority of a public recreation and park agency may vary, the needs of the people, work programs, and the internal staff structure to serve them are similar and could be structured or attached to any of the administrative organization forms shown in Figs. 4-1 through 4-5. The staff structure is based on the administration, programs, special facilities, maintenance, design and construction, and the various work programs discussed earlier.

As an agency grows, the need for other specialized functions develops, and such specialities as public relations, planning and design, research, finance, personnel, and purchasing may be added. In smaller organizations, the recreation executive may handle these responsibilities, if they are not taken care of by central agencies. Smaller organizations may have only three functions (administration, programs, and maintenance and development) with the executive personally handling administration and development.

In a one-man department, the internal staff structure is simple. The recreation executive handles all administrative functions that are not performed by the central service agencies. The secretary, maintenance, and program staff may be part-time or seasonal, supplemented by volunteers. Charting those functions would be as follows:

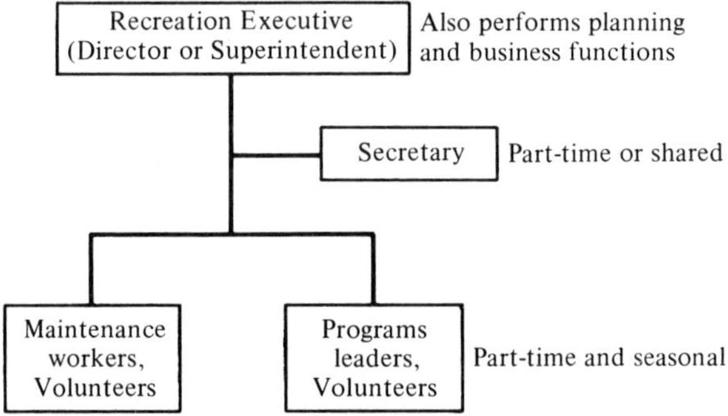

As the services are expanded and new programs are added, the part-time staff may be extended to full-time. Specialists may be added to direct the specialized functions such as "program" and "maintenance." The secretary position may be made full-time to handle secretarial work for all staff as well as to perform some of the business functions.

Agency services may be expanded further by adding specialized facilities such as a *golf course* or a *marina* and specialized agency-wide functional programs such as *athletics* or *horiticulture*. An additional office position, such as a clerk or clerk-typist, would be needed also. These positions could be charted as follows:

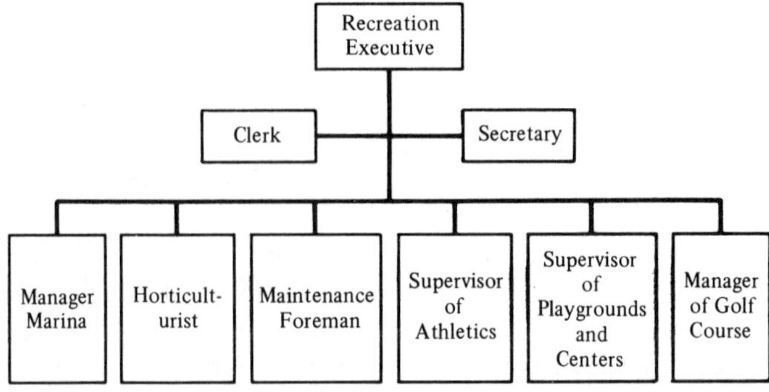

As an organization develops and more staff and specialized services are added, the work load of the executive becomes greater than one person can handle well. A practical solution is to group similar functions and add functional specialists to have charge of each grouping. They would be, in effect, assistant executives responsible for a major unit of closely related agency services. In extending the above example a step further, the marina, the horticulturist, and the maintenance functions which are related to the services for physical properties could be grouped under the park superintendent. The golf course, the athletics, and the playground/center functions which are related to the services for people could be grouped under the supervision of the recreation superintendent. Note in the chart below that the work load would be rather evenly divided between the Recreation Executive, the Superintendent of Parks, and the Superintendent of Recreation. Each is responsible for four positions, including the clerical positions. There is room for further expansion without overloading any administrative or supervisory staff position. These positions may be charted as follows:

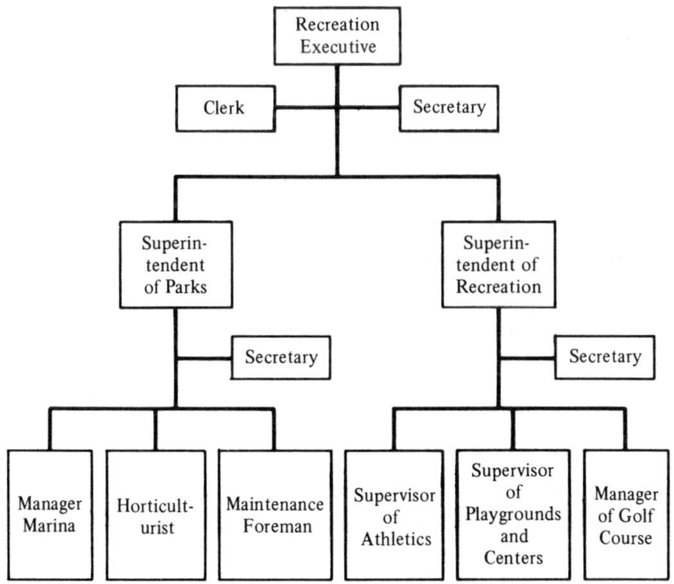

As the functions are expanded and additional services are specialized, new units such as a *Zoo* or *Botanical Garden* could be added to "Parks" and new units such as *Amphitheatre* or *Special Programs* could be added to "Recreation."

When an agency or a function becomes large enough to keep a full-time staff and supporting services busy, the agency services and staff may be organized by areas or districts (as shown in Figs. 4-9 and 4-10).

Almost every locality has central service units that provide specialized functions for all agencies. Such services may include public relations, personnel, finance, accounting, data processing, purchasing, etc. Other departments may provide designing, engineering, roadwork, utilities, the skilled trades, and general maintenance for "Recreation," especially for small departments. If the supporting services are provided by other agencies, the full recreation appropriation may be used for program services. For example, the organization chart for four full-time staff members and director handling sports, may be as shown in Fig. 4-7. In charting an expanding organization structure it is well to provide for future expansion as shown with dotted lines.

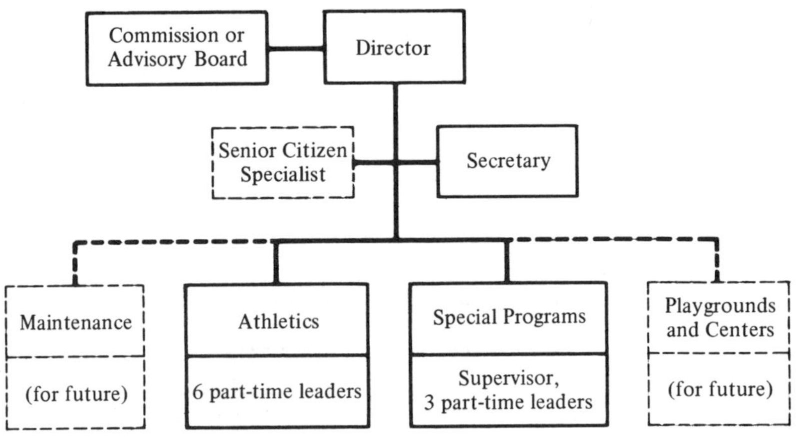

FIGURE 4-7.

The chart for a middle-size city agency might correspond to that shown in Fig. 4-8.

The recreation organization of a middle-size city may evolve with three major divisions, with programs and special facilities combined in one and an administrative assistant acting as business manager. Park special facilities may also be under maintenance. The director often has "staff" specialists attached to his office. The administrative assistant may serve as assistant to the director.

There are basically four types of positions:

1. Administrative positions are those which involves management, policy, and decision making. This includes the executive, staff specialists, and middle management (Fig. 4-8, A, B, and C).

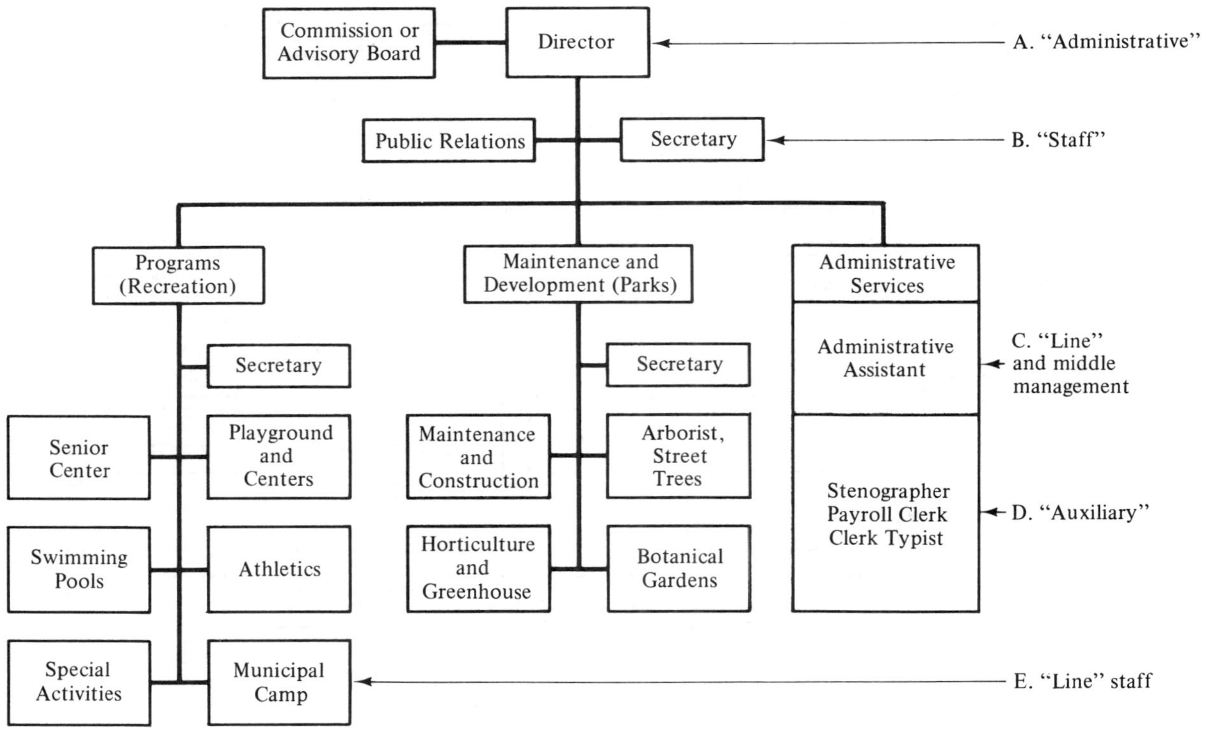
Commission or Advisory Board
Director
A. "Administrative"
Public Relations
Secretary
B. "Staff"
Programs (Recreation)
Maintenance and Development (Parks)
Administrative Services
Administrative Assistant
C. "Line" and middle management
Secretary
Secretary
Senior Center
Playground and Centers
Maintenance and Construction
Arborist, Street Trees
Stenographer
Payroll Clerk
Clerk Typist
D. "Auxiliary"
Swimming Pools
Athletics
Horticulture and Greenhouse
Botanical Gardens
Special Activities
Municipal Camp
E. "Line" staff

FIGURE 4-8.

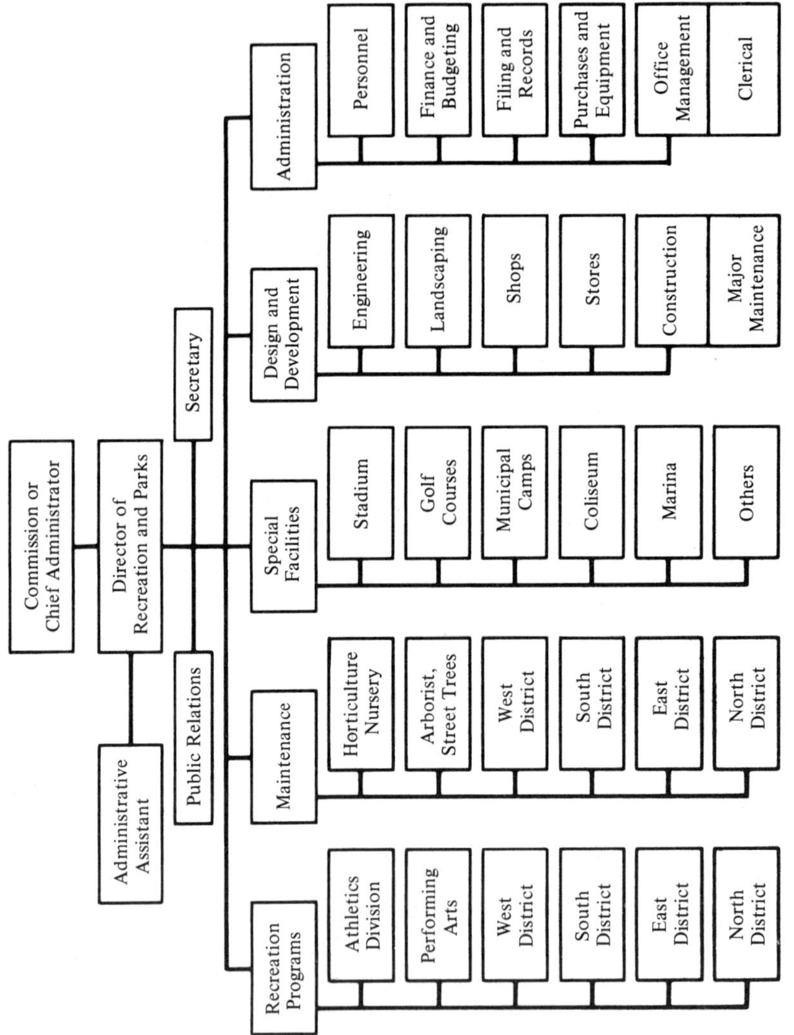
Commission or Chief Administrator
Director of Recreation and Parks
Administrative Assistant
Public Relations
Secretary
Recreation Programs
Athletics Division
Performing Arts
West District
South District
East District
North District
Maintenance
Horticulture Nursery
Arborist, Street Trees
West District
South District
East District
North District
Special Facilities
Stadium
Golf Courses
Municipal Camps
Coliseum
Marina
Others
Design and Development
Engineering
Landscaping
Shops
Stores
Construction
Major Maintenance
Administration
Personnel
Finance and Budgeting
Filing and Records
Purchases and Equipment
Office Management
Clerical

FIGURE 4-9.

2. "Line" positions are program-oriented and are positions of authority in the *line* organization directly responsible for program services to the public (Fig. 4-8, C and E). Line responsibilities are indicated on organization charts by vertical lines.
3. "Staff" positions are advisory, without "line" authority, and are not directly in the chain of command. They usually aid line positions in technical or program matters such as research, planning, and reporting. Staff responsibilities are indicated on organization charts by horizontal lines (Fig. 4-8, B).
4. Auxiliary or ancillary positions are of a general nature which provide essential support services to line and technical positions. These include clerical, stenographic, custodial, and processing personnel. Their purpose is to make line functions more efficient.

The basic organization chart for a larger city may be similar to that shown in Fig. 4-9.

Each locality must design the organization plan that will best serve its needs. The principles of organization apply equally to large or small agencies. In the smaller agency, duties are consolidated under fewer persons. The larger agency will have more levels of supervision, more subunits, more specialists, more complications, and usually more operating functions. A large community is composed of a series of small communities and neighborhoods. As the community grows, another neighborhood may be added to the community and a new area to the organization. In the early stages of development, services are provided by adding new staff and programs to existing units.

In some instances, "special facilities," such as coliseum, museum, stadium, may have their own boards and operate independently.

An example of a recreation staff organization plan for a district, such as "North District" in Fig. 4-9, is shown in Fig. 4-10. This could also be applied to the city-wide program staff organization of a department in which maintenance is a separate work program.

In this plan, the services could be expanded by adding more specialists or dividing the district into two areas and employing an area supervisor for each area. This would add another level of supervision but would double the number of recreation units that could be supervised adequately. It could be expanded further by adding an area supervisor for each five or six additional units. Center B in Fig. 4-10 is a major recreation unit with indoor center, gymnasium and swimming pool in conjunction with a playfield and playground. Staff is under a center director and interchangeable where needed. Sometimes, all units shown under Center B cannot be provided for at one site, but may be dispersed at several sites.

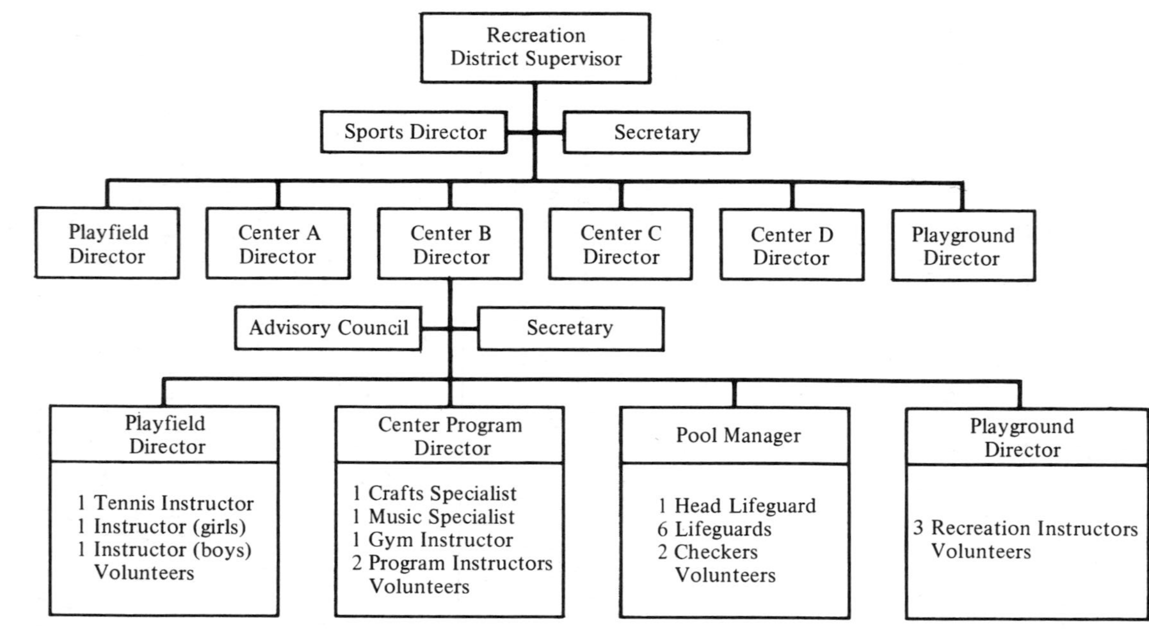

Figure 4-10. District staff organization plan, and division of responsibilities of a major recreation unit staff.

Coordination of Agency Functions

Every unit of the recreation organization performs a specialized function, none of which, by itself, delivers a complete service to the public. Each is dependent to some extent upon specialized services provided by other units. The different functions must, therefore, be integrated and coordinated in order to accomplish the total purpose of the organization. Thus, a unit of skilled tradesmen (carpenters, painters, plumbers) or an athletic unit may contribute to the fulfillment of the objectives of each recreation unit. Administration contributes by formulating policies, standards, rules, regulations, instructions, procedures, and general guidelines for attaining objectives and handling problems plus making resources available, removing obstacles, and planning for future needs. The supervisors contribute interpretation of administrative guidelines, instructions, guidance, training, motivation, coordination, solutions to problems, and other items similar to those of administration but at the work program level.

Administration must have procedures and guidelines that can be applied to every conceivable situation that might develop anywhere in the organization, so that decisions can be made on the spot by functional workers and/or their supervisors without having to interrupt operations to take the problem up the "chain of command." The functioning staff and supervision should be provided with adequate delegated authority and guidelines to make decisions at or near the source of any problem. Although an executive must maintain reasonable control of the organization he heads, he must share information and provide adequate authority for the administrative and supervisory staff to perform their normal duties effectively, efficiently, and completely. Rare and infrequent situations which may not be covered by existing guidelines are expected occasionally to be referred up the chain of command for decision or interpretation but only rarely should it have to ascend more than two levels for appropriate decision.

Questions for Discussion

1. What are the basic work programs in a recreation and parks system?
2. Is there a difference between recreation and park philosophy? Explain your reason.
3. Explain the forms of organizational structure for administering park and recreation services. Which would you recommend? Why?
4. What principles of organization would you use in forming the organizational structure of a park and recreation agency?

5. What would you do as an administrator of a small agency to continue services without interruption if your only sports director terminated at the peak of the season?
6. Explain the major contributions of each of the four basic types of positions in an organization.
7. What do you consider to be the proper role of schools in relation to public recreation organizations?
8. What are the main problems to consider in setting up a municipal recreation organization?
9. What would you do as executive when a staff member develops rapidly and can efficiently supervise more workers?
10. What is the difference in staff organization for a small agency and a large one?
11. Define unity of command? Span of control? Divided authority? Chain of command? Line position? Staff position? Auxiliary position?
12. Why should authority be delegated? What would be the effect of not delegating authority?

Short Problems

1. Prepare work programs for a combined recreation and park agency in a city of 150,000 population and show them on an organization chart.
2. List all of the guidelines an executive uses in preparing an organization chart for a public recreation and parks system.
3. Prepare a plan for transferring administration of recreation from public works to a separate recreation and park department.

References

1. *Recreation and Park Yearbook 1966* (Washington, D.C.: National Recreation and Park Association, 1967), pp. 41, 46.
2. Results of a study made by the Author.
3. "Local Parks and Recreation," *Parks and Recreation*, August 1971, p. 27.

Selected Readings

Albers, H. Henry, *Principles of Management: A Modern Approach* (4th ed.), pp. 63–78. New York: John Wiley and Sons, Inc., 1974.

Athos, A., and R. Caffey, *Behavior in Organizations.* Englewood Cliffs, N.J.: Prentice-Hall, Inc., 1968.

Bannon, Joseph J., *Problem Solving in Recreation and Parks.* Englewood Cliffs, N.J.: Prentice-Hall, Inc., 1972.

Filly, Alan C., and Robert House, *Managerial Process and Organizational Behavior.* Glenville, Ill.: Scott, Foresman and Co., 1969.

Hjelte, George, and Jay S. Shivers, *Public Administration of Recreational Services,* pp. 49–86. Philadelphia: Lea and Febiger, 1972.

Lutzin, Sidney G., and Edward H. Storey, *Managing Municipal Leisure Services,* pp. 109–123. Washington, D.C.: International City Management Association, 1973.

Meyer, Harold, Charles Brightbill, and H. Douglas Sessoms, *Community Recreation: A Guide to Its Organization* (4th ed.). Englewood Cliffs, N.J.: Prentice-Hall, Inc., 1969.

Rodney, Lynn S., *Administration of Public Recreation,* pp. 72–93. New York: The Ronald Press Company, 1964.

Scott, William G., *Organization Concepts and Analysis for Management.* Belmont, Calif.: Wadsworth Publishing Company, Inc., 1969.

CHAPTER 5

External Relationships

Historically, local government has been provided by a legislative process through town meetings, commissions, common councils, and boards of supervisors which pass laws and establish policies but delegate managerial responsibilities to a chief administrator—town clerk, county executive, mayor, county or city manager, to whom the recreation executive is usually accountable. Often the legislative body shares its authority by appointing a policy board or commission to administer the recreation services, in which instance the recreation executive will be accountable to the policy board and is employed by it. Much of the success of the community in general, and recreation in particular, depends on sound policies, progressive administrative practices, competent leadership, and dedicated support provided by the legislative and administrative units, plus the skill of the recreation executive in applying them wisely in execution of the various recreation services.

Public recreation provides leisure time opportunities for the entire community and it uses all of the resources available from other public agencies, private, semi-private, and commercial places. It cooperates with clubs, associations, civic groups, special interest groups, churches, businesses, and all recreation-related activities in the community. The recreation executive, therefore, is not only the director of the public recreation agency but also the leader and coordinator of leisure-time interests and uses of public facilities for the entire community. This chapter will review these different relationships.

COMMISSIONS AND BOARDS

There are two kinds of boards relating to the recreation agency: the policy-making or authoritative board or commission, and the non-authoritative advisory board. Most policy boards have limited powers and their authority is determined by state enabling legislation, charter or local legislation. The terms *board* and *commission* are used interchangeably in describing boards of authority, but advisory boards are seldom called commissions. Recreation is a service very close to the people it serves and commissions and/or advisory boards provide, at the administrative level, a means of active citizen involvement in decision making and program planning.

The Policy-Making Authoritative Board

The recreation policy board of 5 to 9 members (usually 5 or 7) is an independent board similar to a school board with competent citizen membership appointed by the legislative body for staggered terms of three or four years so that the terms of not more than one half of the members will expire during any one year. Sometimes, the terms run concurrently with those of the elected body. Nominations for appointments are usually made by the presiding officer subject to approval of the legislative body. Only rarely is the recreation executive asked to recommend names, but he should be prepared to make recommendations. Sometimes, where the commission has legislative powers, the members are elected. Members serve without compensation, although some may receive per diem and/or expenses for attending official meetings.

Most boards establish bylaws, procedures, and rules to guide them in the conduct of their business. Bylaws may include a statement of policy, duties of the board and committees, board organization, time and place of meetings, rules and procedures for conducting business of the board, order of agenda, and other items necessary for the orderly conduct of its functions.

Laymen accept these non-paying positions out of a sense of civic duty, for honor and prestige, and because of personal interest in various aspects of the services rendered. It is well for members to have interest, knowledge, and ability to analyze facts and make sound judgements concerning the various functions of the agency. The recreation executive and skilled staff can adequately represent the professional and technical fields, but it is well if the board members have areas of knowledge that can supplement the executive's resources in serving the community. It is well to have the points of view of men, women and youth on the board.

Boards usually elect their own chairman and vice chairman. One of the members may be secretary or the department may provide a secretary, who often is the executive's secretary (without vote). The executive should attend all meetings, usually held monthly, and be prepared to make recommendations and explanatory comments. The executive usually is responsible, in consultation with the board chairman, for the meeting agenda and matters relating to the meeting. Funds are handled through normal city procedures, therefore, no treasurer is needed.

It adds interest, facilitates action at board meetings, and gives members specific responsibilities, if committees on specific subjects such as finances, facilities, and public relations are appointed. On the other hand, committees do provide opportunities for persons other than the chairman to make contacts on official matters with the executive phases of the system. Rules, responsibilities and procedures should be carefully defined for each committee to prevent overlap and conflict of authority. Meetings are open to the public and should be held in a central place convenient to the public.

Until recently the recreation commission has been the popular form of public recreation administration.[1] Since 1940, the trend has been towards the combined recreation and parks department under the city manager, county executive or other chief administrator. The August 1971 issue of *Parks and Recreation* stated that most of the 1112 agencies reporting had citizen boards or commissions and most members were appointed. It reported that 45 percent were policy-making; 39 percent were advisory; 9 percent had no boards and 6 percent other.[2]

Commission Functions

The basic functions of the recreation commission, which may vary, as may be determined by the state enabling legislation and local ordinances, include the following:

1. To employ the recreation and park executive and to establish his duties and responsibilities.
2. To establish the purposes, objectives, policies, procedures, and other guidelines for the management of the agency programs and services, refer them to the executive for execution, and give him support. The making of policies is emphasized as the main function of the authoritative board and their implementation is the basic function of the executive. Policies reflect the purposes and aims of the agency and provide general direction. They are value judgments made for general guidance. The expertise of the technician is required to devise the best methods to accomplish the objectives efficiently and effectively within the general guidelines of the policies. For instance, the commission may decide to operate a certain center and approve the budget for it, but the executive decides how it is to be operated, and what program is to be provided there, employs staff and makes specific rules and regulations for management and operations.
3. To establish the standards of quality and the scope of the services to be rendered.

4. To serve as liaison between citizens and agency; to interpret citizen needs and interests and provide programs, facilities and services to serve their needs; to interpret the value of recreation to the public in order to gain their interest, understanding, and assistance.
5. To establish a sound fiscal plan satisfactory to the community; to commend sources of income and to approve the budget and fiscal matters.
6. To keep the general public and public officials informed concerning the status of the recreation and parks programs.
7. To receive and evaluate reports from the executive, and act as a board of appeal on any action not resolved satisfactorily by the executive. Its actions are final since it is the highest authority related officially to the department.
8. To represent the department at ceremonials and official events including budget matters.
9. To make rules for the conduct of the commission's business and meetings. These should be in written form and distributed to everyone involved. Often these are put in the form of "by-laws" and list in orderly fashion the rules, regulations, order of agenda as guidelines for conduct of board business, time and place of board meetings, any committee organization, duties of the board, and sometimes include general policy statements.

Complete minutes and records should be maintained of every official meeting and transaction, and copies provided each member, the secretary, executive, and chief administrator.

Functions of the Executive Under a Commission

The question may logically be raised as to why the functions of the executive should be different under a commission than under a chief administrator such as a city manager. The commission is a creature of the legislative body, appointed by it, reporting to it, and having close advisory relationships with it. Its members are laymen representing the legislative body, which is also composed of laymen but who have legislative powers. The chief administrator is not responsible for the board or its executive. This sometimes creates a problem of cooperation with the administrator. The board and its recreation executive are responsible for the direction of the independent recreation agency and have some responsibilities that are ordinarily assumed by the chief administrator such as approving the budget and evaluating the programs.

The responsibilities of the commission and executive are reasonably clear cut, one making policies and the other implementing them. The relationship should be one of cooperation, reciprocity, and understanding. Because the executive is a paid professional it is considered his responsibility to practice sound management, cultivate good relations with members of the commission, and acquaint them with activities of the department. His relationships will be mainly with the chairman of the board but he should treat all commissioners alike, that is, provide each the same information and assistance. Likewise, the commission should make contacts with the agency through the executive.

It is a good practice to orient newly appointed commission members with a summary of pertinent information, policies, immediate objectives, and problems as soon as they are appointed.

The basic functions of the executive include the following:

1. To select, assign, and develop staff for the agency in accordance with established personnel procedures and formulate rules and regulations for their management, safety, and conduct. It is important that this function be a management function without influence from the commissioners, except with regard to appeals of grievances.
2. To make studies and recommendations to the board based on facts and sound professional judgements.
3. To make problem-solving and policy recommendations to the commission in writing, along with supportive facts, objectives, and judgments as to effects. It is well for the executive to express his professional views on issues before they are discussed by commission members so that his comments will not appear to be influenced by their feelings.
4. To prepare, together with his staff, the annual budget for consideration by the commission.

It has been emphasized that the board makes policy and the executive implements it. Both operate separately but each is dependent upon the other. Executives do not legislate or make policy but, because of their technical knowledge and experience, do serve as consultants to the policy makers and call to their attention matters of concern to them. The executive also directs matters through their proper channels for commission or administrative action. The division of responsibilities should be maintained by the executive's working in harmony with the chairman and the commission as a whole. He avoids dealing with individual members on policy matters requiring commission decision. Discussions and consultations, of course, are held with the chairman. It is prudent to communicate with commission members on official matters in writing with copies to all members. Avoid confidential conversations and commitments with individual members. An "open" policy (same information for all) will tend to prevent involvement in personal differences, politics, feelings of favoritism, "pet" ideas, and pressure tactics.

Strengths of the Commission Form

Members of the commission are usually appointed by the legislative body and are considered somewhat insulated from political pressure groups. As laymen interested in a single department, members are in a good position to represent citizens' interests and to know their needs. Members usually have varying experience, knowledge and talents which can provide different points of view and broad experience in decision-making. They supplement and extend the executive's usefulness. They serve as a sounding board for citizen opinion and can speak with authority in dealing with community problems.

Weaknesses of the Commission Form

The commission is a separate policy-making group set apart from the central administrator and, as such, tends to divide administrative authority. It provides two policy boards (the legislative body and the recreation commission) and divides policy-making responsibilities. It tends to create situations where there is less cooperation and administrative teamwork between the commission and the chief administrator and this, in turn, reduces efficiency. The members of the commission tend to extend their loyalty to the unit that appoints them and sometimes overreach their authority. In this kind of situation, it is easy to see why professional administrators prefer clear-cut and streamlined lines of authority as provided by the single department form of organization, administered by a single executive with the aid of a citizen's advisory board.

The Recreation Advisory Board

The second type of official board is the advisory board consisting of five to fifteen members (mostly 7 to 11) appointed by the legislative body for terms of three to five years, or as provided by the charter or authority establishing the agency. Advisory boards are usually a little larger than authoritative boards. Very often, the advisory board will include a member of the school board, a member of a separate park board, and a member of the planning commission, each appointed by his parent organization, with terms coinciding with their terms on their respective boards. The organization of the boards is similar to that of the authoritative commissions but their functions are purely advisory. Members serve without compensation and without legal authority or direct responsibility for the administration of the recreation agency. The fact they are appointed by the legislative body, however, and serve without compensation and without opportunity for personal gain puts them in a good position to represent the interests of the citizenry. With the guidance of a dedicated chairman and recreation director they can be very effective in supporting action programs, interpreting community needs, informing officials of the values of recreation, and sharing their specialized experiences which are varied and different from those of the executive.

The Advisory Board Needs Strong Leadership

Unless it has strong leadership and sound guidance, the advisory board may deteriorate to a passive role and become disinterested without making any significant contribution to the recreation movement. On the other hand, if it is given meaningful assignments and a feeling of being an essential part of the system, it can be of tremendous aid to the executive and the administration. The contribution of the advisory board is almost directly related to the skill and interest of the recreation executive in directing the talents and resources it contains.

It is important that the membership of the advisory board include a variety of talents and experience to help the executive make accurate decisions on matters relating to technical and professional aspects of the community recreation involvement.

Present Status of Advisory Boards

It is the authors' observation that the authoritative commission was popular earlier when public recreation was a controversial service, politically influenced, not legally defined or popularly accepted. Recreation then was more closely associated with schools, playgrounds, and physical education and some organizers and promoters felt the school board type of administration to be the best for the recreation service. Many independent agencies were, therefore, patterned after the school board.

In recent years, public recreation has been elevated to the status of an essential service and has broadened its objectives. Public administration has been streamlined and as many authorities as possible consolidated under the direction of professional administrators such as a city or county manager, or other chief administrator. In such instances, it has not been popular to divide authority and responsibilities among authoritative boards. The need for and advantages of independent boards have diminished with the advent of the professional chief executive and it has become attractive for park and recreation services to merge and coordinate with other departments under the direction of the professional administrator. The advisory board, as a means of providing community involvement in decision-making, has been considered more compatible with centralized authority and has taken on a new importance.

George Hjelte and Jay Shivers state, "Administrators of recreational service departments heretofore have preferred commissions, but this preference appears to be waning. . . . Until 1940, more than three fourths of American urban departments of recreational services were governed by commissions of laymen. Over the past 20 years the trend slowly has been reversed, although commissions still are in the majority." [1]

The 1971 *Parks and Recreation Yearbook* [2] showed only six percent more policy boards than advisory boards.

City managers and other chief administrators contacted by the author expressed preference for recreation advisory boards rather than authoritative boards. It was their feeling that lines of authority should be clear-cut and not divided between the chief administrator and an autonomous recreation commission. They felt the recreation advisory board provided citizen involvement and was compatible with the popular city manager and county executive forms of government.

Strengths of the Advisory Board Form

The strengths of the advisory board are that it can be added at any level of management without changing normal lines of administrative authority; provides citizen involvement in policy-making, planning, program and facility development; and is a channel for communication between management and citizen interests. Because advisory boards are usually larger than authoritative boards, they provide for broader representation and a wider distribution of talents and knowledge resources for planning and decision-making. Full efforts can be directed to community services and programs since they are not responsible for legislative decisions. An advisory board is very effective in team efforts on matters of interpretation, public information, and community services.

Weaknesses of the Advisory Board Form

The boards are advisory and can make only recommendations and, therefore, they cannot speak or act with authority. This is sometimes frustrating to members. Board members sometimes try to assume authority they do not have. These weaknesses may be avoided or overcome by clearly defined board objectives, rules and procedures; careful orientation of new members; and skilled direction by the recreation executive and board chairman. Board members often lose interest when their recommendations are not accepted. Individual board members sometimes tend to exploit membership for their own interests.

COMMITTEES AND ADVISORY GROUPS

Traditionally, the recreation movement has involved laymen and the public in the various phases of recreation administration from making surveys to making policy. With several levels of supervision in large agencies and centralized administration, government decision-making has gotten too far removed from the people it serves. One way of continuing to involve citizens at the "grass roots" level is through the boards and commissions which where discussed earlier and committees and advisory councils which will be discussed now.

Committees

Committees are usually appointed by a presiding or authoritative officer or organized by a functional person to make a study and report, or to accomplish a specific task, often of short duration. In permanent organizations, however, there may be standing committees that have certain specific assignments.

In recreation, there are both standing committees, usually serving for a year, such as the finance, program, and publicity committees and the committees on special events and girls' sports. Functional, short term committees are organized for a specific purpose such as to make a survey of unmet needs, to help organize and promote a major event, to plan dedication of a new facility, or to sponsor a holiday celebration. These committees may or may not include staff members, but it is wise for the agency to provide a competent staff member, preferably one interested in or responsible for the particular assignment, to be committee secretary and motivator. Such committees are composed of three to seven interested citizens, skilled in phases of the assignment involved. In this way, talent and ability can be obtained that would not otherwise be available, and citizen action becomes involved in the process of planning and decision-making.

Advisory Councils

There are at least six reasons why every recreation agency should have an advisory council: (1) To involve citizens in the processes of policy-making and program development; (2) To make use of unusual talent and interest available in the community; (3) To serve as advisor and liaison between the staff and the citizenry; (4) To perform certain functions such as fund raising, and to supplement the staff at times and provide other services that would not otherwise be available; (5) To assist in planning programs; and (6) To assist with public relations and information.

The councils work with the responsible recreation staff in planning and developing programs that will best fill the needs of the community. They are most helpful when they clearly understand their function and when their responsibility is accepted willingly and enthusiastically. They function in an advisory capacity and *have no legal status.* Care should be taken to make sure this point is clearly understood. It is well to have bylaws and rules for the councils.

Types of Advisory Councils

There are four types of advisory councils in use, namely: (1) Neighborhood playground or recreation center advisory councils; (2) District recreation and/or park advisory councils; (3) City-wide advisory councils; and (4) Special advisory councils, such as for youth, senior citizens, and the mentally and physically handicapped.

NEIGHBORHOOD ADVISORY COUNCILS Such councils are composed of three to nine neighborhood people, preferably participants, parents, or others who are genuinely interested in developing a broad community recreation program for all age groups. Members do not have to be "key people" and should not be selected because of certain political or organization associations. Real interest and sincerity are the main requirements. It helps to have natural leadership and enough dedication to attend meetings. High officials and persons in important positions do not always make good neighborhood council members.

The neighborhood council members, representing all age interest from youth to senior citizens, may be selected by the center director and/or the advisory council. Sometimes youth members are elected by the center participants. For further information on organization, see the appendix.

The neighborhood advisory council assists the center or playground director in planning programs and schedules; serves as consultant on matters of policy, particularly those affecting the neighborhood directly or indirectly; and helps to carry out plans by volunteering services, raising funds, and promoting interest.

Very often the center director will organize a youth council to advise and assist on matters of particular interest to youth. In such instances, it is well for a representative from this group to serve on the neighborhood advisory council.

DISTRICT RECREATION COUNCILS These councils work in conjunction with the supervisor at the district level on matters of area-wide significance, such as district tournaments and other district events, needed facilities and improvements, and coordination of community programs.

The organization and selection of members is similar to the neighborhood council except that the group may be larger and involve representatives of major community organizations interested in recreation in the area such as churches, service clubs, civic associations, parent-teacher's associations, semi-private recreation groups and athletic associations. These councils may provide representatives to the city-wide councils for continuity.

CITY-WIDE COUNCILS City-wide advisory boards of legal stature were discussed earlier in this chapter. If there is not a legally appointed city-wide advisory council for the department, the executive may organize one to assist in policy matters and program development for the department. Membership may include representatives from district and neighborhood and special advisory councils supplemented by interested community leaders.

SPECIAL ADVISORY COUNCILS Special advisory councils may be appointed, as the need arises, to assist with special programs such as those for youth groups, senior citizens, or special interest groups. These are constituted in the same manner as the other advisory councils.

LABOR UNIONS

Although labor unions have been a consideration of management in the private sector since the early thirties, their thrust in the public sector is a relatively recent development, particularly at the local levels of government. The increasing number of public employees makes up the largest labor group which is not yet completely organized. See Fig. 5-1.

Level of government	Average number of employees (in 1000's)	Membership in national unions and employee associations (in 1000's)
Total	13,289.6	4,520
Federal	2,650.0	1,394
State	2,848.4	814
Local	7,791.2	2,312

FIGURE 5-1. Government employment and union/association membership. *Source:* U.S. Department of Labor, Bureau of Labor Statistics, Division of Industrial Relations, March 1975.

Traditionally, wages of public employees have lagged behind those of employees in private industry. Individual employee requests for pay raises make little impression on the politicians, who are more prone to respond to group interests. Pay raises and justified employee complaints are too often put off. Good employee grievance procedures are often lacking, particularly in situations where modern personnel systems do not exist. There is considerable public opinion against strikes and collective bargaining by public employees and a feeling that public employment has many advantages which compensate for low pay. In some states, public employees are denied the right to practice collective bargaining and to strike. There are, however, an impressive number of local unions involving policemen, firemen, sanitation workers, recreation and park workers, and teachers. Local unions have called strikes, slow-downs, "sick days," picketing, and boycotts, and have sponsored political candidates and campaigns to persuade or force public authorities to recognize unions as their bargaining agents. Many state and local legislative bodies have adjusted their laws to permit, or even require, localities to recognize public employees' organizations as collective bargaining agents.

Labor Unions and the Recreation Executive

There are three levels at which the recreation executive may become involved with labor unions: (1) The union organizer or official union representative (not an agency employee); (2) The president, officials, or committees (agency employees) of the local public employees union; and (3) Shop stewards and union members (working employees of the agency) who look after union and employee interests within the agency. They are knowledgeable concerning both union and agency operational practices, especially those affecting personnel.

Unions are an element in administration and supervision which must be considered, not only in situations where unions are established but also in those where public unions are not yet organized. Agencies that fail to provide good personnel practices, good working conditions, competitive wage scales, equal opportunities, fair treatment, and adequate grievance procedures may expect a degree of attention from unions. The relationship is continuous and is not a one time, once a year, affair at contract renewal time. The executive can create the right kind of courteous, cooperative, firm, but reasonable attitude that will bring the best results for the agency.

Union representatives should be considered in management decisions which involve agency personnel, especially those in the non-supervisory classifications. While it may not be legally essential to review these matters with appropriate union representatives, it is usually expedient. The reviews may involve such items as: (1) Changes of personnel such as reorganization, lay-offs, promotions, transfers; (2) Changes of duties and new job functions; (3) Use of labor-saving equipment; (4) Disciplinary actions, suspensions, demotions, dismissals; (5) Handling of employee grievances; and (6) Changes of work rules and work schedules.

The executive should retain full authority to hire, transfer, and make management decisions without interference from union representatives. It is better, however, if team effort and two-way communication are to be maintained, to review changes and reasons for changes, with appropriate members of the agency-union team before they are put into effect. Admittedly, appropriate contacts with unions or employee representatives, like working with community groups and staff committees, is time consuming but it may be expected to be a way of life for the executive.

The union organizer and representative is an expert in his field giving full-time and thought to his specialty. It is well, also, for the executive, likewise, to have a full-time expert who is a specialist in union matters to look after agency-employee-union relationships.

The agency executive and union specialist should:

1. Familiarize themselves and the staff concerning the activities and interests of the union, including procedures, objectives, common practices and relationships, and state and local collective bargaining laws.
2. Take the initiative in recommending practices and contracts that best serve local needs.
3. Keep up-to-date and sensitive to the needs and interests of employees.
4. Maintain good and fair personnel practices with full and complete job descriptions, adequate pay scale, and grievance procedures.
5. Take prompt corrective action to improve unfavorable conditions rather than permit the development of employee or union criticism.
6. Insist that administrative and supervisory procedures be in conformity with approved contract and personnel practices.
7. Welcome facts, information, suggestions, points of view which are pertinent to making sound judgements and appropriate management decisions.
8. Maintain a close consulting relationship with the agency's legal expert on union matters.

Only employee matters (not union business) should be conducted on agency time on agency property.

An agency which takes timely and effective action in employee relations will provide little reason for organized labor to take "forcing" actions.

RELATIONSHIPS WITH OTHER PUBLIC AGENCIES

The local public recreation executive is the number one leader, guide, and authority in the community on recreation matters and has the recreation interests of the entire community at heart. He directs, usually, the largest recreation agency in the community and often has jurisdiction over the only large open spaces and specialized recreation facilities in the community. He has considerable flexibility and freedom of action. Very seldom are the recreation laws specifically restrictive except to define that expenditures must be made for public recreation purposes on public property available to all the citizenry. This flexibility is a special privilege that should be defended with pride and integrity and not abused.

The Executive Coordinates All Public Recreation Resources

Public recreation usually has the flexibility to operate programs both within and without the political boundaries of the jurisdiction and federal and state agencies usually honor the "home rule" policy and support the local recreation program with services or grants. The local director is in best position, and it is his responsibility, to guide and direct all public recreation resources in an orderly manner to the best benefit of the total community.

There should be only one public recreation agency. The presence of more than one public agency providing recreation services in the average community could create confusion, duplication, and competition, resulting in a lowering of the quality of the services. It is not unusual, however, in larger cities for more than one public agency to provide public recreation services by utilizing existing space and resources such as schools, libraries, and police departments. In small and middle-sized communities, public recreation services should be provided by only one public agency.

State and federal parks are usually near urban areas but seldom within a developed city, except for historical and unusual natural sites of state-wide interest. Such sites are usually coordinated with the locality in planning. State plans required for federal grants take into consideration existing and proposed local park and open space sites.

The use of any nearby federal, state, regional, or county parks is taken into consideration when planning local recreation parks.

PRIVATE, SEMI-PRIVATE, AND COMMERCIAL RELATIONS

Every community has valuable recreation assets which are not under the jurisdiction of the public recreation agency. Sometimes, in smaller communities, the non-public resources provide the only recreation opportunities available in the community. Such services include the home, private recreation, semi-private, and commercial recreation. The major industry may provide the recreation area and facility. The United Givers Fund, more recently the United Way, provides recreation for large segments of population in some places. Each makes an important contribution. If it were not for these agencies, public expenditures and responsibilities would be considerably greater.

Home Recreation Relationships

In addition to television, the home is the source of much individual and family recreation initiative such as reading, gardening, sketching, caring for pets, walking or hiking, bicycling, do-it-yourself projects, ceramics, collections, hobbies, electronics, outings, backyard cook-outs, and many others. Many homes do not have indoor or outdoor space for their leisure time interests and, therefore, seek public, private, semi-private, or commercial sources to accommodate their needs. The public recreation agency has three relationships with home recreation: (1) It provides ideas for crafts, hobbies, games and good recreation habits; (2) It provides public facilities which may be used informally by individuals or families; and (3) It provides opportunities for the sharing of talents through entertainment and volunteer services.

Private Recreation

There are various types of private agencies and organizations involved in recreation and they differ in the degree of their involvement with public recreation. Some provide their own resources but may participate in public programs; others are dependent on public and other facilities outside their own organizations; and still others may need only information or equipment.

Businesses and Recreation

Industry, particularly in smaller communities, used to provide its employees, and sometimes their families, with recreation buildings and areas. Some still do, but there is a tendency for industry to support community and public recreation programs, which provide freedom of choice and the whole family may participate as citizens rather than as employees of a specific company, except for company-sponsored teams, outings and employee events. Business and industry use public recreation facilities extensively and are enthusiastic sponsors of teams in public leagues. The company may supply athletic uniforms, equipment and officials, which represents a substantial contribution, and provides an opportunity for some employees to participate who may not otherwise be able to afford to. Business leaders state that good recreation is an important factor in attracting industries to a community and contributes to the contentment of employees.

Businesses sometimes sponsor tournaments, special events, sports clinics, donate program materials and equipment, publish announcements and calendars of events in their newspaper ads, and pay the cost of out-of-town trips. They may also lend the use of areas and facilities or even donate them for public use.

Apartment and sub-division complexes now usually include indoor and outdoor recreation space and sometimes swimming pools, tennis courts, basketball courts, or play equipment.

Institutions and Recreation

Recreation is closely related to the objectives of many institutions of rehabilitation, places of confinement, and nursing and convalescent homes. In recent years an increasing number of such institutions have added recreation and therapeutic specialists to their staffs. Some institutions, particularly smaller ones, have not the funds for specialists and depend on volunteers or public programs. Staff members and clients who are able to get the public facilities participate freely in general or special programs. For the confined ones, the public agency provides ideas, training institutes for staff, consultation services, demonstration programs and sometimes, entertainments.

The Church and Recreation

An increasing number of churches conduct recreation programs and provide facilities such as libraries, social halls, kitchens, game rooms, meeting rooms, and gymnasiums for its membership. Many churches participate in public sports leagues, outings, drama, music, and other events and often permit the public use of their facilities free or at cost when they are not needed for church activities. Public use of church facilities for organized groups, sports and most adult activities works out satisfactorily but attendance at informal, drop-in activities in church facilities tends to be from the respective church membership rather than from the general public. There seems to be a trend recently, however, towards a broader participation. In some cities, church and Sunday school leagues are the basis of the public recreation amateur sports programs.

Semi-Private Recreation

Many quasi-public recreation agencies make major contributions to the total community recreation services. Among these are the United Way agencies, youth service organizations, Y.M.C.A. and Y.W.C.A., Y.M.H.A., and Y.W.H.A., settlement houses, scouting, boys and girls clubs. These organizations may have small membership fees but they are largely financed from private contributions. Some have fund-raising projects and actively campaign for funds. They usually have diversified recreation programs for the entire family but very often are dependent upon public and other facilities for outside programs and mass activities. These organizations provide much needed special services, usually to smaller groups, and on a more personal and individual basis than the public recreation agencies.

Public and Private Agency Relationships

The public and semipublic agencies should cooperate in serving the recreation needs of the community. Professional competition, duplication, and overlapping should be minimized and programs should be coordinated where possible.

In order to provide a means of coordinating, there should be a coordinating organization, a community council or recreation council, composed of executives of the various organizations. An organization such as the Community Chest or the public recreation agency or executive could sponsor such a council.

Commercial Recreation

The desire of the American people for recreation, relaxation, new experiences, hobbies, and relief from routine has developed a multibillion dollar commercial recreation industry. This includes vacation resorts, travel, professional sports and the manufacture of such diverse equipment for the participant as playing cards, pinball machines, athletic equipment and supplies, outdoor gear, and vehicles. If it were not for commercial recreation, the utilization of surplus time would be an enormous problem. Much of our economy is based on the automobile and transportation industry and recreation. Facilities which at one time were thought to be supplied by the user or the public are now supplied by profit-making enterprises. These include beaches and pools, picnicking and camping areas, roller and ice skating rinks, tennis courts, boating and marina facilities, bowling alleys, hunting and fishing areas, and many others.

Public and Commercial Recreation

The recreation executive is involved with commercial recreation in three ways. First, commercial facilities and attractions must be considered in planning public recreation facilities and programs. Second, commercial facilities such as bowling alleys, theatres, circuses, golf courses, professional sports, amusements, rides, and others are often available to the public recreation program free of charge, or at special low rates, during slack periods. Third, commercial enterprises help sponsor certain recreation programs, give awards, and make donations. Commercial recreation merchandises recreation activities to people who have money and are willing to pay.

OTHER COMMUNITY RESOURCES

Many kinds of membership groups, associations and clubs organize around special interests to provide recreation needs for the benefit of their memberships, but sometimes for the entertainment of others. These groups also add a great deal to the total community recreation service. They consist mainly of three different types of groups: clubs, associations and special interest groups.

Clubs

Clubs are formed around some common aim or interest. Some of them are served by a state or national organization. They are usually self sufficient and supported by individual or family membership dues, concessions, rentals, fund-raising projects, donations, fees, and charges for entertainments. There are basically two types of clubs: those that organize around a special interest and do not have facilities, and those that have their own facilities, such as country clubs, and sports clubs of various kinds. Memberships are often limited in numbers and may be restricted by self proclaimed boundaries. They are usually administered by an executive committee or board elected by the members. They sometimes employ professionals. There is generally a minimum of contact between this type of club and public recreation activities except for participation in public programs.

The special interest clubs such as chess and checkers, stamp collecting, folk and square dancing, lapidary, children's theatre, choral groups, nature clubs, photographic, art, and other hobby groups are often dependent on the public department for meeting space, rehearsal room, and some assistance, such as the loan of costumes and props. In return, they often share their talents in agency programs and sometimes provide expert volunteer service and program support which often adds quality to the general programs. These are usually excellent groups to have associated with the agency.

Recreation Associations

Associations, like clubs, consist of two types: those which have their own facilities and those which do not. Those with their own facilities are self sufficient, self directing, and usually have a minimum of relationship with public recreation except to participate in programs. Association facilities are usually planned on the basis of maximum use by the membership, sc that they are generally not available for use by non-members, except guests.

Associations that have recreation as one of their objectives and those based around a recreation-related interest such as, the Rose Society, The Bird Watchers Association, Little League Baseball, Amateur Athletic Association, and American Softball Association may be dependent upon the public agency for facilities to carry out their objectives and may perform a community service that would have to be provided by the public agency if it were not for the service of the associations. Often the public agency does not have the funds for staff to extend services to the many community associations. By cooperative arrangements with self-sustaining, recreation-related associations that can function within the framework of public policy, programs can, however, be extended very effectively at minimum cost.

The executive is obliged to maintain an acceptable balance of activities and use of public facilities with the provision of equal service and opportunities for all. There are some programs and age groupings that could very well occupy a facility full time. It is a responsibility of the recreation agency to schedule equitably.

Special Interest Recreation Groups

Special interest groups are organized, usually, around a single interest, hobby, or service based on any activity recreation in nature. They may be in the form of a club, an association, or a class. Most of them do not have their own facilities and tend to be motivated by the interest and are rather democratic in organization. Often, the groups are organized as an outgrowth of participation in a recreation activity and continue to be dependent upon use of public facilities and accessories. They require little, if any, staff resources but often provide excellent programs, volunteer services in their special skills, and provide an outlet for advanced participants in the regular public programs. Very often, members of the special group will direct or sponsor children's groups in the subject.

Whether the specialty group is departmental or sponsored from outside, it usually makes a fine contribution to the public recreation program.

Questions for Discussion

1. What are the differences between the functions of an authoritative board and an advisory board? Which type of board, in your opinion, is most important?
2. Would it be advantageous to have both an authoritative board and an advisory board? Why?
3. What are the differences, if any, in functions of the recreation executive under a commission and under a chief administrator? Which type of administration would you prefer? Why?
4. What is the difference between a policy-making function and an administrative function?
5. What would you do if the authoritative board assumed some of the responsibilities that are specifically those of the executive?
6. What is the role of the executive in relation to the authoritative board? The advisory board?
7. What makes up the total recreation program for a community? What relationship does the public recreation executive have to each element of the community recreation services?
8. How are lay committees used in public recreation and how are members appointed?
9. What are the purposes of advisory councils? How do they differ from committees?
10. In what respect are advisory councils involved in policy making or administrative decisions?

Short Problems

1. Prepare a complete set of bylaws for an authoritative board and rules of conduct for meetings.
2. In a community of your choice, make a list of the different types

of recreation services that make up the total programs for the community and make recommendations to correct inadequacies and suggest improvements.

3. Provide a plan for involving citizens as much as practical in different aspects of the public recreation program and administration.

References

1. George Hjelte and Jay S. Shivers, *Public Administration of Recreational Services* (Philadelphia: Lea and Febiger, 1972), pp. 88–89.
2. "Local Parks and Recreation," *Parks and Recreation,* August 1971, p. 19.

Selected Readings

Albers, Henry H., *Principles of Management, A Modern Approach* (4th ed.), pp. 123–145. New York: John Wiley and Sons, Inc., 1974. *Committee as instrument of managerial action.*

Corbin, H. Dan, and William J. Tait, *Education For Leisure,* pp. 121–129. Englewood Cliffs, N.J.: Prentice-Hall, Inc., 1973. *Recreation in other institutions.*

Fitch, Edwin M., and John E. Shankin, *The Bureau of Outdoor Recreation.* New York: Praeger Publishers, 1970.

Hjelte,George, and Jay S. Shivers, *Public Administration of Recreational Services,* pp. 87–131. Philadelphia: Lea and Febiger, 1972.

Lutzin, Sidney G., and Edward H. Storey, *Managing Municipal Leisure Services,* pp. 60–67. Washington, D.C.: International City Management Association, 1973.

Murphy, Edward F., *Management vs the Unions—How to Win.* New York: Stein and Day Publishers, 1971. *What the National Labor Relations Act provides and how to relate to organized labor groups.*

Rodney, Lynn S., *Administration of Public Recreation,* pp. 95–112. New York: The Ronald Press Company, 1964.

Shivers, Jay S., and Hollis F. Fait, *Therapeutic and Adapted Recreational Services.* Philadelphia: Lea and Febiger, 1975.

CHAPTER 6

Public Recreation and Public Schools

Although the percentage of public school systems which administer public recreation programs as a secondary function is relatively small, schools have facilities and such a significant relationship to the public recreation program as to warrant fuller discussion at this time. Relationships with other public agencies are discussed in the next chapter.

The August 1971, Special Issue of *Parks and Recreation* magazine surveyed 1119 managing authorities. It showed that school systems administered two percent of the local public recreation agencies.[1] The *Recreation and Park Yearbook, 1966,* showed that 4.5 percent of the 3142 local recreation agencies reporting were administered by school systems.[2]

In recent years the need for recreation areas and facilities has grown faster than the planners and community leaders could provide them. In older cities, especially, the rapid increase had not been anticipated.

Cities find it difficult and very expensive to provide the open space needed for a modern recreation program. The lack of appropriate open space and necessary resources for the expansion of recreation facilities almost makes it imperative that schools, as well as other suitable public facilities, be incorporated into the total recreation plan. Almost all local public recreation executives, whether they are under the direct jurisdiction of the public school system or under that of an independent agency, relate in some way to the local school system. School facilities may provide the only space available for recreation, or they may supplement separate recreation facilities, or the separate public recreation facilities, such as swimming pools, zoos, and nature areas, may be used by the schools to supplement the education program. The recreation executive, therefore, is expected to establish appropriate relationships both with the school administration and personnel and the municipal or county administration with two interrelated points of view in mind. He must, first, consider the best way to accomplish the objectives of the agency for which he is responsible. This will involve establishing effective administrative relationships in cooperation with the school administration and school board. Second, he must keep in mind what is feasible and best for the community. This will involve relationships with the chief administrator, planning commission and other agencies discussed in Chapter 7.

Factors favoring the use of schools for community recreation purposes are: (1) Schools are public property which are not used during a portion of the week when most youngsters and many adults have leisure time; (2) Schools are often the only public facilities with usable indoor and outdoor areas in residential neighborhoods; (3) The objectives of education are broadened to include preparation of the individual for all life situations and the development of extracurricular school activities; (4) Recreation-oriented activities are included in the school curriculum; and (5) educators accept education for leisure as an essential contributing factor in the development of the individual's total personality and maturity.

While these factors foster better understanding on the part of most school personnel concerning the joint use of school facilities for recreation purposes, there are still influential individuals in the school system and recreationists outside the school system who object to the use of school plants for recreation purposes. It can be expected that this kind of feeling on the part of some people will continue to be a problem for the school and recreation administrators.

HISTORICAL RELATIONSHIP

Schools, historically, have played a significant role in providing recreation opportunities for the community, particularly for the youth. Since their inception, public schools in America have been used as places to hold meetings to discuss matters of public interest, lectures, and socials. Although Boston (1901) and other cities used school playgrounds for recreation, Rochester, New York, was the first locality to use a school building as a public community center.

Two major actions of importance affecting the use of schools for public recreation were the approval by the National Education Association in 1911 of a resolution supporting the use of schools for recreation, civic, cooperative and cultural purposes, and the action, in 1918, in which the same organization "organized a department for the wider use of school houses" [3] and published "Seven Cardinal Principles of Secondary Education," one of which was the worthy use of leisure. These two actions by NEA had significant effects on the development of school-centered recreation programs.

The school system is one of several local public organizations that deals with people. Schools and recreation both serve people and both involve the learning process, one formal the other informal, and are more closely related than most other public functions. Also, recreation is part of the planned school curriculum and extends to extra-curricular activity. Whether or not there are other community recreation programs, the school phase of recreation as a training, social and personal development process continues. There is a difference, however, between school recreation activities and public recreation activities. School activities are conducted for the enrollees of the school for training and educational purposes and are usually limited to specific age ranges. Public recreation provides leisure time activities and opportunities for all ages when they have free time and on a voluntary basis. Schools emphasize learning and skills; recreation emphasizes fun, growth, and development.

The school traditionally has been, and still is in most communities, particularly in rural areas, the public focal point for community activities and meetings. School and civic functions plus political rallies are often main group activities, especially in smaller communities. Many schools today provide the only opportunity some folks have for group recreation and meetings, outside of their church and family.

Whether or not the school or an independent recreation agency is responsible for administering the public recreation program, it is absolutely essential that the recreation officials and school authorities cooperate in order to make maximum use of the local resources. There are certain facilities, such as parks, beaches, arenas, auditoriums, golf courses, botanical gardens, picnic areas, zoos, wildlife exhibits, and water areas that are not ordinarily administered by schools, but schools may utilize them. On the other hand, when recreation is administered by a separate recreation and/or park agency it may be necessary to make use of school facilities. Only through maximum cooperation can reasonably adequate services be provided to a community without excessive costs.

In preparing master plans, the planners coordinate the needs and interests of schools and of recreation when considering new sites and structures. In some cities—Seattle, Washington; and Norfolk and Richmond, Virginia, for example—schools and recreation (or parks) jointly have acquired large areas of land and jointly planned, constructed, and used facilities. Each uses the other's facilities to the maximum degree.

THE ROLE OF THE SCHOOL IN RECREATION

Education, at any level, is responsible for the development of the individual to the fullest extent possible. Some activities extend beyond the classroom into trips to the recreation center, swimming pool, botanical garden, wildlife exhibit or camp establishment. Recreation may be involved in the development of skills, coordination, attitudes, appreciation of the arts. Although methods and objectives may differ, education and recreation tend to supplement each other.

The Place of Schools in Preparing for Leisure

The average individual now has about as much free time as he has work time. He does not make enough income above taking care of his necessities to buy recreation to occupy fully his leisure time. Therefore, since schools have the responsibility of preparing the individual for all phases of life, education for leisure of 20 to 48 hours per week becomes a major challenge for schools. Schools had prepared for an average work week of 40 hours, but to add to this responsibility for the expanded dimension of leisure just about doubles their responsibilities and overcrowds their resources.

Like other public services, the school's ability to expand at the present site or to construct new facilities has not kept pace with rapidly expanding needs. Not only has the need for preparation of leisure increased, but the school's involvement in other community services has increased also—traffic control, fire prevention, driver training and safety education, civil defense, various government-sponsored projects, welfare activities, programs for dropouts, and community betterment, to name a few. The school is so involved in preparing for other essentials of life and survival that it does not have adequate time and resources to prepare each individual for his expanded leisure. This is unfortunate because the school is the only facility for training masses of youngsters which has trained guidance and counseling services. Recreationists have found that interests discovered or taught in school are followed up on playgrounds and in recreation settings. As brought out in the "Seven Cardinal Principles of Secondary Education," "Education should equip the individual to secure from his leisure the re-creation of body, mind, and spirit, and the enrichment and enlargement of his personality." [4] Habits and recreation interests developed in childhood very often continue into adulthood. Schools have the responsibility of finding and developing in each youngster at least one good recreation interest, satisfying to the individual, that will be acceptable to society. Recreation, then, can build around that one. Schools provide varied recreation-oriented opportunities to acquire skills —sports, swimming, clubs, art, crafts, music, drama, dance, nature. These are almost identical to the classification of program activities in public recreation. There is excellent opportunity for recreation follow-up. Schools provide the use of buildings, facilities, areas and equipment for leisure programs and provide the individual attention and guidance necessary for some that is not generally available at public recreation facilities geared to informal play groups or mass activities. Schools relate instruction to experience and help the individual apply information, give him experience under supervision and develop attitudes, values and competence.

Recreation is based on voluntary participation. Individuals are not required to participate and they may stop at any time. It is hoped that fun, the appeal of the activity, and the opportunity to improve oneself or accomplish an objective will maintain and continue his interest. The nonconforming, inexperienced, unskilled, timid individual may not be attracted to the group activities of a recreation center until someone can find or develop an interest that motivates him. Because the schools' motivations, external and internal, are different, they have an opportunity to help such an individual find and develop an interest and work jointly with recreation in following it up. In short, the function of the school in relation to recreation is to educate the individual in the use of leisure and to provide training in basic recreation-oriented arts and skills.

Community Uses of School Facilities

Schools have been used for public meetings and places of assembly since their beginning. In order to provide anywhere near adequate recreation opportunities for a community, it is necessary to continue to use or even expand the use of public schools, and many other usable public facilities, that can be made available for recreation. Even now there are athletic teams, groups, and organizations on waiting lists, that do not have a satisfactory place in which to meet when they want to. It is imperative in most communities that school facilities be used for some recreation purposes. There is always a shortage of gymnasiums and often the school auditorium is the only public place in the community where a large crowd can meet. Public schools belong to the people and should be used for public purposes. This use should include civic nonprofit, noncommercial, nonpolitical, nonfund-raising, nonexclusive, nonsecretive community organizations for activities of a recreational or intellectual nature.

Almost all states have enabling legislation now that permits the use of schools for community purposes when they are not in use for school purposes. Some school boards and school personnel, however, do not yet support the general use of schools for recreation. Some state laws are so written that recreation is only a secondary function. Others limit school administration authority to school purposes, which can hardly be interpreted to mean the administration of general public recreation services. Very thoughtfully, however, they do permit the use of public school plants for supervised recreation provided such activities do not conflict with their use for the primary function of education. Recreationists would generally agree that school facilities should be used to the maximum extent possible, but that the programs and recreation services rendered should be a primary function of a separate recreation agency.

Generally speaking, educators have recognized the need for schools to prepare youngsters for their leisure hours and the desirability of a cooperative relationships with community recreation purposes including: (1) making available, with certain qualifications, the use of school property for the community recreation services after school, and on holidays and weekends; (2) adjusting facility planning to serve more satisfactorily the community's recreation needs; (3) developing outdoor areas to permit their use for both school and recreation purposes; and (4) making cooperative agreements and joint policy statements.

The Use of Outdoor Facilities

Schools and recreation have about the same area needs. Recreation, however, needs lighting, outdoor restrooms, concession stands, storage space, and more complete athletic areas. Schools, particularly during daylight saving time, do not have much need for lighting except for high school sports. Public recreation, therefore, should add and maintain the lighting. The indoor school restrooms are adequate for the needs of the school but are not so satisfactory for outdoor recreation and considerable extra staff are required for opening the school building when large crowds use the school grounds. With today's labor costs, it is cheaper over the long run, and much more satisfactory, to include the restrooms, storage, concession, and maintenance complex in the original improvement plans. It is generally easier to obtain funds for construction than it is for maintenance, policing and supervision. Improvements, therefore, should be planned to be as "maintenance free" as possible.

School personnel prefer that recreation not use school outdoor areas for community recreation during school hours, especially play areas near the school building, and that is understandable. There is a matter of safety with added traffic, school buses, and excited youngsters; control of masses of children during play periods; and increased danger of attacks and criminal acts by outsiders involving the school youngsters. Schools have responsibility for the safety and protection of students during the periods they are in school and enroute to their homes.

Some schools with many extracurricular activities and extensive adult education and night school programs, however, present so many conflicts in scheduling that it is difficult to use their facilities for recreation. These may be available only for special events. High schools, especially, often have schedules of their own which are too busy to permit much of this kind of cooperation. Middle schools and elementary schools generally have few conflicts and are usually well located and adaptable for general recreation. They, of course, may not have as many useful facilities as the high schools. The cost of development and added improvements for a full recreation program may, therefore, be greater.

One special problem with the joint use of outdoor school areas is the difficulty of maintenance. The schools use them all day and recreation may use them, with lights, into the night. Maintenance and the marking of fields must be done early in the morning, between games, or at night.

In the joint use of facilities, clear-cut agreement should be reached on the division of maintenance responsibilities. This may be done in one of several ways. The owner of the land may want to assume full responsibility and donate, or be reimbursed, for work done for the other agency. Or each agency may assume responsibility for its own needs. The latter may be a generally satisfactory solution but may involve some overlapping. Each agency will, at least, have clear cut responsibilities. The trouble is that one agency may require a higher standard of maintenance than the other. The result of such a dual standard of maintenance may be that the agency needing the higher quality maintenance may have to upgrade the service to meet its own needs. The double standard situation should be avoided by written agreement when the work assignments are made.

Uses of Indoor Facilities

More complications are likely to arise from the joint use of school indoor facilities than from the joint use of outdoor facilities. It is inside the school building that the *primary* functions of the school take place. Facilities are designed to function on a set schedule at or near capacity during school hours. Maintenance and use must be coordinated with that schedule. Interruptions disturb the planned routine and affect a lot of people. Breakage, vandalism, equipment out of service because of non-school use, the inability of the janitor to do a thorough cleaning job after use by recreation groups sometimes upset the personnel considerably and may become a serious point of contention with regard to the joint use of indoor facilities. Great care should be exercised to keep such developments to a minimum. One rather successful plan is for representatives of both agencies to inspect the facilities before opening for recreation and after closing, note any unusual conditions, and file a joint report. Breakage, damage or loss are, of course, the responsibility of the agency using the facility at the time. Usually the owner prefers to repair in his own way and be reimbursed by the using agency. This policy applies equally to the use by schools of facilities owned by recreation and parks.

School buildings and equipment represent a considerable investment and must be protected. School buildings are generally designed for school purposes only. Recreation usually uses only a small amount of the total space. There are halls, several exit doors, perhaps a second or third floor and basement, so that proper security for the property becomes a special problem. The unused portions of the building may be blocked off. Responsible volunteers, school personnel, or guards may be assigned at the exit doors. It is best to use only one door to a building as entrance. It is suggested that one or more of the school personnel be designated to be responsible for the security and care of the school plant. Desks, tables and equipment should be restored to their original positions at the completion of the program.

It is estimated that the average school plant, depending on age and design, can take care of no more than 30 to 75 percent of the recreation needs of a community. The facilities are not normally available during the day, so that it is impossible to schedule activities for retirees, senior citizens, housewives, and others who have free time during those hours. In addition, of course, some school facilities are simply not adapted to recreation use, and others are not available because of the danger of damage or breakage.

Use of School Personnel

Use of school custodial and maintenance personnel and school guards for the care and protection of the school building and of technicians or specialists as instructors for programs requiring the use of specialized equipment is highly desirable, if not a must. Beyond that, the use of school personnel for recreation is a matter of local circumstances and good personnel management. A principal or a school teacher works a full school schedule during the day and probably has planning, contacts, follow-up work or papers to grade after school. Not many are available for additional after school, night and weekend work. More are available for summer vacation playground work. A good teacher tends to be a good playground leader, too, but all are human and need a vacation before going back to teaching in early fall. If the seasonal recreation job terminates by August 15th it is fine and gives opportunity for a vacation before school opens. If the summer recreation job continues, as most of them do, until the Friday before school starts the school teacher is faced with resigning at a crucial time for recreation about August 15th to allow time for a short vacation and rest before school starts. During the school year teachers may take employment at recreation centers or gyms on a part-time basis. Often a teacher will follow his interest and take charge of a gym, or a recreation group in crafts, drama, music, nature or even coach a team. The trend appears to be, however, that fewer school teachers are taking on extra work with recreation, especially in the schools where they teach.

Employment of school principals part-time as administrator of a school center may work out well in getting a new center started in the respective school, if the principal has the time, supports the program and is interested. Some excellent results have been accomplished in this way. On the other hand, if the principal and custodian of the school are against the school center program it is an uphill task establishing a successful, comprehensive community recreation program in that school. There are fewer and fewer of these kinds of combinations because of increasing community need and support of the programs and selection of administrative personnel with the broader views of the place of education in the modern community.

The demands on recreation as well as schools have become so great the work of each takes the full time and energies of professional personnel of each. Recreation has extended to full-time professionals supplemented by volunteers and half-time para-professionals. The need is for staff to give undivided attention to the participants and programs for them. Schools have a similar need, therefore, there are fewer teachers for part-time recreation jobs.

Advantages of Using School Facilities

In recent years, recreation has taken a place of importance among the basic needs of man along with work, protection, nourishment, and education. Leisure has expanded faster than man's ability to provide especially for it. Therefore, he is obliged to use what is available to him. Schools, in addition to being the most abundant local resource, have other advantages, too, namely:

1. They are already public property and provide services for masses of people.
2. The school facilities, such as playgrounds, gymnasiums, shops, and meeting rooms are similar to those of recreation even though their objectives may be somewhat different.
3. School facilities are generally well distributed throughout the residential districts of the city or county in a manner similar to that of recreation sites.
4. School facilities are not generally in use at times when youngsters and the majority of adults have free time—after school, weekends, holidays, and during summer vacation.
5. Schools are the only public facilities available for recreation in many rural areas.

Disadvantages of Using School Facilities

In making use of school facilities for recreation, a great deal may depend on local, political, and economic situations, as well as community interest and support, the design of the facility, extent of use, availability, and accessibility. Some of more frequently heard disadvantages include:

1. The building may be old and not adaptable for modern recreation activities.
2. Schools are not available when large segments of population have free time such as mothers, housewives, retirees, shift workers.
3. School schedules, including PTA meetings, extracurricular activities, and adult education classes, frequently conflict with regular recreation uses.
4. School principals, teachers, custodians object to school use for recreation and do not cooperate. This is a real handicap and calls for tact and diplomacy. *Handle the problem as close to the source as possible and involve only the minimum number of people.*
5. School facilities and equipment are designed principally for children and many are not suited for all age groups, particularly adults.
6. Schools have practically no storage space for recreation and all equipment must be removed from areas used by education. Temporary storage may be built indoors, if space can be found, or outside if necessary.
7. Only a portion of school building is used but it is necessary to heat and police the entire building.
8. There are people that do not feel at ease or relaxed in going to school for their recreation—drop outs, youngsters that have had trouble in the school, adults because they are not comfortable in the classroom seats.
9. Smoking in classrooms is illegal in some, if not all, states. This makes it difficult for the chain smoker; however, smoking is permitted in some rooms so those that wish may take a break and smoke.
10. Schools are not homey. Initiative cannot be used to fix up a room or leave anything out or on the wall.

JOINT PLANNING AND JOINT USE

Joint planning by local government and school authorities for the selection of sites and use of areas and facilities is in the best interest of the taxpayer and, in the long run, of both schools and recreation. The joint planning should begin with site selection and continue through the consultations with architect or consultant, public hearings, reviews, approval of final plans, and acceptance of the finished facility from the contractor. As a policy, schools should provide recreation with a copy of preliminary new school or school improvement plans for review, recommendations, or approval. Likewise, recreation should provide schools with preliminary plans for new recreation facilities for review, recommendations and comments.

The Process of Joint Planning

Representatives of both agencies should visit sites together, perhaps accompanied by the architect, and agree upon a site most suitable for their joint purposes. It may be that one agency will acquire all the land needed, or they may each buy a specified portion. The second step is to meet jointly with the architect and designers to make specific needs known, including the shape, size and dimensions of the desired facilities and the cost limits. Within a few weeks the architect will present a layout sketch for review, and several weeks later the working drawings. These can be amended. If they are satisfactory, he will prepare perhaps 15 copies and advertise for bids. Both parties should keep informed every step of the way through final construction and final inspection to see that all interests are satisfied.

Planning of Indoor Facilities

Items to be considered in building should include the following:

1. The construction should be vandal resistant, fire resistant, with no recesses or hide-aways. There should be exterior flood lighting under the eaves with no easy means of climbing to the roof. Windows should be vandal resistant and there should be no skylights. Down spouts should be protected.
2. Rooms, gymnasium and auditorium should be arranged with outside entrances, preferably in separate wings, each with its own interior rest rooms. All recreation rooms should be grouped together near the entrance with rest rooms and recessed drinking fountains.
3. There should be movable tables and chairs in the cafeteria.
4. The auditorium stage should have softwood floor.
5. The recreation complex should be provided with adequate storage room.
6. There should be folding metal gates to close off the recreation areas from portions not used for recreation.

7. The gymnasium should be located next to the athletic field.
8. The entrance should be well lighted.
9. There should be automatic heating with zone heating in the recreation area.

Planning of Outdoor Facilities

Recreation and school outdoor areas are very much alike except that recreation areas are more inclusive in order to provide leisure time interests for the entire family.

Most schools have a minimum of surfaced play area, including volleyball and basketball courts, equipment area, bicycle racks, and drinking fountains. Recreation needs to add a baseball-softball diamond, football field, tennis courts, at least a second basketball court, lighting, a storage house, shelter, concession stands, rest rooms, janitor room structure, landscaping and shade, and a passive area landscaped for story telling, puppetry and plays.

AGREEMENT FOR THE USE OF SCHOOLS BY RECREATION AGENCIES

The administrative agreements that establish the working relationships between recreation and school authorities vary from a simple exchange of letters to formal and detailed contracts. Others have the relationship spelled out in the framing of the city charter, as in Richmond, Virginia, which states:

> The Department of Recreation and Parks shall be permitted to utilize grounds and buildings under the jurisdiction of the school board at such hours and on such days as they are not in use for other educational purposes, subject to such reasonable rules and regulations as the school board may establish, and provided that the department of recreation and parks shall be responsible for any damage or extra expense arising from its use of the school grounds and buildings.[5]

This has proven to be a very effective document in setting the guidelines for working agreements between the executives of the two departments and has overcome some strong opposition from individual principals and staff members. This is a much wiser arrangement than the simple verbal agreements that exist in many cities.

School Administration of Public Recreation

Schools administer less than ten percent of public recreation services in the United States. Laws of several states such as, Wisconsin, Michigan, Minnesota, California, New York, Missouri, and New Jersey permit school boards to conduct school community centers with school funds. Milwaukee, New York, and Newark,[6] are examples of cities whose schools render comprehensive public recreation services. Most state laws consider recreation as a secondary function of schools, which leaves recreation in a rather weak position with regard to school administered public programs. While thousands of school facilities are used for public recreation, most of the programs are administered by independent agencies.

The city of Milwaukee, Wisconsin, is a good example of a school-administered public recreation program. It is called the Division of Municipal Recreation and Adult Education and is administered by an Assistant Superintendent of Schools. The recreation staff works under similar rules and working conditions as the school teachers.

RECOMMENDED PRACTICES

There is so much demand for good recreation facilities that it is hard to visualize the time when school facilities will not be needed for public recreation use. Indications are that schools will place increased emphasis on the preparation of the individual for the fullest possible life, and will share its facilities with other agencies.

Recommended practices in relation to schools are:

1. Schools and recreation plan to use each other's facilities jointly with full cooperation of all concerned.
2. Written agreements and contracts clearly defining the relationships, operating procedures and responsibilities of the two parties should be prepared.
3. If there is a recreation board (authoritative or advisory), its membership should include representation from the school board.

Obtaining Permission To Use Schools for Recreation

1. Investigate the existence of legal barriers.
2. Discuss possibilities with the superintendent of schools and ask his advice.
3. Prepare a plan for the recreation activities most needed and most likely to provide early success. Include a committee of interested parties and community leaders at this stage.
4. Organize a steering committee to prepare a promotion campaign.
5. Make a formal request and presentation to the school board.
6. If the approval of the school board is obtained, prepare a formal written agreement.

Questions for Discussion

1. How are the objectives of schools related to recreation?
2. What factors contribute to the support of the use of schools for recreation purposes?
3. What is the role of schools in preparing for leisure?
4. What changes would you make in the school plant to make it more functional for recreation purposes?
5. In what ways should schools and recreation plan together?
6. Why should or should not schools be used for community recreation purposes?
7. Explain the school-park concept.
8. What procedure would you use in obtaining agreement to use the school facilities for recreation purposes?
9. What provision would you include in a recreation-school contractual agreement?
10. What is the best method of administering the comprehensive community recreation program in public school facilities? Why?
11. Should the school personnel be used to conduct recreation programs in the school plant? Why or why not?
12. Would a recreation program using school properties be different from one conducted in separate facilities?

Short Problems

1. Prepare a model layout plan for a combination school-recreation indoor and outdoor unit.
2. Prepare necessary administrative guidelines (policies, rules, regulations, etc.) for conduct of recreation program in a school.
3. Prepare a model contractual agreement for joint use of recreation and school facilities.

References

1. "Local Parks and Recreation," *Parks and Recreation,* August 1971, p. 18.
2. *Recreation and Park Yearbook 1966* (Washington, D.C.: National Recreation and Park Association, 1967), p. 45.

3. Charles E. Doell and Gerald B. Fitzgerald, *A Brief History of Parks and Recreation in the United States* (Chicago: The Athletic Institute, 1954), p. 65.
4. "Cardinal Principles of Secondary Education," *Report of the Commission on the Reorganization of Secondary Education of the National Education Association* (Washington, D.C.: Department of the Interior, Bureau of Education Bulletin No. 35, 1918), p. 15.
5. *The Charter of the City of Richmond, Virginia* (1948), p. 98.
6. *Recreation and Park Yearbook 1966,* Table 41.

Selected Readings

American Association for Health, Physical Education, and Recreation, *School Recreation.* Washington, D.C.: the Association, 1960.

Corbin, H. Dan, and William J. Tait, *Education For Leisure,* pp. 59-75. Englewood Cliffs, N.J.: Prentice-Hall, Inc., 1973. *The school and education for leisure.*

Green, Thomas F., *Work, Leisure and the American Schools.* New York: Random House, 1968.

Hjelte, George, and Jay S. Shivers, *Public Administration of Recreational Services,* pp. 111-131. Philadelphia: Lea and Febiger, 1972.

Hormachea, Marion N., and Carroll R. Hormachea, *Recreation in Modern Society,* pp. 136-139. Boston: Holbrook Press Inc., 1972.

Kraus, Richard G., *Recreation and the Schools.* New York: The Macmillan Company, 1964.

Rodney, Lynn S., *Administration of Public Recreation,* pp. 157-169. New York: The Ronald Press Company, 1964.

Zeigler, Earle F., *Philosophical Foundations for Physical, Health and Recreation Education.* Englewood Cliffs, N.J.: Prentice-Hall, Inc., 1968.

CHAPTER 7

Public Recreation and Other Public Agencies

Administration is a process common to every organization in which two or more people with different skills are brought together to accomplish a specific goal. In early times, when life was simpler and each person was more or less self sufficient, there was less need for organization. With industralization came large concentrations of people and the opportunity for some to specialize and thus make a better living. With specialization and larger working forces came increased need for planning, organization, coordination, evaluation and management as well as specialists for almost every service.

As private corporations grew and developed, specialized departments so, also, did government agencies. Currently, in most incorporated cities, government is one of the largest employers and has the greatest variety of skills and specialized equipment. Recreation and park work has also become a specialized field of work, with the need for many kinds of special services and equipment, some on a full-time and others on a part-time basis.

The recreation and park department maintains service relationships with almost all agencies of local government, including the school board, planning commission, public housing, public works, public utilities, police department, public library, museum, health department, and community action programs.

THE PLANNING COMMISSION

Planning is one of the major functions of administration. In recreation and parks, specialized technical planning is usually done by the executive and program staff as part of their regular duties. Some agencies employ consultants, especially for the planning of large projects or for work with the local planning commission if there is one.

Planning commissions have a wealth of information useful to recreation planners. They make surveys and, in conjunction with the several departments of the city government, prepare the master plan for the entire city, as well as long range development proposals. They regulate subdivisions and land use and, therefore, have information on open space, housing developments, proposals for private use and social and economic trends. They may have useful aerial photographs, charts, maps, and drawings. Sometimes they have landscape architects who can assist with designs.

THE PUBLIC HOUSING AUTHORITY

The public housing authority, usually an independent agency operating under a board or commission, is one of the largest contributors to public recreation. It provides indoor and outdoor recreation facilities, on the basis of a specified amount per family unit, in conjunction with public housing developments. The number of housing units in a particular development determines the size and extent of the recreation facilities provided. Both tenants and non-tenants use the facilities. Local governments may add funds in order to provide larger and more comprehensive facilities to be operated by the public recreation agency for the use of the general public. Public housing officials usually consult with the recreation executive and they jointly plan for the recreation areas and facilities. In smaller housing or "turn-key" developments the "per family unit" allocation for recreation may be contributed in cash to the local government to be used in enlarging or adding specific improvements to nearby public recreation facilities. The recreation agency has considerable freedom of action but is subject to audit by the housing agency for such expenditures. The legislative body, of course, must accept the contribution and be responsible for construction, operation, and maintenance.

When recreation facilities are owned by public housing, the housing management provides the facilities, equipment, maintenance, and custodial services, and the recreation agency provides the program, supplies, leadership, and supervision.

THE PUBLIC WORKS DEPARTMENT

The public works department, which usually is responsible for the city or county engineering, construction, inspections, and maintenance of physical facilities, usually provides these services for park and recreation agencies as well, particularly in smaller communities. The trend is to reimburse other agencies for work performed in order to maintain actual cost accounts and true budget expenses. For instance, the recreation agency would reimburse public works, at cost, for repairs made to park roads. Public works would similarly reimburse parks for tree work. The budgets and work programs of each agency reflect these reimbursement transactions.

Even though another agency performs a service, the agency under whose jurisdiction the property falls is responsible to see that all work is performed satisfactorily. One problem with joint use of services and equipment is that there is so often a backlog of work and the primary agency gives priority to its own work. It is well to have an alternate source of service, such as a private contractor, in the event that the other agency cannot provide a service when needed. Very often the purchasing department has annual contracts with several private firms to provide on-call rental equipment with drivers when needed. Even then, equipment may not always be available when it is needed most. For this reason, park and recreation agencies like to provide all of the services possible themselves.

PUBLIC UTILITIES

Water, gas, electricity and sewer utilities are provided by local government in some areas and by private companies in others. Recreation is a big user of utilities for floodlighting, fountains, irrigation, heating, drainage, and public rest rooms.

The water utility may have lakes and watershed areas which may be developed for hiking, picnicking, nature education, golf, fishing and other activities that would not contaminate the water supply.

THE POLICE DEPARTMENT

Some police departments have established centers, clubs, and camps for boys and young men, particularly the disadvantaged. They are intended as both a human relations activity and a voluntary interest for policemen. Most public recreation agencies, particularly the smaller ones, are dependent upon the police for security and protection. Larger agencies sometimes have their own park police force. However, the recreation staff must assume full responsibility for discipline and conduct of participants.

It is well to invite police to drop in at recreation events and facilities occasionally to promote a friendly image as much as possible. When time is not a factor, the police on call should quietly inform the recreation director of the reason for his call. The recreation staff should cooperate to the fullest.

The problems of crowd control, drugs, threats, confrontations, and riots require special training, equipment, numbers, and quick response in quantity and skills that most recreation departments do not provide. On the other hand, police departments do not have the manpower or budgets to assign police personnel regularly to all recreation areas. Also, when police are around there is a human tendency for the individual and group to be less careful of their own responsibilities for protection, law, and order. In recreation systems where park police are provided there should be the greatest cooperation between park and regular police. Usually, the authority of park police is limited to recreation areas or law violations originating on recreation areas.

There is need for some park police, or regular police assigned to duty in parks, to handle parking, traffic, security, and minor violations. More serious crimes are matters for regular police jurisdiction.

THE LEGAL DEPARTMENT

Most local governments have either a well-staffed, full-time legal department or an attorney (full-time or part-time depending on the size) to handle legal matters. Although the respective agencies, including recreation, handle paperwork and fact finding, or even make drafts of proposals and ordinances, it is well to consult with the legal department and have them review or prepare all legal documents before they are signed officially or submitted for legislative action. It is much harder to change a law or correct a legal document once it is approved than it is to get it done correctly in the first place.

The legal department advises the executive on all legal matters, such as the interpretation of laws, liability, insurance, property acquisitions, agreements, and easements, and prepares written opinions, ordinances, contracts, court cases, and condemnation suits.

THE LIBRARY

The public library not only provides reading and references for the public but also has professional books and references on games, hobbies, crafts, music, drama, and conservation useful to the staff. It may provide a monthly list of new publications and magazine articles on recreation. Some libraries conduct story telling for youngsters, both in the library and on playgrounds, and some have organized craft, music, and dramatic groups and lend films, records, and sheet music.

Some libraries have lecture halls for exhibits, forums, book reviews, musicales, and educational features and may provide branch or mobile libraries in or near parks and recreation areas. In some places recreation and libraries are combined in a single agency.

THE MUSEUM

The museums of today not only are buildings for the display of art and collections of literature, crafts, science, and natural history, but also exhibit the performing arts and conduct classes, workshops, and lectures on a variety of subjects. Space may be used by community groups when they are not needed for museum purposes. Museum exhibits and performances may serve as another outlet for recreation skills and cooperative programs. Museum staffs are good sources for training, demonstrations, lecture programs, and traveling units.

THE HEALTH DEPARTMENT

The public health agency provides three main services for recreation. The first is health and sanitary standards and the periodic testing and inspection of swimming pools. The second is the conducting of physical examinations required for participation in resident camping and certain strenuous sports. The third is the control of rodents and insects. It is very helpful to have the health department "fog" spray for mosquitoes prior to a late evening outdoor performance.

The health department may sometimes use public recreation facilities for dog inoculation clinics, health clinics and health programs that are compatible with recreation uses.

COMMUNITY ACTION PROGRAMS

Community action programs, funded by the Office of Economic Opportunity and other governmental departments, and administered locally by a board of directors composed of representatives of public and private sectors of the community, began in the mid 1960's to provide programs for the disadvantaged and the poor. The scope of these activities was determined largely by the initiative and ingenuity of the local board and staff. Several of the anti-poverty programs involved public recreation. Often, the recreation executive, or his representative, served on the C.A.P. board of directors and helped coordinate the programs. The projects involved work, education, self-sufficiency, play, business training, community cooperation, and many others. The purpose was to find ways of preparing the untrained, undertrained, unemployed and underemployed for jobs and to make job opportunities for them. Recreation, schools, community agencies, civic leaders, government, business, planning, law enforcement, health and welfare agencies were heavily involved.

Public recreation participated in several programs and often sponsored them locally, such as:

1. *New Careers in Recreation,* which involved enrolling young people with recreation potential from low income areas, training them for Civil Service recreation-aide positions, and working them on-the-job under instructors.
2. *Summer Youth Work in Recreation,* which provided training and experience as recreation aides under close supervision.
3. *Summer Jobs Corps,* which included training and recreation work.
4. *Neighborhood Youth Corps,* which provided work experience in recreation for teenagers.
5. *Summer Recreation Support Program,* which provided recreation camping, and experiences of innovative nature.
6. *Transportation* for trips of recreational and educational nature for youth.
7. *Summer Food Supplement Program,* which provided free lunches for low income participants under age 21 in organized recreation programs.

Some cities have added apprentice or recreation trainee classifications to provide for employment of individuals from ghetto and low income areas as recreation aides.

Recreation was used in the modified role it had in the 1930's which was to combat crime and delinquency; to rehabilitate the individual and family; to involve the hard-to-reach and to help them develop a better way of life through recreation contacts. It gave more consideration to the total needs of the individual, provided a means of communication through recreation, provided opportunities to develop self respect and a "wholesome" way to find recognition and leadership.

With the termination of the Office of Economic Opportunity and the reduction of federal support for several antipoverty programs in the early 1970's, several localities increased contributions and others carried on selected C.A.P. programs either as new units of local government or as added responsibilities to existing agencies, including recreation. Recreation thus took on a different role, particularly in areas with large numbers of the disadvantaged, by communicating with the hard-to-reach, "cooling" the emotions, providing special recreation programs, creating job opportunities, and referring individuals to places which might serve other unmet needs.

OTHER DEPARTMENTS

Relationships with other departments and agencies are less significant or functional.

Model Cities programs, involving larger old cities, have public recreation-sponsored programs ranging from trips, senior citizens clubs, and improvement of park areas, to the operation of multipurpose centers sponsored by the public recreation agency.

Urban renewal, operated sometimes in conjunction with redevelopment and public housing authorities, acquires slum areas and clears land for redevelopment. This provides the recreation agency a real opportunity to acquire and develop adequate recreation space and facilities at reasonable cost to the agency. The park division would be involved in planning for street trees and park space. Recreation and schools are sometimes planned together in urban renewal areas.

The *assessor's office* has records of all public and private real estate property in the locality. This information is useful in preparing plans for land acquisition and estimating costs.

The *fire department* assists in flooding areas for ice skating and in safety training programs. Often, members are skilled in first aid.

ADJOINING PUBLIC JURISDICTIONS

Many of the older cities have developed solid to their boundaries. They have no space on which to build attractive new residences and modern industries. Surplus population from farms and outlying areas gravitates to cities for jobs and better health and welfare services. As municipalities expand in population, it is necessary to expand in area and in services. The need for more space invariably brings city interests into conflict with adjoining county interests. No politician or official likes to give up areas of jurisdiction and power. Administrative authorities of adjoining political jurisdictions, therefore, often are looked upon with suspicion when they seek cooperative arrangements or consolidation of efforts. Sometimes there is little cooperation between city and county. Generally, however, professional and technical staffs cooperate and work together very well within the jurisdictional framework established for them.

It is impractical to put an imaginary wall around a city, county, or other political jurisdiction and keep out nonresidents. There are friends, relatives and citizens who want to join together for recreation whether in city or in county. Overcrowded urban areas cannot accommodate their own population as well as adjoining areas without expanding their territory and facilities. There is usually tremendous opposition to annexation or expansion of jurisdiction especially where it means higher taxes for urban services.

There are several solutions: (1) complete separation of activities by jurisdictions, (2) friendly cooperation between jurisdictions, (3) agreement by a jurisdiction to provide service for an adjoining jurisdiction, (4) creation of a metropolitan government, (5) creation of special districts, and (6) creation of regional authorities.

Local cooperation, contract agreements for service, metropolitan government, and creation of districts have been partially successful in minimizing municipal-county conflicts. Mergers and consolidations of local governments have proven very successful. Districts will be discussed in Chapter 8 and regions in Chapter 9.

RELATIONSHIPS WITH THE STATE

Recreation services provided by a state to its subdivisions are similar to those provided by the federal government, except that they relate to the specific interests and needs of the people as well as to the specific resources of the state. State agencies preserve natural features and historic sites not included in local or federal jurisdictions and provide information, planning, consultation, and advisory services to its political subdivisions. The state, of course, maintains and administers state forests and parks, including recreation areas and facilities, cabins, and camp sites; nature, hiking, bicycling and bridle trails; beaches, game and wildlife preserves, and highway waysides. Educational institutions with outreach programs may provide state grants for senior citizens and youth and administer certain federal grants such as Bureau of Outdoor Recreation funds. The recreation executive usually maintains close contact with the various state services available to the locality. Nearby state areas and facilities are used extensively to supplement local services.

RELATIONSHIPS WITH FEDERAL AGENCIES

The federal government, with its more than 72 agencies involved in recreation in some way, makes it a near necessity for the recreation executive to be an expert in the interpretation and application of federal laws, practices, procedures, and communications if maximum benefits from federal services are to be obtained.

The traditional role of the federal government in recreation is to preserve national recreation resources of historic interest and unusual natural beauty and administer recreational areas within the national parks, forests, and other federal lands. More recently it provides special funds, revenue sharing arrangements, and grants to state and local governments. Federal guidelines are also provided for their use, often requiring the upgrading of standards, the establishment of protective codes, and citizen participation.

In larger agencies, executives often assign an aide full time to handle federal and state contacts, contracts, implementation, expediting and reporting on grant-in-aid projects. Smaller agencies may assign the executive or an aide part time as contact person for grant programs. In any event, it is good for the contact person and the executive, if possible, to keep up-to-date on every aspect of these programs and all changes in policy relating to them. Lack of conformity to precise contract items, failure to maintain accurate records, and incomplete implementation can lead to loss of funds or disapproval of reimbursement payments. Sometimes, uncommitted federal funds become available on short notice. The executive who has plans ready and is in a position to implement a program promptly may get priority on assignment of such special funds.

Certain federal grants such as land and water conservation funds are administered by an agency of the state in conformity to a state master plan; therefore, the executive should make contact with the assigned state agency.

There are several federal agencies, other than federal grant programs, with which the recreation executive might have relationships.

Department of Agriculture The department administers the United States Forest Service, which protects the federal forest preserves, as well as provides the use of appropriate areas for recreation purposes including organized camping, fishing and hunting, nature education, picnicking, water sports, winter sports, consistent with the primary purpose of the area. The extension service provides consultant and advisory services, field demonstrations, home demonstrations, 4-H Club activities, and publications, particularly for rural areas. The soil conservation service provides advisory service and soil information and preserves natural resources for recreation.

Department of the Army The Corps of Engineers protects and maintains navigable rivers and waterways for navigation and flood control. It provides the use of areas for water sports, hiking, camping and other outdoor activities consistent with their primary purposes. Military facilities, standby, abandoned and unused property may also be available for recreation purposes.

Department of Health, Education and Welfare The Children's Bureau and Office of Education provides publications and information on recreation and provides motivation for recreation services.

Department of the Interior The National Park Service which is responsible for national parks, monuments, national historic sites and scenic areas of interest to the public also controls battlefield sites and other areas so located that they may serve a local use. The Fish and Wildlife Service protects national fish and wildlife resources and enforces game laws but permits the use of areas and facilities for recreation when such use is compatible with their primary purpose. The Bureau of Reclamation permits the use of its reservoirs for swimming, boating, fishing, hiking and camping.

Other agencies that provide information, consultation and their resources in various ways for recreation purposes include the Departments of Housing and Urban Development, Labor, Transportation, and Commerce; the National Capitol Parks and Planning Commission; the Tennessee Valley Authority; and various temporary and emergency type programs that are initiated from time to time for specific purposes.

It is well to contact federal agencies in the community to determine what facilities under their control may be used for local recreation purposes. Use of such facilities and services may be coordinated with local resources to enhance the local program and make the local appropriation go further.

The federal government also, upon occasion, sponsors national conferences which involve recreation interests, such as the White House Conferences on Children and Youth and the White House Conference on Aging.

Questions for Discussion

1. What recreation agency services may be provided by the local planning commission? By the department of public works? By the utilities department?
2. In your opinion, is it better for the recreation and park agency to provide its own complete auxiliary services or to use services of other government units? Why?
3. What kinds of services are performed for the agency by private contractors and under what circumstances?
4. Is the recreation agency justified in operating a public housing-owned recreation facility when the participants are almost all from the housing project? Why?
5. How would you recommend policing and security on public recreation areas be handled?
6. In what way did the anti-poverty programs of the 1960's affect public recreation agencies?

7. What would you recommend as the most effective way to handle public recreation services in urban communities involving two or more city and county jurisdictions?
8. As recreation executive, what would you do if 45 percent of the attendance at a public recreation area regularly were residents of adjoining jurisdictions?

Short Problems

1. Prepare policies and suggested agreements between the public recreation and housing agencies for operating housing facilities as public centers.
2. Prepare a practical plan for a recreation agency to administer recreation services for an adjoining jurisdiction.
3. Using the acquisition of open space and its full development for a public playground as an example, outline how each agency of government discussed in this chapter would be involved.

Selected Readings

Corbin, H. Dan, and William J. Tait, *Education For Leisure,* pp. 131–151. Englewood Cliffs, N.J.: Prentice-Hall, Inc., 1973. *Recreation on the federal and state levels.*

Federal Interagency Committee on Recreation, *The Role of the Federal Government in the Field of Recreation.* Washington, D.C.: Federal Interagency on Recreation, 1961.

Hormachea, Marion N., and Carroll R. Hormachea, *Recreation in Modern Society,* pp. 130–136. Boston: Holbrook Press, Inc., 1972.

Meyer, Harold D., Charles K. Brightbill, and H. Douglas Sessoms, *Community Recreation: A Guide to Its Organization.* Englewood Cliffs, N.J.: Prentice-Hall, Inc., 1969.

Recreation and Park Yearbook 1966, Washington, D.C.: National Recreation and Park Association, 1967. *A nationwide inventory of public recreation and parks services of local, state, and federal agencies.*

Smithee, Kenneth J., *Federal Assistance for Recreation and Parks.* Washington, D.C.: National Recreation and Park Association, 1967.

Sundquist, James L., and David W. Davis, *Making Federalism Work,* pp. 1–129. Washington, D.C.: The Brookings Institution, 1969.

CHAPTER 8

Rural Recreation Services

Recreation in the United States is thought of as having had its beginning in the urban population centers. Only a few county governments had expressed interest in public parks before the turn of the century and there was even less concern for public recreation.[1] The busy families of the sparsely settled rural areas had neither the time nor the transportation for recreation as we know it today.

Traditionally, urban and rural are thought of as opposites: the urban, dealing with factories, congestion, traffic, pollution, crowds, noise, and manufactured products; the rural dealing with open space, gardens, fields, streams, animals, clean air, quiet, and natural products. Although that was the way the country was in earlier times, the differences between urban and rural life are becoming less each year.

The recent "population and transportation explosion" has spread the urban population into the hinterlands and, aided by the efficiency of farm machinery, has transplanted the surplus workers from farm families into the congested cities. Large portions of former rural counties which adjoin cities are rapidly becoming urbanized. Most of the one third of the nation's population that still live in rural areas, now enjoy the same conveniences as urban dwellers—expressways (or good roads), telephones, television, radio, electricity, running water, modern plumbing and heating. Really, the significant differences now between urban and rural living are means of livelihood, space, tempo, distance, and hours of work.

Rural land near cities is rapidly being occupied by business and industry, apartment developments, housing subdivisions, and former city dwellers who want to continue to receive the services to which they were accustomed in the city. They are, therefore, exerting strong pressure on nearby rural-oriented governments to provide such services. Most of the rural young people also want urban type services.

Two types of local government evolved originally: one for urban needs and one for rural needs. All cities, except those in Virginia and a few other independent cities, are in counties. Thus, people living in cities are subject to two layers of local government (including the payment of taxes) and each performs an area of service. Unincorporated villages and towns are generally associated with rural government. Although the conditions have changed over the years, the styles and patterns of local government have remained basically the same.

RURAL GOVERNMENT

"The county" is the main unit of rural government. In the state of Louisiana, it is called a "parish." Counties may be divided into districts. In some New England and North Central states, they are divided into townships. The idea of the county as a unit of government for rural areas is of English origin and was established in the colonies, first by Virginia, and later adopted by some of the other colonies and most of the states.[2] Delaware has 3 counties, the smallest number, and Texas has 253, the largest number.[3]

Counties are local subdivision units of the state for the assigned purpose of making state services and functions reasonably available to the rural population. Counties were established at a time when communication was mainly by personal contact and transportation was by horse, and they have changed little in basic structure since. Counties operate under state law to carry out the basic functions designated by the state, such as to collect taxes, conduct elections, administer health, welfare and education programs, maintain the peace and administer justice, register land titles and vital statistics, and build and maintain county roads. Functions may vary slightly from state to state. More recently, county residents, particularly those in urbanizing communities, have demanded and received additional services, such as drainage and flood control, fire protection, water and sewer service, garbage disposal, airports, libraries, parks, recreation, and some have planning, zoning, and building regulations. This about closes the gap between the types of services urban and county governments provide.

Characteristics of Counties

The 1970 U.S. Census reports that there were 3,043 counties varying in size from 23 square miles in New York County, all of which is occupied by New York City, to 20,119 square miles in San Bernardino County, California. About 15 percent of counties are near urban population centers and have both urban and rural areas. Some, such as Arlington County,

Virginia, next to Washington, D. C., are distinctly urban in character. The vast majority of counties are, however, distinctly rural with less than 25,000 population. Counties range in population from 164 in King County, Texas to 7,040,697 in Los Angeles County, California. Topography may be flat, rolling, mountainous, prairie, wooded, desert, swampy or a combination of these. Most of the typically rural counties are found in New England, parts of the South, the Midwest and Far West.

Counties with streams, lakes, interesting natural features and appropriate topography are beginning to attract numbers of vacationers, campers, and city dwellers who enjoy getting away from the stresses of the city. The open country counties attract the adventurer, sportsman, snowmobiler and skier. Catering to these kinds of activity provides a livelihood for many villagers and county residents and, at the same time, provides extended recreation services to the local population.

Consulting planners visualize that future population will reside in strips, or corridors, along the rivers, coasts and highways and they propose the establishment of strip parks, recreation areas, and hiking and bicycle trails along these corridors, such as Sligo Creek Parkway in Montgomery County, Maryland. The modern parkway may well be the connecting link between places of interest and the forerunner of the strip park and recreation area of the future.

A most critical concern of planners, politicians, and citizens is how to coordinate effectively the resources of the several government units which currently exist in metropolitan areas and which provide duplicating, overlapping, and competitive services. County leaders are concerned also that the congestion and other problems of the cities should not spread through the suburbs and rural sections. County, regional and state planning units and zoning boards are working with park and recreation authorities to preserve open space for present and future community use.

BRIEF HISTORY OF COUNTY PARKS AND RECREATION

The first identifiable, rural, public park-like area was the courthouse square. Children played on the lawns and adults used them for drills, meetings, and agricultural displays. Some are still in use in the Eastern states. County fairs provided a source of rural recreation at least once a year, and made facilities available for community use at other times.

Open spaces, forests, and parks were acquired or received as gifts and used for passive recreation long before public recreation was established as a public function. Although, land had been received by counties as gifts before 1890, most of it remained as undeveloped public space.

The first county park system to be established was "in Essex County, New Jersey in 1895, but the provision of parks by counties did not occur generally until considerably after 1900. By 1930 seventy-four counties had established parks." [4]

During the depression years of the 1930's, county governments and public school districts sponsored hundreds of federally-funded Works Progress Administration recreation, music, drama, and handicraft projects for rural areas. For instance, in the state of Virginia, 43 of the 100 counties sponsored recreation programs under the WPA emergency work programs. Some counties continued the programs, some under the supervision of school boards, after the federal emergency funds were phased out in the early 1940's. Such programs were the forerunners of public recreation in several counties throughout the nation.

In the decade following World War II there was a 64 percent increase in the number of counties reporting recreation and/or park departments.[5] Since 1965 especially, the land and water conservation fund, other federal and state grant-in-aid monies, and federal revenue sharing funds (beginning January 1, 1972) have helped citizen groups considerably in obtaining approval from county boards of supervisors to inaugurate county recreation services. Since 1970, the expansion of county recreation departments has been extensive. For instance, in Virginia the chief of the State Office of Recreation reported to the authors that 13 of Virginia's 95 * counties had established recreation departments in 1973, but there were 22 in 1974, an increase of 9 in one year. Several were in distinctly rural counties not near any city. This is significant and indicates the universal need for recreation and group activities, even in rural areas. Each of the new agencies is a separate recreation or recreation and park department, and several have acquired and developed park lands for community use.

SCOPE OF RURAL RECREATION SERVICES

Life in a strictly rural setting moves at a slower pace than in the city. The general pattern is to work longer hours, including Saturdays, and to attend church on Sundays. People do as much of their own maintenance and repair work as possible and tend to be self-sufficient, sometimes because of economic necessity. There is pride, considerable reluctance to accept certain government programs, and a tendency to conform to custom and tradition. There is less governing and fewer legal restrictions in rural government resulting in a great deal of individual independence,

* In recent years five Virginia counties and cities have merged.

all of which is reflected in the value judgments and philosophy of the rural dweller and county government officials.

Until recent years, public recreation has been identified almost entirely as an urban service. Since the beginning of public recreation in 1885 with the sand gardens in Boston, programs in urban environments have been developed with the growth and changes in cities. However, a few notable counties have developed outstanding programs and facilities. Rural areas have not changed so much, except those affected by urban and industrial developments. There are, therefore, three kinds of county situations today: the majority that are distinctly rural, those that are partially urbanized, and those that are completely urbanized. Those that are completely urbanized have adjusted legally and structurally to provide urban type services.

Traditional Rural Services

The traditional rural services involving recreation are adjuncts of the state and federal government agencies, farm organizations, and service groups.

The public school is often the center of social, cultural, and recreational life of the rural community. The school sports program, clubs, choral groups, bands, school socials, educational trips, and other extracurricular activities may be the only group recreation available other than the Sunday school and church.

The church is one of the most effective influences in rural life. It provides spiritual, social, drama, sports, outings, games, holiday celebrations and other group recreation activities for the rural family.

The cooperative extension services of the land grant colleges and universities assist rural people as consultants in the planning and developing of recreation areas, and provide training, homemaking courses, nature clubs, festivals and, in some places, regional camps and other recreation opportunities.

Rural-oriented organizations such as the 4-H Clubs, The Future Farmers of America, and The Ruritan are membership organizations which provide experience, training, trips, educational and recreational opportunities for youth and adults. The National Grange, the American Farm Bureau, and Farmers Union not only motivate better community life and recreation for youth and adults, but also sponsor legislation of interest to the farmer.

State colleges, universities, and community colleges are often located in rural areas and may provide consultants, technical advisors, planners, research, field services, and sometimes traveling entertainment and program demonstration groups. The campuses and physical plants may be used for meetings, training, and special recreation functions.

Branch libraries and bookmobiles provide excellent services to rural areas. Sometimes they have storytellers, lending service for films, sheet music and records.

Other recreation resources include participation in nearby municipal recreation programs and organizations, Little League and other nationally sponsored youth sports programs; and the use of state and national parks and forests. There is considerable visiting among families, hunting and fishing, political rallies, group picnics and outings.

Some counties have been prevented from adding permissive functions, like recreation, because of lack of legal authority or enabling legislation. However, most states have urbanizing county areas which, no doubt, will be sponsoring appropriate enabling legislation for the operation of county recreation programs if it does not already exist.

County Park and Recreation Services

The scope of county park and recreation services is limited only by the legal authority given by the state and the funds available. In urban and urbanizing counties, the scope of the recreation services is similar to municipal recreation services but with emphasis on larger parks and open spaces, streams, conservation areas, lakes, beaches, scenic drives, parkways, and the use of school and other public properties such as courtrooms.

Parkways tie in with urban parkways, where possible, to provide a continuous park effect. They may have lookouts and turnouts at interesting scenic and historical places. There is a popular practice of acquiring adequate space on both sides of roadways and along streams for turnouts, parking, picnic areas, tennis courts, nature education, and other appropriate recreation opportunities as well as space for hiking and bicycling. The parkway and the strip park serve as connecting links in the county park system. An example is Westchester County, New York.

County parks are similar in development to municipal parks. Since most urban parks are small and often overcrowded, planners recommend larger county and regional parks, particularly where open space is available. Although county school facilities are emphasized for use as active recreation areas, sometimes it is necessary to use a portion of a park for tennis courts, playing fields, playground and other recreation purposes. Rural people have expressed the hope that county parks will have adequate space, will continue "rural-like" in appearance, and will not look like city parks.

Rural parks are of two types: one, the local park to provide for the recreation needs of those within a 1–1½-mile radius; the other, regional parks which provide natural areas, streams, lakes, and facilities for golf, camping, picnicking, and similar activities. A few counties have acquired large reservations of open space to preserve plant life and provide for winter sports, camping, hiking, water sports, and other acivities that require considerable land space.

Playing fields, playgrounds, and recreation areas are also needed in rural areas. Rural-oriented county boards of supervisors are prone to use schools for public recreation uses. Usually, there is adequate open space around rural school buildings for the purpose, but often these must be lighted and improved, and new facilities added. Improvements are planned jointly with school administrations for the mutual benefit of both agencies. Where school facilities will not serve the purposes, additional space is sometimes acquired, or parks and other properties are used.

Because of distance and scattered population, organization is more difficult in counties but it is overcome by working closely with participants, advance planning, careful coordination, and careful scheduling with a minimum of last minute changes. Groups may not meet as often as in the city. Most general everyday programs are conducted in populated areas, such as towns and villages with, perhaps, special extension or traveling programs into more rural areas.

Traditionally, programs provide for the normal active population but in counties, too, there are numbers of handicapped individuals, senior citizens, and disadvantaged groups for which special programs should be provided.

MANAGING AUTHORITY FOR RURAL RECREATION

The type of managing authority for rural park and recreation services, and how such services are administered locally, depends greatly on the kinds of subdivisions a state has and what authority the various states have given their respective subdivisions. The county, of course, is the principal unit of rural government. There are also towns, townships, different kinds of special districts and regions as well as agencies of the state and federal governments.

The County Managing Authority

Until recently, many state enabling laws did not permit counties to conduct public recreation programs. This was considered a function of urban government.

Local officials are expected to initiate requests for changes to meet new needs. Too often, county officials are content to provide the usual, traditional rural services. Admittedly, it is easier that way, especially when the urbanizing areas within the county's borders incorporate as towns and cities and provide their own services, which they may do by authority of a different set of state laws which apply to incorporated communities. Such laws *permit* urban governments to perform special services, such as recreation and parks, and use tax money to finance them.

Urbanized portions of counties usually want urban-type services and they may incorporate or form special districts to provide the services they need. This relieves the pressure on the county governments to provide the extra services. Some county governments, therefore, continue to provide the traditional county services and operate with lower tax rates, which accounts somewhat for the reluctance of some officials to ask for a change in enabling legislation.

When residents of an urbanizing portion of a county demand a new service, like recreation, and the county does not yet have authority to establish a separate recreation and parks agency as such, the authorities sometimes assign administration of the services to an existing, traditional agency that is interpreted as having the necessary authority. The managing authority may be the board of education, the planning commission, a special committee, a forest-preserve district, or even the county road commissioners, as in Michigan.[6] Some counties operate only a seasonal or limited program.

The park and/or recreation board and the separate park and recreation agency are the two most common forms of county managing authorities.[7] With the increased use of the county executive form of administration and central management control, the trend in county recreation management is to the separate agency with or without an advisory board. In recent years, most states have enacted laws permitting county governments to acquire, develop, and maintain parks, and several states specifically have empowered counties to conduct recreation programs. If the authority is vested in the general laws, it applies to all countries alike. If it is vested in special laws, it may apply to a single county or all counties with the same identifiable characteristics, such as population. In urban counties, the management and programming of public recreation services are much the same as they are in cities, except for the government structure.

Towns and Townships

Towns and townships represent the smallest units of government authorized by the state. An increasing number of towns conduct their own recreation programs. In the New England states, where towns are governed by the historic "town meeting" process and board of selectmen, even the unincorporated town has a significant place in providing rural services, including recreation. In other places towns conduct full-time or part-time programs suited to their needs.

The township form of rural government was designed to provide basic services, such as roads, for rural areas when transportation and communications were difficult. Only in a few states, such as New Jersey, New York, and Pennsylvania have they provided significant services.[8] Relatively few have been involved in recreation and park services. When transportation and communications were improved, counties took over many of the services some townships had been providing.

Special Recreation Districts

Special districts are sometimes established to provide recreation services which are not, or cannot be, provided by existing government processes. They may be totally within a political jurisdiction or they may cross jurisdictional lines, usually encompassing a population or service area. They are autonomous units governed by a board appointed by the state authority, county board of supervisors, or elected. When a district is totally within a county, the county board of supervisors may act as the governing board. Request for establishment of a special district is made by petition of voters to the county board of supervisors in the event of a single jurisdiction and to the state in instances were multiple jurisdictions are involved. Depending on the circumstances, either the state, or the county, under authority given it by enabling legislation, may establish the special district.

A special recreation district is really a political subdivision of the state similar to a school district, county, or township. It has only those powers given it by the state. Usually, it may acquire and develop property, tax and raise funds, sue and be sued, and perform the usual recreation functions. There may be a number of special districts, each performing a different type of service. Taxes for districts may be collected by the normal tax collection agencies of the counties or by the districts.

The special district is especially useful as a means of providing recreation services for portions of counties that want and are willing to support public recreation while other parts of the county are not. It provides a vehicle for obtaining federal and state grants for the acquisition and development of park and recreation space. It is a means of crossing jurisdictional lines and providing a unified recreation program. It is a method of getting services that are impossible to obtain by conventional methods. Also, district boards are independent and free from political influence and the complexities of artificial political boundaries.

The disadvantages are that another layer of government is added, responsibility divided, and the complexity of government in the areas involved is increased. They are independent units usually confined to the single interest which they pursue vigorously, often without adequate coordination and balance with other government activities. Sometimes, there are also special districts for parks, parkways and roadside parks, conservation, libraries, and housing which may perform overlapping or duplicating services. It is more economical to operate all services under a single unit of government. Finally, once they are established and entwined in the life and activities of the communities, it is nearly impossible to merge services or change the political and authoritative structure. Although special districts for other public services have been common for many years, special districts for rural recreation are recent developments and are used thus far in only a few states.

CHANGING CONCEPTS OF COUNTY SERVICES

The counties in America were originally designed primarily to administer state government services to rural areas of the state. Most of those services were oriented to agriculture and products of the soil. Emphasis was on roads, education, 4-H Clubs, care of livestock, good farming practices, farm management, housekeeping and gardening. There was interest in helping the farmer improve his status and to use the best techniques. Numbers of unincorporated towns developed to serve the rural areas. Following World War I, tractors and automobiles replaced horses in fields and on highways. New techniques, efficient machinery and faster transportation increased the farmer's productivity with less manpower. He expanded his acreage and still there was not enough work to occupy all members of the customarily large farm families. Many, therefore, left for a better life in the cities. By the time of World War II, new residences and expanding industries had occupied most of the vacant spaces in the cities. Except for war activities and related housing, there was little construction during the war years. Until this time, there had been a nominal amount of residential and industrial development in rural areas adjacent to the cities. Counties continued to perform the traditional rural services and cities continued to perform the usual urban services, but the needs of the rural families began to be more like those of city families.

Traditionally, cities have favored rural areas. They needed the products, the rural market for their manufactured products, and they needed the weekly business to maintain their central business sections.

Traditionally, also, nearby county residents have had the advantage of participating in urban services (airports and transportation centers, medical centers, expressways, parks, and recreation opportunities) without participating in the costs, except to patronize the business district. With the "population and the transportation explosion" and the flight of people, business, and industry to the suburbs, counties can provide both natural and manufactured products and are not so dependent upon city resources. The incorporated areas can no longer absorb, economically or space-wise, the masses from the suburbs and the hinterlands who now seek the "permissive" services which are provided by incorporated areas. The situation has created conflicts of interest between urban and rural governments with practical solutions, short of consolidation or mergers, not yet in sight.

The Status of Urban Counties

Many counties have their own industrial sections and modern shopping centers which help provide a good tax base. Rural residents no longer have the need they once had to patronize the central city business district. The expressways to the central city business district still carry rural workers by the thousands to and from jobs and some urban dwellers to suburban shopping centers and some county shoppers to the central business district.

The suburbanite enjoys more space, a lower tax rate, and fewer problems, but he also wants the services to which he has been accustomed in the city. He lives in unincorporated suburbs outside the city limits. Except, perhaps, for an appropriate sign, one cannot tell where the city jurisdiction ends and the boundary of the county begins. The streets, utilities, street lights, traffic lights and other urban services continue. Recognizing the many problems of the central city, counties are attempting to prevent the extension of those problems into their areas.

In former years, cities would annex adjacent populated county areas but, since 1950, there has been stronger opposition on the part of lower tax-paying county residents and a trend away from annexation and incorporation. There has been an increase in consolidations and mergers.

Many state legislatures have updated their enabling legislation to permit counties to provide most, if not all, of the urban services as indicated earlier. Many counties have provided urban services to the unincorporated areas adjoining cities, therefore, making it difficult for a city to expand its borders.

Families that live in distinctly rural sections are expecting the same kinds of urban services the county provides its metropolitan areas. An increasing number of typically rural counties are, therefore, providing urban services, including recreation. An increasing number, also, are employing professional county administrators and some are changing to the county manager form of government. The trend in development of county service is towards total services according to need and available resources. There is little difference between rural and urban authorities and functions.

Questions for Discussion

1. Explain the differences between functions of a city government and those of a county government.
2. What would you consider to be the differences between city and county recreation services?
3. What were the principal events in the history of county parks and recreation?
4. What are the basic characteristics of a county? How are they different from those of a city?
5. What is the scope of the rural recreation services?
6. How do "traditional" county recreation services compare with the "metropolitan" type of recreational services?
7. What are the differences among the types of managing authorities for county recreation?
8. What is a special recreation district and how is it used in recreation?
9. How would you justify a recreation service for a distinctly rural county?
10. What are the significant characteristics of city, county, regional, and state parks?

Short Problems

1. In a county of your choice, list the different recreation opportunities available to county residents, identify any unmet needs, and make recommendations for improvements.
2. Prepare a suggested model recreation plan for a typical county which has one city of 75,000 population, three incorporated towns and 25,000 population in rural and unincorporated areas. The area of the county is approximately 300 square miles.

References

1. Charles E. Doell and Gerald B. Fitzgerald, *A Brief History of Parks and Recreation in the United States* (Chicago: The Athletic Institute, 1964), p. 6.
2. Lynn S. Rodney, *Administration of Public Recreation* (New York: The Ronald Press, 1964), p. 171.
3. 1970 U.S. Bureau of the Census Report.

4. Doell and Fitzgerald, *A Brief History of Parks and Recreation in the United States,* p. 6.
5. *Recreation and Park Yearbook 1966* (Washington, D.C.: National Recreation and Park Association, 1967), p. 44.
6. *Ibid.,* p. 152.
7. *Ibid.,* p. 45.
8. *Ibid.,* pp. 104–130.

Selected Readings

Finlayson, Judith, ed., *Guide to County Organization and Management.* Washington, D.C.: National Association of Counties, 1968.

Hjelte, George, and Jay S. Shivers, *Public Administration of Recreational Services,* pp. 132–160. Philadelphia: Lea and Febiger, 1972.

Levin, Melvin R., *Community and Regional Planning: Issues in Public Policy.* New York: Frederick A. Praeger, Inc., 1969.

McDonald, Austin F., *American State Government and Administration,* pp. 237–271. New York: Thomas Y. Crowell Company, 1961. *Government of counties, New England towns, townships, villages, and special districts.*

Rodney, Lynn S., *Administration of Public Recreation,* pp. 171–190. New York: The Ronald Press Company, 1964.

Sundquist, James L., and David W. Davis, *Making Federalism Work,* pp. 130–166. Washington, D.C.: The Brookings Institute, 1969.

Torrence, Susan Walker, *Grass Roots Government The County in American Politics.* Washington–New York: Robert B. Luce, Inc., 1974.

CHAPTER 9

Regional Recreation and Park Services

For nearly 200 years, the pattern of city and county government has served the nation well. The services provided by each, the conditions, needs and life styles of the people, interests, means of making a living, resources and products were so different, one tended to complement the other. The towns and cities depended on trade, food, and raw materials from the rural areas. The rural areas depended on the manufactured products, human services, and resources of the cities. For a century and a half, transportation and communications were limited largely by the distance a horse or a bicycle would travel and return in a day, about 10 miles. Walking was the main mode of transportation and, therefore, people lived near the places where they worked. Often, industries provided houses, a store, and recreation space for their employees. Changes were slow to come.

By 1920, the automobile had increased the span of communication to 40 or 50 miles. Cities and industries began to grow and spread more rapidly, often extending into adjoining jurisdictions. Since 1925, highways, telephones, and economical transportation further increased the span of communication and spread of population. In order to serve new needs within legal authority and existing political structures, new services were added in different ways and with varying boundary lines. Local government often established autonomous authorities, boards, commissions, and special districts with single purpose jurisdictions, such as public housing, sanitation, health, libraries, planning, recreation and parks, expressways, conservation, environment, antipollution, and many others. When these were added to the conventional layers of government, complications, confusion, divided authority, duplication, inefficiency, and conflicts resulted.

Currently, most counties have open space to which residents and industry may continue to expand; most cities do not. Cities are overflowing with people and problems. The more affluent families and many needed civic leaders are migrating to the suburbs. Citizens, planners, and local, state, and federal authorities have been seeking solutions to the massive problems of the metropolitan areas. They realize the multi-jurisdictional conflicts have become too great and too complicated for local governments to handle. The solutions, not simple, tend towards consolidation and metropolitan and regional planning. Some urban governments continue to maintain clear-cut responsibilities and perform their functions well.

Consolidation

Most states provide for the consolidation (merger) of two or more services or jurisdictions, or annexation by majority vote of the electorate of each jurisdiction involved. In other states, boundary lines may be changed by court decision. In instances where the economics and interests of two or more jurisdictions are closely interrelated, and the complexities of the jurisdictional units have not yet become too complicated, counties and core cities have voted successfully to consolidate or merge their governments. Two cities may merge and counties and/or cities may merge, usually taking the name of the unit with the larger population. In these instances, the respective departments and services of each jurisdiction are consolidated into a single department.

Sometimes populated areas of counties incorporate as a city, or two local units of government consolidate to avoid being annexed by a city. The lower tax rate in counties, plus the problems of the city, are often the reasons county residents and industries give for opposing annexation and consolidation with cities. It is nearly impossible to get an electorate to vote for annexation, consolidation of areas, or anything that will increase their taxes, especially when the farmers say they do not get any advantages from the city services. Consolidation arranged by local effort is a good solution and is successful in the less complicated situations, but new solutions must be found for the many more complicated and deeply involved multi-jurisdictional local government services. This may be accomplished either by extending the form of government to metropolitan or regional or by enlarging the single purpose jurisdiction to district or regional level. In any event, effective planning must be on a regional basis.

THE CONCEPT OF REGIONAL GOVERNMENT

The concept of regional government is based on serving common interests and handling common problems of the citizenry, regardless of man-made political boundaries. Regional government is made up, therefore, of two or more local governmental jurisdictions for the purpose of coordinating all functions under a single administrative organization. It may add or subtract units as needs change. Very often, a region consists of a core city, or a major urban center, and several towns or counties which have common needs, interests and interrelationships, such as transportation, economics, resources, industry, and employment. The units which make up the region share the costs and advantages of the whole region. The theory is that the whole is greater than any of its parts and each part makes a vital contribution to the welfare of every other part. Sometimes, regional governments are established to provide services that cannot be provided in any other way.

Recreation and parks may be administered at the regional level in two ways. First, they may be administered as a function of a metropolitan or regional government. Second, they may be administered as a regional park and/or recreation authority.

The Metropolitan Region

The rapid expansion of urban populations without the preservation of adequate space and new problems of the congested urban areas make it reasonably clear that most single urban governments cannot meet the park and recreational needs of metropolitan areas. Therefore, metropolitan districts and regions have been formed. The first metropolitan park district was established in Boston in 1892.[1] This was used as the pattern for other metropolitan districts and served as the forerunner of more recent metropolitan regions. The metropolitan region is primarily a core city, or major urban center, and the interrelated urban communities around it. The central city and satellite communities complement each other and make up a useful, more or less self-reliant, whole. Fortunately, in their earlier stages of growth, the various units of member communities were developed in such a manner that the balance of services, unity of interest, and important interrelationships could continue in spite of rapid growth and expansion. This meant that opportunities for those services important to man and his security—utilities, sanitation, transportation, housing, employment, education, protection, parks and recreation, and others—were reasonably provided for all component units.

In a few instances, the jurisdictions within a metropolitan region have formed a metropolitan regional government. The governing board is made up of equal representation from each member unit. Members of governing boards may be elected or appointed, depending on the authority given the respective jurisdictions by the state. In most instances, however, the interests, jurisdictions, politics, authorities, and services are so fragmented, separated, and entangled with independent, unequal, unrelated satellite authorities that no practical solutions have been found to meld them into a unified metropolitan operation. The organization of successful metropolitan districts to provide essential services, such as utilities and parks and recreation, have been encouraging and may be the forerunners for the formation of additional regional governments in the future.

THE REGIONAL PLANNING UNIT

A *region* is thought of as an indefinite portion of a territory, usually of considerable extent.[2] There is no single definition that clearly identifies, without question, just what a planning region is. In government, a region usually refers to a large part of the whole which has common or interrelating factors. In the nation, it might be based on the major use of the land (farming, industry). In the state, it might be topography (mountains, plains, or tidewater). In a locality, it might be geographic (northern, western). Locally, a region is an indefinite portion of the state but it may be the whole of some city or county jurisdiction plus portions of others, or it may be composed of portions of several jurisdictions. A single county, or portion thereof, would not be considered a region. It could be considered a district. The economics, resources, and problems of a cluster of local governments freely cross political lines and are very much interrelated. The effective regional planning unit, therefore, includes strong representation and depends upon complete cooperation from each political jurisdiction involved.

Regional Planning

Until recent years, planners and planning commissions were primarily associated with urban governments. More recently county governments have added planners. Scientific planning arrived almost too late to be really effective because, prior to 1940, most urban areas just grew and developed without very much planning. New master plans, industrial developments, and parks and recreation plans have been implemented on inadequate space. The planners and existing conventional governments do not have the powers and resources to handle effectively the mixture of jurisdictions and human problems with which they are now faced. Since 1960, especially, an increasing number of regional planning commissions have been established to make surveys, studies and master plans and to coordinate planning for the several counties, cities, and political jurisdictions of a region. A regional planning commission may consist of an equal number of representatives, generally appointed by the respective legislative bodies, often including a professional planner, a key citizen, and a member of the legislative body. They may receive funds from federal and state grants and pro-rata payments from member jurisdictions. Members serve without pay.

The regional commissions give advice on matters of concern to member jurisdictions, encourage cooperation and joint planning, and sometimes clear federal grant-in-aid projects, environmental impact studies, and other regional matters. They are expected to be involved in land use, economics, resources, designs, subdivisions, transportation, conservation, and other planning functions for the region. Generally, their function is advisory.

STANDARD METROPOLITAN STATISTICAL AREAS

The public recreation executive is confronted with the term "standard metropolitan statistical area" (SMSA) in dealing with federal and state grants and programs that affect or involve areawide problems and influences. In the past decade, agencies of the federal government, planners, and research personnel have used the SMSA's of the Bureau of the Census to identify and define metropolitan areas.

The Bureau of the Census recognizes 243 standard metropolitan statistical areas in the United States and four in Puerto Rico, making a total of 247 in the 1970 census. Each time the census is taken, the SMSA's are updated and new SMSA units and boundaries are defined.

The Bureau of the Census defines SMSA as follows: Except in the New England states, *a standard metropolitan statistical area* is a county or group of contiguous counties which contains at least one city of 50,000 inhabitants or more, or "twin cities" with a combined population of at least 50,000. In addition to the county or counties containing such a city or cities, contiguous counties are included in an SMSA if, according to certain criteria, they are socially and economically integrated with the central city. In the New England states, SMSA's consist of towns and cities instead of counties.[3]

Since 1965 some form of voluntary organization of municipalities and counties has been established in the different states to attack area-wide problems. Almost every one of the nation's 247 SMSA's had a regional council of some type (Councils of Governments Economic Development Districts, Regional Planning Commissions).[4] Although they began as voluntary or advisory units, some have won (or aspired to win) governmental powers. For instance the Minneapolis-St. Paul area's Metropolitan Council now has taxing authority and power to plan and carry out anti-pollution measures, solid waste disposal, noise abatement, and zoning in a seven county area.[5]

In addition to the tendency to acquire governmental powers, there are some that administer federal and state program funds. The standard metropolitan statistical area, therefore, is important for planning and program purposes. It may be a principal concern in developing a metropolitan or regional authority.

REGIONAL PARKS AND FACILITIES

Very few cities have space for regional parks within their boundaries. Some counties no longer have suitable open space for regional parks. In order for many metropolitan communities to experience natural areas, lakes, water sports, golf, camping, and winter sports it is necessary to go beyond the city and county boundaries. Authorities and conventional thinkers give considerable resistance to approval of the use of tax funds for the acquisition, preservation, or development of large parcels of land beyond the city boundaries, unless they are related to the water supply or other essential city need. City authorities often express the objection that such a city-owned facility would be of greater service to the jurisdiction in which it is located and why should the city pay for it. Consequently, cities and urban counties continue to adjust their local recreation and park program to small, inadequate spaces.

In the previous chapter, we emphasized the importance of county park systems to provide the larger and regional type parks under a single county jurisdiction. The counties, however, that do not have large open spaces are in about the same position as are the cities. Others may not have a recreation or park service or may not have sufficient resources to support one. They may, therefore, look to a regional park and/or recreation authority to serve their needs.

The Regional Park Authority

The need for regional parks to serve large urban populations is growing in importance. If for no other reason, it is important for people to have a place where they can escape the crowding and constant pressures of urban living. The regional park also provides counties of limited resources with a means of having recreation services.

A regional park, as the name implies, is one that serves people of a large area, perhaps a 50-mile radius, in addition to serving the local communities. The desirable size is more than 500 acres. Sometimes, however, because of lack of available open space, city and county recreation and park departments may be able to provide only a 200-acre space which they must make do. In a cluster of urban communities, it is not quite realistic to expect a single jurisdiction to provide regional park services for the entire metropolitan area. Several governmental units may combine resources and form a regional park authority. They are authorized by state governments and have all the powers of counties and cities. The members of governing boards may be elected or appointed depending on the respective state enabling legislation. Their responsibilities are usually limited to the single functions of recreation and park services. In several instances, regional park authorities have been established near metropolitan centers. For instance, in Virginia near Washington, D.C., six participating counties and cities formed the "Northern Virginia Regional Park Authority." A statement from their 1973 report gives the purpose and background information.

> The Northern Virginia Regional Park Authority was created in 1959 under State legislation for the purpose of planning, acquiring, developing, and operating a system of regional parks in Northern Virginia.
>
> The NVRPA has provided a cooperative arrangement whereby its six-member governments—the counties of Arlington, Fairfax, and Loudoun and the cities of Alexandria, Fairfax, and Falls Church—have been able to preserve more than 6000 acres of natural and historic areas for public enjoyment and outdoor recreation. These parklands represent a public investment of twenty-one million dollars.
>
> The NVRPA serves a population of almost a million people. It operates two comprehensive recreation areas, two marinas, a wildlife sanctuary and the beginnings of a historic park.[6]

NVRPA is administered by a board of twelve members (2 appointed from each of the six participating member jurisdictions) and a staff of 54 full-time employees. Funding is through annual appropriations from member governments based on population and supplemented by federal and state matching grants.

The regional park authority may provide a comprehensive recreation and park program for the region or it may provide for special interests, such as park areas and facilities. Some obstacles may be the failure of a key jurisdiction to participate, conflicting political and independent administrative authorities, unwillingness of a jurisdiction to support a regional jurisdiction as well as its existing recreation and parks programs or, on the other hand, expecting the regional authority to provide total services for a jurisdiction.

METROPOLITAN AREAS AND FACILITIES

Metropolitan areas and facilities usually supplement those provided by local jurisdictions in order to make possible a comprehensive park and recreation program for the entire region. They usually include the larger areas and facilities the separate jurisdictions have not been able to provide. A regional-type administrative organization provides an opportunity to use vacant space in outlying areas for recreational uses which it is not possible to provide in the fully developed core areas. It may be that some of the larger spaces will have to be acquired and developed beyond the metropolitan boundaries.

The factors to be considered in planning metropolitan properties are the types and locations of areas and facilities which are provided by the separate political jurisdictions; the sizes and locations of available spaces that can be acquired and developed; the unmet recreational needs of the citizenry; useful natural and historical features that may be included; the amount of funds available for development, operation and maintenance; and the maintenance of a desirable balance of services. The natural features may include lakes, streams, safe and interesting water areas, large wooded areas, wilderness and undisturbed natural areas, and sites of scenic, scientific, and historical interest.

The areas and facilities of a metropolitan community are generally regional in nature and include facilities for camps, camp grounds, picnicking and outings, bike trails, hiking and bridle trails, boat ramps, marinas, boating and water skiing facilities, beaches, swimming areas, winter sports, sports centers, golf courses, rifle and archery ranges, nature study and nature centers, outdoor theatres, botanical and zoological gardens, arboretums, museums, observatories, planetariums, controlled model airplane areas, skooter and mini-bike areas.

The sports centers may include facilities for several or all of the following: baseball, softball, football, soccer, rugby football, and a battery of four or more tennis courts. The sports centers should be at least every five miles in built-up residential sections. A regional sports center would require 40 to 50 acres.

Indoor facilities may include a tournament center with seating for basketball, tennis, volleyball, handball, and swimming together with the necessary appurtenant facilities.

Certain recreation and park facilities in conjunction with highways and thoroughfares add considerably to the metropolitan recreation services. These include parkways, roadside parks, turnouts, look-outs, picnic sites, hiking and bicycle trails, recreation areas, and roadside rest stops.

RELATIONSHIPS WITH LOCAL UNITS

Local recreation authorities, programs, and facilities are centered around local needs and interests. They generally include playlots, playgrounds, centers, playing fields, gymnasiums, special facilities, and neighborhood and large parks which serve neighborhoods primarily within walking or bicycling distance—a radius of ½ mile to 2 miles, usually. The centers, playing fields, gymnasiums, large parks, and special facilities may attract users who travel by automobile or public transportation. Parking facilities are, therefore, needed in conjunction with them.

The regional areas, facilities, and services complement and supplement the locally sponsored ones and are generally larger and more spacious to provide for activities which require large areas or special topography. The facilities and services are adapted to regional needs and interests rather than those of the neighborhood although regional facilities are used extensively by families of the neighborhood. There should be cooperation and coordinated planning to minimize duplication and overlapping and to make maximum use of the total resources.

Questions for Discussion

1. Why did regional services develop? What is the purpose of regional services? Do you think they are necessary? Explain.
2. Does consolidation of local governmental units solve the urban problems of recreation? In your opinion what is the best way to administer a recreation and park service for a large urban community with several governmental jurisdictions? Explain.
3. How are local government units involved in regional planning?
4. What is the concept of regional government and how does it affect recreation and parks?
5. What is a regional park? What are its purposes?
6. Should a local governmental unit operate a regional park or recreation facility? Explain your reasons.
7. What is the purpose of a regional park authority and how is it organized?
8. What is the difference between a district and a region?
9. What are the appropriate relationships among city, county, district, and regional recreation authorities?

Short Problems

1. In a metropolitan area of your choice describe all of the public jurisdictions that provide recreation and park services and how each relates to the others. Recommend a model plan to administer a comprehensive recreation and park service for all of the metropolitan area.
2. List the advantages and disadvantages of establishing a regional park authority.

References

1. Charles E. Doell and Gerald P. Fitzgerald, *A Brief History of Parks and Recreation in the United States* (Chicago: The Athletic Institute, 1954), p. 33.

2. *The Reader's Digest Great Encyclopedia Dictionary,* 3rd ed. (1969).

3. Bureau of the Census, *United States Summary* (Washington, D.C.: Government Printing Office, 1970), pp. xii–xiii.

4. Melvin B. Mogulof, *Governing Metropolitan Areas* (Washington, D.C.: The Urban Institute, 1971), p. 1.

5. *Ibid.*, p. 2.

6. Northern Virginia Regional Park Authority 1973 Report, p. 1.

Selected Readings

Gille, F. B., *Basic Thinking in Regional Planning.* New York: Humanities Press, 1967.

Hufschmidt, Maynard M., *Regional Planning: Challenge and Prospects.* New York: Frederick A. Praeger, Inc., 1969.

Levin, Melvin R., *Community and Regional Planning: Issues in Public Policy.* New York: Frederick A. Praeger, Inc., 1969.

Rodney, Lynn S., *Administration of Public Recreation,* pp. 327–337. New York: The Ronald Press Company, 1964.

Sundquist, James L., and David W. Davis, *Making Federalism Work,* pp. 167–214. Washington, D.C.: The Brookings Institution, 1969.

Torrence, Susan Walker, *Grass Roots Government The County in American Politics,* pp. 139–167. Washington–New York: Robert B. Luce, Inc., 1974.

PART II

Management Responsibilities

CHAPTER 10

Staffing the Public Recreation Agency

Recreation is dependent on quality personnel for a quality program. The success of the agency depends more upon its program personnel than upon any other factor. The agency board, city council, or county board of supervisors enact legislation, determine policy and set the political climate. The executive working in harmony with the policy makers brings about necessary legislation, translates the legislative and administrative decisions into specific programs, mobilizes resources both physical (including budget) and human, and establishes practices and procedures. The staff is the means of bringing about action (achievement). Personnel practices and policies determine to a large extent the quality of the staff the agency can attract and retain. The quality of the staff (including the executive) determines the quality of services the agency can provide. The staff is by far the largest item in the agency budget. Three fourths of the operating expenditures of a recreation agency is for staff services. Therefore, the competence of staff as well as the efficiency in selection, management, and development of staff are of major interests to all concerned, especially the recreation executive. The staff not only contributes to the effectiveness and quality of the agency program but also has the greatest impact on the budget and the income, if income is involved. But the efficiency of the staff and organization is also affected to a great extent by the effectiveness of management and management practices and policies. Hence, the two must work in harmony and really serve to support each others' efforts. Techniques used to attract, retain, motivate, develop and challenge personnel plus providing conditions that produce a pleasant, stimulating environment are basic concerns of personnel administration. Personnel is involved in all agency matters, therefore, staff at every level is involved in how well the agency provides its services and achieves its objectives.

FUNCTIONS OF PERSONNEL MANAGEMENT

Like most areas in the general field of recreation *personnel management,* functions, organizations and responsibilities vary with local conditions. These functions may be carried out by a separate government agency (personnel department) that serves all units of the government jurisdictions including recreation; a unit (personnel division) of a large recreation agency; one or more individuals on the administrative staff in the smaller agency (personnel director), or a part-time assignment of an administrative staff member or included as one of the responsibilities of the executive in a small operation. The procedures in each instance may vary and the functions listed in greater or less detail, but the principles of administration and major functions are the same and include:

1. Job analysis, classification and specification.
2. Recruiting, advertising, reviewing, screening.
3. Testing, investigating, rating.
4. Selecting, interviewing, inducting, placing, orienting, probation.
5. Promoting.
6. Providing compensation plan, salary, increments.
7. Providing good work rules, personnel practices, conditions of work, health, welfare, safety.
8. In-service training, education and development.
9. Disciplinary action, transfers, suspension, demotion.
10. Evaluation, interviews, appraisals, motivations.
11. Separation, transfer, resignation, dismissal, retirement, death.
12. Records, research, reports.

Job Analysis, Classification and Specification

Analysis involves in-depth review of the elements of the position, kind and variety of duties, degree of difficulty and complexity, amount of skill needed, amount of supervision required, experience and training required, unique features of the job, and responsibilities.

Classification is concerned only with what is required by the job. It serves as the basis for intelligent staffing, personnel selection, salary evaluation, training, planning, budgeting, and orderly personnel transactions. The classification plan of an agency is a basic management tool and must be kept up to date. Needs of agencies change and duties of positions change, particularly in recreation agencies, therefore, positions and classifications should be reviewed periodically and adjusted, if needed. Classification should accurately reflect the duties performed in each position. Sometimes agency program needs require a change and often the conscientious worker will see things that need to be done or find a better way to do them, take on new responsibilities and provide a better service. His job then needs to be reevaluated and reclassified if the new importance justifies it. This may mean allocating the position to a higher class. The *classification plan* is a job inventory which groups under the same title all positions that are alike in responsibility and qualifications required.

Specification involves the requirements, duties and responsibilities of a title for the purposes of classification, establishing appropriate compensation, and recruiting. It is often called job description or specification. It may become the employee's contract after employment. Job specifications and classification plans lay the foundation for a sound personnel system and is the beginning of the recruitment process.

Job needs in recreation in the same general class (recreation professional) are so varied (sports, drama, music, arts and crafts, nature) that personnel experts have not yet found a completely satisfactory way to classify and recruit recreation leadership generalists and specialists without preparing specific job specifications for each program category. This becomes rather voluminous. Personnel specialists like to keep the number of position classification to a minimum, but it is not practical to recruit "generalists" and "specialists" from the same general specifications. For example, the leadership position of "recreation instructor" may serve all categories of recreation programs from music to sports, but it is not practical to get a recreation instructor who is interested and skilled in sports to be the recreation instructor for a choral group even though they both are called recreation instructors and work with groups. The best solution is to provide appropriate job specifications for specialists in each program category and also for generalist positions.

Recruiting, Advertising, Reviewing, Screening

Recruiting is the securing of competent and qualified personnel. Recreation staff, whether recruited by a central personnel department or staff of the recreation agency, should be selected on the basis of merit. Too often this is not the case. In some places the pay may be low, trained and experienced recreationists are not available, or the locality wants to employ local people. Even so, there should be job specifications and selection on the basis of merit. Most of the recreation budget goes for personnel, the recreation product depends on personnel and the community should get the best possible for its money. If recruitment is performed by a central agency, advice and assistance should be obtained from experienced personnel in the recreation field. Recruitment must be performed objectively and impartially. The recreation expert is directly responsible for determining the minimum qualifications, duties, selection, development, and management. The personnel expert provides the services for the program units and has no authority for recreation staff and program management except to see that the laws and general rules pertaining to personnel are known and enforced.

Recruiting involves making contacts and announcements through the news media, state recreation services, professional publications, professional organizations, colleges and universities, convention job marts, direct correspondence and other available sources of qualified applicants; receiving and reviewing information, references, education, work experiences, legal aspects and other requirements in the job specifications to see if they conform; eliminating those applications that do not meet qualifications; and preparing a list of qualified applicants for testing. Sometimes there will be a hundred applications for a key position. If only one person, such as director or division head; is needed, the lesser qualified applications are screened down to perhaps fifteen names or less for final testing.

When a number of professionals and specialists are needed, sometimes a recruiting team visits training institutions for direct contacts and personal interviews with prospective candidates.

Recruitment for full-time, part-time, and seasonal workers follows the same procedures. This has the advantage that seasonal and part-time personnel are excellent candidates for permanent full-time positions. Many seasonal and part-time workers are preparing for careers in recreation and are excellent prospects for later recruitment. Even though the personnel staff is primarily responsible for recruiting, it is in the best interest of the recreation staff to assist in recruiting in every way possible.

Recruitment announcements are usually carefully worded, brief announcements including job title, a brief description of duties and qualifications, location, salary, closing date for applications, name and mailing address of person to contact. Sometimes an agency provides standard application forms that can be filled out and returned, in which case the announcement would invite interested applicants to request application forms. This has three distinct advantages. It provides a guide to the applicant, provides for uniformity of information and tends to discourage the "nuisance" application which is a copy of an autobiography prepared for mass distribution with no direct relationship to the position advertised.

Employment Opportunity (*Name of City*)
Department of Recreation and Parks Pop. 250,000

SUPERINTENDENT OF RECREATION

Closing date, June 16-__

SALARY RANGE:	$15,158-19,344. Six steps.
SELECTION:	Appointments are made by Director of Recreation and Parks from eligibility roster of six top names. Appointments are probationary for six months.
FUNCTION:	Under administrative direction has charge of and is responsible for planning, organizing, promoting, developing and coordinating programs and functions of the bureau of recreation which has staff of 155 full-time and 200 seasonal leadership personnel. Responsible for operations of playgrounds, play fields, community centers, school centers, swimming pools, gymnasiums and all facilities.
MINIMUM QUALIFICATIONS:	Thorough knowledge of the philosophy and objectives of public recreation: use and benefits of all phases. Extensive knowledge of functions and principles of management. B.A. degree with major in recreation, M.A. degree in administration desirable. Seven years of successful experience in field of recreation, four years of which must be in supervisory or administrative capacity. Valid operator's license.
MERIT EXAMINATION:	Will be competitive and consist of four parts, namely (1) evaluation of training and experience, (2) assembled written test, (3) oral board and interview, and (4) medical examination.
METHOD OF APPLICATION:	Application forms are available and must be mailed not later than the closing date shown above. Only candidates meeting minimum qualifications will be eligible for examination. Make application to Personnel Department; (*Address*)

(*Agency*) IS AN EQUAL OPPORTUNITY EMPLOYER

FIGURE 10-1. Example of Recruitment Announcement.

Testing, Investigating, Examining, Rating

Testing is a procedure used to select the best qualified applicant for the position to be filled. It involves making contact with individuals on the qualified list of applicants recruited; arranging appointments for oral, written, practical or oral board examination or other tests; confirming educational background and any pertinent items that are unclear; rating applications in order of priority based on total grades received in the testing plus any special points the system allows for such items as veteran's priority, exceptional and unique training in addition to requirements of the specifications; sending to the using agency for selection a list of the six top rated applicants (or the number specified in the local system), if there are that many who qualify.

Sometimes in examining for key jobs, particularly where the position involves major contacts with the public, oral boards consisting of perhaps five citizens knowledgeable in major elements of the job are set up to examine and rate the applicants. It is helpful if the person from the using agency who is doing the hiring sits in on the oral board hearings. This may provide essential information, save time and duplication of questions later.

Examinations are designed to obtain pertinent information about the knowledge, skills, capabilities, expertise, and future potential of the applicants and to rate them in order of merit. Tests of intelligence, achievement, general aptitude, health and physical conditions may be included. There is also some interest in adding psychological tests to discover personality and emotional tendencies that might adversely affect the job. The tests provide the using agency with uniform and comparable information on which to rate the qualifications and competence of the candidates in relation to the requirements of the duties to be performed. It tends to reduce pressure to employ unqualified, political patrons, and others lacking in competence.

There is one more important phase of testing and that is the probation period which comes after selection in sequence in steps of employment procedures.

The testing and examination procedure is very much a team effort. The personnel expert handles the mechanics and paper work dealing with applications, such as planning and scheduling, documentation of information, checking, screening, and evaluating information, conducting written or oral examinations, correspondence, and rating applications. The recreation expert provides professional and technical information and is involved mainly in phases dealing with the applicants—oral board examinations, performance tests, personal interviews, character examination, and arranging medical examination. The two aspects, of course, cannot be separated but this does show how the team process works and indicates how skills of experts are used in management to take advantage of specialized knowledge in bringing about a better product for the using agency. A problem can develop, if the two units fail to cooperate to the extent necessary.

In the testing process the "job description" for the specific position is the basis for the testing program. Each requirement needs to be examined in terms of the applicant's ability to perform the duties best and meet or surpass the minimum qualifications.

Job descriptions include minimum *education* and *experience* requirements. Most testing procedures rate them in determining scores for the respective candidates from the information available to them. This emphasizes the importance of complete and accurate information on the application form and the necessity for checking it. This is one reason personnel agencies have provided their own application forms. Education and experience in recreation are so variable that it is difficult to make a true evaluation of its values unless the reviewer is familiar with the specific situations. This is where the recreation expert is of valuable assistance.

The *oral examination* in testing procedures is used to evaluate the personal qualities, appearance, attitude, philosophy, personality, ability to express himself orally, individual characteristics all of which are important in the field of recreation. However, final judgement on these items will be made by the agency in the selection process. Oral examination here is for grading purposes. Sometimes an oral interview is necessary to clarify information or omissions. To be most useful the information must be recorded and added to the applicant's record; therefore, in effect it becomes a written examination using the interviewer as a recorder. As a testing procedure, the oral examination is of limited value except in evaluating personal qualities of higher level personnel such as administrators. Then the oral board is sometimes used.

The *written examination* is a most important phase of the examining process for determining a candidate's knowledge pertaining to skills and professional competence. It may include an aptitude test as well as general, technical and professional questions related to the specific job. The recreation expert assists in providing suggestions for applicable questions or emphasis he wishes to make. The tests generally are administered to all applicants assembled at one time at an appropriate location. This is known as an *assembled examination.* Sometimes tests are given continuously over a short period of time in special situations and sometimes tests are given in other cities by the civil service commission or personnel department of that city as a convenience to applicants. Individual tests known as *unassembled examinations* are often used for higher level positions. An increasing number of jurisdictions pay travel costs of out-of-town applicants for high-level, hard-to-fill positions. In such instances testing and job interviews are scheduled on the same day.

The *practical test* requires the applicant to demonstrate his skills or competence by performing a job assignment relating to the position he seeks: a lifeguard may demonstrate life-saving methods; craftsmen may make an object; recreation instructors may organize and conduct group activities; a recreation superintendent may prepare an organization plan for the department and show how he would staff it. This is successful in testing for professional, technical and administrative positions.

A satisfactory *physical examination* at agency expense is required by most agencies before a new employee can begin work. The purpose is to make sure the individual is physically capable of performing the task of the position and reveal any health or physical defects that might impair the efficiency of the employee on the job. It is also protection against communicable diseases, sick leave, and future claims against work-connected disability ailments such as back trouble, hernia, heart and respiratory conditions that reduce or stop his production capacity, and/or create continuing medical costs for the agency. Often these examinations reveal conditions that the candidate does not know he has but which can be corrected satisfactorily.

Investigation of character, sometimes a sensitive area of testing, is used in varying degrees by most public agencies. This is especially important in positions of responsibility, policy making, handling funds, and influencing people such as in recreation. Some information relating to convictions, drugs, alcohol, legal matters, and patriotism may be received through questions in the oral interviews. They need to be checked out with police and F.B.I. records in appropriate situations, references, former employers, and acquaintances. Much information and satisfactory explanations can be obtained in the personal interview. The use of a confidential questionnaire, although not perfect, is one of the more successful methods of obtaining useful information about an individual. Personal contacts, in person or by telephone, have the advantage of two-way live communication and are most satisfactory.

The Assessment Center

Courts recently have raised doubt concerning "fair and equal" treatment aspects of the conventional written tests indicating that minority and underprivileged groups or lesser educated individuals could not receive equal treatment based on written tests. An assessment center approach has been developed which is an assessment of behavior and qualities of applicants by trained assessors. It is a formal procedure designed to identify individuals who have potential as supervisors or managers; to identify the participants' strongest abilities and specific areas for improvement; to establish development programs to prepare them for increased responsibility; and to provide input information for human resource planning and development.[1] While the procedure has been used, to some extent, at the federal level, it is a relatively new approach at local levels such as Richmond, Virginia. It is particularly effective for evaluating employees for promotions and testing and rating of applicants for positions such as administrators, supervisors, professionals and others where responsibilities affect or involve people in a variety of conditions, differing cultures and life styles, intangible or immeasurable factors, personal behavior, judgments, opinions, likes and dislikes. These are related to different kinds of people responses. The process is looked upon more favorably by the courts than written tests by the applicant.

The Assessment Procedure

The assessment center approach utilizes simulated situations based on extensive job analysis of the duties and responsibilities of the respective position. Critical behavioral dimensions are identified as prerequisites to successful performance on the job for which the applicants are being tested. All candidates are given the same practical problems and exercises. Exercises and problem-solving matters may be presented to the group (usually not exceeding 10 candidates) which may then separate as individuals to work out solutions and later come together for the group to determine together a single best solution. A panel of five to seven observers, professionally trained, observe each individual and record an applicant's behavior and performance in the exercises to appraise the degree to which he possesses the behavioral characteristics and skills necessary for successful performances in the position. Observers may be professional consultants or especially trained agency personnel who are in higher positions than the position concerned.

Observers may consider such items as personal approach, initiative, techniques, leadership, priorities, reactions in group situation, personal behavior, emotions, skills, setting of objectives, completeness, judgments and other qualities and characteristics that are related to the job.

The testing sessions last from one to three days for candidates and two to five days for the assessor team. The assessors devote the last periods to discussion and evaluation of the behavior observed of each candidate as they relate to each other and performance on the job. They rank the individuals and prepare a comprehensive report which includes individual strengths, weaknesses, and areas for improvement.

There are a number of advantages to this procedure. Several qualified persons make the evaluation, usually from different points of view, not just one. The assessors are trained in objective evaluation techniques. The evaluation is based on the candidate's abilities to successfully demonstrate behavior important to supervisory and managerial functions. Finally, the evaluation is based on the candidate both as an individual and as a member of a group in several situations.

The disadvantages are that it is very time consuming and relatively expensive, especially when there is a large number of candidates which may be as many as 200. In such instances more than one panel of observers may be used which, then, raises the question as to whether different panels would provide the same and equal treatment.

The results of the assessment are used as an intregal part of the total selection of an appointee for the position.

The main responsibility of the recreation executive in this process is to prepare a personnel requisition form for the position and clearly identify the major prerequisites, duties and responsibilities for the position, and then cooperate with consultants in making contact with department staff, in making job analysis and perhaps use of staff in the assessing process.

At the completion of all testing the personnel expert, who has ranked the qualified applicants on the basis of test scores, prepares an eligible list and certifies the top names (usually three to six) to the using agency for consideration.

Selection, Interviews, Induction, Placement, Orientation, Probation

Selection, which is done by the hiring agency, is the most crucial step in the recruiting process. Employees should be selected entirely on merit. Literally, at this point it is the privilege of the hiring agency to select the most capable individual from a list of the available most competent applicants in the country, or maybe in the world. Anyway, it is an important action; for the applicant because he may have given up a secure job, home and community ties to move to a new community, to a job that is not secure, at least through the probation period; for the agency because it has to make the right decision from a sampling of information compiled during the short testing time and to make a character and personality judgment from relatively few bits of select information the applicant and his friends or acquaintances have provided for the occasion. It involves separate personal interviews with all candidates; follow up of references, education requirements, and work experiences; evaluation of physical and character examination; and finally selection of the right candidate and promptly advising unsuccessful candidates of the decision.

Appointments are made at the first step of the pay range for the class, except for unusual qualifications. Then follows induction, placement, orientation, and probation. Names usually remain on the eligible roster for 12 months and additional appointments can be made from names on list without recruitment during this period to fill vacancies that may occur. The eligibility list is usually terminated at the end of 12 months. After that, the recruitment process is begun again, as needed upon receipt of a request from the using agency and a new eligible roster is established.

Sometimes persons are laid off because of seasonal employment, reorganization, or curtailment of budget. These names may be placed on a preferred eligible roster which means they will be first to be certified for employment when vacancies occur. The preferred roster is not dissolved. In some cities personnel rules recognize seniority which provides that a person with more years of service, in event he is laid off, may "bump" (claim the job) a person in the same class with less years of service.

It is well, as a part of early orientation, to tour facilities or show slides and discuss agency operations, perhaps the first day if appointee is from out-of-town. It is well, too, to have brief handouts concerning benefits and information about the agency that he can read at leisure and share with his family. It is well, also, to have a check list of items that make up a good employee orientation program and check each item off as it is completed and then filed permanently in the employee's personnel folder. It is too easy to forget, neglect or omit items without a written list. Too often an appointee is not informed until he runs into trouble, just what is expected of him in his job. It is the supervisor's responsibility to see that this does not occur.

The probation period is the final and most important step of an employees testing period. The appointment is not considered final until the employee has demonstrated his ability to perform his work satisfactorily during the probation period. It is usually the first six months of employment for new employees and three months for promoted employees. In unusual circumstances rules may provide that the using agency may extend the probation period an additional six months or three months respectively. In such instances the appointing authority must discuss with the employee the reasons for extending his probationary period and confirm same in writing with copies to others concerned (including the personnel experts) before the end of the original probation period. At the end of a probationary period the employee becomes a permanent employee and has all the rights and privileges of permanent personnel including right of appeal. During the probation (or testing period) the employee has few privileges except sick leave earned.

During the probation period the appointing officer is expected to evaluate the fitness of the appointee for the job he holds and to judge strong points and weaknesses in a realistic way. Opportunities may be provided to test capabilities in different ways. The agency should make special effort to learn all about the individual and observe his responses and future potential. The work habits and working relations established then have a good chance of continuing. This is also a trying time for the appointee. This is the orientation period. He needs to know what is expected of him on the job; what resources are available to him; where he can go for assistance and how; what the goals, policies, rules, practices, and procedures of the agency are, and his relationships to his unit and the relationship of his unit to other units with which he has contact; what his rights and privileges, incentives, motivations and opportunities are; what are some of the improvements relating to his unit or nearby that need to be accomplished. It may just be that one or two of them will be his challenge. The supervisor must be helpful and objective. If the worker does not succeed, it must be entirely his doings and not lack of assistance from the supervisor.

Promotion

Promotion is the advancement of an employee to a higher position within the agency usually higher paying, more difficult in nature and different title. Filling vacancies by promotion is a preferred policy of most agencies. It rewards the employee for exceptional service, helps employee morale and incentive, greatly reduces period of orientation, minimizes the uncertainties involved in assimilating into the system a relatively unknown person, and enables the agency to make greater use of the more experienced workers of proven competence. It tends to attract more capable individuals with good potentials into the service. Most employees look for opportunities for advancement and are willing to take subordinate positions if chances of advancement are reasonably good. A frustrating problem develops when persons of lower rank cannot meet the qualifications of higher positions.

It is necessary to have higher requirements as one goes up the organization ladder and it is necessary to have higher salaries to compensate for it. Agencies keep these promotion factors in mind in setting up organization plans and setting requirements for positions but even so at some place there has to be a point where education requirements change from minimum of a high school degree to minimum of a college degree. Experience is attainable in a reasonable time but it takes considerably longer for a worker to get a baccalaureate degree while working full time. Some agencies will share the cost of educational courses that relate to improvement on the job or lead towards a high school or college degree. There is a trend, however, towards even more emphasis on experience than in the past. Therefore, recreation agencies have developed acceptable alternatives, where possible, in preparing job specifications. This does not mean that essential qualifications are lowered or that doors are opened to lesser qualified persons. It is intended to emphasize the importance of satisfactory work experience. Every effort should be made to develop and promote competent workers with meritorious service but this cannot be the only consideration. Promotions should be on the basis of merit, therefore, all applicants must meet requirements specified, be examined and rated.

Some agencies permit closed promotional examinations for employees only when there are several persons within the organization that meet the qualifications and are interested in promotion. If this restriction is applied too often it tends to reduce the true effectiveness of the merit system to attract the most competent person possible. Agencies avoid the use of the closed promotional procedure when only one person within the agency is qualified for a position. The open recruitment process, where any qualified person can apply, should be used but employees should be urged to apply. They have experience with the agency and should not have problems qualifying. In higher level positions it is generally best to have open competition rather than "closed promotional" procedures.

Usually employees must have at least six months service in a position (complete probation period) before they can be promoted. Also, promotions and new appointments usually involve advancing one, two, or three ranges at a time as a matter of common practice but are not necessarily restricted to that. Sometimes promotions "jump" a class in unusual circumstances but if it occurs in the same unit of the organization it often creates an employee morale problem among peers and those skipped over. The feeling is usually not so strong when such a promotion is made to another organization unit.

Compensation Plan, Salary, Increments

The compensation plan consists of a salary range for each position class in the classification plan of the agency, which provides for regular increments within such range to be earned by length of service and satisfactory or better service rating. Each range is related to the salary ranges for other classes and to the relative difficulty, complexity, and responsibility of characteristic duties of positions in the class, minimum education and experience requirements, the prevailing rate paid for similar employment outside the agency and other factors that may properly be considered to have a bearing upon fairness, equity, and adequacy of the range. Based on these guidelines the personnel expert prepares a comprehensive pay plan for approval by the administrator and finally the policy board with or without amendments or modification. Usually the policy board accepts the recommendations of the technicians. After adoption by the policy board it is law and cannot be changed by anyone except by amendment adopted by the policy board. The compensation plan must be very complete and relate to every known or anticipated condition within the agency. It is the basis for the preparation of the largest expenditure of the agency budget—personnel services—and is the law in dealing with personnel practices relating to expenditures of funds for services. It relates to many personnel rules: pay, hours of work, overtime pay, differential pay of various kinds, vacation, sick leave and other leaves of absence. It establishes the work week usually conforming to the Fair Labor Standards Act. Until recently pay was commonly based on annual and monthly salaries for administrative, professional, supervisory and office personnel and annually and hourly wages for skilled, semi-skilled and labor classifications. The hourly wage earner received overtime but the salaried personnel did not. This created a problem in emergency overtime work when the hourly worker got paid time and a half for overtime and foremen, professional, office and other personnel did not. With the standard 40-hour work week and most jobs below a specific rate receiving the same privileges, the common practice is to convert all compensation into hourly pay based on the 40-hour work week. This provides for a flexible work schedule, equal treatment and means of paying full-time, part-time, and emergency work on the same pay schedule. Usually individuals who are not authorized overtime pay may be permitted compensatory time off equal to the actual time worked.

Compensation plans provide that all new appointments, including promotions, shall begin at the first step of the pay range for that class. However, there may be provisions for exceptions for unusual circumstances: (1) When reasonable recruiting efforts fail to secure eligible applicants at the beginning rate; (2) When an employee with several years of increments in present range is promoted to a higher position where the beginning rate is less than his existing pay; and (3) When an individual on the eligible roster has qualifications (more than minimum) equivalent to a higher level within the same range.

Leaves of absence in good standing vary with the practices in the respective community. Sick leave, vacation, and compensatory leave times are limited to the amount accrued and should not be given in anticipation of time not yet earned. Types of leaves may include:

1. *Vacation time* is usually earned at the rate of 1 to 1½ days per month of work status to accrue to a maximum of 24 months. Agencies

should insist on employees taking vacation each year. This is a part of compensation, therefore, employees at time of termination should be paid for earned, unused vacation time.

2. *Sick leave* is usually accumulated at the rate of 1 day per month of work status and may accrue to a maximum of 90 to 120 days. It is the intent of sick leave to provide security and full pay for those who are actually sick. It is a privilege; however, many workers consider sick leave earned leave and use it for time off with pay as if it were free time. Some agencies in hardship cases of long illness allow a maximum equivalency of ½ day per month extraordinary sick leave for total months of service. This is in addition to ordinary sick leave. A certification from a physician may be required in cases of sick leave.
3. *Injury leave* is given when an employee is totally incapacitated by an illness or injury which has occurred because of his employment and performance of duties with the agency. It may involve medical expense and full pay for periods and amounts equal to full pay not covered by Workman's Compensation or it may involve lesser amounts in other communities.
4. *Civil leave* is any absence necessary for serving on a jury, serving in court under subpoena as a witness, and sometimes for voting in an election. Not all cities provide for these leaves with pay. When the worker is paid for civil leave functions, some agencies may require leave without pay or vacation time.
5. *Military leave* with pay is permitted in some cities for a period not exceeding 15 calendar days in any calendar year when it is necessary to be absent from the job for field training or active duty in military reserves, National Guard or emergency duty.
6. *Education leave* with pay may be granted for short periods to pursue a course of study to improve his service with the agency. Conventions, institutes, inspection trips to other cities, and water safety training courses are examples.
7. *Compensatory leave* equal to overtime worked and work on holidays and assignments beyond their work week is sometimes granted to employees not eligible for overtime pay. It must be used within a specified time, perhaps a year.
8. *Leave because of death* not to exceed three consecutive working days may be permitted with pay in case of death in immediate family which is regarded as parent, spouse, child, sister or brother of the employee, or any other close relative of the employee or his spouse who actually resides in the household of the employee.

9. *Holidays* may vary in number from 5 to 15 including most national holidays and one or two of particular local interest.
10. *Insurance and pension* benefits are increasingly important to employees. In order to be competitive with community practices, increasing numbers of agencies are paying all or part of an employee's hospitalization insurance, group life insurance, liability insurance, and sometimes employee pensions.
11. *Differential pay* may be added to regular pay for more hazardous, difficult and responsible work as working in a deep trench, unusual height, work at night (other than shift work), working foreman, and recognition for special and outstanding service. Each factor may add five percent to the normal pay scale which is usually the differential of one step in the respective pay range.

Good Work Rules

Good work rules relating to pay are sometimes included under "Compensation Plan." Others are more like everyday conveniences important to the agency personnel. There is considerable variation in the types of these services communities provide. They include employee medical services, physical examinations, credit unions, payroll deductions for savings plans, cooperative purchasing plans, legal aid, employees' recreational services, staff lounges, rest periods, coffee breaks, snack bars, cafeterias, participation in formal education programs, paid expenses to educational conferences, rewards for meritorious service, employee recognition programs, free parking spaces, death benefits, more pleasant working conditions, other professional development and employee welfare services. All of these fringe benefits tend to make the working environment more pleasant, more convenient, more attractive for the staff, and they usually pay good dividends.

In-Service Training and Education

Very seldom does the training and previous experience of a new appointee prepare him exactly for the new job to be done. Also, very few administrators, professionals, and technicians can keep up with needs, techniques, and new ideas in these rapidly changing times without on-the-job training. Training begins with the personal interview before selection, placement, and continues through staff indoctrination, orientation, and evaluation. From this point agencies may differ in need and approach.

Most agencies have regular staff meetings at all levels. These are for the purpose of interpreting policy, administrative and supervisory plans and instructions; discussing problems common to the respective group, recommended changes, suggestions for improvements, problems and solutions, new ideas, group cooperation, and joint action if needed.

Once or twice a year, it is well to provide for specialized training appropriate for the group, for example, supervisory techniques, problem solving, program evaluation, and innovative programming.

In-service training provides motivation for improvement of skills, techniques, and methods to increase effectiveness on the job and develops opportunities for advancement. Recreation interests are so varied and change so often with fads, new developments, national events and publicity, whims of people and government grant guidelines that there is constant need for training, retraining, and untraining just to stay even with the times.

In-service training is not a substitute for formal education, but it does help to acquaint the employee with the goals, policies, rules, regulations, forms, reports, records, personnel policies, procedures, plans and responsibilities of the agency and how to relate to them. Later, if emphasizes improvements, growth, development, capabilities, competence, skills, and opportunities. Time used in this manner in in-service training is multiplied many fold by understanding, individual initiative, less need for supervision, better decisions, fewer problems to solve, and a better product.

In-service training is greatly influenced by the local resources that are available. These may be found within the agency, in other departments of the city, in other levels of government and adjoining jurisdictions, institutions of higher learning, private agencies and businesses. Many have similar services and problems. Since many government services, particularly local government services, were first initiated and demonstrated by private agencies and organizations, it may be they have considerable expertise to offer.

In recreation, many employees come into the organization from other fields and through seasonal and part-time employment. They have not had the benefit of formal planned preparation for professional recreation positions. Often they are enthusiastic, interested workers but need in-service training to develop professional skill and confidence. Too often, an employee is appointed and left to his own initiative with little or no orientation from the supervisor except a hurried interview or brief job description and the title of the job to be filled. If he is experienced, he will know what to do in a general way. If it is his first job or he has limited experience he may soon run into difficulty, because of inadequate orientation, wrong decision, or conflict with policy. This may lead to criticism, reprimand, poor impression which is the fault of the supervisor. In-service training is essential and good business at every level. It is a continuous process.

Disciplinary Action

In this context, discipline refers to orderly conduct and systematic training in obedience to rules and authority. In personnel administration it refers particularly to policy, rules, and procedure for orderly and uniform corrective actions. Anything that affects prestige, pride, welfare on the part of the employee and morale, prestige and production on the part of the agency is a concern of management. These are sensitive areas involving equal treatment and equal opportunities for employees. Fair and equitable rules of operations and uniform application are important elements of a personnel system. Improper application on the part of the individual worker, whether subordinate or supervisor, leads to disciplinary action which may vary in degree from a simple friendly suggestion to dismissal or court action. All are time consuming to a degree and affect not only the production but also the prestige of both the individual and the agency. The ideal situation is to have such adherence to rules of conduct and application of policies and procedures that all disciplinary action would be on the positive side—constructive and educational suggestions. Since behavior, emotions, interpretations, and applications vary with different people in spite of good personnel and good supervision, a necessity for disciplinary action develops. Management, therefore, anticipates the kinds of actions that will be needed in the specific agency, prepares fair procedures for handling them, both for the individual and the agency, and makes them known to all employees. All aspects of personnel rules, including disciplinary actions, grievances, and appeals, should be a part of the employee's orientation.

The agency is responsible for establishing policies, procedures, rules and regulations and accepted standards of personal conduct with integrity and justice towards each employee, recognizing his individuality as a human being and his right to fair, decent and understanding supervision. Even more important, the agency is responsible for seeing that each employee understands the rules of conduct and conforms to them.

Types of Disciplinary Actions

Disciplinary actions range from a simple reprimand for minor infractions to a warning, a suspension, an unsatisfactory service rating and delay in step increase, a reduction in pay, a demotion for cause, and finally to dismissal as a last resort. The constructive suggestion, reprimand, warning and similar actions are preventive in nature and tend to avoid need for more serious action. Actions after warning become corrective measures of varying degrees and much more involved, because they deal with unlearning old methods and learning or substituting correct methods and dealing with attitudes.

Suspensions are made for reasonable periods of time, usually not more than thirty calendar days, for severe violations to impress the employee with the seriousness of his improper actions. This happens only after the worker has failed to respond to other discipline. It usually takes effect immediately upon commitment of a serious violation and continue without pay for a specified period of time.

A *delay in step increase (increment)* occurs when an employee's work performance is less than satisfactory. Increments are not automatic. At the effective date of increment, the employee's service rating must be satisfactory or better in order for pay to be advanced to the next step in the pay range.

Reduction in pay is moving back the pay of an employee to a lower step in the pay range for his class. It is used as a disciplinary measure, usually in chronic situations when other actions have failed to bring about the desired results and the employee has potential but is not performing at the level expected.

Demotion for cause is moving the employee to a lower pay range because of his failure or inability to perform the tasks in the present range. The employee can perform the tasks of the lower position. This action may prevent dismissal proceedings and be of benefit both to the individual and the agency, by providing a job at the level he can perform well and saving the investment the agency has in him.

Dismissal is termination of services and completely separating his relationships with the agency unless there are vested rights as personnel privileges that carry over such as vested pension rights and right to convert insurance. Dismissal is used in very serious violations—theft, assault, murder, criminal acts, bribery, absence from duty for long periods without permission—or as a last resort, when employee fails to respond positively to other forms of corrective action. The employee should be advised of rights to appeal and proper procedures in writing at the time of notification of termination.

Appeal from Disciplinary Action

There are occasions when employees feel they have been treated unjustly and desire an appeal of supervisory decisions. Procedures should be available for this purpose. The usual procedure will provide for the worker to appeal to his immediate supervisor, then the general supervisor. Most complaints should be satisfied at this level. If not, the appeal should be heard progressively up the chain-of-command to the executive. A few may not be satisfied at this point and may go on to the general administrator (city manager) or policy board. In some instances the procedures provide for the policy board to appoint a personnel board, which in addition to other functions, hears appeals as final authority.

Evaluation

The orderly appraisal of an employee's work performance against his capabilities and what is expected of him in the job is a means to determine the effectiveness and efficiency of the respective employee. This is more useful in larger organizations. In small agencies the executive knows each worker personally and is able to counsel on weaknesses and develop their strong points for the good of both the individual and agency. In a larger organization there are too many people to know intimately and not enough time to counsel and work out their individual differences in the same way.

There is no standard system for evaluation of recreation workers. Evaluations, sometimes called efficiency or performance ratings, are used in determining pay increases, promotions, transfers, discipline and appeals, some legal matters and movement of personnel. Because of the intangible nature of recreation leadership, and lack of measurable standards, its efficiency cannot be measured accurately. Most cities, however, use for recreationists the same forms and same procedures that are used for engineers, utility workers, and sanitation workers. Items frequently used in rating recreation workers are quality of work, dependability, attitude, courtesy, cooperativeness, personal appearance, loyalty, initiative, attendance and promptness, judgment, leadership, organizing ability, and stability. It is recognized that ratings should be made periodically, usually once a year and as often as needed in addition for discipline, probation, and personnel transactions. Timing should be on anniversary date of step increase or birthday or staggered scheduling so the supervisory work load of regular reviews can be spread over the year.

Except for information and personnel transactions, the main benefit of the performance rating is to get the supervisor and subordinate together in proper atmosphere to talk seriously about the job, the individual, achievements or lack of achievements, and means of improvement. Almost everyone likes to know how they are doing and they like constructive suggestions if given in a sincere and objective manner. One problem is that the supervisor tends to compare the individual with others rather than rate the employee's performance with what is expected of him in his job. Also the supervisor may avoid issues and rate unrealistically high rather than being fair and honest in discussing his true feelings. When rating is not done realistically, it is still in the agency's permanent records to remind the supervisor, executive and agency personnel later when something goes wrong. In the meantime the employee has a false sense of security, or a distrustful attitude, or a lowered morale. It may mean the agency is overruled in event of an appeal from a later disciplinary action. On the other hand, an employee has good reason to be resentful if he was led to believe by his supervisor that his performance was satisfactory but he received a low rating at review time.

In some agencies, the immediate supervisor only rates the worker. In other agencies, the next level of supervision also reviews and comments on the rating. This has the advantage of a double check and tends to cause the immediate supervisor to rate more realistically.

In all rating systems the supervisor discusses objectively his reasons for ratings with the respective employee. The employee signs the form to indicate it has been discussed with him. If he feels he was not properly evaluated, he may appeal to the next higher level of supervision and in writing on to the agency executive.

It is recognized that ratings have their weaknesses, but they are a means of recognizing and recording excellence in service as well as deficiencies of performance. When properly used they provide incentive for the employee and do bring about team work and improvements in the agency services.

Separation

Separation is the termination of employment. It may be temporary or permanent and may orginate either with the employee or the agency. Temporary leave usually originates with the employee who takes another job, goes back to school, goes into military service, husband or wife is transferred out-of-town, or employee is laid off and returns later. Permanent separation may be through resignation, layoff, dismissal, retirement, or death. The separation should be on a friendly basis if at all possible. It is good human relations for the agency to continue contacts with retirees, and others where appropriate, after separation.

Resignation. Some employees, from time to time, find it necessary to terminate their services with the agency to take a position of greater responsibility and pay, to complete education, or for other personal reasons. Most of them will want to resign in good standing. It is recommended that employees at administrative and high levels of responsibility give written notice at least four weeks in advance and others give at least two weeks written notice before the effective date of the resignation. However, custodial type positions may give only one week written notice.

Layoff. It sometimes becomes necessary for an agency to reduce its working forces because of lack of funds, changes in program, completion of program, or for other reasons. Therefore, it becomes necessary to abolish positions and release employees through no fault of their own. When this happens, the agency should try to transfer the permanent personnel to other phases of its operation. Any that cannot be transferred should be given as much notice of termination as possible and placed in first priority on the eligibility roster for reemployment as soon as a vacancy exists. The agency, of course, is as helpful as possible in referring names to other places of employment and assists wherever possible.

DISMISSAL. Every agency, at one time or other, is faced with serious disciplinary action that, as a last resort, involves permanent termination of the employee's service for just cause. In most instances, agency procedures provide a means of appeal before an impartial body. The purpose is to make sure the reasons for dismissal are justified and not a result of emotions or arbitrary action on the part of a supervisor. Usually an employee who has permanent status feels secure in his job and personnel practices tend to support that feeling. Agency personnel should be sure beyond any doubt that the failure was on the part of the employee and not a weakness or failure of the agency. In dismissals, it is essential to have complete records and documentation of all actions for the last several years. The negative side must greatly out-weigh the positive side of employee's conduct record and the agency must have documented proof that it was fair and objective in all of its actions. Too often, agency records are incomplete, policies unclear, or employee not informed of his failures until they become serious. Grounds for dismissal may be serious crimes, unwillingness to render satisfactory service, insubordination, habitual over use of intoxicating beverages and drugs while on duty, willful damage to agency property, falsification of official agency documents, bribery, and similar items.

RETIREMENT. Most recreation agencies have a retirement plan where both the individual and the agency contribute into a pension fund a specified percentage of salary each pay period. A few agencies pay the full amount and the employee pays nothing. A retirement plan is one means of attracting and retaining recreation personnel and adding a feeling of security, particularly for older employees. Pension is planned insurance for disability or retirement after a specified period time (varies from 5 to 15 years of service) and after a specified age for retirement, usually 60 or 65. Sometimes there is earlier age (50 or 55) at reduced benefits or after a specified number of years of service (30 or 35). Sometimes agency rules provide that an employee, upon request of the executive or policy board, may extend his services of employment beyond age 65 to 67, 70, or above. Each extension should have a definite termination time subject to review and approval annually in order to minimize controversies and misunderstanding. Employees have choice, rights and privileges through contract period of employment from permanent appointment to the established retirement age for the agency. After that he serves either full time or part time basically at the will of the agency subject, of course, to fair and reasonable treatment practiced by the agency but without rights of appeal. The major decision is based on willingness of the individual to continue plus his continued good health and competence which can change rapidly in older ages.

Very often, agency retirement plans also include participation in Social Security.

Every agency should prepare its employees for retirement beginning at least five years before effective date so it will be something to which he will look forward. Too often, retirement is without preparation and is a severe mental and emotional shock that should be avoided. Some agencies provide orientation sessions and hand out kits of things to do, privileges available to them and contacts for jobs if they so desire. It is good business for the agency to keep in touch with its retirees after their retirement. This is done by sending them copies of general news letters, or information of interest to them; inviting them to department functions such as annual meetings, Christmas party, special programs; or even asking them to volunteer on occasion.

Records, Research, and Reports

Needless to say, the personnel unit has its share of records and reporting. Program units look to the personnel unit as the source for central information involving personnel. Usually, outside inquiries about present and past employees are referred to and handled by the personnel unit.

Records. The program units usually maintain rather complete records of personnel transactions involving employees in the unit but this is not all. There are transfers, retirees, policy boards and other actions that are not maintained within the program unit, therefore, the personnel unit maintains the follow-up records of individuals before and after they leave a unit.

The personnel unit maintains individual files and roster of all persons in the service by class and position held, the salary, any changes in class title or pay; every appointment, transfer, promotion, evaluation, appraisal, demotion, dismissal, vacancy, change of salary rate, leave of absence, absence from duty, medical record, termination and any other changes of status for every temporary or permanent worker.

Research. One of the functions of personnel management is to research labor market, salaries, policies, practices, and work conditions of like jobs within the community and record information for comparison in establishing wages and salaries. They also research training methods, innovative programs, techniques, motivations, educational opportunities, personnel benefits, new personnel development programs, safety, and any matters affecting personnel of the agency. In addition, they check violations of personnel rules, policies, and laws and see that they are correctly followed; and check and certify payrolls to see that all transactions are legal and completed.

Reports. The personnel unit reports its research findings to the executive and usually a copy to any affected agency for information and appropriate action, if any is needed. Except for confidential information, it is a good policy to send units involved copies of memorandums, letters, and reports with information pertinent to their interests.

SUGGESTED PERSONNEL POLICIES AND PRACTICES

A policy is a declaration of intent and plan of action, in this instance, to achieve the agency's goals. A policy is one of the general guidelines of management. A "practice" is an established custom or accepted way of doing things. Procedures are methods for implementing policy. A rule is an authoritative direction for the control of action. Policies set standard or quality of product. Personnel policies establish the general scope of operation within which the agency must operate to achieve its purposes.

Personnel Policy Statements

Personnel policies, rules, and regulations are established for mutual protection and benefit of individual and agency. The following are examples of policy statements.

Each appointing authority is responsible for seeing that the employees under his supervision thoroughly understand and comply with personnel rules and policies.

There shall be a special personnel unit which shall consist of a director, personnel board and such staff as are necessary to carry out its functions.

The personnel unit is an auxiliary agency to assist other units with their personnel management needs but in no way will it assume authority or responsibility of program units and their personnel.

The policy of the agency may be:

— To provide a fair and equitable wage for its employees that is competitive with other employees in like positions in the community.

— To provide good work environment and work rules that apply equally and fairly to each employee.

— To act with integrity and justice toward each employee, recognizing each person's individuality as a human being and his right to fair, decent, and understanding supervision.

— To assure, insofar as possible, security, steady work and permanent employment.

— To help each individual progress in the service of the agency in accordance with his individual capacities.

— To alleviate, in so far as practicable, the adversities occasioned by illness, injury, age and death.

— To promote an atmosphere conducive to harmonious personnel relationship, friendliness, mutual helpfulness, and team work.

— To encourage individuals to better themselves by training and experience for advancement and to give existing employees with satisfactory service records every opportunity for promotion.

— To make new appointments at the beginning rate of the pay range except where the candidate has unique qualifications and applicable experiences above the minimum requirements for the position to be filled.

— To conform with the spirit and letter of all applicable laws, federal, state, local, including those that pertain to employment, working conditions, labor relations, old age benefits, Selective Service, Workmen's Compensation, Fair Labor Standards Act, civil rights, Social Security Act, and Internal Revenue regulations.

Prohibitive Practices

Although it is well to state rules and regulations positively, there are items in every agency that deal with negative elements. Some of these may be stated as follows:

— No person shall willfully or corruptly make any false statement, certificate, mark, rating, or report in regard to any test held or certification, or appointment or in any manner commit or attempt to commit any fraud preventing an impartial execution of personnel rules.

— No officer or employee of the public agency shall continue in such a position after becoming a candidate for nomination or election to any public office.

— No person seeking promotion or appointment to an agency position may give money or anything of value in connection with a test, advancement or appointment.

— No employees or others may campaign on public property during working hours.

— No employee of the agency may accept any gift of value from any person or firm interested in business dealing with the agency or accept any gift or favor that might influence the employee in the impartial discharge of his duties.

— No agency employee may be a party to or interested in any contract between the agency and any person, firm, or corporation.

NOMENCLATURE

Personnel departments find it almost impossible to compare positions, titles and salaries in the field of recreation because there is no standardization of job titles and duties. Each position may be called by five or more names even in the same state. A recent survey in one state revealed there were 17 titles used to identify recreation positions. There is no one title that identifies the recreation professional like a physician in the medical profession or a teacher in the education profession. The titles "play leader" and "playground worker" were common titles in early stages of recreation development and are still used in some places. As recreation grew in importance, complexity, and skills, other titles developed, too. Personnel experts, committees of professionals, and civil service commissions have tried to standardize job titles. A committee from the American Park and Recreation Society in 1972 reviewed all of the job titles and descriptions available, which were several hundred, and recommended 166 titles with appropriate job descriptions. These include the general fields of both parks and recreation. The committee combined many existing job descriptions similar in nature under a recommended title. It is hoped this will prove a big step towards standardization of titles. The recommended title for professional leadership position was "Recreation Group Worker" which most nearly describes the work a leadership person does—"works with a group."

The top position in the recreation agency may be designated director, superintendent, general manager, or commissioner in order of frequency beginning with the one most frequently used. The title *director* is most generally used as top executive of a recreation and parks department although the other titles are used in some instances. The title *superintendent* is more frequently used to designate the head of a division of parks, of recreation, or head of separate agencies. Common usage is *director* heads a department; *superintendent* heads a bureau and *supervisor* heads specialists or field program. In larger agencies there may be district or area supervisors under the superintendent. The *center director* or *playground director* is the head of a major local facility. The *recreation group worker* (or recreation leader) is the professional and *recreation instructor* (or junior recreation leader) is the para-professional. *Interns* are personnel in training.

Types of Positions

Organization of a recreation agency involves a minimum of three basic functions: (1) administrative services—technicians, business, clerical, and other office staff; (2) leadership and program services—supervisors, specialists, group workers, recreation instructors, interns, volunteers; and (3) planning, maintenance and construction services—general foreman, foreman, specialists, skilled trades, custodial, security, and laborers. The organization plan is one guide the executive uses to assist him in making new agency program assignments. The general administrative, maintenance and construction personnel are recruited from the general labor market because their duties and qualifications are similar in nature to those of other agencies. Recreation leadership and supervision, recreation and park technicians and specialists have distinct functions not generally in common with other types of agencies. Experience is a major consideration in selecting personnel for these positions. The strong points of these categories are the ability to interest, organize and motivate people.

Recreation leadership personnel may be either *generalists* who have training and experience in the broad field of recreation leadership or *specialists* and *technicians* who have concentrated training and experience in a specialized field of recreation leadership. Employment may be full time, seasonal, or part time. Usually there is expansion of staff and programs during the summer school vacation period. This provides seasonal summer time employment for many advanced recreation students and teachers and provides a good source for expanding seasonal staff for recreation agencies. In communities that have the twelve-month school program the recreation leadership programs are spread more evenly throughout the year, however, the summer months with their greatly expanded outdoor program opportunities will always provide an impact on recreation agencies. This is especially true in areas of colder climates.

REQUIREMENTS AND QUALIFICATIONS

In the beginning of the recreation movement, requirements and qualifications for recreationists emphasized love for children, pleasing personality, honesty, helpfulness, good influence, as well as the ability to read, write, count, and record the attendance regularly. Recreation served a few people, mostly children. The importance of recreation has grown until now it is considered a necessity of life and it has become more complex, requires more skill, and serves all the people. Requirements and qualifications of staff, therefore, must equal or exceed those of the people they serve. In some places, persons with general recreation training and experience provided the leadership and basic skills needed. As opportunities in education, leisure time hobbies, cultural interests, and skills of individuals increased, so did demands for skilled and more expert staff. In 1955 the Personnel Practices Committee of the then American Recreation Society (later American Park and Recreation Society) recommended the minimum requirements for registration of professional recreation personnel. They were adopted by the Administrative Council and used by state societies in setting up state registration plans and personnel standards. These requirements were a baccalaureate degree with specialization in recreation (or extra years of experience) plus a minimum of twelve months of successful recreation experience plus good personal habits. These are used as minimum standards for employment of professional, supervisory and administrative personnel. Local communities, states and specialist groups since have increased education, experience and other items of these minimum requirements to include master's or doctorate degrees in recreation. Considerable emphasis is being placed on successful recreation experience by personnel administrators, politicians, and policy makers to permit alternates for some of the educational requirements. This is giving professionals considerable concern especially since society (and pay schedules) has put such emphasis on college graduation.

JOB DESCRIPTIONS

There is a job position in every classification plan. The organization plan shows where the position is in relationship to other positions vertically and horizontally. This will indicate the general function of the job and relate horizontally to the difficulty of the job and general requirements. The *job description* gives the specific requirement for the specific position. Few recreation jobs remain static. Needs and interests of the participants change, therefore, needs and duties of the staff will change. Hence, job descriptions must be flexible and all inclusive for any future possibility at that level of position, yet specific enough to be an administrative and employee guide for performance on the job.

It is well to use simple words that have a single meaning in making job descriptions, if possible. A job description has several uses; it is used by administration to set up the duties and essential requirements of the job, for recruitment, for evaluations, as a guide for supervision, as a reference for promotions and disciplinary action, and it often becomes the work contract.

Format for Job Descriptions

Most job descriptions must be adapted to fit the situation and they may need to be amended periodically. A good sample of a job description usually can be adapted to almost any situation by adding and subtracting items if it follows a good format. The basic elements of a format are:

1. Identification of agency
2. Job title
3. Brief statement of job functions
4. Supervision:
   - (*a*) Who responsible to
   - (*b*) Who responsible for
5. Examples of basic duties and responsibilities of the job (not all inclusive)
6. Minimum requirements
   - (*a*) Education
   - (*b*) Experience
   - (*c*) Alternates, if any
7. Special requirements, such as—
   - (*a*) Must type 40 words per minute
   - (*b*) Must live on premises
   - (*c*) Must have valid operator's license
8. Desirable qualifications, such as—
   - (*a*) Red Cross First Aid Certificate
   - (*b*) Skills in conducting sports tournaments
9. Salary range

In a small department duties will be many, while in a large department duties tend to be more specialized because extra staff members are added and work load divided by functions or skills. (See Appendix H for examples of job descriptions.)

TRAINING AND DEVELOPMENT

Personnel experts state the average person will be retrained equivalent to three complete times during his life because the nature of his work will change that much. The best practice in training is to keep up with changes as they occur. The primary purpose of recreation is to provide services to people. People look to the professional recreationists to provide those recreation services and to take the leadership not only in modifying existing programs but also in developing new programs to challenge new interests and improved skills of the participants. Participant interests soon lags when opportunities for learning and improvement of skills decline. The isolated recreationist, except in unusual instances, soon exhausts his reserve of ideas and innovations. He may not have time or opportunity to develop additional ideas. Although the local media and the community may provide some recreation problems, few will help him to develop professional solutions or think up more effective ways of providing services. Most professionals desire and need fellowship with other professionals not only to "refresh their minds and spirits" but also to share problems, possible solutions and test ideas. The professional, therefore, needs professional fellowship with other professionals. As participants and community leadership grow in experience and knowledge so must the professional (the leader) grow and develop in order to keep his relative position of leadership and confidence. The administrator not only is paid for his professional knowledge and ability but also is paid to be "an authority" in his special field. This means he must keep abreast of developments in the field. It is common procedure for councilmen, city managers, and board members to want to know what the profession thinks or what other cities are doing about certain areas of recreation. Prestige and confidence get a boost when a ready answer is available. Too many sincere and well intended "I don't know but I'll find out" answers often lead policy boards and general administrators to find other approaches less favorable to the agency executive or the professional.

The administrator or the supervisor cannot be expected to know answers to all technical and professional problems. He may know many but he expects and depends on the technicians and professionals in the agency to keep up-to-date and be the best authorities available in their respective specialties. Many agencies have liberalized their personnel policies and resources to encourage training, but the individual and/or his supervisor must take the initiative to take advantage of training and personal development opportunities.

Agency Practices Concerning Professional Development

Most agencies have training and development programs for their employees. While many of the training activities are geared to greater efficiency on the job, many are geared to and certainly relate to professional development leading towards promotions and better paying jobs for the individual. Even before an individual is eligible for appointment, cities participate in training programs for undergraduates, providing field work experiences, part-time jobs, summer jobs, and summer internships. They also share in tuition expenses of their full-time employees, who take special or formal education courses that are related to their jobs or in preparing for higher jobs with the agency. In these instances the agency may reimburse the individual for half or more of the enrollment costs if he has a passing grade in the course.

Cities, also, conduct professional institutes and workshops, permit time off, pay all or a portion of expenses to attend national and state professional conferences; and allow educational leave of absence(usually without pay) for individuals to take specialized training of their own choice for periods up to twelve months.

Most agencies subscribe to professional magazines and technical publications. Many agencies have a professional and technical library within the agency, especially the larger departments. Some have a working arrangement with the local or state public library to have the use of certain professional books. Some cities have a liberal policy concerning "inspection trips" to projects in other cities. A few pay membership dues in professional organizations if the agency feels it will benefit from the employees' belonging to it by receiving announcements and new ideas.

Professional Identification and Growth

In recreation, leadership personnel are obliged to develop and grow in knowledge to keep up with the community and ahead of the participants. This is done by belonging to, attending, and being active in professional recreation organizations available to him. These may be local, regional, state, or national. Many professionals are active in all of them. The professional also subscribes to and reads the best professional magazines and publications including new books; accumulates a good professional reference library including publications on standards, research, evaluation, personnel, and program practices; attends professional meetings and conferences; serves on committees; attends training institutes or special workshops at least once a year; writes articles about successful projects for professional publications; makes talks on recreation subjects; and participates in community and civic activities. A professional needs to identify with his professional organization and he needs to be identified as a professional in his community.

REGISTRATION AND CERTIFICATION

More than 30 state recreation societies have systems of registration of professional recreation and park personnel. Registration is performed by state societies and by special interest branches of the National Recreation and Park Association. The procedures and minimum qualifications were established by vote of the membership of the respective recreation professional units. It is designed to identify qualified professional personnel and to discourage employment of incompetent persons.

Registration means that the professional organization certifies that the minimum professional requirements pertaining to education, experience and code of personal conduct as established by the profession have been met and names placed on the roster of qualified registered professional recreationists. Registration is administered by the recreation profession and has no legal connection with government. Registration is closely tied in with the *code of ethics* of the profession. The purpose is to set and maintain minimum standards for professional recreation and park personnel and to establish a system of identifying professional personnel that can be adopted by government for legal certification at an appropriate time. Registration has been very effective in establishing minimum uniform qualification in the recreation and park fields at all levels of government. The National Recreation and Park Association's National Registration Board provides standards for registration, a model registration plan, encourages reciprocity between state plans, maintains a national roster of registered professionals, promotes employment of registered personnel and generally guides the registration programs.

Certification, as contrasted with registration, is considered to be legal certification administered by an agency of government. A few states have state certification of recreation personnel, for example, Georgia and New Jersey.

CIVIL RIGHTS

Protection of the rights of the individual is not new but it has important new emphasis which affects the recreation executive and modern personnel practices and procedures. Every recreation executive, personnel manager and staffs involved in personnel actions should fully understand federal civil rights legislation and guidelines. Civil rights began with the U.S. Constitution. The thirteenth amendment (1865) provides in Section 1:

> neither slavery nor involuntary servitude, except as a punishment for crime whereof the party shall have been duly convicted, shall

exist within the United States, or any place subject to their jurisdiction.

The fourteenth amendment (1868), Section 1, states in part:

> no State shall make or enforce any law which shall abridge the privileges or immunities of the Citizen of the United States; nor shall any State deprive any person of life, liberty, or property, without due process of law; nor deny to any person within its jurisdiction the equal protection of the laws.

Both amendments give the Congress the power "to enforce, by appropriate legislation" the provision of the amendments. Statute 42 U.S.C. Section 1983, Civil Rights Act of 1871 states:

> Every person who, under color of any statute, ordinance, regulation, custom, or usage, of any State or Territory, subjects, or causes to be subjected, any citizen of the United States or other person within the jurisdiction thereof to the deprivation of any rights, privileges, or immunities, secured by the Constitution and laws, shall be liable to the party injured in an action at law, suit in equity, or other proper proceeding for redress.

These due processes and federal protections are duplicated by most states by similar constitutional and statutory provisions.[2] States and localities tend to administer them according to their separate needs which leads to lack of uniformity in application.

The Civil Rights Act of 1964

Although there are many other general federal and state laws which affect public agency management and personnel actions, none has greater effects on general personnel practices than the Civil Rights Act of 1964 as amended in 1972 by Public Law 92-261. In it, Congress outlines in detail its modern application of the U.S. Constitution as the basis for protection of individual rights, privileges, uniformity, and corrective remedies of abuses particularly as pertains to public agencies. Title VII of the act as originally passed in 1964 did not apply to state and local governments but the act was extended to include them by the Educational Amendments in 1972 (March 24). It supersedes any state or local laws that might be in conflict with it.

The purposes of the act are:

> to enforce the constitutional right to vote, to confer jurisdiction upon the district courts of the United States to provide injuncture

> relief against discrimination in public accommodations, to authorize the Attorney General to institute suits to protect Constitutional rights in public facilities and public education, to extend the Commission on Civil Rights, to prevent discrimination in federally assisted programs, to establish a Commission on Equal Employment Opportunity (EEOC), and other purpose.[3]

Title VI, Public Law 88-352, 88th Congress H.R. 7152, July 2, 1964, Section 601, states:

> No person in the United States shall, on the grounds of race, color, or national origin, be excluded from participation in, be denied the benefits of, or be subjected to discrimination under any program or activity receiving Federal financial assistance.

Nonconformers were subject to withdrawal of federal funds. This, together with supervision by EEOC, the U.S. Civil Service Commission, various federal agencies and the jurisdiction of the district courts, is a very effective means of getting public agencies dependent on federal funds to conform to the letter of the law.

Title VII of the Act forbids discrimination on account of a worker's or applicant's race, color, religion, sex or national origin and provides administration, guidelines, procedures, remedies and means of correcting nonconformance to the act. A summary of requirements of the act which involves recreation administration is:

1. Any locality with 25 or more public employees is subject to the act.
2. Exemptions (Sec. 702): employment of aliens outside any state or a bona fide occupational qualification (BFOQ) where an employer can prove a particular religion, sex, or national origin is absolutely essential to the normal operations. Very few, if any, exemptions are considered valid. However, hardship cases may be submitted to EEOC for consideration.
3. Unlawful employment practices for an employer (Sec. 703) are:
    a. To fail or refuse to hire or to discharge any individual, or otherwise to discriminate against any individual with respect to his compensation, terms, conditions or privileges of employment.
    b. To limit, segregate, or classify his employees or applicants for employment in any way which would deprive or tend to deprive any individual of employment opportunities or otherwise adversely affect his status as an employee.
    c. To discriminate in employment practices, training and retrain-

ing because of his race, color, religion, sex, or national origin except as may be especially exempted (BFOQ).

4. Section 704 prohibits employers from discriminating against any employee because he has opposed an unlawful practice or made a charge, testified, assisted or participated in any manner in an investigation, proceeding, or hearing under this title, or from printing, publishing, or causing to be printed or published any notice or advertisement relating to employment indicating any preference, limitation, specification, or discrimination, based on race, color, religion, sex, or national origin except bona fide occupational qualification for employment.

The remedies vary from usual fines and punishments to injunctions; withdrawal of federal assistance funds; payment of back pay, legal fees and court costs and court orders for public agencies; reducing tax exempt status, affecting economic sanctions and court actions for non-profit organizations; and boycotting, blacklisting contractors, executing economic sanctions and court actions for business and professional segments.

The Civil Rights Act involves the recreation executive in two ways. First, he must provide equal and fair treatment of citizens and participants. This involves equal protection of the law, freedom of speech, freedom of assembly, unrestrained use of public areas without harrassment or invasion of the individual's privacy, freedom from unreasonable searches and seizures, maintaining appropriate conduct of staff, protecting the rights and privileges of everyone, even informing the individuals taken into custody of their legal rights and privileges including the right to be silent. Second, he must provide equal, fair treatment and equal opportunities for employees as outlined in this Act.

Equal Employment Opportunity Commission

The Civil Rights Act of 1964 as amended creates an Equal Employment Opportunity Commission (EEOC) composed of five members and a General Council (appointed by the President with the consent of the Senate) to administer the Civil Rights Act.

The Commission shall have power (Sec. 705g):

(1) To cooperate with and, with their consent, utilize regional, state, local and other agencies, both public and private, and individuals.

(2) To pay to witnesses whose depositions are taken or who are summoned before the Commission or any of its agents.

(3) To furnish to persons subject to this title such technical assistance as they may request to further their compliance with this title.

(4) Upon request of any employer whose employees refuse or threaten to refuse to cooperate in effectuating the provisions of this title, to assist in such effectuation by conciliation or such other remedial action as is provided in this title.

(5) To make such technical studies as are appropriate to effectuate the purposes and policies of this title and to make the results of such studies available to the public to prevent (706a) any person from engaging in any unlawful employment practices set forth in Sec. 703 or 704.

This includes (706b) investigating charges of persons claiming to be aggrieved, serving notice on respondent and trying to bring about remedies by informal conference, conciliation and persuasion. If in the case of a government agency or political subdivision (706f), the Commission is unable to secure from the respondent a conciliation agreement acceptable to the Commission, it shall refer the case to the Attorney General who may bring civil action against such public respondent in the appropriate U.S. district court. In civil suits, the agency executive is usually named as defendent.

The Commission (Sec. 709a) or its designated representative shall at all reasonable times have access to and the right to copy any evidence relating to unlawful employment practices being charged. The Commission also shall have authority (713a) to issue, amend, or rescind procedural regulations to carry out the provisions of the act.

The prohibitive activity under the federal requirements is state action rather than action of individuals. State action is interpreted to include any activity authorized by state law, county and municipal ordidances, or acts of public agency executives and their employees functioning in the performance of their official duties.[4]

One purpose of Congress in establishing EEOC was to provide a means of preventing unlawful employment practices or illegal procedures and to provide civil remedies through the district (federal) courts and redress for abuses by government officials when the state courts did not provide adequate remedies.

In instances of alleged unlawful practices by government agencies or personnel the act (Sec. 706f) provides for appointment of an attorney upon certification "that the case is of general public importance," provides for temporary relief (restraining orders), expediting action by the courts and remedies (Sec. 706g) in the form of enjoining the respondent from such practice and "orders such affirmative action as may be appropriate," such as reinstatement with or without back pay, hiring of employees, or "any other equitable relief as the court deems appropriate." The Commission (Sec. 706i) may "compel compliance with such order" and allow the prevailing party "a reasonable attorney's fee as part of the costs."

The Act has generated many alleged violations and complaints and a tremendous backlog of correspondence, unanswered claims, pending suits and investigations. Opposing forces tend to appeal decisions or use this route to settle differences.

Every employer is required (Sec. 709c) "to make and keep such records (a minimum of 2 years) relevant to the determination of whether unlawful employment practices have been or are being committed" or as may be necessary. The EEO-4 forms are provided by EEOC to all public employers with 100 or more employees on which to report annually data concerning the sex and minority composition of their work forces.

Every employer (Sec. 711) "shall post and keep posted in conspicuous places on premises . . . a notice to be prepared or approved by the Commission setting forth excerpts from, or summaries of the pertinent provisions of this title and information pertinent to the filing of a complaint." Willful violation is subject to $100 fine.

Equal Employment Opportunity Coordinating Council

Section 715 of the Civil Rights Act of 1964 as amended establishes an Equal Employment Opportunity Coordinating Council composed of the heads of five federal agencies (EEOC, Civil Service Commission, Civil Rights Commission and Departments of Labor and Justice). This Council has "the responsibility for developing and implementing agreements, policies and practices designed to maximize effort, promote efficiency and eliminate conflict, competition, duplication and inconsistency among the operations, functions and jurisdictions of the various departments, agencies and branches of the Federal government responsible for the implementation and enforcement of equal employment opportunity legislation, orders, and policies."

By July 1 of each year the Council transmits to the President and Congress a report of its activities, together with recommendations of legislative or administrative changes desirable to further promote the purposes of the act. The act further provides (Sec. 717b) that the Civil Service Commission should have authority to enforce the provisions of the act concerning all personnel actions affecting federal employees or applicants for positions in the competitive service and shall issue rules, regulations, orders, and instructions to carry out its responsibilities. Basically, the Commission relates to federal agencies as EEOC relates to nonfederal agencies.

Every recreation executive, personnel director and staff member involved in personnel actions should be thoroughly familiar with the provisions of Title VII, as well as the EEOC regulations and guidelines, some of which are:

1. Qualifications and personnel actions must be based entirely on realistic requirements of doing the job.
2. Activities which tend to favor or discriminate against a class is prohibited.
3. Illegal employment practices include pencil and paper testing of application as a basis for selection; qualifications or tests that adversely affect a class and not specifically related to performance of the job; prehire inquiries not related to selection for the job such as age, religion, national origin, photograph, number of children, marital status, arrests (criminal convictions cannot be used as a reason to refuse employment if they are unrelated to the job—example, a clerk convicted for speeding); testing procedures which have not been validated by EEOC; and the same questions not being asked of all applicants.

Charges (of alleged violations) may be made by three parties: (1) an aggrieved person, (2) a person acting on behalf of an aggrieved person, or (3) a Commissioner. A charge must be filed within 180 days of the alleged violation.[5]

Other Pertinent Legislation

The *Equal Pay Act* (1963) for equal work, Part 800.100 of the Fair Labor Standards Act as amended, 1974, establishes the same pay for men and women doing substantially equal work with substantially equal skill, effort and responsibility under similar working conditions in the same establishment. It is enforced by the Wage and Hour Division of the Department of Labor. Either the Secretary of Labor or a private individual may bring suit.

The Age Discrimination in Employment Act prohibits discrimination in all aspects of employment against persons between the ages of 40 and 65. For example, the Act prohibits discrimination in wording of advertisements; e.g., "male," "female," "ages 25 to 40" which are restrictive are violations of the act. The act is administered by the Wage and Hour Division of the Department of Labor.

Questions for Discussion

1. What are the advantages of the merit system? How is it applied in public recreation?

2. Why is the recruitment process important in a recreation system? What steps would you take as an administrator in filling vacancies in your agency?
3. What is the difference between an assembled and an unassembled examination and how is each used?
4. Should there be a difference in education requirements for professional recreation workers, supervisors, and administrators? Why? Why is experience important in recreation positions?
5. What is the purpose of the position classification plan and how is it used by supervision?
6. What are the purposes of worker evaluations in personnel management?
7. How does a supervisor or administrator motivate staff?
8. What are the basic functions of a good personnel system?
9. What comprises a good staff training program?
10. How is the job description used?

Short Problems

1. Prepare administrative rules and guidelines for overtime work and pay.
2. Complete a job description for a city-wide sports specialist or other professional recreationist position.
3. Prepare "good work rules" for a recreation agency.
4. List common job titles for each position in a public recreation agency from executive through recreation trainee and include alternate job titles sometimes used for each position, underline the one you think should be made standard for each position.

References

1. Memorandum on "Assessment Center," Personnel Department, Richmond, Virginia, August 20, 1975.
2. *Managing Municipal Leisure Services.* (Washington, D.C.: International City Management Association, 1973), p. 100.
3. Civil Rights Act of 1964, p. 1.
4. *Managing Municipal Leisure Services,* p. 99.
5. *Equal Employment Opportunity Handbook.* (Richmond, Va.: State Division of Personnel), pp. 135–136.

Selected Readings

Albers, Henry H., *Principles of Management: A Modern Approach* (4th ed.), pp. 208–233. New York: John Wiley and Sons, Inc., 1974. *Management staffing and succession.*

Athos, A., and R. Coffey, *Behavior in Organizations.* Englewood Cliffs, N.J.: Prentice-Hall, Inc., 1968.

Donovan, J. J., ed., *Recruitment and Selection in the Public Service.* Chicago: Public Personnel Association, 1968.

French, Wendell, *Personnel Management Processes.* Boston: Houghton Mifflin Co., 1970.

Harvey, Donald R., *The Civil Service Commission,* pp. 3–91. New York: Praeger Publishers, 1970.

Hjelte, George, and Jay S. Shivers, *Public Administration of Recreational Services,* pp. 163–200. Philadelphia: Lea and Febiger, 1972.

Kraus, Richard G., and Joseph E. Curtis, *Creative Administration in Recreation and Parks,* pp. 57–83. St. Louis: The C.V. Mosby Company, 1973.

McChesney, James C., *Personnel Policies.* Washington, D.C.: National Recreation and Park Association, 1966.

Municipal Personnel Administration (6th ed.). Chicago: International City Managers Association, 1960.

Otto, Calvin P., and Rollin O. Glaser, *The Management of Training, A Handbook for Training and Development Personnel,* pp. 1–55. Reading, Mass.: Addison-Wesley Publishing Company, Inc., 1970.

CHAPTER 11

Supervising the Programs

Supervision is one of the most important functions of management. It not only has management responsibilities but also has direct responsibilities for agency program. Supervision is usually thought of as being in the middle, representing management on the one hand but responsible for interpretation and production. The executive also is a supervisor. He supervises the administrative staff (planners, public relations officers), top line officers (heads of divisions and bureaus), and sometimes consultants. He is also "in the middle"—between the policy board or general administrator and administrative staff but functions rather independently with minimum direction except guidelines. There is always somebody higher until authority gets to the people and always somebody lower in the organization plan until authority runs out at the base of the organization pyramid where there are only individuals, but very important individuals (program people) in the production line of the agency serving the public directly. They have no staff to supervise, but they do supervise volunteers and participants.

THE RECREATION EXECUTIVE

The recreation executive is at the top of the organization pyramid. He is the top authority within the organizational structure. The authority above him (board, city manager, general administrator) is outside of the agency structure, therefore, the executive is the last word within the agency in decision making. He holds the only position of its kind in the entire agency, no matter how large or how small it is. What he says and what he does affects the agency, its staff, its program, and the community many times more than anyone else in the agency. Poor judgment, wrong decision, procrastination, or misconduct at the executive level has serious effects on the agency programs, its image, and credibility. Every problem in the agency may become the executive's problem if it is not properly handled at the source. Every employee, every facility, every piece of equipment, every program, every dollar in the budget is the executive's responsibility but one individual cannot be skilled in all things. He, therefore, must assign duties, responsibilities and resources to dependable and competent staff that can supplement his abilities and skills. In selecting staff, the executive usually selects individuals and needed skills different from his in order to provide a good balance of knowledge and experience.

The Role of the Executive

In simple terms, the role of the executive is to get the job done in the most efficient manner possible. An executive will delegate as much as practicable to his staff. He always has more than he can do effectively himself. This involves knowing his resources, both material and human, then organizing them in an effective way to accomplish the goals of the agency. A more detailed discussion of the executive's role follows.

The executive should be familiar with laws applicable to the agency operations and see that all agency staff and board actions conform to them. The executive may be aided in legal matters by a staff member, a consultant, an agency legal department or a combination.

The executive should cause needed legislation to be enacted by researching information, checking results in other cities, listing exactly what needs to be done accompanied by justifications, getting approval of the administrator, having legal department prepare legal document for approval of policy board, and informing staff and interested citizens.

It is the executive's responsibility to translate legislative and administrative decisions into programs of action. After sufficient orientation and discussion, this may be assigned to a staff member, usually a program (line) person.

The executive should determine the short and long term needs of the community by talking to community leaders, organized groups, program staff, observing news media and agency reports, and being alert. This can be assigned to a staff member.

The executive shall determine policies, rules and regulations, procedures for management and guidance for functions of the agency. The executive seeks advice and recommendations from his professional and technical staff and anyone involved that may be interested or that can provide useful information to him. He may assign a staff member to research information related to the subject, particularly information from other jurisdictions and professional or technical sources. After all possible facts are collected a proposal is documented, distributed to appropriate individuals for testing over a period of time to see if it applies equally to all situations, staff and programs it is suppose to regulate. If not, it is amended and re-checked by the same process. If so, and it is within the authority of the executive, it is adopted, publicized and put into effect. If the executive does not have authority for adoption, it is documented with justifications and recommended to the appropriate authority for favorable action. Of course, the executive and supporting interests would be present to support the recommendation when it is scheduled for consideration in committee or at public hearings.

The executive is held almost exclusively responsible for rules, regulations and procedures pertaining to employment, working conditions, health, safety, welfare, development, assignments and conduct of staff. He keeps close watch on staff actions but usually delegates the details, mechanics of operations, authority to interview candidates for jobs and to recommend the names for appointment to staff under whose jurisdiction the appointee will work. However, the executive must give final approval for personnel actions, but may delegate signing of routine official documents to a staff member.

Making resources available to staff is priority role of the executive. This includes personnel, budget, facilities, materials, equipment, clearing roadblocks, forecasting resource needs, and keeping the staff and operations in production. It also includes counseling a staff when needed. Certain phases can be delegated such as personnel, budget preparation, purchases, engineering, and research.

The executive also coordinates resources of the agency in both short term and long term projects. Quite often it is necessary to change priorities to meet changes of need and unanticipated circumstances like emergencies. In emergencies, the executive coordinates programs if there is no prepared advance plan. Alert executives will have prepared plans for any emergency or disaster that might be expected in the area and that might involve the agency. Usually the executive, even in pre-planned procedures, will be available in any emergency of major significance for prompt decisions, coordination of resources with other agencies and to assist where needed. If an emergency involves services of a technical unit only or a single service division it is well, in most instances, for the division head (the expert) to take the leadership as he would in his regular services. The executive then arranges for additional resources needed outside the division including supplies, meals, and equipment. This permits "the expert" to give full attention to direction of resources with the close support of the executive. Too often the executive tries to take over supervision in emergency that could better be done by line staff.

Coordination is bringing together in an orderly, harmonious manner the various segments of the organization to achieve an agency objective. Coordination does not necessarily guarantee success. Friendly leadership and motivations must be added to it. The director is constantly in a leadership role. To be a good leader one also must be a good follower. He must follow the needs of the community and sound recommendations of his technicians.

The executive determines the nature, scope, and direction of program. Recreation service to the people is the primary function of the recreation agency. The executive, therefore, must keep resources directed towards the agency goals. Very often special interest groups, pressure groups, and people working for a special cause outside the agency guidelines will try to turn agency resources to their special advantage at the expense of routine agency programs. First, the executive should have anticipated and checked out these types of requests with legal department, the administrator, policy board and obtained in advance a documented policy, authority to deal with it, or justification for rejecting the request. If the idea is good and he has not checked it out before, he will express his honest feelings, check it out, and promptly advise the contact person. He must direct the programs and staff in accordance with laws, policies and other approved guidelines which should be in writing and widely distributed to staff, board members and key people. The directing is accomplished through line staff, conferences, and written communications.

The executive is constantly evaluating program efficiency in terms of standards and goals; staff in terms of achievement; and areas, facilities, new programs, reporting, budget in terms of community needs and priorities. One of the executive's constant problems is priorities, including priorities of his own time and staff time. Each staff member, each organization, and each neighborhood in the community can justify that its project should have the highest priority. It is well to take first and second level supervision to agency budget hearings to hear directly some of the reasons budgets are cut and as a training process. It also gives them better understanding of how to prepare acceptable justifications for their own budget requests.

The executive has the same human limitations as everyone else, yet his single position is the communication and control center for all of the agency. He, therefore, must evaluate his time and establish priorities. Reports to him are made brief. Some are on standard forms for uniformity and easy reading. Longer reports have a summary sheet on front, giving key points, pertinent changes, recommended action to be taken, money involved and where it comes from, benefits, effective date and other pertinent information. The secretary and staff handle everything they can. No two executives will assign the same priorities on their time.

Interpreting policy matters and major program changes to staff and the public is a primary responsibility of the executive. Public interpretation and public relations have become so important that most agencies have either a full-time or part-time public information officer to whom is delegated research and public information responsibilities using news media, printed reports, leaflets, brochures, house organs, professional and technical publications, speeches, and demonstrations.

Planning and supervision is involved in setting up an agency and its program plus keeping it in operation. An experienced staff can keep it going when things go well. The executive then gives special attention to improvements, problems, and future plans. Actually one of the most important roles of the executive is looking ahead, calling on his reservoir of knowledge and experience and that of his technicians to visualize future needs, also visualizing what could happen in every phase of agency operations and being prepared to meet any adversity in an orderly manner before or as it develops. The executive develops his ability to sense or feel when things are going right and likewise when things are not going as well as they should or when "trouble is a brewing." When he senses a trouble spot, or a potential one, he gives it priority attention in a quiet discrete way without disturbing the staff and operations. His procedure might be personal observations, talking to staff, reviewing records and reports, checking complaints, observing unusual reactions of staff and participants, or checking any unusual changes in relationships. The review might indicate a weakness in supervision, need for a change in administrative policy or procedure, personality conflict, personal problems of a staff member in his personal life, or something else. Whatever it is, the executive should cause appropriate improvement or corrective measures to be taken promptly. If delayed, it might become worse, involve more people, become more complex, hinder production or create tension. The solution at that point might be helpful suggestion to supervision, a better interpretive program, better communications, a special type of training, a change in administrative procedures, personal counseling or assistance to a troubled employee. If the executive finds all is well then appropriate comments and commendations are in order. The executive is careful at all times to work with and through subordinate staff and not take over or interfere with their responsibilities.

In planning for programs and facilities, the executive obtains the interests and needs from key contacts in the community, neighborhood organizations, the planners, and the staff. Most details of this can be delegated to technicians, but the executive provides guidelines, evaluates information, establishes priorities, determines time schedules, and translates needs, resources, and finances into action.

Contacting policy board, general administrator, peers, and high level officials is usually handled by the executive. Sometimes he assigns a key staff member (with or without briefing and instructions) to represent him at "information" sessions, as differentiated from policy sessions, and to submit afterwards a summary oral or written report to him.

Administering all the functions of management is the broad role of the executive. To do this the administrator must keep in mind the goals and objectives of the agency; the general purposes and concepts of public recreation, agency resources, and changing conditions in the community; reappraise agency programs and resources continuously; make changes as needed; protect and defend the agency and staff against unsound and irresponsible actions.

The executive of recreation agencies achieves goals by leading and motivating people and getting people to work together harmoniously. The example set by the executive affects the entire organization and its image. It must be good if the agency is to thrive.

Qualification of the Executive

Under "The Role of the Executive" were discussed the strategic position the executive holds in a recreation agency, the broad variety of responsibilities and strong influences the position has on the agency programs, staff, and community. The judgments, decisions, controls, and directions which are made at this single executive position in the agency affect the lives and may even determine for many the direction those lives will take because it is through the broad opportunities recreation provides and contacts with an understanding recreation staff that many youngsters find an interest, avocation, or vocation they pursue through life.

The person who adequately serves in the role of recreation executive must be one of broad cultural background with interest in people and ability to deal with them in all kinds of circumstances. It may be too much to expect one person to have all of the qualities desired in the top position, but honesty, integrity, sincerity, fairness, impartiality, understanding, good judgment, initiative and sense of humor are among the essential personal qualities. Possession of natural traits of leadership is an advantage. Patience is a good quality, too, but at the executive level, time soon runs out on patience because a delay in decision at executive level may delay action and production of many others.

The executive should be thoroughly familiar with the general field of recreation and knowledgeable in administration. A good combination is a bachelor's degree in recreation and master's degree in administration. Education provides the reservoir of knowledge on which to draw for sound judgments and good decisions and experience to give feeling, meaning, skill, understanding, and right choice for the particular situation. This is why an executive likes to inspect an area to see for himself, "to get the feeling," to help him make a better decision that words alone do not communicate. Also because words have different meanings to different people, decision makers sometimes need to inspect a site in order to get the true meaning of some of the words or phrases the staff uses in describing the situation orally or in written reports. If a decision maker has had previous or similar experiences relating to the situation being considered he can call on his education, experience and feelings to help him make proper judgments quickly. This saves everybody time and keeps production moving without delay of on-site inspections. This is one reason a person with broad experiences is more valuable.

In order to advise, instruct, maintain confidence, and review recommendations the supervisor needs to know more and have a larger reservoir of knowledge and experience than those he supervises. Hence, as one goes up the pyramid of organization he finds duties become more complex, require more skills, education and experience. The executive at the apex, then, requires the most. Educational requirements range from a minimum of a bachelor's degree in smaller agencies to doctorate degrees in larger agencies. Most common at this point is bachelor's degree with the variable being experience. Experience requirements range from three to ten years, usually five to seven years. Beyond that point the requirement of education is increased rather than adding years to requirements for experience. Most people get the greatest variety of experiences before age 35 during which time they are changing jobs to advance or changing to jobs with more potential or to ones they like better. After that they tend to stay longer in one position; then extra years of experience may be just more of the same thing. After age 45 it is increasingly difficult to change jobs except by promotion within the agency or in instances of those with outstanding success. "Outstanding" is relative, therefore, there are only a few who qualify in that manner. Most agencies like to think new appointees would have a potential of at least ten years of service with the agency and, hopefully, a lifetime, including advancement if they are good. A check with both private and public agencies confirmed the observation that none employed executives or supervisors without successful work experience in the respective field of service. Also it was confirmed that most agencies prefer to fill vacancies by promotion from within. However, both public and private agencies emphasized open recruitment, particularly in administrative positions.

Because of the wide range of programs and need for broad experiences in decision making, recreation executives are usually generalists rather than specialists unless, of course, they are dealing with a specialized field of service.

Age restrictions may eliminate valuable applicants with just the qualities needed. It is well, therefore, in setting experience and educational requirements to make them high enough to cover approximatly the minimum age limit desired. For instance, if a minimum age of 30 years were desired the specifications might be "master's degree and seven years of successful recreational experience, four of which must be in a supervisory or administrative capacity." In this way emphasis is on quality rather than on age.

Relationship With Chief Administrator

Although administrators have different needs and perhaps may not think to communicate what all of them are until the subordinate executive fails to anticipate the need, there are some relationships that generally are expected by all chief administrators on which the executive may base judgments. Basically, they are matters of human relations. In a way, that is what administration is. First, the executive candidate should find out by asking questions at the time of his interview for employment just what is expected of him in the job, and what is expected in terms of relationships with the administrator. The administrator will take more time then, and give it more thought, perhaps, than later. Anyway, this is the time for the candidate to find out all he can about the job and what is expected of him. It may have a bearing on his decision and success of his future. This is where laying the foundation for team work begins.

The administrator usually expects the executive to:

1. Refer to administrator, with brief notes or pertinent facts, status, purpose, recommendations, and possible results of any action or matters involving the administrator or the policy board. If a matter involves other agencies, clear it with them before sending it to administrator for action. Sometimes a joint recommendation signed by all executives involved should be attached.
2. Discuss with him personally in planning stage any proposed major changes in agency program, policies, facilities, and resources (human and material).
3. Inform him promptly of any information that might be useful to the administrator in carrying out his functions and take initiative in performing those functions related to the situation that come under the jurisdiction of the agency or that the agency can provide in event the service is not a function of another agency. The executive's attitude should be that he is the assistant administrator, as an individual, specifically responsible for all the functions of a specialized agency but also, as a team with his peers and the administrator, is re-

sponsible for the welfare and prosperity of the political jurisdiction as a whole. A little more may be expected of the recreation executive than is expected of other agency executives, because, after all, he is trained and experienced in leadership. This is not intended to imply that the recreation executive can neglect his agency responsibilities in any way. Indeed not, but it does imply that his job carries sole responsibilities for a single agency and cooperative responsibilities for the overall jurisdiction of which the agency is a part.

4. Send the administrator, for his information, copies of correspondence that may involve directly or indirectly the administrator or his policy board and matters of controversy that may arouse the citizenry.
5. Inform him immediately of any crisis, mishap, major accident, disturbance, and similar items that involve loss of life and property, serious injuries, liabilities, local politics, finances, conflict of policy, or interfere seriously with services.
6. Take the administrator on tours of major activities of the agency, new facilities, and problem areas that may involve budget.
7. Inform him concisely of matters, plans, and actions that are important to him along with main pertinent facts and items he requests. Involve the administrator only in matters affecting him or the policy board. The executive should handle everything himself that he possibly can within the authority assigned to him.

The matter of what to refer to the administrator is largely a matter of judgment, circumstances, and sometimes experience. A good criteria is "what would you as an administrator need in that position or like to have." It is well to have a regular time, at least monthly, to meet with the administrator. At this time, achievements, failures, progress, plans, problems, information of mutual interest can be presented and discussed where needed in an orderly manner. It also saves time. A brief listing type of report of status or progress once a month between the regularly scheduled meeting is very helpful and provides two contacts per month regularly. There, of course, can be special communications at any time circumstances warrant. Some matters may be cleared through the administrator's secretary with whom there should be established a good relationship.

Relationship With Subordinates

The executive deals primarily with his immediate staff—division heads, administrative assistant, other "staff" personnel, and administrative secretary. A recent survey by the author indicated that an executive works most efficiently with three to five (usually three) subordinates depending on size, diversity, and complexity of the agency services. Most of his time is involved in administrative functions—coordinating resources, making assignments, channeling information and materials, planning, dealing with the public and administrator (or policy board), conferring with staff, and removing obstacles, in order to keep the agency personnel and equipment in full operation and as efficient as possible. Generally, his subordinates are experienced experts in specialized fields who require minimum supervision. In a way, the executive is like a policy board which determines the policies, guidelines and services while the staff carries them out. It is an orderly way of dividing work loads. In a small department the executive may do program work in addition to administrative work. As the staff and programs are increased, functions are divided and staff assigned specialized tasks to fully utilize skills and talents of individual workers. There is more of a family-type closeness between the executive and his immediate subordinates than with some other levels of supervision, perhaps, because administrative personnel have different interests in common from production personnel. Then, too, they are rather dependent on each other and obliged to work as a team. The executive generally makes resources available and the staff translates them into achievement and makes technical recommendations to the executive.

Some specific items involving relationship with subordinates are:

1. To see that information flows freely and that all channels of communication are kept open. Information (except confidential, certain legal matters, and types that may not be in the best interest of the agency or that may be harmful to members of staff) should be provided all personnel.
2. To counsel staff where necessary—improve competence.
3. To support and defend staff where necessary, but help them correct errors, improve weaknesses, and utilize strong points.
4. To coordinate functions and liquidate differences.
5. To delegate authority commensurate with responsibility assigned and refer to subordinates matters of decision making that come within their scope of authority.
6. To respect and support judgment of subordinate staff.
7. To require advance clearance on matters of policy, major or significant changes, and problems.
8. To provide training and learning experiences at every opportunity.
9. To provide subordinates broadest opportunities possible to participate in formation of policies and plans.
10. To keep subordinates well informed on matters of importance to

the agency, particularly those matters involving their units. They are assistants and technicians that determine to a large extent the success of the unit.

ADMINISTRATIVE PROCEDURES AND POLICIES

The recreation executive and supervisor usually have more to do than they can get done and often overcommit themselves. This may lead to work on weekends and holidays, taking work home, over-time pay for staff involved, neglect of some functions, hurried decisions without complete facts, poorer quality performance, procrastination, slowed staff services, tension and nervousness, and other negative factors which should be avoided. Because leisure time needs vary and come at different times for different people, the recreation executive and supervisory staff are called on to administer the planning, construction, maintenance and business affairs of the agency during normal work day but perform their main program and supervisory functions evenings, weekends and holidays. In some places administrative and supervisory staff are responsible for round-the-clock operations. In most places, they have what is equivalent to two-shift operations with administrative housekeeping functions and some programs during the normal day and program functions in the evenings and at night. The shifts cannot be clear-cut because some administrative functions (meetings, inspections, courtesy visits) must take place after normal work hours, weekends, holidays, and emergencies, and some program supervisory functions must take place during the normal workday. It is not practical to split supervision in the same program function in such instances; therefore, administrative and program supervisory personnel schedule their services to serve both types of operations, both shifts as needed. In personnel rules, provisions are made for overtime for staff and compensatory time off, or flexibility in rescheduling time for supervision. The Fair Labor Standards Act is often used as the guide for formulating local policy.

Recreation is unique in some of its management responsibilities. Its program services are varied and changeable. Program sites are variable, often borrowed, leased, temporary, or makeshift, or are on facilities of other agencies with considerable limitations. Program sites are far flung throughout the jurisdiction and considerably different in character and services. Some are limited to a particular phase of program or one activity, such as swimming. Others are seasonal and part time with a broad program. Still others provide a full service year around, indoor and outdoor. Policies, therefore, have to be broad and inclusive. Supervision needs to be broad in order to provide service and keep duplication at a minimum.

Special facilities and skill programs are often operated with a great deal of independence under the supervision of a generalist. The majority of agencies do not have sufficient staff positions to provide supervisors for specialized programs except, perhaps, sports.

The recreation executive and supervisor especially need to find ways to use time most effectively and minimize need for close and constant supervision. One way to do this is to have good center, facility, and unit directors, and then delegate sufficient responsibilities to them to perform their tasks. Another way is to provide written copies of agency and program guidelines and make periodic field visits.

Important Administrative Factors

The recreation executive, because of the flexible nature of recreation, is subject to requests, pressures and influences from many sources—political, community services, personal interests, and special causes. A human service that is not specifically assigned to another agency is often referred to the recreation agency for handling and to absorb the extra costs. Sometimes this can be a rather large item of staff time and budget expense. The recreation executive, in setting or recommending policies and procedures, should visualize in advance all of the possibilities with which he may be faced in the future and formulate a policy, if it is within his authority, or cause to be adopted an appropriate policy if it is outside his authority, to deal with a situation before it develops. Once it develops, it becomes a personal matter for the individual participant or organization involved and it becomes a more sensitive problem for the policy board, personnel board and administrator.

All policies and practices are directed towards achieving certain predetermined goals and objectives. One of the major objectives is to make best use of resources, personnel and materials, at all times. Use of materials and other resources depends on personnel. Therefore, the prudent administrator will formulate policies and rules that will help personnel function at maximum efficiency with minimum effort. The supervisor takes into account the goals, the skills and ability of staff, and causes and results of actions. With his reservoir of knowledge and experience, he chooses techniques and methods that are most apt to bring about desired results. Some supervisory factors of high priority are to:

1. Provide adequate, clear, and concise guidelines and direction.
2. Have complete factual information before making decisions.
3. Apply rules, guidelines and opportunities uniformally, fairly, justly, impartially, without bias or prejudice.

4. Be consistent and make changes promptly when need is clearly indicated.
5. Instruct, interpret, direct, motivate, evaluate, improve, and correct to accomplish staff functions.
6. Encourage individual initiative and self-direction. Provide training opportunities and learning experiences. Resolve conflicts and differences promptly. Counsel and assist subordinates where needed. Improve their competency and opportunities.
7. Make observations and visitations, evaluate, and recommend desirable changes and improve techniques.
8. Provide incentive programs—in-service education, promotions, awards for outstanding accomplishment, recognition for outstanding or unusual service.

Some Common Weaknesses in Supervision

Everyone needs motivation and everyone needs supervision. Without supervision or checks and balances, individuals tend to be careless. Maybe in a small way at first. If not corrected, it tends to become greater and more serious. One of the purposes of supervision is to improve efficiency and to help individuals utilize their strong points and strengthen their weaknesses. Often individuals do not recognize their own weaknesses or fail to do anything about them until someone or some incident calls it vividly to their attention. The persons in supervisory positions have the responsibility of correcting their subordinates. To some, it is an unpleasant responsibility and often is delayed or neglected until a small crisis develops. Then, at that point, disciplinary action may be involved and the supervisor finds himself in an awkward position because it was really his neglect that let the crisis develop in the first place. The weak supervisor then tends to look for ways to save face and, too often, finds a way to relieve his conscience by blaming the subordinate or someone else. The subordinate, of course, is a likely target, because he had an uncorrected weakness and was already in trouble. The supervisor's supervisor then has a responsibility to correct a weakness in supervision.

Some common weaknesses in supervision to avoid are:

1. Failure to apply all important administrative factors adequately and uniformly.
2. Failure to communicate adequately. Restricts scope of involvement of other people in matters affecting them.

3. Procrastination; failure to clear matters promptly, therefore, holds up staff.
4. Indecision.
5. Inadequately and unequally applying work rules; shows partiality.
6. Poor judgment in values, priorities, decision making.
7. Desire to reserve authority, powers, decision making for self.
8. Thoughtlessness, lack of consideration, and understanding.
9. Indiscretion, blaming others, "passing the buck," dealing in half-truths.
10. Failure to face unpleasant issues fairly, squarely, and promptly.
11. Setting a poor example. Failure to follow the rules others are expected to follow.

SUPERVISION

Supervision is generally thought of as the phase of management between the executive and the individual at the base of organization structure. Supervision begins when an individual is responsible for all or part of the activities of one or more other individuals, usually two to eight, mostly three to six. It is not considered efficient for an individual to supervise the activities of just one other individual, known as *one over one,* an example of which would be a supervisor over *one* assistant supervisor.

The purpose of supervision is to organize and direct agency resources into effective action towards achievement of specific objectives. It involves planning course of action; interpreting administrative directives, goals and guidelines; organizing, motivating and scheduling staff resources; coordinating and directing activities of groups and individuals both within and without the agency; selecting, training, and developing workers to their highest potential; evaluating progress, services, and staff; and adjusting, correcting, improving competency of staff, methods, and techniques of operations.

The Role of the Supervisor in Management

The supervisor is identified and associated with management and is goal oriented with the basic responsibility of carrying out the functions of management at the worker level. He helps and manages people. The supervisor may relate to other supervisors, as in middle management, or may relate to production workers as in a community center staff. The first type may involve considerable administrative responsibility, broader functions, and general supervision; while the second type will involve more face-to-face leadership and instruction, showing individuals what and how to perform. In either instance, the supervisor is responsible for translating administrative objectives, rules, regulations, other guidelines and assignments into effective and efficient programs of action. A supervisor is usually assigned a specialized area of work (facility, area, skill, project, program, function) with workers who have appropriate skills and knowledge to perform a variety of assignments pertinent to their overall responsibilities. The supervisor, knowing the capabilities and potentials of staff and resources available, is responsible for arranging and implementing an appropriate plan of action. He is the leader of a team which not only is interested in efficient production but also interested in the health, welfare, and development of each member of the team. He provides the direction and know-how or takes necessary steps to get information, needed skills or resources if he does not have them within his jurisdiction. He must choose the most effective methods and techniques that will motivate others to achieve desired objectives.

The supervisor operates on a two-way street. He is responsible for transmitting and interpreting communications to subordinates from higher authority on the one hand, and on the other hand reporting to higher authority plans, progress, major problems, accomplishments, and information of special interest to management. In addition, the supervisor makes recommendations, counsels with his supervisor on matters of mutual interest, and assists management in carrying out its functions.

Supervisory Techniques

Supervision is a leadership process. Hence a supervisor, a leader in the management of people, should have and practice the qualities of leadership, including loyalty to agency and staff, consideration of others, deep sense of understanding, common sense, and good judgment. Since individuals are so different, a supervisor needs to know different techniques and approaches to problems. He also needs to know the expected results from each technique. The supervisor is expected to develop rapport between individuals; encourage growth and development of workers by providing learning experiences; encourage creativity, imagination, individual initiative by making assignments with just the right amount of explanation and maximum freedom of action in order to develop self reliance, self direction, and self confidence. In addition, he should only supervise as much as needed to develop trust and faith, lead and suggest rather than demand and force, and recognize and utilize strong points and strengthen weaknesses. Incentive programs that will stimulate varying individual interests and talents such as awards for outstanding achievement, should also be developed; a simple pat on the back for simple things, public recognition and praise for larger things and raise or promotion on big things.

The supervisor should encourage self-evaluation and help the individual to understand how and why he reacts as he does. He should also assist the worker in gaining information by explaining and interpreting how it relates to plans and how it relates to the individual. It is important to encourage self improvement by counseling, interviews, staff meetings, letters and memos, bulletin boards, house organs, informal conferences, observation and suggestions, visitations and inspections, and on-the-job training. The attitude and approach of the supervisor does much to create receptiveness on the part of the worker.

Supervision may be applied in several ways the most common of which are by criticism, prevention, instruction and cooperation.[1] *Criticism*, unless handled very objectively, can create defensive and sometimes a belligerent attitude on the part of the worker. In this frame of mind some workers are not in a very receptive mood for corrections. However, others respond well to this method. Most conscientious workers like to improve and are very receptive to objective and constructive criticism when given in an acceptable manner by supervision. The supervisor would be expected to have a sincere concern both for improvement of work methods for the agency and improvement of skills of the individual. Criticism by itself without a suggested corrective measure may create ill will. A supervisor should be careful not to appear to be finding fault without definable reasons and should have a practical solution to offer. Sometimes it may be better to delay criticism until an appropriate solution or procedure is thought out except, of course, when situations are completely wrong and must be stopped or changed immediately. To correct a mistake in supervision and recover dignity, prestige, and confidence is twice as difficult as making a proper decision in the first place because one has a degree of undoing in the wrong direction before starting in the right direction. A little delay for a more effective solution may be time and energy well spent at supervisory level but one justified delay should not be the occasion to form a habit of delaying other solutions. A quick decision based on emotions, excitement, ignorance of the situation or incomplete facts may turn into a calamity, but a quick decision based on experience, knowledge, and fact is a real asset.

Preventive supervision anticipates problems before they develop. It follows the philosophy that it is better management to prevent a problem from developing than to deal with it after it develops. This is a good point if appropriately handled and surely is in line with good recreation objectives. If problems can be prevented or reduced in intensity, certainly the staff can save the unknown effort and energy that they and the agency would have used in solving the problem. Also it would reduce interruption of program and any negative results, including costs and staff feelings. This kind of supervisory attitude is an asset. On the other hand if the supervisor watches every move of subordinates, expecting problems to develop, directing each activity, then he tends to assume all initiative and not only delays progress because he cannot be every place at once, but also greatly reduces individual initiative, judgment, confidence and development. Preventive supervision is good in planning and in creating new jobs or changing directions in old jobs and has a place, but it should not be used to the extent that it interferes with growth and development of individuals' capabilities and initiative to anticipate and solve his own problems. Emphasis should be on achievement.

Supervision by instruction refers to informing subordinates of what has to be done, identifies possible problems or weaknesses, tells or demonstrates to individuals how they may be avoided or overcome. The supervisor, in this kind of a situation, is a source of advice. It emphasizes the superior-subordinate relationship where the supervisor has the knowledge and control and the subordinate has the physical resources to achieve the objectives.

Cooperative supervision puts emphasis on team work and gives worker maximum freedom to use individual initiative and capabilities. The supervisor provides resources, opportunities, advice, and leadership when needed but encourages self reliance and self improvement. In recreation both the supervisor and the worker are professionals and can relate to each other as such. The team or democratic approach proves very practical with the supervisor putting more effort into planning, coordinating, innovating, training, evaluating, assisting, developing, and promoting. The worker puts his efforts into implementing plans, organizing, conducting, instructing, improving, and recommending. Each becomes more skilled in his respective areas of responsibility, yet they complement each other in the team approach for more effective results. The success of one tends to help the success of the other. Likewise, the failures of one tend to reduce the successes of the other and are a motivation for joint efforts towards improvements.

The same technique of supervision may not fit all occasions and all types of individuals. It is likely that the astute supervisor will use all techniques and devise some of his own in order to deal effectively with the wide variety of situations confronting him. Also with today's changing times and values, old approaches may have to be adjusted frequently to modern needs, therefore, the supervisor that has techniques for many types of situations and combinations will have a distinct advantage over those with conventional techniques only.

Types of Supervisory Problems Encountered

Supervision is obliged to be responsive to changing conditions in the community, particularly those that affect changes in agency programs and services. Changes of all kinds, such as interests, personnel, values, and needs, cause the supervisor and staff constantly to reevaluate and redirect emphasis in services. Changes in personnel require considerable effort on the part of the supervisor to arrange a way to fill the void of a vacancy which means, perhaps, that priorities have to be changed, something left undone, and other workers oriented to take on, at least temporarily, new duties in addition to their own routine functions. Usually, there are no relief workers, therefore, some have to do double duty in order to carry on essential services. It may mean overtime for some workers or employing substitute workers if the nature of the work is such that it cannot be combined with other staff functions. The substitute is seldom as efficient at first as the one experienced in the job whom he replaced. The supervisor must change priorities on his own time in order to recruit, orient and train a new appointee for the position, therefore, reducing temporarily time available for routine supervision and assistance. It takes from two weeks in less complicated situations to, perhaps, six months in more complicated high level supervisory situations to fully orient a new appointee to all of the responsibilities of the respective position. An overlap of time in changing supervision is recommended but very seldom possible because the outgoing supervisor often has to report to another job before a replacement can be recruited or he leaves under negative circumstances where his advice may not prove to be in the interest of the agency. Once a time is set for an individual to terminate services with an agency, his interest becomes divided (except in unusual circumstances), and his interest in the agency tends to wane in spite of good intentions. Therefore, it usually turns out that the outgoing worker and the supervisor orient a substitute worker who carries on until a permanent appointment is made. Then the substitute worker and supervisor orient the new appointee beginning with the simpler functions and progressing to the more complicated ones which take longer.

Differences in personalities, temperaments, responses, sensitivity, emotions, understanding, approaches and similar items require different methods and techniques in supervision to accomplish desired results. Sometimes a very knowledgeable person may be limited in techniques and runs into trouble in dealing with problems that do not fit into his techniques.

There is a tendency initially to be fearful of supervision, particularly in organizations that emphasize the superior-subordinate relationship or where supervision is set apart and treated differently by management in contrast to production workers. With this kind of an atmosphere the supervisor may be looked upon as a boss with a punitive and threat of punishment attitude which should be avoided rather than a leader and co-professional team approach attitude which is desirable.

One of the greatest problems of management is communication. The larger the organization, the more difficult it is to keep communications open in all directions. This is brought about by thoughtlessness, selfishness and a feeling of insecurity, carelessness and procrastination, incomplete information, failure to explain, friction between workers, personality conflicts, jealousy and holding information. It is to the advantage of supervision and administration generally to keep communications open and especially keep the levels of supervision above, below and to each side of the operations as well informed as possible about basic functions and objectives.

Personality differences and supervisory attitudes often are real trouble spots and include lack of loyalty to agency, peers, and subordinates. The supervisor should have self respect, pride in the agency, confidence and respect for his workers. Much of his attitude, good and bad, will be "caught" by others with whom he comes in close contact. Showing favoritism rather than being impartial in action and in words is a common fault of supervision. Indiscretion in conversation, inappropriate behavior, poor judgment, ridicule, tolerating gossip based on unfounded facts, passing-the-buck, sidestepping decisions, and bypassing supervision are common situations confronting supervision.

Other problems may be lack of worker involvement in planning and decision making affecting them; violations of agency rules, regulations and guidelines; unauthorized absences and tardiness; incompetency; inefficiency; and use of agency time, equipment, supplies for personal benefit. Sometimes personal problems carry over and affect job situations. The supervisor counsels and assists where he can. It is to the agency's advantage to cooperate in assisting employees with personal problems where appropriate.

The supervisor must be fair, impartial, and demonstrate personal integrity at all times. He should deal with problems promptly. All members of the agency should understand the laws, concepts, policies, rules, regulations, personnel practices and other guidelines of the agency. It is one of supervision's responsibilities to see that all personnel conform. How well he performs will depend largely on how well he communicates, how he applies his knowledge, how he handles human relations, how he exemplifies leadership qualities, and how he relates to other human beings.

Disciplinary Action

Discipline as related to personnel rules and practices was discussed in Chapter 10. It will be discussed here from the point of view of the supervisor.

In supervision, discipline involves correcting failures of conduct, negligence, infraction of rules (tardiness, indolence, carelessness, breakage, and damage), violation of laws (theft, bribes, extortion, immorality, embezzlement, assaults, all crimes), unauthorized absences, nonconformance to safety practices, intoxication, abuse of people and equipment, any breach of conduct, and misbehavior. A worker is employed to perform the tasks outlined in the job description for his particular position. One of the responsibilities of every individual is to conform to the laws of the land and policies and rules of the agency for which he works in a manner generally acceptable to society and the agency. When the employee fails to perform these duties at a reasonable level expected of the position, interferes with performance of other staff, violates rules of conduct (legal or civil) or harms and seriously offends people, some appropriate action of correction needs to be taken. This is a responsibility of supervision. The action taken depends on facts of the occasion; complexity of the situation; values involved; number of persons implicated; temperament of the individual, his receptiveness and what will best cause him to respond favorably; and, of course, the seriousness of the situation. Certainly the supervisor wants to get all of the facts without expressing his personal views until all facts have been considered and he has decided what is best to do to bring about desired change. Depending on the seriousness of the situation and the ability of the individual to respond to objective suggestions, the appropriate action may be a friendly discussion, a suggestion, careful instructions, verbal reprimand, written reprimand and warning, probation, transfer to another unit of the agency, a suspension (without pay), a demotion, or dismissal.

In considering disciplinary action the supervisor should make sure the individual or individuals involved are responsible for the action or lack of proper action rather than supervision and management. The worker should not be disciplined on matters of management's failures if he has no responsibility for them, but they should be resolved and corrected immediately. On items for which the worker is responsible, the supervisor is expected to handle the action promptly. After considering all of the facts involved, goals of the agency, seriousness of the violation, the temperament of the individual, previous actions, and kinds of discipline to which he responds, the supervisor must select the type of disciplinary action that he thinks is adequate to bring about proper results. Discipline is a corrective measure. It is not a punitive one and should not be used or thought of as such. If an individual cannot be corrected after reasonable efforts then he may be dismissed for cause. This is not intended as punishment, it is elimination of a situation that cannot be corrected.

The supervisor's goal is to accomplish an objective and to mobilize resources to accomplish that objective effectively and efficiently. To do this, he must keep his personnel in full production. If an individual or crew of workers takes themselves out of production (slow up, are tardy, "goof off", or are absent) or if management takes them out of production by suspension, hearings, or dismissal, it has a negative impact on production and accomplishment. In determining appropriate disciplinary action, the supervisor considers both the short and long range effects of actions to be taken and the possible effects it would have on others. He, therefore, is expected to consider all factors relating to the agency as a whole and select an action that will bring about the desired change. The objective is to resolve the problem at the unit level as quickly as possible and to keep the individual in maximum production, if feasible. Taking a worker out of production by suspension and dismissal are actions of last resort.

In discipline it is most important for the supervisor to be fair, reasonable, realistic, and objective with decisions based on facts. Sometimes a worker will ask to be permitted to resign instead of being dismissed. This may mean he terminates in good standing instead of bad standing and is in position after termination to direct activities against the agency and its personnel with considerable retaliatory effect. This kind of situation should be avoided by handling each disciplinary action on its own merits realistically and completely. If a worker has committed a violation serious enough to be dismissed, it does not seem fair to others or to the agency and supervisor to permit him to leave in good standing as a favor to him and provide a potential later problem to the agency. This is an instance where the supervisor lets the accomplishment of a short term objective interfere with a long term objective.

Fair treatment in discipline is more than a consideration of just the worker involved in a violation. It involves fair considerations for the agency, the supervisor, other workers, and sometimes for the participants. Although the supervisor should consider the proper disciplinary action for each separate situation, he should consider also treatment he has given others under similar circumstances and be as consistent as possible realizing, however, that some workers may require more intense treatment than others. Also the disciplinary action gets more severe with second and third offenses and with the seriousness of the offense.

Every situation has accompanying problems for which the supervisor should be prepared. Frequently in public service, the worker will present his side of the story in such a way that it stirs up the emotions of the public and politicians which results in preparation of detailed, time consuming reports and sometimes improper decisions. This has a demoralizing effect on staff and is one reason the immediate supervisor should resolve a grievance or complete a decision on disciplinary action fairly, decisively, and as promptly as possible at the supervisory level.

Handling Complaints and Grievances

Complaints and gripes are as natural in a democratic society as life itself. In a way, they are useful means of telling management how it is doing. They may also be considered gentle warnings or advisory messages. Management and supervision are expected to answer them realistically and promptly before they become grievances. If the complaint is not heeded or resolved, it may later be documented and presented as a grievance.

Grievances, imagined or real, should be handled by the immediate supervisor, if possible. Sometimes grievances develop because of lack of proper information or inadequate explanation of certain administrative and supervisory actions. Most of them are related to work rules, compensation, promotion opportunities, physical environment, treatment of supervision or lack of uniformity in application of personnel practices.

Every agency should have a grievance procedure. All complaints and grievances should be resolved as near their source as practical. However, communications should be kept open so an employee may reach his desired destination progressively through the chain of command, if necessary, to the chief executive or appeals board. Often a complaint or grievance can be resolved easily by a frank, honest discussion with the supervisor. However, there are times when it cannot be satisfied at the supervisory level. In such cases the immediate supervisor without prejudice should explain to the worker the proper procedures to follow and make an appointment for the worker to present his grievance to the next level of supervision. It is preferable, from management standpoint, if the immediate supervisor goes with the aggrieved worker until the grievance is resolved or reaches the final authority (the appeals board). The grievance process is a normal procedure of management; therefore, the supervisor and management should handle matters in an objective, professional, business-like, and helpful manner as in any other job function and guard against derogatory remarks, prejudices, and negative reactions. Indiscrete discussions with third parties should be avoided.

It is important that all employees know that a procedure for handling grievances exists and that they will be heard fairly, objectively, and without prejudice. Good supervisory practices, uniform application of personnel rules and regulations, fair treatment of personnel, good work rules, good working conditions, and alert supervision do much to minimize development of serious complaints and grievances.

Motivating Workers

Most people need motivating challenges to make their jobs more interesting and to increase their capabilities. It has become a priority function of supervision and management to provide attractive and challenging incentives to motivate workers. This may be done in several ways but most of them relate to personal improvement, individual prestige, and opportunities for the individual but they may have direct and indirect benefits for the agency. They may be grouped in three classes related to (1) compensation; (2) improvement of capabilities; and (3) recognition and prestige.

Good compensation is the base incentive and provides the opportunity for further participation. Pay range increments are incentives to get personnel to remain with the agency. Some cities, in addition to pay differential for more difficult work conditions, add 5 to 10 percent for unusual qualifications above the job requirements, such as working foreman and acting in administrative capacity for long periods. This encourages workers to take those hard-to-fill jobs. Monetary awards for exceptional service is sometimes added to pay for a specific period of time. There is the agency's participation in group insurance for employees, credit union, medical services, hospitalization, and supplemental retirement system. These are in addition to Social Security benefits and when combined add up to quite an impressive figure. These extra opportunities for the worker are almost entirely to the benefit of the employee.

The group of incentives for improving employee *capabilities* are of benefit both to the agency by improving competence and to the employee by improving work opportunities for advancement and better jobs. There is a wide variety of on-the-job training programs that increase the workers capabilities. These will be discussed later under in-service-training. More and more cities are participating in student field work, internships and tuition payments for courses connected with the specific job assignment or promotion within the agency. In certain areas of specialized training or special problems (water safety, park ranger, park security, lighting, special programming, federal grants), institutes and workshops are conducted locally or individuals are sent (expenses paid) to places of training.

Recognition and prestige programs are of great interest to most employees. In a way, it is a counterpart to disciplinary action and should be utilized to the fullest. Developing and maintaining pride, prestige, and dignity is of interest to the individual and often a strong motivating force used by supervision. Important factors are properly screening and placing individuals in positions they like, giving them freedom to act, and involving them in planning and decision making. More and more agencies give recognition for long service (perhaps give a service pin), safety certificates for periods without accidents, safe driving awards for a year or more of accident-free driving, a certificate and, perhaps, monetary award for outstanding suggestions used by the agency. Supervision should strive to put each individual in a place where he can be recognized as leader in his field. Some agencies add points in applying for promotion to those who have passed five or more specified in-service education courses or have a degree higher than the minimum required in specifications for the job.

PROFESSIONAL GROWTH AND DEVELOPMENT

In modern times interests and needs in recreation are changing so rapidly the recreationist must continuously strive to improve his skills in order to keep up with the times. Training, therefore, is a vital part of the supervisor's responsibility to keep himself up-to-date on latest supervisory developments and techniques; to keep the worker up-to-date on latest program ideas; and also to help qualify those with leadership potential to become eligible for promotion to a more responsible position. This may involve enrollment in night school or regular college classes or it may involve organizing special classes in specific subjects for development of supervisors. It may mean providing more opportunities for worker involvement, assuming more responsibility, doing research, making surveys, and preparing plans and justifications.

In-Service Training

No candidate is completely trained for the variety of recreation jobs he has to do. During orientation and probation period the appointee needs training in agency philosophy, purposes, goals, administrative policies, rules and regulations, procedures, prohibitions, responsibilities and resources available. Later training is geared to increase confidence and competence, broaden skills, acquire new techniques to increase capabilities and abilities to serve public needs. Recreationists recognize that in-service training reduces the potential of problems and improves the quality of the program. Increased capability of leadership increases participation and broadening of program. One advantage of in-service training is that it applies acquired knowledge to a practical situation in which the participants are involved.

In-service training is especially beneficial in introducing new programs or changing old programs, introducing new techniques and orienting new appointees, especially the worker who has just been appointed supervisor and who finds himself in a situation with a new set of problems. In some agencies, series of courses are provided especially for supervisory development. They include job relations training, job instruction training, personnel rules and procedures, supervisory methods, safety for supervisors, effective letter writing, effective speaking, report writing, human relations, job analysis, personnel evaluation, and introduction to the humanities. For higher levels of supervision, professionals, and those preparing for advancement, the various management courses prepared by the International City Management Association are often used, sometimes sponsored by the local colleges and universities.

Questions for Discussion

1. What are the main responsibilities of the executive?
2. How does the executive's position differ from that of the superintendent? How does the superintendent's position differ from that of a supervisor?
3. What are the differences in requirements for an executive of a large city department as compared to an executive of a small city department?
4. How would you deal with a situation where a worker is absent without official leave?
5. What would you think the public would consider to be the most important positions in a public recreation agency? Why?
6. What are personal qualities of a good supervisor?
7. What would you consider most important in selecting professional recreation workers—personal traits and qualities, education, or experience?
8. What guidelines do supervisors use in making decisions?
9. How would you handle the situation where a worker is seeking a city councilman's influence to get himself promoted to a higher position?
10. How would you deal with an employee who claims to be out on sick leave but you have good reason to believe he is just "goofing off"?

Short Problems

1. Prepare a full job description for a recreation executive for a city of 100,000 population.
2. Outline the steps to be taken in dismissing a playground worker including handling of the worker's appeal of the dismissal action.

Reference

1. George Hjelte and Jay S. Shivers, *Public Administration of Recreational Services* (Philadelphia: Lea and Febiger, 1972), pp. 221–22.

Selected Readings

Albers, Henry H., *Principles of Management: A Modern Approach* (4th ed.), pp. 495–524. New York: John Wiley and Sons, Inc., 1974. *The problem of motivation.*

Bannon, Joseph J., *Problem Solving in Recreation and Parks.* Englewood Cliffs, N.J.: Prentice-Hall, Inc., 1972.

Bittel, Lester, *What Every Supervisor Should Know.* New York: McGraw-Hill, 1968.

Hjelte, George, and Jay S. Shivers, *Public Administration of Recreational Services,* pp. 202–222. Philadelphia: Lea and Febiger, 1972.

Kraus, Richard, and Barbara Bates, *Recreation Leadership and Supervision.* Philadelphia: W.B. Saunders, 1975.

Nigro, Felix A., *Management Employee Relations in the Public Service,* pp. 5-53. Chicago: Public Personnel Association, 1969.

Otto, Calvin P., and Rollin O. Glaser, *The Management of Training, A Handbook for Training and Development Personnel,* pp. 341–373. Reading, Mass.: Addison-Wesley Publishing Company, 1970.

Rodney, Lynn S., *Administration of Public Recreation,* pp. 55–71. New York: The Ronald Press Company, 1964.

Stokes, Paul M., *A Total Systems Approach to Management Control, Controls for Employee Relations and Development,* pp. 112–121. New York: American Management Association, 1968.

Van Dersal, William R., *The Successful Manager in Government and Business.* New York: Harper and Row Publishers, Inc., 1974. *About organizations, career development, training systems, performance appraisals, goal setting, staff work, communication systems, reports and reporting inspections, and self improvement for managers.*

Wilson, Howard, *Understanding and Motivating Employees.* Deerfield, Ill.: American Research Association, 1969.

CHAPTER 12

The Recreation Program

In public recreation services, the term *program* generally refers to the entire range of recreation activities and services for all groups and ages. However, in some general situations the terms *program* and *activity* are used interchangeably. Usually, however, *program* refers to the total and *activity* refers to a specified unit or a single item of the program.

The recreation program is based upon the many and varied activities which involve the entire gamut of human interests. These activities provide for leisure time needs of the whole family from pre-school age through the retiree. A total community recreation program includes private, semi-private, public, and commercial activities and facilities. Each provides for a different leisure time need. Public recreation is generally thought of as providing open space, large facilities and a variety of recreation services for mass activities and groups although some specialized programs provide for the individual often on his own initiative. Rodney classifies public recreation programs in three general categories:

1. The provision of recreation areas, buildings, and facilities for recreational enjoyment.
2. The furnishing of professional leadership for organized individual or group activities.
3. The giving of assistance to individuals or self-determining groups who wish to enjoy recreational pursuits or opportunities through their own continuing membership.[1]

The *purpose* of the public recreation program is to provide appropriate areas, facilities, leadership, varied program opportunities, pertinent supportive services (concessions, consultation), and a wholesome environment to serve the many leisure time interests of the population throughout the year as needs arise. The activities may be regularly scheduled for specific times, organized, informal, supervised, self-sustaining, special, occasional or "drop in."

The recreation executive not only must be sufficiently knowledgeable to guide the policy makers in establishing effective agency guidelines but also he must be sufficiently knowledgeable in program methods and services to direct staff in efficiently achieving the agency program goals and objectives.

PROGRAM GOALS AND OBJECTIVES

Goals and objectives may vary considerably with situations in different communities depending on size, needs, interests, resources, scope, quality of services and so forth. Statements of program purposes, goals, and objectives are among the guidelines used in planning program services. There may be an overall guideline to give direction such as "program emphasis is placed on growth and development" and/or a series of statements relating to specific features. All programs also relate to the purpose and general objectives of the agency towards which effective administration works. Program then becomes the method through which goals and objectives are accomplished.

Recreation programs and services may be so broad and flexible and requests so extreme that specific guidelines are necessary in order to keep programs within available resources. For instance, it is tempting for citizen pressure groups working for a special cause or politicians and administrators who have inadequate funds for pet ideas to call on recreation resources (staff, equipment, maintenance personnel after hours at overtime pay) to help with projects, especially one-time affairs, that look like use of leisure time but which are only remotely related to recreation functions and their related services. Too often, the public recreation agency is used for staging such events and providing custodial type services for a community group, business, church, or private agency for which funds are not included in the budget. These types of services can be quite a drain on the agency resources and, of course, unless provided for in the agency budget or by reimbursement for the service rendered, takes resources away from normal recreation programs. This also has a negative effect on staff morale. If these types of services to community organizations are to be provided by the recreation agency they should be included in agency objectives and funds provided for them in the agency budget. Services should be restricted to those recreation in nature and care should be taken that the public agency is in a position to provide the same services to all alike.

Program goals may be defined as design plans or courses of action to reach an ultimate end (agency purpose). They involve long range actions and may never be reached completely, because they may be changed with time and progress. For instance, a recreation goal might be "to enrich the lives of individuals and provide a better community environment in which to live." It is long range and perhaps not attainable because individuals can continue to progress and recreation programs can continue to enrich by progressively raising their standards. The stopping point is indefinite. Likewise, there is no definite stopping point for "better community environment."

Program objectives are short range, attainable ends leading towards ultimate goals. Goals are especially meaningful to the executive and policy makers while specific attainable objectives are more meaningful to staff, participant, and the community.

Suggested Program Goals and Objectives

The general purposes, goals and objectives of the agency, legal authority, and legal limitations suggest to some extent the areas to which the program goals and objectives can be directed. Since "recreation for all" is the basic function of the public recreation agency, the program goals may be, in effect, a statement of purposes of the agency, except in situations where the agency has responsibilities in addition to recreation functions (street trees, coliseum, cemeteries). The different levels of government, or units of government, will have different program goals and objectives.

The federal government may emphasize operation of areas and facilities for agency personnel and their families; visitor use of public areas and facilities; research, preparation, and distribution of information; and allocation of funds to federal, state and local agencies. State governments may emphasize programs similar to federal governments but increasingly are adding advisory services to assist state and local recreation agencies with their recreation problems such as setting up new programs and developing staff. Local agencies provide a multiplicity of recreation programs, facilities and services for citizens, visitors, special groups such as the handicapped, and in special settings such as hospitals and institutions.

The suggested goals might be to:

- Provide recreation opportunities for all of the people all of the time, or
- Provide a constructive leisure time outlet for the maximum number of all segments of population, or provide recreation areas, facilities, program opportunities the year around for all citizens and visitors.

The goals would be supplemented by specific objectives such as to:

— Provide a wide variety of recreation opportunities in different types of activities (arts and crafts, dance, drama, games, music, nature) for all age groups and both sexes.
— Provide opportunities for individual self-expression as well as opportunities for participation in group activities at progressive levels of skills.
— Provide activities for participation of the entire family, either as a unit or as individual members, or both.
— Provide programs for all seasons of the year, indoor and outdoor.
— Develop recreation programs around leisure time needs and interests on neighborhood as well as city-wide levels.
— Provide activities that will carry over into adulthood interests.
— Make maximum use of community resources. Involve neighborhood groups and individuals as much as possible.
— Balance every day pursuits of the individual, providing opportunities for developing leadership, with emphasis on "growth and development" of the individual and group.
— Provide a broad leisure time program where the major groupings of recreation activities are developed, correlated and adapted to the needs of participants under qualified leadership.
— Extend old interests and develop new interests.
— Provide general and special recreation areas and facilities conveniently available to all areas of population according to accepted national standards.
— Provide for special population needs for groups such as the handicapped and senior citizens.
— Integrate the leisure time programs into the community life, established activities, interests, and future planning of the neighborhood and locality.
— Provide cultural, passive and creative activities as well as those more physical in nature.
— Provide for different periods of time to serve the needs of people when they have free time.
— Provide for self sustaining, self directed groups.

Some of the objectives which relate to by-products of recreation may be:

— To develop body and mind through physical, mental, educational, and creative activities.
— To develop personal qualities, citizenship and respect for self and others through group associations, leadership, and satisfying recreational activities.
— To develop social graces and strengthen family relationships through family participation and group activity programs.
— To help individuals find themselves by exposing them to a variety of interesting recreation experiences which may lead to an interest in a vocation, avocation, or lifetime hobby and better living.

Participant Motivation

About the best motivation for continuing participation is the satisfaction the individual gets from the activity. Individuals have a strong tendency to pursue recreational activities with which they are somewhat familiar. For example, most people are familiar with sports and games, either as participants or as spectators. It is generally easier, therefore, to stimulate interest in sports than in any other major grouping of recreation activities. Recreation interests (drama, music, dance, crafts, sports, nature) learned and promoted in the local schools carry over into recreation interests outside the school and are also easier to organize in the recreation program.

In planning recreation programs, the professional not only considers the usual types of facilities and programs, but also the people's desires and motivations one of which is the satisfaction individuals get from participation. The more satisfying recreation activities involve achievement of some kind such as creating something, developing a skill, making a friend, discovering a new idea, learning, having a new and interesting experience, exercising one's emotions, relaxing, witnessing something beautiful, improving one's confidence, earning recognition, winning a championship, gaining prestige, overcoming a weakness, helping others, or becoming a leader.

It is through recreational activities in pleasant environments that individuals with opposing views, different backgrounds, education and cultural differences find a common interest, respect for each other, a means of communication and understanding, a sense of achievement, and a feeling of satisfaction, a contributing factor to happiness. The recreation professional knows the purpose of each game or recreational activity, the effects each is supposed to have on participants, and he earns his standing as a professional by his ability to fit together appropriate recreational activities, facilities, leadership resources, and human personalities which have needs for particular services in particular ways which are satisfying to them. Experience has proven that the satisfaction from achievement, learning, improving, gaining prestige, being wanted and needed, and recognition in addition to fun are major motivators for continued recreation participation.

PROGRAM PLANNING AND SCHEDULING

The program is the end product of recreation and the means for attaining recreation goals and objectives. From the administrator's point of view, all programs are directed towards reaching the goals of the agency. The rate of progress depends greatly upon the initiative and progressiveness of leadership, including the skill and initiative of the executive, plus the resources the locality makes available to them. However, lack of certain resources could have a wholesome effect on the program and the recreation professional for it creates a challenge to improvise ways of supplementing agency resources. This includes developing volunteers for leadership and fund raising for special projects, developing nature activities to the fullest including the converting of natural materials into attractive craft projects, improvising instruments for rhythm bands and toy orchestras, and emphasizing uses of whatever is available in the community such as using old clothes from the attic and props for plays and dramatic productions. This is an example of recreation leadership and community involvement that emphasizes several principles of recreation and is a real asset to good program development, particularly in smaller communities.

With an expanding leisure and the ever changing needs of people, considerable emphasis in planning is placed on flexibility and future opportunities for changes, expansion, and adjustments.

Program planning involves all the facilities, activities, and services which the agency proposes to provide and use. It is based largely on recreational interests of the people, unmet needs of the population, anticipated future needs, the quality and scope of services to be rendered, the amount of resources (leadership, areas, facilities, budget, community involvement) the locality expects to put into its recreation program, and, of course, the agency purpose, guidelines, goals, and objectives.

Program Planning

Program planning is the formation of a method, design, or mode of action that leads towards attainment of objectives and goals. It not only considers the present but also extends into future years. The plans must relate to the locality's financial resources. Before attempting to prepare a plan, the planner determines community needs, has available all of the necessary facts, and has a rough outline of pertinent subjects to be included as well as agency goals and guidelines.

The steps in program planning include (1) determining aims and objectives as described above; (2) determining needs of individuals and groups; (3) evaluating resources (budget, staff, facilities) available to the agency in terms of objectives, existing services, adjustments, areas of expansion, and priorities; (4) determining sites, quality and scope of services; (5) selecting balanced program to serve needs in line with principles of program planning.

The "determining of aims and objectives" was discussed early in the chapter under "goals and objectives."

Determining the Needs. The recreation needs of families, neighborhoods, and communities vary greatly and change from time to time. Therefore, it is imperative that the planners and administrators continuously strive to keep up-to-date on needs and bring about necessary adjustments in the program. A certain amount of information is obtained from staff passing on ideas from their contacts with participants and community leaders, from reports, news media and normal contacts with advisory boards, community organizations, meetings, and socials but this is not enough. Recreation is for the total population and as much of the total population as practical should be involved in planning. City-wide advisory boards appointed by the governing body and neighborhood and youth advisory councils organized by the agency are used to advise staff on needs, but some residents do not come in contact with them either; therefore, contacts are made with the planning commission, community councils and agencies, parent-teachers associations, Chamber of Commerce, special interest groups, community action groups, youth commissions, youth councils, commissions on aged and others for further information.

Sometimes recreation surveys are made of school homerooms or of participants at recreation areas but these may not reach school drop-outs or those that do not attend public recreation areas regularly. The use of check lists where people may indicate their interests is sometimes used to determine interests. The U.S. Census report provides information on items such as age and economic conditions. School surveys may provide helpful information on child population. Information is considered on existing and proposed services, facilities and locations of other recreation and recreation-related agencies such as private, semi-private (including The United Way funded agencies), recreation clubs and membership associations, hobby and special interest groups, residential development complexes, and commercial recreation. Some information on needs comes directly from the participants to staff and headquarters office. Day-to-day observations plus a summary of findings from the community contacts give the experienced program planner a very good insight into the needs and interests of the population.

Evaluating the Resources. Program evaluations are generally made once a year, usually at budget time, or at the end of a completed program while impressions are fresh, then held for later use. Invariably program requests and needs are greater than the available resources. Also, invariably, there are program activities that can be strengthened, completed or replaced. There are, also, requests that do not have enough participants to justify costs, requests that are not within policy and functions of the agency, or requests for skills in leadership and facilities that cannot be made available within resources. They, of course, are eliminated or delayed to more favorable times.

Resources available to the agency are staff, areas and facilities, and budget which determines the limits of agency provided services. These may be supplemented by volunteers, donations, sponsored activities, self-supporting and self-directed activities, and rentals which may provide for extension of programs considerably.

Recreation workers are selected on the basis of funds available and the specific skills needed to conduct the program activities proposed. The matter of costs, available skills for instruction, and adequate number of enrollees often determines whether a specific activity can be provided. Sometimes an individual, or committee of interested individuals, will organize an interest group, or help the staff locate and organize into a group, individuals with common interests.

Self-directed, self-supporting groups have a place in the total recreation plan and should be considered in allocation of available time and space. The self-directed groups generally require a minimum of agency resources and are often emphasized when leadership and agency resources are limited.

Determining Sites, Quality and Scope of Services. Most public recreation agencies operate programs at more than one site, usually to serve different neighborhoods and different needs. Large organizations may provide as many as 300 or more different recreational activities. Not all of them will be provided or needed at a single site. Some may be suitable for winter and indoor use and others may be suitable for spring, summer or fall and outdoor use. Some programs may be operated full time, some part time. Most systems are operated year round, but some only seasonally. The information on needs will indicate where interests are and when the most people have free time. The program planner then will determine the most appropriate times and sites for the activities.

The quality and scope of services are determined largely by availability of funds, staff with necessary skills, and appropriate facilities. Very often, especially with adults, the group is self-directing and self-supporting. In such instances, individuals furnish their own materials and share the cost of an instructor by collecting dues or dividing the costs among the members. These types of groups are often used to expand the scope of the program.

SELECTING BALANCED RECREATION PROGRAM. A balanced recreation program includes a cross section of recreation opportunities at progressive levels of skills from the several program categories for both sexes, all ages, special interest groups, and special settings. This would involve a variety of activities in arts and crafts, dance, drama, music, games and sports, nature, special events, miscellaneous features and their supportive activities which make up the work programs. Every planner uses guidelines and standards for the total recreation system. This does not mean that programs in each neighborhood should be standardized. Indeed not, because programs may be as different as the recreation habits of the people that make up the neighborhoods. In program planning, the guidelines are stated in the agency purpose, policies, goals, planning principles, and program objectives.

Factors to Consider in Planning Programs

Certain factors (interests, age, sex, time, place, degree of skill, purpose) which were mentioned in a general way in the statements of program objectives become major considerations in selecting specific activities for a balanced recreation program.

A sound recreation program must be developed around the *interests* of individuals and groups to be served. Usually children, eager to learn, can be interested in a wide range of activities. Youth, particularly older youth, and young adults, make up a large portion of the public recreation attendance especially in team games, organized groups, and social activities. Older adults and senior citizens have broad interests but tend to patronize the individual sports, educational subjects, passive and spectator activities. Adults express more interest in activities in which they have had experience or those that serve a personal need at the time.

Capabilities and interests of the individual vary considerably with *age* and even with individuals the same age, particularly in sports and physical activities. Yet physical activities and games have a natural appeal to the growing child. Interest span of younger children may be short. Then children like to go from one activity to another, therefore, a variety of activities at different levels of skills and equipment is needed for each age group. After age 65, or retirement, many individuals continue in normal mixed age activities but many, also, like to be with their own age groups for their recreation. This brings about the need for senior citizen groups.

Sex differences still are a consideration in planning sports and forms of recreation involving physical ability, but are not of the same importance in other activities as they were a few years ago. Boys and girls under ten years of age are nearly alike in physical abilities and can participate together in the same activities.

Time is a significant factor in determining when most activities are planned. The free time of the participants must be taken into consideration. For instance, children are free after school hours in the afternoon, weekends, and holidays and non-working mothers are available for programs during mornings and early afternoons while the children are in school. Holiday and special day features have more meaning on or near the special day.

Place and space required for different activities vary from a quiet nook to read a book to a mountain range ski jump. Lack of space (indoors or outdoors) eliminates or restricts many recreation activities, but sometimes an imaginative staff can adapt the activity to a "mini-version." Program planning requires knowledge of space requirements, safety factors both for participants and spectators, and ancillary needs for each activity; also when, where, and under what conditions the best results can be obtained. A suitable place in pleasant surroundings contributes much towards the success of the activity.

Distracting noises interfere seriously with effectiveness of dramatic productions, story telling, most musical programs, senior citizen activities, listening and discussion groups, or any other similar kind of event. This makes it necessary to arrange areas and facilities so quiet activities can be grouped together, and physical, noisy, action-type activities can be grouped with an appropriate buffer space or activity between them.

Effective planning includes the fitting of activities to the *skills* and abilities of prospective participants and providing opportunities for all age groupings to progress to higher levels of skills. It is particularly important in competitive sports to match teams and individuals with others who have equal or near equal abilities, for greater satisfaction both to the participant and to the spectator. Close competition is a strong motivator in sports.

The general recreationist is prepared to provide for the normal range of individual interests. Specialized service groups such as nursery ages, and physically and mentally handicapped are better served by specialists trained and experienced in the specialty and conducted in facilities that are properly equipped for the purpose.

Other factors to consider in program planning include *characteristics of the neighborhood* which the program serves such as economic status, culture, education, nationality groups, how residents make a living, and community efforts. For instance, activities which appeal to a college community may not arouse the interest of those in a mill area.

The size of the group is a concern of planning. In pre-school groups where individuals require considerable attention, the group is small, usually less than ten. In some arts and crafts, musical, drama, and dance groups, and athletic teams which require considerable instruction, the organized groups are planned to be small, perhaps under twelve. Most groups may be expected to average 20 to 35 and more.

Scheduling

Scheduling means coordination of location, time, dates, leadership, and activities. Programs may be based on two major periods of time, namely summer and winter, with summer programs emphasizing outdoor, nature, and informal activities and winter programs emphasizing indoor, instructional and more highly organized activities. In warmer climates, however, programs may be scheduled on basis of the four seasons: spring, summer, fall and winter with spring and fall being transition periods with emphasis on outdoor activities. Often the spring and fall outdoor programs are planned part time to avoid conflicts with school schedules and use of school facilities when they are used for recreation purposes.

Factors to be considered in making up schedules for municipal recreation programs include:

1. *Nature of the activity:* quiet, educational, informally or formally organized, regular or special, single activity or competitive.
2. *Facilities available:* outdoor or indoor, regular or specialized, self directing or supervised, participant oriented or spectator oriented, seasonal or year-round, lighted or unlighted.
3. *Staff available:* supervised or self-directed, routine or highly skilled, professional or volunteer. Are staff or volunteers available who have required skills?
4. *Funds available:* self-sustaining or supervised, free or fee. Are adequate funds available for supervision, maintenance, equipment, supplies, transportation?
5. *Characteristics of participants:* age, sex, level of skill, health condition, normal or handicapped.
6. *Time requirement:* length of period required for the activity and how often, what time period (morning, afternoon, evening).

There is a tendency to provide supervised recreation seven days a week. The periods are often divided into three-hour sessions such as 9:00 A.M. to 12:00 noon (except Sunday); 2:00 to 5:00 P.M.; 6:30 to 9:30 P.M. (or 7:00 to 10:00). It is well to give the staff a break at least every three hours.

Time should be provided for free play, practicing skills, and group instruction such as sports clinics, swimming and life saving classes. Often the mornings are used for group instruction. In warmer climates free play, swimming or the less strenuous activities are scheduled in summer during the hot part of the day—12:00 to 4:00 P.M.

Most departments organize their recreation programs within the usual time periods—daily, weekly, monthly, seasonally, and yearly. Usually programs are expanded during the summer months when children are out of school. In planning outdoor programs it is well to include several "rainy day" programs that can be conducted indoors in event of inclement weather.

The daily schedule should provide something for each age group (both sexes) to do. If staff and space are available, a variety of activities (both active and quiet) may be scheduled for each age group. Different levels of skills may be scheduled on alternate days. The skilled group often enjoys helping the beginner group. It is well to have an interest activity such as a contest, preliminaries of a tournament, or competitive sport to provide a climax of interest; also an activity that leads up to a weekly interest climax like finals in a tournament, or crafts for exhibit, or play practice for a later special event to tie interests together. Daily schedules will vary with needs of the participants and skills of staff, but the format might be adapted from the following multiple choice ideas.

1. Opening ceremony, raising of flag, playing a patriotic recording
   Clean up
   Inspection of area and equipment for safety
   Brief discussion of plans and schedules for the day
2. Organized sport instruction (baseball, tennis, basketball)
   Beginners swimming
   Badminton instruction
   Story telling
   Crafts class, play practice, dancing, music
3. Life saving instruction or water safety instruction
   Preliminaries for tournament (paddle tennis, horseshoes, shuffleboard)
4. Free time, improving skills, informal play
5. Team games, league play (softball, baseball, basketball, football, tennis, hockey, soccer), etc.

6. Nature activity (gardening, nature craft, hiking, outing)
7. Game tournament, final playoff, puppet show
8. Practice for special event
9. Free time
   Clean-up
   Flag lowering ceremony
   Check in equipment, report any unsafe condition
   Meeting of junior volunteers
   Announce plans for next day

A number of groups and classes would be conducted at the same time if there are sufficient staff.

The weekly schedule would be a series of daily schedules plus a staff meeting perhaps at the beginning of the week and one or more special features like a movie, a play, a social, special program, a hike, or major contest or tournament perhaps at the end of the week. It provides for a diversity of activities scheduled one, two or three times per week. There may be a theme for the week which may emphasize a phase of the theme for the season.

The monthly schedule would add a special event, a bigger special feature, play day, family day, holiday celebration, track meet, watermelon feast, bicycle rodeo, pet show or similar activity.

The seasonal schedule would add the final play-offs for leagues and tournament, major seasonal closing program and exhibit showing cross-section of accomplishments for the season coordinated into a major special event like neighborhood fair, arctic carnival, harvest festival, pageant, or anniversary program. The seasonal program highlights the activities for the season and provides for different levels of skills in each activity culminating in a special event program. A theme for the summer is often used to stimulate imagination and initiative and broaden interest.

The yearly schedule takes into consideration community events that might affect the recreation activities such as opening and closing of schools, holidays, major church activities like vacation bible schools, religious holidays, summer school, community celebration or activities like county or state fairs, historic events, seasonal changes in program and major special events. It serves as a master calendar.

Program Policies and Procedures

Policies are used as guidelines to provide equal consideration of matters of like circumstances and faster decision making. Suggested program policy statements might state that the public recreation agency:

1. Coordinates and cooperates with, but does not attempt to duplicate or compete with local efforts. The programs should be planned to obtain fullest cooperation of public and private agencies. It co-operates with private agencies in sponsoring short-term projects of benefit to the community.
2. Promotes and conducts programs at specified public locations where the public feels free to go such as parks, public school facilities, and recreation centers.
3. Organizes and promotes recreation activities during hours when majority of people have leisure time.
4. Provides programs which are generally open to the public free of charge. The agency may conduct some activities where charges are made. Clubs sometimes charge their own members club dues. Private, semi-private and non-profit organizations such as special interest clubs, Boy Scouts, Girl Scouts, bridge clubs, garden clubs and other groups recreational in nature may use public facilities if the use does not interfere with regular agency-sponsored activities. Paid recreation personnel may not be permitted to direct activities of private clubs, groups or organizations which are governed by policies of other agencies even though the particular organization may conduct meetings at the public facility. Agency leaders may assist with their recreation activities, if it does not interrupt regular city-sponsored programs. Members of all groups may be invited to join activities at a recreation center.
5. Promotes health and safety. Activities such as boxing, wrestling, weight lifting, football, and track require parents' written consent, a physical examination by a doctor approved by the agency, safe and proper equipment and facilities approved by the agency, and qualified and adequately trained personnel.
6. Provides facilities, equipment, program materials and supplies for group activities which are sponsored by the agency. Supplies and materials used by the individual such as tennis balls, racquets, handcrafts projects, uniforms, and baseball gloves usually are provided by the participant. Tools and certain materials used for instruction and demonstration purposes only often are provided by the agency.
7. Organizes an advisory council composed of five or more interested representative citizens of the neighborhood to assist in planning and developing the programs for each community center or playground.

CLASSIFICATION OF RECREATION ACTIVITIES

Classification of activities is used by the executive and the planner as a guideline in selecting a balanced program of activities and in satisfying different needs of participants. Each class of recreation activity serves a particular purpose or provides a specific type of satisfaction and pleasure to the participant.

Recreation activities may be classified in several ways such as indoor and outdoor; age or sex of the participants taking part; individual or group; mental or physical; active or passive; participant or spectator. The most common classification is by types such as arts and crafts, dance, drama, music and rhythm, nature and outings, sports and games, educational, service, special events, and miscellaneous. Some recreationists add other classifications such as socials, hobbies, contests, and tournaments. More careful analysis, however, shows these classes could be included within the 10 classifications listed above. Socials could be dancing, games, nature or an outing. A hobby could be drama, music, nature, dance, sports, arts and crafts, or an educational endeavor. A contest or tournament could be held in sports, games, drama, music, or dance. The 10 classifications are adequate. Some agencies reduce the classes to eight supervised types including educational and service classes under miscellaneous grouping. Each classification may be divided into sub-units.

The 10 classifications are briefly discussed below. The suggested activities under each class are listed in Appendix I.

1. *The arts and crafts* category provides opportunities to develop the creative interests of individuals. It offers the satisfaction of making and completing something, which often leads to a lifetime hobby or avocation. It provides for individual as well as group expression.
2. *Dance,* in various forms, provides opportunities for expression of natural movements and rhythm of the body; develops coordination, grace, and beauty through movement. It is a means of expressing emotional and physical feeling, and is used for social development.
3. *Drama* is a means of communicating through voice, action and emotions. It stimulates imagination, creativity, and is often used by recreationists to bring out the timid and teach impressive lessons of conduct, improve poise, memory, and conversation.
4. *Music and rhythm* provides a variety of opportunities for the individual, group, and spectator to express emotions and natural rhythm through voice, instrument, or ear. It provides a universal means of

communication and is applicable to all age groups in some form. Almost everyone enjoys and participates in music in some way.

5. *The nature and outings* category usually applies to activities out-of-doors involving nature in some form (wildlife, plants, animals, birds, products of land, water and air). Particularly important is to counteract man-made environment of brick, steel and concrete of the urban areas, and to stimulate the emotions of love, beauty, and appreciation of living things as they relate to human lives.
6. *Sports and games* are for the development of the body, coordination, health, teamwork, cooperation, obedience to rules, general self-improvement, and character building. Activities include individual, group, and spectator participation both in competitive and non-competitive forms.
7. *The educational category* (not included elsewhere) is for mind development and information. Every experience is educational to some degree even though it may be incidental and not a direct objective in the activity performed. Learning may be formal or informal, individual or group situation, short or long range. Activities in this category emphasize learning and information aspects such as reading, lectures, and research.
8. *Services* performed for others develops satisfaction of giving, helping, being wanted, and being needed. This category includes volunteering, supportive activities such as serving as hosts, officials, judges, and leadership, and serving on committees and boards.
9. *Special events* may include combinations of activities in regular program categories, but they are used to add "spice" to the program and serve as a major climax of interest. They broaden interests of participants and attract new enrollees. They serve as a means of stimulating research. Further, they aid in the discovery of new talents, develop imagination and unity of purpose, promote understanding between groups, and foster loyalty at the location. Lastly, they promote good human relations. A good special event combines activities of two or more major program categories to form a different and exciting exhibition type of event entertaining the participants and spectators. They basically emphasize achievements of the program over a period of time or talents discovered and may include exhibits of items made or collected, demonstrations of skills learned or talents developed, performing arts, athletic contests, live demonstrations of activities programmed, spectator participation, and social events. These and other ideas may be worked into a central theme representing the activities learned at the center or

playground such as a hobby show, neighborhood fair, or space exploration.

10. *Miscellaneous* includes activities that do not fit into other categories such as father and son banquet, family reunion, or trip to a national shrine.

Special Features

These are special treatments of some of the activities in an existing category like a contest, tournament, display, banquet for athletic team, hike, picnic, outing or trip. It is distinguished from a special event because it generally involves one activity or a single program category.

Leadership

The minimum staff for a program location for boys and girls is one female instructor and one male instructor. If a general location justifies only one staff member, it is suggested it be a female because females generally seem to be more acceptable to the neighborhood in dealing with small children, girls and washroom problems.

PROGRAM ORGANIZATION

Program is the vital element in a public recreation agency. Administration, maintenance, planning, personnel, and facilities are important adjuncts to the recreation program, but it is the program that has most exposure and meaning to the using public. All functions should center around and support the program. Emphasis is on organization and leadership; organization to group and coordinate requests, activities and services and set priorities; leadership to fit physical and human resources into priorities and provide continuing direction. Program organization involves development of many different activities and services into a combined program schedule which will serve all segments of the population.

Factors to Be Considered in Organization

Individuals participate in recreation voluntarily. Opportunities are provided and they make their own choice of activities. They may attend or leave when they wish. They enjoy complete freedom of choice and tend to resist regimentation and domination by others, including staff. Program is not an arbitrary plan imposed on participants by staff, but it is planned and developed in response to needs and participant involvement. The participant expresses the need or interest. The recreation professional knows how to bring about satisfying results. In so doing he considers (1) basic needs; (2) available resources (staff, facilities, equipment); (3) balance of opportunities; (4) potential of individuals and level of their skills; (5) how often the group should meet; (6) time period the group should meet; (7) how the activity relates to other activities; (8) the number of individuals enrolled (does it meet minimum agency requirements); (9) essential criteria and guidelines of the agency; (10) age interest; (11) priorities; (12) size of group; (13) opportunities for growth; (14) self directed or supervised; (15) amount of supervision needed; (16) relative importance of the activity; (17) amount of patron involvement; (18) indoor or outdoor; (19) whether similar activities are already scheduled; and (20) opportunities for development and expansion.

It is inadvisable to plan the same program for all locations alike because the needs, interests, leisure time habits, staff, and facilities are not the same. The program for the week, or month if possible, should be posted in a convenient place so all may see it. Suggestions should be welcomed. The director, staff and interested individuals should promote interest in planned activities continuously. This would include announcements on bulletin board, posters in places of interest in neighborhood, and fliers for participants to take home or to distribute in the neighborhood.

OTHER AND SUPPORTING PROGRAM SERVICES

Although program is the end product of a recreation agency, other, less important elements are involved such as rules, transportation, permission of parents, medical examination, personal contacts, awards and prizes, sponsorships and costumes.

Rules and Regulations

Recreation is most effective in a relaxed and tension free situation where freedom of choice and flexibility may be practiced to the fullest, however, there are some who need some guidance. A minimum of rules and regulations needs to be established and equitably enforced in order to provide order and the most effective service and maximum program opportunities. The more rules that are provided the more staff effort will be involved in enforcing them and the less effort will be left to put into program direction. The minimum of rules should be established with participant involvement to provide for *safety* of people, the *protection* of properties, and the fair and orderly use of facilities. It is advisable for the governing body to adopt into law all rules involving control of the public use of facilities. Examples of safety rules might be dogs in parks and playgrounds must be on leashes, no discharge of firearms or projectiles (arrows), no hitting of baseballs or golf balls except in places designated for the purpose by the director. Examples of rules that protect property might be no walking on surfaced tennis courts with track or baseball shoes; no walking, riding, or driving on wet clay tennis courts, and ball diamonds; and tennis or gym shoes required on tennis courts and gymnasium floors.

Transportation

Because of liability involved, commercial transportation or properly insured agency owned vehicles are generally used to transport participants. For the same reason, it is recommended that private cars or personally owned staff cars not be used for transporting participants unless proper insurance and safety precautions are taken. The insurance premium on private cars is considerably higher when the car is used for transporting participants and in some states is subject to cancellation unless appropriate policies are acquired. Sometimes bus tokens are provided for participants. There is increasing public pressure for agencies to provide transportation to and from recreation areas similar to the practice in public school. There is also a movement to amend laws so public school buses can be used for recreation purposes.

Intermural competition, primarily sports leagues, creates serious problems of transportation both for staff and participants. An instructor is expected to travel with them. This leaves his home center without his services during the time he is absent with a team or a substitute must be provided to work at the home grounds. It is not very practical to have the substitute go with the team unless he is also coaching the team. Considering the cost of employing a substitute plus travel expenses, it is difficult to justify the high cost per participant in the usually limited recreation budget. It would be well if a dedicated dependable volunteer would coach and travel with the team. However, the problems of dependable transportation would still exist. Unless transportation is provided, youngsters tend not to keep appointments and games are forfeited. This causes, not only the participants on the individual team to lose interest but also affects adversely all other teams in the league. It is recommended not to participate in intermural leagues unless dependable transportation and supervision (paid or volunteer) can be provided. An alternative is intramural competition at the home grounds with the winning team in each age grouping progressing to the district and citywide championship tournaments.

Permission of Parents

Every recreation agency has occasions to take participants out of the neighborhood (on trips, picnics, sports competition, education tours) or to participate in agency programs where there is physical strain (track, football, boxing, wrestling). In order to participate it is common practice to require a signed statement of approval from the parent (or guardian) of a minor. This helps the parent to know what the child is doing, indicates interest of the agency in the health and welfare of the child and sometimes is a means of discovering health conditions that should be considered. Although the agency cannot sign away its legal responsibilities nor can parents sign away the legal rights of their children, signed permissions do help public relations and minimize the potentials for legal claims.

Medical Examinations

In order to safeguard the individual's health, reduce possibility of injury, and protect the agency against unusual health weaknesses, it is well to require a medical examination and declaration of physical fitness by a competent medical authority in addition to parents consent before persons are permitted to participate in activities involving physical strain (boxing, wrestling, track, football) or where the individual leaves home for a period of days such as in camping, canoe trips and tours. These examinations may be performed by the individual's family doctor, health clinics, or volunteer physician approved or arranged by the agency.

Personal Contacts

It is very helpful and good public relations to follow up with a personal contact or visit in the home in some instances such as injuries, accidents, hospitalizations, deaths, illnesses, misunderstandings, outstanding honors or awards, weddings, or if there are any unusual situations related to recreation or welfare of individual and neighborhood. A friendly note or telephone call would be appropriate for congratulatory, recognition, inquiries, and positive matters but a personal follow-up visit should be made to the home of one injured on recreation area, accidents and serious or long term illnesses of participants. Follow-up of serious misconduct, misunderstandings, discipline matters such as suspensions, could well be discussed in the privacy of the office.

Awards and Prizes

The strength of recreation is in doing. It is voluntary and should not identify with monetary benefits for the individual. It emphasizes participants' growth and development rather than winning and prizes. Giving of awards, trophies, or prizes of material value puts emphasis on winning, favors the best players, tends to discourage general participation, and raises questions concerning legal use of tax money for the purpose. Participants do like recognition and something to show "he is a winner." Public agencies, therefore, usually give no prizes or awards of material value, but instead they give ribbons or certificates which have no value except as recognition to the recipient. Sometimes plaques, cups or banners are given teams and groups. However, it is a common practice to include in the franchise fee of organized leagues a small amount for trophies or appropriate awards for the winning teams. In this way the sponsor or the individuals (not the public agency) pay for their own trophies. Sometimes a sporting goods firm or local business will donate a trophy.

Sponsorships

Business firms, industrial organizations, churches, civic clubs, special interest groups and similar organizations sponsor and pay for the operating expenses (uniforms, balls, equipment, officials) of organized teams which participate in public leagues and use public facilities. This is the way most adult leagues are financed. Businesses, hobby, and special interest groups also regularly sponsor other recreational activities, campers, tournaments, tennis instruction, banquets, outings, special days, performing arts events, and similar activities which are directed by the agency staff or volunteers and under agency rules, regulations, and direction. Sponsored programs which have little cost to the agency add quantity and often quality and variety to the overall program. Agency budgets which are made up once a year do not provide for unforeseen needs that may develop during the budget year. Sponsors often make a donation to assume the costs of the activities of special interest to them and the agency.

Costumes

A system with a good drama program is almost obliged to have a costume unit. Many costumes can be improvised by altering, adding to or combining old clothes from the attic. Others can be made of *flame proof* paper or inexpensive cloth. Others can be rented from costume rental concerns but these are usually too costly for playground and casual use. It is very helpful to have basic costumes but it takes a person to care for them, keep them clean and sanitary, and direct the service. A good costume reserve can be built up over the years by saving donations from store displays, cleaning out attics, saving costumes from previous events, and donations of unsold clothing from stores. The agency should avoid competing with costume rental agencies and local businesses. It should, therefore, provide costumes for its own purposes and not for non-public groups and individuals.

SELF SUPPORTING GROUPS

Most recreation agencies do not have sufficient staff to use all facilities to capacity all of the time. At little or no additional expense rooms and facilities can be scheduled for use by self sustaining, private recreation groups, and non-profit organizations.

Self Sustaining Groups

One of the goals of recreation agencies is to make groups self sustaining and self directing, or provide advice, consultation and just enough staff services for them to be self sufficient. This helps spread agency resources and serves more people, usually youth or adult groups such as social, athletic, and special interest clubs; choral, music, drama, dance, and nature groups whose membership is open to the general public. Some cities may charge rent, as determined by the governing body, for semi-private use of a portion of the facility. Sometimes members in such groups provide an excellent source of volunteer leadership especially if no rent is charged.

Private Uses of Recreation Facilities

When public facilities are not in use for recreation agency-sponsored programs, private, non-profit groups which have exclusive membership are often permitted by written permit to use public recreation facilities. There is usually a small charge which is collected at the time application is made and income deposited in the general treasury. Groups sometimes employ, at their own expense, private teachers to give special instruction to their membership. Care should be taken to prevent commercialization and exploitation of public facilities for private gain.

It is questionable, without council approval, if public recreation administrators legally can permit private non-recreation uses of public recreation facilities. Decisions vary from place to place, therefore, this matter should be checked out with the respective city legal department for local application. The public recreation administrator should take the position that public law intended recreation facilities and resources to be used for recreation purposes and no funds, staff, or other resources should be expended for non-recreation activities. Some local governments permit civic and non-profit community organizations to use vacant space in school or community centers when there is no cost to the government and its use does not interfere with uses for recreation purposes.

INVOLVING THE COMMUNITY

A public recreation program is so broad, so diversified, and includes so many kinds of interests and activities the recreationist needs to involve the community in all aspects of planning, decision making, policy making, program and facility development at all levels of management in order to bring about meaningful and effective programs. At the executive level, a representative advisory board of 9 to 15 interested lay citizens and ex-officio agency heads advises the director on matters of policy and major plans. At the neighborhood level, likewise, a representative playground or center advisory council of 5 to 15 interested neighborhood laymen, including youth and participants, advises the playground or center director on program needs, interests of the different age groups, best hours of operation, handles fund raising projects, provides volunteer help and generally promotes the activities of the center.

The advisory council may be supplemented at each location by a youth advisory council composed of 5 to 15 boys and girls of varying ages to advise the center director on programs and items of interest to youth. A boy and girl from the youth council should be members of the center advisory council. City-wide special interest committees could be organized to assist in planning, promoting, and assisting with city-wide special events like a Christmas pageant or historical pageant or with city-wide programs such as activities for senior citizens, the mentally and physically handicapped and similar programs. It is recommended that the laymen and participants be involved in policy making, program planning and services, promotion, facility development and other items affecting them at every opportunity possible.

MATERIALS, SUPPLIES, AND EQUIPMENT

An active recreation schedule of program activities requires a considerable variety of materials, supplies, and equipment and occasional replacements. *Supplies* are items consumed and become a part of something in maintenance and operations such as building, office, janitor and program supplies (paint, nails, writing paper). *Materials* are items that may be formed or reshaped to make useful objects and usually do not lose their identity such as wood, plastics, clay, metal and crafts. Both materials and supplies are expendable. *Equipment* are more durable items expected to last at least one season such as uniforms, tennis racquets, baseball gloves, mitts, tables, chairs, benches, and protective items and tools. The agency usually furnishes supplies and materials for children's activities, instruction, and demonstrations. Great emphasis is placed on the use of natural and salvage materials. There is a tendency to expect adult groups to be self-sustaining and self-directing.

Control and inventory of materials and supplies is generally a problem. Procedures vary. Some agencies have central warehouse and storage. Others are decentralized. The preferred system is the central storage with perpetual inventory by locations. Supplies, materials and equipment are provided and inventoried at beginning and end of season for seasonally operated locations and perpetually for year round locations. Permanent records by locations are maintained. Replacements are made by requisitions approved by the supervisor. Staff is expected to account satisfactorily for all items. Items used only occasionally may be checked out on loan and returned. One of the responsibilities of supervision is to check periodically the use of materials and supplies and inventory the condition of equipment.

Questions for Discussion

1. What guidelines are used in program planning?
2. What services should a public recreation program include?
3. Explain the steps in building a comprehensive program.
4. What are the basic recreation needs of individuals?
5. What makes up a balanced recreation program?
6. What are the principles of program planning?
7. How are program goals and objectives determined?
8. What factors are considered in preparing a program schedule?
9. What are the purposes of the special event?
10. What is the difference between a special event and a special feature?

Short Problems

1. Prepare a balanced weekly program schedule for a community center with 5 activity rooms, a gym and swimming pool for the third week in January.

2. Prepare the rules and regulations needed for the operation of a summer playground. (No indoor facilities except storage house and boys and girls restrooms.)
3. Prepare recreation program policies for a city population of 100,000.

Reference

1. Lynn S. Rodney, *Administration of Public Recreation* (New York: The Ronald Press Company, 1964), p. 193.

Selected Readings

Athletic Institute, *The Recreation Program* (rev. ed.). Chicago: the Institute, 1966.

Avedon, Elliott, *Therapeutic Recreation Service.* Englewood Cliffs, N.J.: Prentice-Hall, Inc., 1974.

Butler, George D., *Introduction to Community Recreation.* New York: McGraw-Hill Book Company, 1967.

Corbin, H. Dan, *Recreation Leadership* (3rd ed.). Englewood Cliffs, N.J.: Prentice-Hall, Inc., 1970.

Danford, Howard G., *Creative Leadership in Recreation* (rev. ed.), ed. Max Thirley. Boston: Allyn and Bacon, Inc., 1970.

Hjelte, George, and Jay S. Shivers, *Public Administration of Recreational Services,* pp. 426–465. Philadelphia: Lea and Febiger, 1972.

Kraus, J., *Nature of Art.* Englewood Cliffs, N.J.: Prentice-Hall, Inc., 1969.

Kraus, Richard G., and Joseph E. Curtis, *Creative Administration in Recreation and Parks,* pp. 204–217. St. Louis: The C.V. Mosby Company, 1973. *Manuals and guidelines.*

Ottoman, Robert W., *Music for Sight Singing.* Englewood Cliffs, N.J.: Prentice-Hall, Inc., 1965.

Shivers, Jay S., *Camping: Administration, Counseling, Programming.* New York: Appleton-Century-Crofts, Inc., 1971.

Stein, Thomas A., and Douglas H. Sessoms, *Recreation for Special Populations.* Boston: Holbrook Press, 1973.

Vinal, William, *Nature Recreation.* New York: Dover Publications, Inc., 1963.

CHAPTER 13

Financing Public Recreation and Park Agencies

Public finance is so broad and complex a subject that it may be approached from many angles. The following approaches and viewpoints involve the financing of recreation. The taxpayer and user of recreation services pay the costs in some way. The legislative body has the powers and responsibilities for determining fiscal policies (purposes, amounts, sources of revenue). The chief administrator recommends and administers general policies. The assessor determines the value of properties and maintains property records. The finance director, who is advisor and aide to the chief administrator on fiscal matters, maintains accounting and finance records, and the operating department head provides services to the public. In some agencies, particularly larger ones, a budget director (specialist) also aids the chief administrator on budget matters (revenue, operating, capital improvements). Accounting, budgeting, collecting, safeguarding and disbursing of funds, personnel, purchasing, debt and investment management, post-auditing, and projections also involve financing. This chapter will consider briefly those fiscal matters concerned with management of the operating department.

Financing is a growing concern for recreation executives because of increase in leisure time, increasing needs for expanding recreation opportunities, increased cost of operations, and difficulty finding sufficient sources of additional revenue. New and developing recreation agencies not only have to compete for tax dollars to maintain normal extension and improvements in services but also for acquisition of suitable space, construction, maintenance and operation of much needed areas and facilities. Since the early 1970's, increases in sources of revenue have not kept pace with rapidly increasing costs of government, therefore, all city services have experienced a tightening of budget, greater attention to fiscal management of department activities, improved community involvement and budgetary support. The quality and extent to which facilities and programs can be provided depends upon the amount of money the public authority makes available for recreation purposes.

FISCAL POLICY: BASIC CONSIDERATION

Fiscal policy deals with the political phases of setting standards and guidelines for public services and providing funds for implementing the programs. It involves taxation, revenues, and allocations of funds for various services and is affected by the local and general economy; public interest; availability of revenue and additional revenue sources; money expended on existing programs; priority interests; public demand for additional services; and background, attitude, knowledge of the subject, and supporting information the politician obtains.

Tremendous advancements have been made in recent years in changing attitudes of public and politicians towards providing public recreation services at all levels. Until recently, recreation was considered a personal matter and the individual was expected to use his initiative and funds to provide recreation for himself and family. Now, a person has more free time than he has work time and the average citizen does not make enough money to buy commercial recreation to occupy his free time plus that of his family. Nor does the average family in an urban setting have the space to play. Citizens, therefore, tend to look to public programs and facilities for much of their recreation. The more vocal groups may affect fiscal policy. The public has come to realize that recreation concerns the total community, therefore, recreation is a public function that should be supported by public funds.

Costs for public recreation have increased dramatically in the past decade. For example, the 1971 yearbook issue of *Parks and Recreation* magazine reported the average per capita operating expenditures for parks and recreation in 11 selected cities increased from $5.63 in 1960 to $10.96 in 1970. Some of the increase, of course, was due to inflation. However, it does show the cities almost doubled their appropriations for parks and recreation and the need for added revenue.[1] The public has demanded broader and better quality programs which has involved better leadership and new and better facilities. As urban populations spread into adjoining rural subdivisions, the county families either return to the city during their free time for recreation or cause the establishment of a county public recreation program, or both. New federal land acquisition policies and scarcity of suitable land conveniently located for urban families increased the cost of space. Costs of public recreation have increased as the American dollar has decreased in purchasing power. In spite of inflating costs and expanding recreation programs and services, citizens have demanded greater appropriations and governments at all levels have responded with increased appropriations.

The financing of public recreation by taxation is considered the most economical and practical method for providing essential recreation space, facilities, and programs for all the people. As governments approach their legal debt limits, population, costs, and needs for space and facilities continue to rise. As the sources of additional public funds dwindle, competition for the public tax dollar becomes more acute. The recreation executive, therefore, is being called on to improve efficiency of programming and fiscal management.

It is not possible in a few pages to consider fully all aspects of recreation financing, but some of the main items of concern to the executive will be discussed briefly.

Fiscal Management

Fiscal management is the administration, custody, protection, and control of all revenues received by the recreation system from all sources and properly expending funds for approved purposes. Money is the basic tool of administrative control.[2] A good business policy is to have financial matters (collections and authority for expenditures) pass through at least two persons.

The purpose of fiscal management is to handle and be responsible for all money matters (financial records, accounting, collections, protection, controls, investments, expenditures, conformance to laws and administrative directives, property inventories, debt services, and other items of value).

A special bureau, department or office of controller under the chief administrator is usually established by law to be directly responsible for all financial transactions, accounting, records and fiscal matters. Usually methods of collecting, accounting and expenditures must be approved by the authorized representative of this unit before any transaction can be completed. One reason is that the fiscal officer must certify that sufficient funds are available and the transaction meets all legal requirements. The chief administrator, therefore, can control through the director of finance (or controller) all money matters and operations of various line departments. Internal and external auditors usually check and verify the books and financial records of the finance agency, rather than those of the separate departments. However, all records are subject to and are reviewed by auditors from time to time, including use of petty cash.

Government organizations may have other fiscal officers, such as treasurer or tax collector who collects taxes, assessor who determines the value of properties for tax purposes, and auditor who sees that all funds are legally and properly accounted for.

Even though there is a central finance officer, the various line departments for purposes of internal operations and management control perform accounting functions, recording of financial transactions, collections, inventories and expenditures within the respective department. The recreation executive legally is responsible for all transactions of his agency, but he usually delegates certain responsibilities and authority to specialized staff.

Petty cash is sometimes a problem because it is for small expenditures and emergencies and not subject to as many processes of "checks and balances" as routine expenditures are. Staff tends to use petty cash, because they can buy small items promptly, can inspect what they are getting, and can select the item that suits them best. Auditors and fiscal officers feel the use of petty cash avoids procedures of "checks and balances," is often misused, and costs more because of payment of sales taxes, otherwise exempt, therefore, its use must be rigidly controlled. The following guidelines should be used:

1. Use for small purchases only in emergency.
2. Limit the amount that can be expended for an item to a reasonable figure of perhaps $10.00 or less.
3. Under no circumstances can a receipt be divided to purchase an item greater than the limit.
4. Receive approval of department fiscal officer in advance.
5. Present the receipt for reimbursement promptly.
6. Under no circumstances may petty cash be used for purposes other than those specified.
7. Permit only one person (or a minimum number) to have a petty cash account.

SOURCES OF RECREATION FUNDS

Like many public services, the values of recreation were demonstrated initially by private initiative and funded by private means in many communities before local government took them over. Private funds, to varying extents, continue to be an important source of funds for demonstrating new programs or extending old ones. Many of the present valuable parks, particularly those in the older cities, were gifts from private citizens and corporations. As populations grew, needs increased and the tax structure changed, major gifts became less frequent. Private sources could not finance a total program and government was called on to acquire, develop, operate, and maintain a variety of public recreation areas, especially in the larger urban communities. At the turn of the twentieth century a good portion of recreation for the public came from private funds. Today, except for occasional special programs, public recreation programs and facilities are supported through public sources, if we include collections of fees and charges. The sources of recreation funds are appropriations from general revenues, millage tax, special taxes, special assessment, concessions, government grants, federal revenue sharing, gifts and bequests, rents, leasebacks, sale of surpluses, fund raising events, fees and charges, sale of bonds for capital improvements, and miscellaneous such as pay telephone receipts, and permits.

Appropriation From General Revenues

The largest source of funding for public recreation is from appropriations from general revenues. At the local level, the main source of general revenue is from the property tax. Other taxes may include sales tax, taxes on personal property, machinery and tools, utility sales, prepared food, transient lodging, admissions, bank stock, personal income (pay roll tax), private franchise, and other smaller items. Other sources of general revenue may include licenses, permits, and privilege fees (business, professional, dog, vehicle, etc.); revenue from federal and state agencies (library, courts, planning, safety, welfare, health, traffic, public housing, recreation and parks, schools, flood relief, federal revenue sharing); service charges (all types of public service operations from library to airports); fines and forfeitures (library, courts, legal); miscellaneous (interest on investments, income from utility operations, rentals, fees, sale of surplus properties).

As a matter of law and public policy all general revenues, except otherwise authorized by the governing body, are collected under the direction of the chief fiscal officer or treasurer, as the case may be, and placed in a general fund. The governing body then appropriates monies from the fund to finance the various budgets on an annual basis. All monies collected by any public agency including the recreation agency, unless otherwise predetermined by law, city charter, or the governing body, must follow the same course and be authorized by the legislative body before expenditures are made. Matters of rates, salaries, fees and charges, rentals, fines, admissions, refunds, contracts committing the governing body, and all units of income and expenditures are determined and authorized by the governing body in some manner. Sometimes certain authority, with limitations, may be delegated to divisions of government such as the finance department or to individuals such as the chief executive, fiscal officer, purchasing officer, and heads of departments and agencies. The recreation executive makes studies and recommendations but refrains from setting salaries, fees, charges or handling money except as specifically authorized by government body, fiscal officer, or chief administrator.

In order to protect the taxpayer, every state has established maximum limits for local taxes but the governing body may determine the ratio at which property is assessed for tax purposes. There is a growing tendency to assess at fair market value. Some localities, particularly cities, are assessing at full market value. Rural areas tend to assess at a lower ratio of value but the tax rate is often higher. The ratio of assessed values to true values may fluctuate from one political subdivision to another. For instance, a city may assess at 100 percent of true property value and have a tax rate of $2.00 per $100, and a nearby county may assess at 25 percent of true property value and have a tax rate of $3.75 per $100.

Most revenues of local and state government are placed in the general fund; however, there may be special funds, gifts, bequests, grants, or bond funds that are earmarked for specific purposes and, therefore, are maintained in separate accounts for a specific purpose.

The Millage Tax

Some states permit localities to make a special tax levy of a few mills per dollar of assessed valuation, known as a millage tax, the income of which is earmarked for recreation purposes. It is collected by the governing body in the usual manner and placed in a special fund for recreation. This method tends to provide a dependable source of income with minimum political control, because the rate can be changed only by amendment to the charter, either by a vote of the electorate or a vote of the state legislature depending on how the respective local charter is authorized. It also has the disadvantage of being rather rigid and often does not provide for all the present recreation needs of the people. Sometimes these funds are supplemented by other funds. Only a small percentage of localities use this plan of financing. The number seems to be dwindling in favor of funding from general fund revenues.

Special Taxes

In a few places communities levy a special tax on such items as liquor, tobacco, amusements or other merchandise and earmark for recreation the income collected. The rationale being to tax less desirable forms of activities to finance the desirable forms of recreation. The cost of collecting and separating funds in this manner is higher than the cost of collecting general revenue.

Special Assessments

This plan is used for acquisition, development, and operation of recreation areas in urbanizing districts where the cost of the service is assessed against the property of those who would benefit from the project. Assessments are usually specified amounts which may create a hardship on poor families as compared to the more affluent. The cost of administering isolated assessments is high and it is difficult to grade assessment charges according to proximity to facility and relative benefits. This plan may prove successful in providing services to an area of the city that is willing to pay for the costs when it would be impossible to get a favorable vote from the total political jurisdiction on a bond issue or increase the tax rate for recreation services that would benefit only a portion of the jurisdiction.

Government Grants

After taxation, the greatest source of income for the development and operation of some local recreation and park departments is state and federal grants.

Many state youth commissions make grants to local recreation departments to provide specific programs for youth, sometimes on an established amount per capita. Likewise, many state commissions for the aging provide funds for recreation programs for older citizens.[3] Also, states provide matching funds to state and local recreation and park departments for federal Land and Water Conservation (BOR) funds for acquisition and development projects. Some states provide financial aid for planning, regional parks, crime prevention activities, recreation for the mentally and physically handicapped, and certain advisory services.

During the depression and period of unemployment following the stock market crash of 1929 the federal government through federally funded programs (WPA, NRA, CCC, and NYA) in an effort to provide employment provided personnel and some program monies for recreation projects. In many instances these demonstration projects marked the beginning of many recreation programs and provided for extension of almost all local recreation programs in operation at the time. Many local governments later took over the financing and operation of those federally funded emergency type recreation programs when federal funding was discontinued in the early part of the 1940's. In the late 1960's with inflation, increased costs, and increased financial strains, the state and particularly the federal government agencies allocated funds to provide special programs for economically and socially disadvantaged people and to add public open space, recreation and park resources. During this period local governments reported that essential expenses were rising at a much greater rate than their revenues. Some sharply cut back their less essential services and reduced personnel in order to balance budgets. Also some cities in an effort to provide new schools, recreation, anti-pollution, and other essential services borrowed for capital outlays up to their respective legal debt limits, established by law. New sources of local revenue were available only in small amounts, therefore, the only solution locally was to cut expenses and services to the level of income in order to balance the budget.

As a result, government grant programs were rapidly expanded with certain accompanying controls, minimum requirements and varying percentages of local matching funds in kind or in cash. Some states and localities prepared well for use of the grants and benefitted considerably. Some were less prepared, had difficulty with delays, deadlines, local resources, available qualified personnel and many other problems which resulted in low quality performances.

Almost every major department of the federal government sponsors grants-in-aid programs which includes the Departments of Agriculture, Commerce, Health, Education and Welfare, Housing and Urban Development, Interior, and Transportation; General Services Administration; the newer agencies of Bureau of Outdoor Recreation and Model Cities. Some examples of grant programs for recreation follow.

Department of the Interior. The Bureau of Outdoor Recreation (BOR) administers the Land and Water Conservation Fund which is allocated to states for use by states and localities to acquire open space and develop their outdoor recreation and park resources. Preference is given to land acquisition, however, grants include development of regional and district parks, wilderness areas, neighborhood parks and playgrounds, mini-parks, recreation beaches, swimming pools, marinas, golf courses, nature recreation and camping areas, campgrounds, equestrian, nature, hiking and bicycling trails. Grants generally are provided on a matching basis with state and local funds. The states have general supervision of allocations but localities, within general guidelines, have considerable freedom in planning and management as long as they are for recreation purposes. Developments must be in harmony with an approved long range state outdoor recreation plan.

Department of Housing and Urban Development. This department provides several types of grants to local governments for recreation purposes such as for multipurpose neighborhood centers, a comprehensive unit involving health, welfare, recreation, and other needed services primarily for low income families; federal neighborhood facilities program, which provides financial assistance to local governments for neighborhood youth centers, senior centers, and other buildings for recreation and recreation related purposes; and open space and urban improvements, which includes acquisition and development of land for parks, recreation areas, and facilities.

Department of Agriculture. The Department of Agriculture provides surplus foods and funds for supplemental lunches for low income participants under age 21 in organized recreation programs.

Federal Revenue Sharing

In 1972, the federal government changed its method of providing grant funds to states and localities by initiating the federal revenue sharing program. The purpose of this program was to reduce federal control and decision making functions and permit states and localities to determine how best to use federal grant funds in their respective jurisdictions.

The plan was approved on a trial basis for a period of five years at which time Congress was to make an evaluation and decide whether to modify, extend, or terminate it. State and local response to the procedure is good and it appears Congress is agreeable also and extension is expected.

Although Congress gave the states an almost free hand in administering grant funds, localities were required to confine revenue sharing funds to eight categories, namely (1) safety, (2) environmental protection, (3) public transportation, (4) health, (5) recreation, (6) libraries, (7) social services, and (8) financial administration. One third of federal revenue sharing funds was to go to the states and two thirds were to go direct to localities.

There are three procedures by which the federal government provides grant funds to states and localities which are as follows:

1. *General revenue sharing* of a general nature related to the above subjects which are made direct to localities and paid by check from the United States Treasury every three months based on a formula involving population, local tax efforts, and personal per capita income. These funds may be used for recreation purposes.
2. *Block grants* (or special revenue sharing) to states for administering, except in a few instances where cities with population of 150,000 or more may be prime sponsors and receive grants direct. Projects include law enforcement assistance, manpower training activities, and summer employment which may involve recreation related activities.

3. *Categorical grants* to states or localities. Examples are Land and Water Conservation Fund grants, and environmental protection projects such as waste water treatment and air pollution control. In some instances the states also add a percentage to federal grants on a matching basis.

Gifts or Bequests

In early stages of the recreation movement, there were many gifts and bequests of significance from private sources such as structures, parks, and playgrounds. Many public parks in older cities today were gifts, former estates, and memorials. Private sources included individuals, business firms, foundations, United Way Funds, public spirited families, clubs and organizations. Many of the gifts and bequests have been accepted with the stipulation the property would be used solely for recreation purposes. This stipulation played an important part in preserving several of the fine parks and recreation areas in use today.

In recent years, gifts from private sources represent a small proportion of funds for operation of public recreation programs; however, major industries, business firms, civic clubs, and special interest groups sponsor or give financial support to specified projects and events.

Leases and Rents

Small amounts of income may be collected from leases and rents of surplus properties or properties awaiting improvements rather than letting them remain idle.

Leasebacks

Leaseback is a procedure used occasionally whereas private resources construct facilities to agency specifications with agreement to lease it back to the government over a period of time at an annual rate to cover the cost of liquidating the investment.

Concessions

The sale of refreshments, recreation commodities, and services in some manner is almost essential in major recreation facilities. Concessions may include parking automobiles; renting boats, space at marinas, horses, bicycles, towels, swim suits, golf clubs, and various kinds of recreation equipment; amusement rides, pony rides, skating rinks; conducting tours and excursions; operating refreshment stands and vending machines; sale and repair of sports accessories; instruction privileges such as tennis, golf, swimming, and similar items needed by patrons of the facilities. Generally, public operations try to avoid competition with private enterprise and emphasize services more than profits. Concession services may be handled by the agency, private operations, and volunteer group operations with profits used for programs. Often concession facilities and vending machines are targets for vandals, unless well protected. In the tight budget situation and increased problems with commercially motivated concessionaires, more concession services are being operated by public agencies, particularly where operations justify a full-time merchandising specialist.

Concession privileges are awarded to private operators on the basis of a flat sum per year, percentage of gross receipts, or a fixed amount per admission where admissions are involved such as a stadium or auditorium. All collections are subject to inspection and audit. The agency should include in the concessionaire contract rules for health, safety, quality of merchandise and service, setting of prices, approval of personnel and merchandise, periods of operation, advertising practices and signs, methods of vending, sanitation and cleanup. A cash deposit or performance bond should be required to insure satisfactory performance of contract plus a public liability and property damage insurance policy including the municipality as one of the insured. Contracts are often awarded for one year with the agency having the right to extend the contract one or two additional years.

Sale of Surpluses

Some revenue may be realized from sale of property no longer needed for recreation, sale of used equipment, scrap metal, surplus trees and shrubbery, and residue of land.

Fund Raising Events

Small communities, rural areas, and neighborhoods often raise money for memorial buildings, play areas, and recreation services through fund drives and special events such as fish fries, sale of candy and cookies, community barbecues, suppers and entertainments. Some counties such as Baltimore County, Maryland, provide the school areas, facilities, and general supervision and the neighborhood councils provide special leadership and program materials through fund raising events and charges.

FEES AND CHARGES: POLICIES AND PRACTICES

The recreation profession, to date, has not been developed into an exact science where philosophy, standards, procedures and means of financing are the same for each community. Recreation professionals and politicians have not decided or agreed upon any one best way to provide much needed recreation and relative services. Communities have different needs and they have different ways of paying for the services rendered to them. Each may feel his is the best way; and, it may be the best way for his particular community. There are convincing reasons why various charges are justified, and there are equally convincing reasons why charges should not be made. Almost every public recreation agency makes charges for some privileges or services. The big problem is how and where the charges are appropriate. There are localities that tend to support their operations by assessments, fees, service charges, revenue-producing undertakings and with less tax revenues. They emphasize self-sustaining activities. They have few poor families. There are others that prefer to support services through taxation. Then there are some that have a large influx of seasonal tourists which feel the tourist should have a part in paying for recreation and benefits provided them. They emphasize fees. Recreation financing, however, will need to be in harmony with the basic financial pattern established in the respective locality.

A *fee* may be defined as a charge for admission, privilege, or service. The common practice in most communities is to provide for general recreation and park activities, especially those for juveniles, to be free. To a varying degree, charges are made for adults, specialized or high cost facilities, and personal services of special benefit to the individual.

Legal Aspects

Authority to make charges is vested in the governing body, except as may be delegated by ordinance or other legal means to administration personnel. Care should be taken to conform to the legal requirements; refer to the respective state enabling act, city charter, ordinance, special legislation and administrative directives on the subject for guidelines, or check with legal departments.

Court decisions as to a city's liability often rests on whether a fee is charged, the profit motive intended, the amount of the charge, whether nominal or competitive with private enterprise, or whether the municipality was performing a governmental (public, essential) or proprietary (voluntary, permissive) function. It is the general opinion that making charges for use of public recreation facilities increases the liability of government for accidents. Many cities have adopted the policy of carrying liability insurance where charges are made as protection against damage claims.

There is considerable difference of opinion among administrators concerning charges.

Reasons Against Charging

1. Public services and general public law provide equal opportunity for all. Charges tend to favor those willing and able to pay; tend to restrict those unwilling and unable to pay; and often eliminate those who need the service most.

2. Staff, paper work, and procedures for making collections and accounting for funds add to the total costs and sometimes exceed actual income.
3. Attitude of public is more exacting where charges are made. Some claim "competition with private enterprise." This is a major factor politically in some communities.
4. Charges tend to emphasize income rather than services to participants.
5. It is more difficult to obtain volunteers and donations where charges for public services are involved.
6. Charges encourage politicians to want to extend charges to more activities.
7. There are often pressures for exceptions, i.e., free rides, which get forced approval.
8. Charges in the eyes of the courts tend to increase agency liability.
9. Handling of money adds responsibility and divides the attention of the staff.

Reasons for Charging

1. Charges make it possible to provide activities that would not be available otherwise, therefore extending the program.
2. Charges eliminate some of those less interested and aid control.
3. Charges supplement agency income and make it easier to get budget approval.
4. Participants should pay for special services.
5. Participants have more respect for an activity when a charge is made and are more regular in attendance.
6. Fees permit higher quality services than might be available otherwise.

Kinds of Charges Commonly Made

Some localities make no charges for general recreation services and facilities. Others make nominal charges for a few services and others make charges for many services. Each may be guided by different policies and amounts charged. Charges may include special instruction for small groups where per capita costs are high or not generally available to everyone; use of facilities where per capita costs are high such as health clubs, resident camps, swimming pools, golf courses, ice rinks; privileges and services of personal nature such as parking, transportation, locker space, checking; consumable items such as craft materials and food; admissions to events such as entertainments and special events; rentals of space and equipment such as exclusive use meeting rooms, boats, horses, bicycles; and franchises and service charges such as use of park for art show, entry fees in sports leagues, use and cleaning of costumes.

In times of increasing costs, greater need for recreation services, tight money, and search for additional sources of revenue, it can be expected that fees and charges will be a growing source of revenue for expanding or even maintaining existing recreation services.

Suggested Guidelines for Making Charges

Although the policies and practices concerning charges vary with needs of different communities, guidelines for comparable situations are similar. Except for national and state organizations, charges for recreation services and amounts are determined by conditions in the respective local community, usually on an actual cost basis, with or without interest and amortization of investment. However, some fees may be figured on all expenses above the average costs of other services. Few cities have clear-cut written policies. Too often, decisions are based on the merits of each situation and influenced by tradition and local public sentiment. It is recommended that each agency adopt the best set of policies possible for its situation and widely distribute them to the staff and throughout the community. If it is necessary to charge for recreation services, the following policies, not necessarily in order of importance, may be considered.

1. The majority of general recreation programs, areas, and facilities are free for public use except as may be provided otherwise by ordinance.
2. Fees, charges, admissions, rentals, services, privileges, rates and all items of revenue are authorized by the governing body which also determines any special terms and conditions.
3. Charges for services shall be applied to everyone alike.
4. Services shall be emphasized rather than profit. Charges may be made on an actual cost basis, if costs are known; on estimated cost basis, if actual costs are not known; on supplemental cost basis, for special privileges costing more than normal activities; on all or a por-

tion of high-cost programs, leadership, facilities investment, and equipment; on all the costs for personal services and special privileges, food, consumable items, and items of value; and on rentals, user fees, admissions, service fees, and special use facilities necessary to sustain the service at actual or estimated cost and when activities must be self supporting, such as trips, use of commercial facilities, special programs, and special use facilities.

5. When there is overcrowding, reservations, or scheduled use of facilities, local residents shall have priority. Non-residents, where fees are charged, may be charged a higher fee than residents.
6. When not needed for agency-sponsored activities, recreation areas and facilities may be used by eligible non-profit community groups for a nominal fee on a cost basis and in keeping with the policies of the department.
7. Clubs and classes may charge their own members dues but they must collect and handle their own money. (Agency personnel are permitted only to handle agency funds and then only as may be assigned as a function of their jobs and appropriately protected.)

Objectives of the agency, purposes of the charge, results desired, actual costs of the service and the relationship of the charges to the user's ability to pay are major considerations in determining charges and rates. Communities with a relatively high percentage of low income population tend to have fewer and lower charges than communities with little or no low income or disadvantaged population. If a fee is too low or if number of users is low, it may cost more to make and process the collections than if the activity were free. High cost tends to reduce number of users many of which need the services most.

The tendency to charge higher rates on holidays and weekends reflects practices of profit-making enterprises which are not in keeping with the usual goals and objectives of public agencies. If the situation is such that it costs the public agency more to provide the service on weekends and holidays, then the increased costs may be justifiably reflected in charges made.

It is a common practice, also, to make charges for special adult activities and expect them to be self-sustaining. The self-sustaining group is a real assest to the recreation agency. It leaves the initiative for program, collecting, and accounting for money with the using group rather than with the government. The group is self-supporting, collects its own fees, arranges its own leadership, manages its own affairs, spends *all* of its money for its *own* purposes and the agency accomplishes its objectives without having to take a high percentage of fees collected for agency expense. The agency provides the use of the facility and general staff, as it would do if the agency sponsored the group, and the group by "do-it-yourself" method gets the full control and full use of all money collected and selects its own program with or without aid of the general recreation staff. This procedure should be strongly supported by the agency.

BONDS AND BONDING PROCEDURES

Governments, like businesses, have urgent needs for new and improved areas and facilities. Current revenues generally are not sufficient to pay for them, especially the more costly items. Also these items (capital improvements) will last a long time and serve the future as well as the present. One method of financing them is to borrow money through the sale of bonds, the principal and interest of which may be paid back from current revenue sources over a period of 10 to 40 years, but not to exceed the useful life of the improvements. The maturity dates of such bonds are usually 20 or 30 years and are used for financing capital improvement projects rather than current operations and expendable items.

In recreation, bond funding may be used for such items as acquisition, development and equipping of land and such major facilities as zoos, botanical gardens, stadiums, sports facilities, centers, playgrounds, swimming pools, and golf courses. One or several projects may be included in a single bond issue. Usually small items are financed from current revenues. Bond information is important to recreation executives when they are involved in preparation of a bond issue.

Bonds

Bonds may be classified according to the method of retirement, namely, term bonds, callable bonds, and serial bonds [4] or the manner in which funds are provided for payments such as general obligation bonds, revenue bonds, and assessment bonds.

A *term bond* is one that is paid at the *end* of the specified time agreed upon. Interest may be paid at specific intervals. Funds are usually set aside annually, as in a "sinking fund," to pay off the principal at maturity. Any special fund, like a sinking fund, in government operations is vulnerable for other purposes and is not popular.

A *serial bond* is one where the principal and interest are paid in annual installments. The debt is reduced each year. It requires a minimum amount of paperwork and administrative costs. It is preferred for long-term borrowing.

A *callable bond* provides for an option, either of "calling in" bonds for retirement at any time or paying them at maturity. If interest rates drop, they can be called in and reissued at a savings, however, this type of bond is less attractive to buyers and may require higher interest rates than bonds with specified maturity dates.

General obligation bonds refers to those paid for, including interest, from general tax revenues.

Revenue bonds refers to those paid for, including interest, with income from the revenue-producing facility which was built with the bond funds, such as coliseum, golf course or marina.

Assessment bonds refers to those paid for, including interest, from a special assessment or special tax imposed upon property that benefits especially from the public improvement through increased services and higher property value.

Payment of Bonds and Limitations

The best way to pay for all public services is through current revenues without resorting to borrowing. Few governments are that fortunate. Few can finance from current funds a new coliseum, a stadium, auditorium, large park, community center complex and similar facilities without increasing taxes. The question is raised: "Why shouldn't the future citizen help pay for the facilities he will be using?" Borrowing money, like in business, and the sale of bonds in some form most suitable to the community are the methods used by most cities to provide needed improvements and to spread the cost over a period of years. Government bonds are desirable, especially those from governments with good credit rating. They have an income tax advantage; they are a safe investment because they have the security of all the worth of the government unit (public land, facilities, equipment), plus its taxing resources. Usually cities have good payment procedures. Interest rates, therefore, tend to be lower. However, payments of bonds must come from the usual revenue sources of the government.

In order to protect the taxpayer, the federal government and all states have legal debt limits. In the states, bond limits vary from 2 to 18 percent of the assessed value. This does not provide much opportunity for comparison because of the flexible and varying rates at which property is assessed. In the early 1970's, some cities had reached their debt limit for borrowing and curtailed spending.

Sale of Bonds

Authority for issuance and sale of bonds must be authorized by the legislative body and approved by at least a majority vote of the electorate, except in a few instances. A few cities require more than a simple majority approval and others require majority approval of owners of real estate only. A few city charters provide a procedure involving public hearings, legislative approval, a period of news media advertising, and opportunity for electorate (10 percent) to call for a referendum, which if requested must be held and approved by a simple majority vote of the electorate. In any method, the recreation executive has a serious responsibility of involving the public, preparing sound justifications and convincing information, then guiding procedures to a conclusion. Since bonding processes and laws are quite technical, the fiscal officer or recreation authority secures expert legal assistance usually including services of a bond attorney. State laws and local charters regulate the procedures for issuance of bonds. A bond prospectus with appropriate information is prepared. Specific information relating to sale of bonds is well advertised and, after competitive bidding, bonds are sold to the highest responsible bidder. This may appear to be a simple process but it is not. A long period of preparation precedes the sale of bonds.

Preparing for Bond Elections

Preparation for a bond election really begins with the involvement of the public which includes determination of needs and priorities, handling of public information, and public relations during preparation and following adoption of the long range "master plan" for capital improvements. A good master plan will help greatly in setting the stage for a successful bond election.

The recreation executive (and staff) should provide information and guidance but the people should be the promoters of the effort and be enthusiastic spokesmen at every opportunity. Suggested order of procedures are as follows.

In line with the master plan, determine the greatest needs and priorities by specific project. Determine which projects the public is ready and willing to support. It might be better to delete a highly controversial item or treat it as a separate project, or finance it through other means rather than stand the chance of including it with a group of acceptable projects and risk a negative vote on the entire package. On the other hand, if needs are great and interest for other projects is strong, it may be well to include it with the strong vote getters. This is a matter of judgment.

Prepare fact sheets and brochures with supporting information and give them wide distribution.

Prepare a plan of action for informing the public and gaining public support. Get the support of the news media. Organize a strong citizens' committee with sub-committees representing different segments of the population, including children's interests. Orient members well. The executive should be secretary to the main committee. Assign an agency staff member to be secretary to each sub-committee to coordinate activities, to maintain records, and to keep them motivated. It would be well to have a "speakers bureau" with members that could communicate well with different groups such as civic clubs, parent-teacher associations, businessmen, women's groups, labor organizations, recreation clubs and sports groups, churches, professional groups, senior citizen clubs, and student groups (voting age).

Provide children with accurate information they will understand. They very often may interest their parents. Have a sub-committee to discuss facts with individuals on individual basis key persons who appear not to understand or are in opposition.

Promote a "get out and vote" campaign, telephone, announcements, news media, and word of mouth. Be careful to avoid expenditures of public funds for advertising, general mail-outs, entertainment, and controversial practices.

If the bond issue is approved, implement adopted plans promptly and effectively, keeping public informed of progress, any changes, and reasons.

COLLECTION OF REVENUES

Generally, collection of basic government revenues (taxes, fines, licenses, rents, gifts, bequests) are made by a separate finance agency. However, it is the general practice for agencies to make collections for programs and services for which they are responsible, but under general procedures of the central fiscal officer. Recreation agencies have many miscellaneous and widely scattered situations for which charges are made. In most instances, amounts involved are too small to justify a specialist and the usual system of receipting and accounting. Proper accounting for public funds is a controversial area which must be protected against dishonesty and public criticism. One of the following methods may be used.

Collection at Administrative Offices

Recreation personnel are experts in "giving" services and not universally skilled at "taking" and accounting for funds. Adding collection of revenues to their duties adds confusion and divides their interests. It is best to require that collections be made, whenever practical, at administrative offices by other than program personnel, if possible. Such collections could include permits, franchises, entry fees, charges for camping, and similar items of a general nature not confined to a special location. Numbered receipts should be used and checked in daily.

Collection at Sites

Recreation activities are so widespread, and many times collections are so small and so much a part of the activity, it is necessary to make collections at the site or even as an adjunct duty of staff. Where volume justifies (swimming pools, stadium, auditorium), it is well to use tellers, cashiers, ticket takers, or personnel who are accustomed to dealing with money. Program staff have many distractions such as discipline, emergencies, time consuming appointments, and classes which, if interrupted for collecting, will cause inconvenience to others. Therefore, they should not be used for collections except as a last resort and then only at scheduled times when collecting is their main responsibility at the moment or does not interfere with their program responsibilities. In public work, the public is quick to criticize and take advantage of loose handling of any funds (public or private). For the protection of integrity of staff, accounting for money, and minimizing temptation and errors, collection procedures should require pre-numbered tickets, pre-numbered receipts, or mechanical counters (meters, cash registers, turnstiles), and participation of two employees or in smaller operations, a minimum of a mechanical device, numbered tickets or receipts plus one employee. Payment by check or credit card should be encouraged where possible.

Some collections can be made by coin-operated metered turnstiles (admission to enclosure), coin activated electric switches (stoves and water heaters at camp sites, floodlighting tennis courts and athletic facilities), and coin-activated parking meters. They require daily collections and checking.

Punch cards which may be purchased at central locations may be used for admissions, cash purchases, handcraft supplies, etc. Tickets for activated parking lot gates may also be purchased at central location.

Pre-numbered tickets, pre-numbered receipts, cash registers, coin meters, metered turnstiles, and counters are used as checking devices to account for collections. The use of at least one is recommended for every cash transaction.

Receipts should be written on triplicate forms of different colors with exact carbon copies: original to payee, a copy for central files, and a copy remaining in the receipt book for collection site record.

Admission prices, fees, concession prices, golf fees, and other charges should be posted for public viewing and policing. Public funds and private funds should be kept separate.

Security Measures

Collections are balanced with receipts daily and those at central locations and sites involving larger amounts are deposited daily. Collections occurring after bank hours, if large amounts, are put in a night depository or held in a secure safe or vault. Collection should be made from mechanical devices, checked against meter reading, and recorded daily. At the same time check for malfunctioning. Daily collections in outlying areas of small sums may be held in a safe or vault and deposited weekly, or as specified by the fiscal officer. It is not an acceptable practice to hold money in drawers, file cabinets and similar insecure places. All employees who handle money should be bonded. Burglary insurance should be carried in amount exceeding the total amount expected to be in possession at any one time. In outlying areas, it is well to have burglar alarms or building security. Large amounts of money should be transported in armored or guarded vehicles or with police escort.

All unused tickets and receipts should be kept locked in a central administrative office and signed out when needed by the responsible employee. Ticket takers should cancel in some way or tear off stubs from tickets at the time they are used for accounting purposes to prevent re-use of them.

ACCOUNTING, RECORDING, AUDITING

The general fiscal functions and fiscal services of a unit of government are usually performed by a central agency or agencies under the chief administrator except the post-audit functions which are performed by a unit under the legislative body. The chief fiscal functions include assessing, budgeting, accounting, collecting, safeguarding, and disbursing of funds, purchasing, debt services and investment management. The executive makes rules or causes rules and procedures to be made for management and control of fiscal matters within the respective operating agencies, including recreation. To a degree and on a smaller scale, the operating agency has similar fiscal functions, but they are regulated by the fiscal officer or other authorized agency head which in reality acts as an arm of the chief administrator. The central agency, or agencies, provides all units of the government general accounting services, record keeping, auditing, and financial data. The operating unit, therefore, is involved mainly in providing information, processing financial transactions (revenue, disbursements including payroll, inventories) originating within the agency, and maintaining specific fiscal records needed to effectively manage the agency's functions.

Accounting and auditing are companion functions of government. Accounting, under direction of management, involves the controls, computation, records, transactions, financial data methods, and procedures essential for operation. Auditing, under direction of the legislative body, provides a means of checking and verifying accounts and transactions to see that they are made properly and in conformance with the law.

Common Accounting Terms

A few terms as they apply to fiscal management are defined here.

Appropriation *is the amount of money approved by a legislative body for a specified purpose, budget or separate enactment.*

Fund *is a sum of money set aside for a particular purpose and readily available. It may be a gift, appropriation, part of an appropriation, but accounted for separately—trust fund, bond fund, sinking fund, capital fund.*

Expenditure *(disbursement) is the amount of money properly authorized and paid out.*

Encumbrance *is a commitment or hold on an amount of money for expenditure until the respective transaction is completed satisfactorily.*

Unencumbered balance *is the amount of money still available for spending after all expenditures and encumbrances have been deducted.*

Fixed charge *is an obligatory overhead expenditure essential to the operation and usually a fixed amount—rents, retirement and social security payments, utilities, insurance.*

Contractual service *is one that is performed by another agency of government or private enterprise.*

Force account *refers to work performed by personnel of the agency.*

In kind *refers to agency resources used (cash; use of personnel, equipment, facilities at cost or an estimated fair cost value) usually in terms of sharing costs or matching funds for state, federal or other grant funded projects.*

Accounting Within the Agency

Since most of bookkeeping, computing, and record keeping is processed by modern mechanical equipment and coordinated and maintained by a central finance agency, the accounting responsibilities of the recreation agency involve, mainly, providing accurate information for data processing and recording; attendance figures; figures for cost accounting; preparation of budget figures (revenue and expenditures, capital improvements); preparation of budget allotment figures; completion and verification of time sheets, payrolls including authorized deductions; property inventories; personnel information (vacations, sick leave, compensatory time, etc.); preparation of requisitions, verification of deliveries and certification of vouchers for payment; collection, safeguarding, recording, and processing department revenues; preparation of fiscal and operating statements; maintenance of necessary files and records; and reporting monthly, annually or as otherwise required.

Government accounting is based on the same concepts and principles as business, but the accounting problems, sources of funds, and objectives are different including conformity to legal requirements and regulations, methods of control and safeguarding the uses of public funds.

Although the agency, especially the larger ones, may have data processing technicians, the recreation executive should be well oriented concerning the uses and potential of data processing equipment and helpful services that can be provided for effective management of his agency.

Cost accounting is a determination of actual costs per measurable unit of service (personnel, administrative, materials, rent, equipment). It is used in recreation as a means for evaluating efficiency, for comparisons, determination of unit charges for services, for planning, for figuring costs in preparing budgets, for justification of changes and additions to programs, facilities and budget. With tight budgets and data processing equipment, cost accounting is increasing in importance as a management tool. Where cost of gathering pertinent information continuously is great, it is reasonably effective to obtain basic information by spot checks and samplings for a specific period of time.

Records

The kinds of financial records to be kept by the agency will depend largely upon what the law requires, what the administrator and fiscal officer expect, what is provided by the central agency, and what is needed to control fiscal transactions of the agency to properly carry out its functions. The central agency maintains most permanent records, but the operating agency needs to keep duplicate records of payroll, personnel, capital projects, gifts and special accounts, revenue, expenditures, financial reports and statements, cost accounting data, property and equipment inventories, budgets and allotments. Also records relating to reports received from the field and reports to be made to the administrative offices should be kept.

Auditing

Auditing is inspection and verification of accounts, petty cash, fiscal transactions and related matters to determine accuracy and whether such matters were made properly and in accordance with legal requirements. There are two kinds of audits, namely (1) *internal* (current) often called concurrent or preaudit because it involves daily checking by agency staff before payments are made, and (2) *external* (independent) or postaudit because it is performed for verification purposes after financial transactions are made and recorded. The postaudits are made by a separate agency of government usually on a continuing or annual basis and often supplemented annually or at least every five years by the state auditor or an independent auditor preferably selected by the governing body and in no way under the control of the chief administrator. The auditor reports his findings, good and bad, to the governing body and, usually as a courtesy and for information, sends a copy to the chief administrator and department head involved although this usually is not required. Postaudit by a private concern is preferred. Some state governments conduct postaudits. Errors and improper operations should be corrected promptly. Handling of funds and properly accounting for funds (revenue and disbursements) is a touchy situation, therefore, all transactions must be carefully checked before payments are authorized or receipts made and recorded.

Reporting

Financial reporting (statements) are made daily, weekly by payroll period, or monthly, as well as annually depending on needs. The reports from the field—revenues, deliveries, requisitions, payroll—should be at least once a week, except time sheets which can be once per payroll period.

Statements of revenues and operation expenditures are prepared by fiscal officer monthly, annually, and at budget preparation time, except expenditure statements which may also be prepared daily and weekly if they are prepared by data processing. Expense statements should include capital improvements and special projects, total appropriation for each object, allotment to date, expenditures to date, encumbrances outstanding, and unencumbered balances for each object. Sometimes the statement shows percentage of appropriation unencumbered. The agency prepares for its own use any supplemental information needed or it may request the data processing unit to provide the information.

Questions for Discussion

1. What are the sources of revenue for financing a public recreation agency?
2. What is meant by the term *assessed value?* How is it determined?
3. What is meant by *fiscal management* and how does it involve the recreation executive?
4. Describe the flow of money by steps from the time it is collected until it is audited after expenditure.
5. What is meant by *a general fund? A capital expenditure? A tax limitation? A bond limitation?*
6. Do you recommend fees for recreation services? Explain your reasons.
7. What guidelines would you use in recommending *fees?*
8. What types of bonds are there and how is each used?
9. Explain the ways to finance a *capital improvement.*
10. How is *cost accounting* used in recreation?
11. What safeguards and protective measures are necessary in handling public funds?
12. What are the recommended steps in preparing for a successful bond election?
13. What are the functions of the *accountant?* The *auditor?*

Short Problems

1. Outline a plan for presenting a bond issue for land acquisition and development of a major recreation complex costing $1 million.
2. Prepare for legislative action, a proposal for establishing fees and charges to supplement financing a public recreation agency, including legal authority, guiding policies, specific activities for which charges are to be made, recommended rate of charges, estimated income from each, justification, and effects.
3. Prepare a procedure for collection of fees and charges in a public recreation agency, which has many sites for collection, and provide necessary safeguards and protection for handling and accounting for the monies.

References

1. *Parks and Recreation* (Arlington, Va.: National Recreation and Park Association, August 1971) (Yearbook issue), p. 21.
2. George Hjelte and Jay S. Shivers, *Public Administration of Recreational Services* (Philadelphia: Lea and Febiger, 1972), p. 316.
3. Richard G. Kraus and Joseph E. Curtis, *Creative Administration in Recreation and Parks* (St. Louis, Mo.: The C.V. Mosby Company, 1973), p. 164.
4. Lynn S. Rodney, *Administration of Public Recreation* (New York: The Ronald Press Company, 1964), p. 235.

Selected Readings

Council of State Governments, *State Planning and Federal Grants.* Chicago: Public Administration Services, 1969.

Hanna, L., and Barry Hanna, *Preparing Proposals for Government Funding.* Englewood Cliffs, N.J.: Prentice-Hall, Inc., 1968.

Hines, Thomas I., *Fees and Charges.* Washington, D.C.: National Park and Recreation Association, 1966.

Hjelte, George and Jay S. Shivers, *Public Administration of Recreational Services,* pp. 315–339. Philadelphia: Lea and Febiger, 1972.

International City Managers Association, *Municipal Finance Administration* (6th ed.). Chicago: the Association, 1962.

Maxwell, James Ackley, *Financing State and Local Government.* Washington, D.C.: The Brookings Institution, 1965.

Moak, Lennos L., and Albert M. Millhouse, *Concepts and Practices of Local Government Finance,* pp. 1–65. Chicago: Municipal Finance Officer Association, 1975.

Powers, Stanley Piazza, F. Gerald Brown, and David S. Arnold, eds., *Developing the Municipal Organization.* Washington, D.C.: International City Management Association, 1974.

CHAPTER 14

Budgeting for Public Recreation and Park Agencies

Budgeting for the public recreation agency and the efficient implementation of it are the most important functions of the recreation executive. All functions of the agency depend on an adequate budget (money) properly administered (efficiency). Knowledge of budget preparation, principles, and budgeting process is vital to the recreation executive. Every organization and every individual which is involved in finances is concerned with two kinds of transactions—*income* and *disbursements*. Each, also, is concerned with orderly and effective accomplishments (program). In government, state statutes and local charters require that money must be on hand or legally authorized by the appropriate legislative body before a disbursement can be authorized. Analysis of needs, planning objectives and accomplishments, work programs, legal authorizations, management and controls, estimated income, and estimated expense are brought together in the budgeting process.

Budget, in a recreation context, may be defined as the agency financial plan which specifies revenues, expenses, programs and services, operation, development, and other fiscal requirements for a definite period of time, usually one year. The budget expenditures cannot exceed funds available.

Rodney states that, "Today budget may be defined as a financial plan used by management that forecasts the estimated income and expenditures of an operating organization for a given period of time, usually one calendar year." He further states, "the budget is a planned work program expressed in terms of dollars and cents." [1]

In recent years, three emphases have been added to recreation budget management: the recreation executive and staff must give more careful attention to (1) fiscal matters and efficient programming; (2)

involvement of the public in the process of decision making, and (3) realistic forecasting of revenues and expenditures (needs) for at least five future budget years.

Although budgeting is the most important function of management, the attitude of the executive may be the most important contributing factor in determining the degree of its success in fiscal management. Each public agency executive is competitive for the public revenues with every other agency executive plus the competitive interests of some pressure groups and dedicated community leaders. No longer can the modern executive make all the decisions by himself, or pad the budget to allow for cuts he knows are going to be made, or spend everything to prove he did not receive enough appropriation in the first place, or forget about the budget once it is passed (except the total), or overstate estimates and program, or get all he can from his peers and practice the "dog-eat-dog" attitude all the way. These attitudes have been frequent, but with computers, highly skilled financial experts, skilled administrators, tight budgets and closer looks at budgets, and change of times a positive and realistic approach to budget administration is a must.

In a democratic society usually more than one person is involved in the better decisions. Discussions and testing of ideas tend to bring about refinements, strengthen weak points or even result in better choice of words. The positive attitude and realistic approach to budgeting includes (1) involving citizens and citizen groups in studies, determining community recreation needs, making and interpreting rules and policies, and other decision matters that vitally concern them; (2) involving the staff in program planning, budget preparation, procedures, safeguards and other budget matters that vitally concern them; (3) cooperating with peers and administration; (4) anticipating future needs and changes and being prepared for them; (5) reviewing, analyzing, changing, and emphasizing efficiency and savings, yet requesting and defending strongly what is needed; (6) following budget plan carefully, spending money where needed but not spending more than is necessary; if necessary, requests surpluses be transferred where they are needed; and (7) being realistic in estimates and in describing situations.

Dealing with money, particularly public money, is a delicate subject. The taxpaying public and a competitive staff are aware constantly of the executive. Accounting for public money is an exacting function. Accounts must balance, money must be spent for the purpose intended, programs must be of good quality, and plans proposed in the budget must be carried out as if they were under a contract with the executive each to be performed within the year. The executive needs a good image for the public and for the staff. Budget, the most important document and management tool, affects all elements and segments of an operation and must be given prime attention of the executive. In dealing with the budget and other fiscal matters the executive must maintain the highest integrity and credibility at all times. How the executive deals with budget matters sets the tone for the functioning of the entire agency.

PURPOSES OF BUDGETING

The budget not only is a financial plan but also is a means of setting objectives, priorities, and determining the quality, quantity and extent of program. This also means in-depth planning, reviewing, analyzing, researching, selecting, improving, modifying, justifying, and maybe eliminating (programs, facilities, staff, expense, objectives, procedures).

Budgeting is a necessary procedure for organizations and agencies which deal largely in goals and objectives such as profit-making enterprises; clubs, fraternal and civic organizations, non-profit agencies and others which must raise their own budgets; and government agencies which by law must have an estimated balanced budget of income and expense.

Public budgeting is different from other areas of budgeting in two respects. It involves services to the citizens that pay the cost (taxes) and it must conform to general laws which are made by people (state and federal) that have no direct involvement in the specific local services. The purposes of public budgeting are very broad. They include the interests of law, politicians, administration, management, and citizens in the following ways:

1. Provides a balance between revenues and expenses based on estimated funds available and expenditures required.
2. Safeguards the public against overspending.
3. Provides for review of needs by involvement of public in studies, evaluations, services required and sources of funds.
4. Provides means of determining quality of service (level of skills), standards and quantity (number of units), and scope of services (variety and range of program).
5. Establishes realistic and attainable objectives.
6. Provides uniform information for all concerned:
    a. To the politician for facts, program, basic information, needs and services rendered for deciding policy, revenues, and allocation of appropriations;

   b. To the administrator for comparisons, relationships to needs of other departments, budget savings, coordination, measures of control;
   c. To management for comparison, setting priorities, guidelines and work plan for staff reference, document for planning; and
   d. To the general public for basic information and understanding, proposals, to inspire public confidence.
7. Informs officials and taxpaying public how money is being spent.
8. Serves as a basis of future planning and modification of services.
9. Serves as a basis of regulation and controls.
10. Serves as a basic tool for determining future budget requirements.

ELEMENTS OF BUDGETING

Elements that make up a budget vary with conditions and circumstances. Some localities include capital improvements that are funded by general revenue (not bond money) and all funds in one budget document. Others, particularly larger units, may have separate documents divided in different ways—personnel; expense; new additions, expansions, and extensions of services; capital improvements; explanations, justifications; and the administrator's budget message. Capital budget elements may be a project in a division of the general operating budget with general description and lump sum amount, or it may be a separate document with complete details.

The basic elements of a maintenance and operating budget generally include the following areas.

Objectives and scope of activities are included in a statement at the beginning of each department or division budget unit to describe briefly the general responsibilities of the respective unit. An example is "This Department is responsible for the conduct of organized and supervised public recreation programs. It is responsible for the operation and maintenance of park and recreation facilities, the maintenance of trees on the city streets and in the public parks."[2]

Summary of general and special fund expenditures are broken down by separate work programs and separate special fund listings so viewers can see at a glance the totals and status of each unit. The special funds may be set up for any legal purpose the council may designate.

Receipts and revenues summary from all sources by types or sources of revenue (rentals, concessions, light meters, federal grant, sundry) are listed. These funds generally go into the city's general fund and are appropriated (allocated) to equal the amounts of approved agency budgets. Actually, as a matter of practice, monies are held in the general fund (or invested) and paid out upon receipt of proper authorization from the agency to the limits of the appropriation.

Work programs and performance are described; the work programs identify the work unit such as administration, general maintenance, and street trees, while dramatics, music, sports and the performance describe the units of work or what is to be accomplished during the budget period. This element is included for each separate work program of the agency.

Expenditure elements are basically three kinds, namely, personnel, expense (non-personnel operating items), and capital improvements. In larger cities or where projects are funded by grants, gifts or bond issues, capital improvement accounts may be separated from operating budget and capital funds may carry over to the next period because construction often takes more than a year. Maintenance and operation budget funds terminate at the end of the budget year, except where law provides that the actual amount legally committed under contract or by purchase order when merchandise has not been delivered at the close of a budget year may carry over to the next budget year for payment. Budget programs and expenditures should be completed in the same year in which appropriations are made, if at all possible.

Supportive information in the way of brief explanations are sometimes included in the "comments" column on budget request forms, however, space is often too small and extra sheets must be added for full explanations, particularly when a new commodity or change is being requested.

TYPES OF BUDGETS

Budgets are thought of in two ways, namely the subjects they deal with (revenue, operating, capital) and the way the budget is prepared (line item, object, function, program performance).

The *revenue budget* involves estimates of all income and the sources. The *operating budget* involves all estimated expenditures and what will be accomplished with them during the period. It is the ongoing base budget for management, staff, program, maintenance, housekeeping, collection of revenue, security, and related costs. The *capital budget* involves estimates of expenditures for improvements of permanent nature, such as land, structures, long lasting equipment, and improvements. It usually increases the value or net worth of inventory. It may be noted that budgeting is influenced by advances in techniques, collecting information, and accounting methods.

Line Item Budget

This type of budget lists in detail every separate item estimated to be needed such as 12 dozen pencils, 2 tractors, and 40 tons of coal. This method emphasizes items and quantity. Appropriations are made and controlled on item basis. For instance money appropriated for coal cannot be used for gasoline. Past expenditure for the item and comparison is the usual basis for figuring line budget requests. Line item budget making in some form is carried over into other budget types.

Object Classification

This type is broader than the line item budget and is based on groupings of estimated expenditures by several major categories. It is commonly used, is more flexible, and relates to the accounting system used by the fiscal officer and auditor. The basic expenditure classifications, originally developed by A. E. Buck,[3] are used by various government agencies which adapt them to their local needs; they include:

1000. Services, personal: salaries and wages, regular, part-time and temporary.
2000. Services, contractural: includes work, services, materials provided by outside contract (transportation, printing, utilities, repair work, laundry).
3000. Commodities: food, fuel, materials, supplies, clothing.
4000. Current charges: rents, insurance.
5000. Current obligation: fixed charges (interest, pension).
6000. Properties: equipment, furnishings, tools, vehicles, plants, animals, structures, land improvements.
7000. Debt payments.

Like the line item type budget the object classification type emphasizes items and quantity. Therefore, it is used in combination with other types of budgets to give program and function more emphasis. Rodney provides detailed coding by objects.[4]

Function Classification

This budget type lists estimated expenditures by functions (playgrounds, centers, swimming pools, programs for handicapped) often in combination with object classification in order to put more emphasis on function.

Administration is sometimes treated as a "function" classification along with facilities and special services (program). This kind of budgeting involves considerable breakdown and keeping of records. No one classification plan is in general use.

Performance Budget

The performance budget takes program, makes evaluations, and determines units and costs. This type of budget is a modification of the object and function budgets combined. It involves planning and setting of objectives. Single unit costs are figured from previous work experiences for measurable work units of performance. More emphasis is given to performance. The amount of work units necessary to accomplish the planned objectives for the year are multiplied by the unit cost to obtain budget totals. For example, the budget would show how much money is spent on staff, supplies, equipment, and transportation for a specific phase of service such as programs for the handicapped. Expansion or reduction of performance is obtained by adding or subtracting numbers of units. This type requires extensive accounting and cost analysis. Unit costs may be refigured on fluctuating costs as new records are incorporated into the system and averaged out. However, there are recreation programs, services and benefits that are not measurable, therefore, there are often modifications and various combinations with the traditional character and object classification type budget. As techniques and use of computer improve for reporting and record keeping, the use of the performance type budget is expected to be more extensive. Emphasis is placed on work units performed rather than on money spent or commodities used. The performance type budget is adaptable to any size agency.

Program Budget

Program budgeting, as currently used, is a combination of performance budget and character and object classification with emphasis on program and accomplishments based around agency work programs. It involves careful planning at budget preparation time, setting of objectives, and work units to be accomplished. Such programs, in keeping with agency goals and objectives, are determined by the needs and local policy. They are separated and clearly identified. They may be basic agency functions, programs, activities, major interest groups, program catagories, operation of areas or facilities, tree maintenance, nursery, and administrative offices. Work units need to be determined for each work program such as enrollment, participant-session, acre, square foot, each tree. Costs are maintained by work program (drama, music, tree maintenance) which, in turn, may be broken down into unit costs for the work program. For example, the budget would show the estimated number of units (participant-sessions) at the average cost per unit of a program, such as drama. It might show as 60,000 participant-sessions at $.50 per session or $30,000. All expenses must be figured in determining the unit costs. Planner, administrator, politician and public are informed of participation, total costs, and unit costs for the program. It provides, also, a means of checking performance and progressive record of accomplishments, as well as expenditures.

THE BUDGET PROCESS

The preparation of the agency budget is the most important single responsibility the recreation executive has to perform. Although the procedure may be adjusted slightly to conform to size and administrative structure of the agency, the principles of budget making, responsibility of the executive, administrator, and policy making body remain the same. In a small agency the executive, after consulting with his staff, may prepare the budget himself or in any size agency he may have to present his budget directly to a recreation board, a commission, or a committee of the legislative body rather than, or in addition to, the chief administrator.

Processing the budget, from planning through execution, is a team effort. The recreation executive will consult with his staff and citizens and delegate planning, preparation, and, later, implementation to assistants and key department personnel, particularly heads of the separate functions. At the higher level, the recreation executive (and staff) prepare and execute the budget. The chief administrator reviews, evaluates, develops policy, coordinates, controls, and recommends to the legislative body. The legislative body examines the budget document, sets standards of service, rejects, modifies, approves, and provides appropriation for implementation. The citizens, of course, pay the taxes (fees) and receive the service. This identifies the phases the budgetary process passes through, namely, preparation, review and adoption, and implementation of the budget plan.

Legal Basis for Budgeting

The legal basis for the budget is usually provided for in state enabling legislation, city charter, or special laws which are general law and permissive legislation only, and applies to a variety of circumstances and conditions. In order to adapt it to the local situation, the local legislative body must establish an operating recreation unit, make policy, regulations and appropriations which usually require that an itemized listing of expenditures and revenues be submitted to the legislative body for review and approval.

The general legislation may set dates, define method of presentation, require public hearings, and establish alternate methods of approval in event the legislative body fails to act. It may also provide for emergency financing in event of a serious disaster.

The type of administrative and legislative structure may determine who is designated to formulate the budget—the president, governor, mayor, city manager, county executive, chairman of the board of supervisors, commissioner, a committee; or in large agencies, a budget officer or other designated official. The person in charge of finances and the budget officer hereafter will be called fiscal officer.

The usual items that are included in basic budget laws are the date the fiscal year commences, date budget is to be transmitted to legislative body, date prior to beginning of fiscal year the budget must be adopted, alternate method for approval in event legislative body does not act, general scope and extent of the budget, and designated authority who has responsibility for preparing and implementing the budget plan. They usually specify that only the legislative body may authorize charges of any kind, make appropriations, or permanently commit monies or property.

The Budget Calendar

Budget making requires the effort and time of many people, sometimes at the same time; therefore, it requires careful scheduling in order that department heads, chief administrator, legislative members, and the public may be present when needed and be given adequate time to review budget materials, check out needed information, and make sound decisions. Agency heads need time also to prepare figures and other information that may be requested specifically. Legislators may want time to inspect certain conditions and operations during their review of the budget. A budget calendar or timetable is prepared to show in chronological order the dates action must be taken in preparing and processing the budget. Usually the fiscal officer will give the agency head a master budget calendar showing dates set by the administration which conform to the law and administrative needs—dates for submission, review hearings, council action and adoption. Agencies can then add the dates set by the agency for its use.

Since budget making is an annual and continuous process, often the fiscal officer will provide agencies a budget manual which includes pertinent legal information, copies of forms and how to use them, administrative rules and procedures governing budget preparation, and the budget calendar which is updated at the beginning of each fiscal year. Fiscal years may vary with the locality. Usually, they extend from July 1 to June 30; in other instances it may begin April 1, January 1, or some other date. The important fact is that they are all for a 12-month period. The dates in the following suggested timetable for the fiscal year beginning July 1 may be adapted to fiscal years which have different dates by figuring the same time span.

Suggested Budget Calendar For Fiscal Year Beginning July 1.

When	Who	What
September 10	Agency Heads, Key Staff	Attend meeting with administrator and fiscal officer concerning budgeting.
October 15	Staff	Give executive capital proposals
October 20	Staff, Executive	Review capital proposals
October 25	Staff	Submit final form, 5 copies, capital proposal
October 30	Executive	Submit to fiscal officer 3 copies of capital proposals
November 15	Executive, Administrator	Review capital proposal
November 30	Executive, Administrator	Review capital with Planning Commission
December 15	Staff	Begin preparing operating budget proposals
January 10	Staff	Give executive budget proposals
January 15	Staff, Executive	Review budget proposals
January 20	Staff	Submit proposals in final form, 5 copies
February 1	Executive	Submit proposals to fiscal officer, 3 copies

Suggested Budget Calendar (Continued)

When	Who	What
February 23, 24	Executive, Staff	Review proposals with fiscal officer
April 7	Administrator	Submit budget recommendations to Policy Board
April 25	Administrator, Fiscal Officer, Executive, Staff	Review recommendations with policy board
May 3	Administrator, Executive, Policy Board, Staff	Attend public hearing on operating budget
May 10	Administrator, Policy Board, Executive, Staff	Attend public hearing on capital budget
May 15	Administrator Policy Board	Make amendments
May 31	Policy Board	Take final action on capital and operating budget
June 1–30	Executive, Staff	Planning, setting up accounts, submitting quarterly allotments to fiscal officer
July 1	Executive, Staff	Implementation of budget plan; begin preliminary preparation—studies, analysis, improvements, planning for next fiscal year

PREPARATION OF THE BUDGET

Although the budget is a financial plan, it was first a less tangible program-service plan. A good budget plan is based on a good program plan. Many days of observing, evaluating the needs, and determining the most effective method of providing for programs have taken place before the budget is prepared. Budget preparation, like budget management, is a continuous process. Budget plans for the next fiscal year begin before the previous budget is adopted. Also, budgets are prepared from estimates at least a year in advance. During that time interests may change; then program plans need to be changed with them. Budget and program, being prepared together, cannot very well be allowed to go in different directions without causing loss of credibility with someone. It is the responsibility of staff and supervision to see that the program conforms to the budget plans at all times, or if needed, to get appropriate approval to make a change that will improve the program yet conform to the budget plan. The staff, therefore, is administering the budget of one fiscal year while it is evaluating existing programs and planning for needs of the next fiscal year.

In the budget process, it is well to keep in mind some of the influences that may affect budget approval such as pressure groups, public opinion, interests and intent of politicians and strong community leaders, emotional situations, ability of spokesman to convince, past and current commitments, prejudices, experiences, even though limited, controversial issues, lack of information about a subject, and others.

Guidelines for Preparing Budget

Since budget making involves the purposes for which the agency exists; the quality, quantity, and scope of program services; income, and the life and existence of the agency, preparation of the agency budget requires great effort and attention.

Because the budget involves all of the agency operations, the guidelines relating to its purposes, existence, and programs are important in considering recommendations for the budget year. Even though most guidelines have been discussed previously, general guidelines important to bear in mind in preparing the budget are:

1. Legal authority, laws, powers, restrictions, jurisdictions.
2. General concept and purpose of the agency.
3. Established policies, rules, and regulations.
4. Established goals and objectives.
5. Administrative directives and instructions.
6. Accepted standards based on experience and sound research.
7. Established objectives for the year.

Other more flexible factors and situations that serve as important guides to the budget maker are:

1. Existing programs and level of service. This is one of the most uni-

form guides for budget makers, but in recreation they seldom can be used without changes. However, when they are used without critical reviews annually, inferior programs are perpetuated along with successful programs.

2. Need for continuing existing programs, areas, and facilities. This must be established after objective reviews and sound justification of each separate unit or division of a unit.
3. Need for new or expanded services. This is established by objective review and evaluation of existing programs by staff, plus information from all kinds of contacts with users and public.
4. Political, economic, social conditions, and attitude of the public.

Priorities, while not guidelines, must be considered. They include:

1. Fixed charges such as payroll for permanent personnel, rents, utilities, insurance, pension costs, debt payments, interest and long term contracts, and employee benefits.
2. Continuing programs.
3. Completed improvements previously committed and being put into operation for first time.
4. Commitments made by administrator, policy board or change in laws during the year such as acceptance of gifts, acquisition or disposal of property.
5. Costs made necessary by changes in other agencies such as charges for school custodians, increase in inspection fees, sewer charges, reimbursements.
6. Changes in costs of commodities, rents, contracts.
7. Revenue producing items.

Work Programs and Work Units

In preparing budgets, primary emphasis is on program and achievement (performance), secondary emphasis is on money. The program and services (often intangible) are presented. Money is the tangible means of obtaining programs and services. For purposes of explaining, measuring, accounting, recording, and evaluating, work programs and work units are used. Certain intangible benefits of recreation and parks, such as quality, carry-over interests, preventive and corrective activities which take much time and effort, have no satisfactory measurable unit. Enrollment and attendance are sometimes used for the lack of anything better.

With improvement in technology and methods of record keeping, data processing and accounting are providing more and more recreation agencies performance figures in measurable units as well as dollar figures. There is a push to find realistic ways to measure all activities and services. It may be that the intangible values will be measured by computer from different relationship values to the measurable tangibles taking into consideration the pluses and minuses of human characteristics, environment, and hereditary factors of separate individuals, if necessary for close refinement.

All recreation agencies have *work programs.* Smaller agencies may have one (sports and games) and operate every service from the one work program by doing their own typing and marking of fields. Another agency (public works or schools) may perform the maintenance work. As agencies become larger, they add specialists and more work programs. These are measurable as a unit as well as many of their subunits.

A work program is an essential element of program and performance budgets, a spending unit composed of closely related activities. It may be a major unit with specialized or subordinate programs and activities. Examples are drama, music, nature, park maintenance, tree maintenance, golf courses, camp operation, and administration. Performance is reported by work units.

A *work unit* is a standard of measurement that refers to volume of performance. It is based on sound research and experience. It may be expressed in acres of grass cut, number of trees planted, number of playgrounds, participant-hours, linear feet or miles of curbs trimmed, or loads of trash removed. It does not measure quality. Often work units are influenced by organization structure, facilities, and accounting practices. They are essential for accounting, program and performance budgeting, and, for that reason, are increasing in importance.

Preparing Revenue Estimates

The recreation agency income is part of the total government revenue budget. In local government, the revenue budget as well as the expenditure budget is a factor in determining the tax rate for the year. While the separate revenue and expenditure budgets of each agency, including recreation, may not balance, the total local government operation budget must be balanced without using borrowed money. The agency revenue in itself should not be the basis of recommending new services or expanding programs, except in self-sustaining types of functions, but it is an aid in planning and forming policy. In instances where the recreation agency is funded by fees or a special tax, the budget may be expected to balance.

Revenue is income collected from sources under the jurisdiction of the agency—fees, charges, rentals, concessions, admissions, registrations, pay telephones, direct donations and grants, and sundries. Total receipts for the year from each source are estimated and listed in the revenue budget. Judgments are based on comparisons with past records, comparable and closely related operations, plus advice from technicians and experts in the field. Each revenue producing unit, like expenditure units, is analyzed and evaluated continuously with an in-depth review at budget preparation time, including objectives, operational methods, types of equipment used, hours of operation, fee structure, patronage, and need for change.

The key personnel at each separate operation are usually responsible for preparing and presenting both revenue and expenditure estimates as well as maintaining appropriate records.

Preparing Expenditure Estimates

Although the recreation executive is solely responsible for presenting the recreation budget, good management dictates that staff members responsible for executing the agency programs should also be responsible for recommending and justifying the budget for their respective units. Several months prior to the beginning of the fiscal year, depending on local conditions, the executive will provide the head of each spending unit with a copy of the budget calendar and request estimates of revenues and expenditures for the next budget year including justifications and supplementary information. He also passes on any pertinent suggestions and instructions. At this point, actual fiscal needs are the main considerations. Types of information and scope of the programs will be as varied as the activities and the needs of the locality. The budget forms and budget calendar dates will be provided by the fiscal officer. The fiscal officer may hold a general informational meeting with all agency heads and key staff.

Guidelines, discussed previously, are used in determining programs. Information for estimates is obtained from experience records, data processing, purchasing agent, personnel department, fiscal officer, engineers (public works), utility departments, private contractors, technicians, businesses and catalogues.

Estimates for continuing routine programs can be judged rather accurately by comparing like expenditures with the two previous years, taking into consideration any differences or changes. Avoid using budget categories of miscellaneous, sundries, and other, unless items are not clearly identified.

Estimates for extensions of existing programs and adding of new programs can be judged rather accurately by comparing costs with those of similar existing units.

In starting a new recreation agency, the policy board very often will appropriate a lump sum amount for recreation and then employ the executive, who then budgets the lump sum amount. Several alternates are possible. The executive, with approval of the administrator or policy board, may delay starting program services or conduct them on a reduced scale, or the policy board may appropriate additional funds from contingency funds, or transfer from surpluses of other agencies. In preparing first year estimates of expenditures, the executive will then rely on his past experiences, experiences of other local agencies, the local businesses and personnel services.

In larger agencies, and where computers are used, budget printouts are made including individual names of personnel plus necessary historical information and expenditure accounts for the past two years. The budget maker then makes any corrections, fills in the estimates for the next budget year, attaches program information, supportive materials, justifications, summary, and returns it.

In localities that do not have access to computers, all the work, of course, is done by personnel. Whatever the situation, plans, or figures for budget year, supportive information is prepared by agency staff.

Some cities prepare expenditure budgets in two phases. The first phase includes new programs, additions, expansions, extensions, putting new facilities in operation for first time, or any increases. These requests are usually presented on different colored forms, for easy identification, and submitted, perhaps, two weeks in advance of the second phase which includes the normal, routine ongoing programs and expenditures.

The Budget Forms

Standard forms on which to prepare budget together with explanatory instructions are usually provided by the fiscal officer. Such forms conform to legal requirements, local needs, data processing, and the accounting system used. (See Appendix J.)

The basic budget form consists of several column headings numbered for easy reference. It is on standard size paper stock that will fit in standard or wide-carriage typewriters. The 8½ × 11-inch size is preferred because most attachments are that size and it is a convenient size for reproducing and general use. Sometimes 8½ × 13- or 8½ × 14-inch sizes are used to provide for needed columns. In binding them, these sheets are folded once to fit with the regular 8½ × 11-inch size material.

Most budget expense forms provide a column for object code, item and quantity; a column each for actual expenditures for past two years; a column for estimated expenditures for current year; a column for current budget; a column for proposed budget; a column for final budget, and sometimes a column for remarks.

The budget forms for personnel provide columns for position title, salary range, columns for each of the past two years, current year (estimated), current budget, proposed budget, final budget, and remarks.

Some communities provide work sheets, forms for supportive information, and forms for financial summary of division or work programs.

Forms for revenue estimates provide columns for accounting code no. and description, actual income for two previous years, current year (estimated) and budget year.

Forms for capital improvements (only one project on a form) provide identification with accounting code, descriptive title, and columns for estimated total cost, prior authorizations, budget year, and column each for four additional fiscal years. The columns only use the top third of the page. The remainder of the page is used for description and pertinent information. Sometimes a large project will be programmed over two or more years and have appropriations each year. Some cities, as a policy, program construction work for two years; land acquisition and preparing of architectural plans the first year and construction the second year. Capital projects usually have a backup form providing for breakdown of costs by categories such as land, planning, structures, equipment and furnishings, landscaping, and contingencies. Sometimes there are spaces for suggested financing, especially where grants are involved. And most important, there is space for estimated annual maintenance and operations cost after project is completed. This is to aid in considering continuing costs for future operating budgets.

Supportive Information

The essential elements to include in preparing budgets have been outlined previously and need not be repeated except to list them in order to be presented in preparing budgets: (1) general statement of objectives and scope of activities and title as an introduction to the department and each major division; (2) financial summary of the department or division, as the case may be; (3) receipts and revenue summary; (4) work programs and performance; (5) expenditure budget; and (6) supportive information, which is pertinent to discuss now.

Preparation and presentation of supportive information (attachments) is one of the most important features of budget preparation. It, if effectively done, presents exactly what the program technician and executive had in mind to accomplish with the budget. Only a brief explanation can be put on the budget sheet under the column "Remarks." The objective is to present concisely facts pertinent to the situation, after considering effectiveness and efficiency of performance, other alternatives and service benefits (need, production, safety, durability, low maintenance and operation costs, labor saving methods, and how acceptable and appealing it is to the public). Extra sheets may be attached. Pictures and brochures of new equipment are added. Provided also is breakdown of items that make up budget account total such as 40 tons of lime, 60 tons of fertilizer and cost of each. This is line item budget material, but it is in form of attachment for benefit of persons reviewing budget at different levels of administration such as supervisor, division head, executive, fiscal officer, and administrator who makes final decisions and recommends balanced budget to policy board. At this point attachments may have been removed, but held for further reference, and budget information condensed into administrator's budget message and budget summaries.

The operating agency needs to keep its budget notes and work sheets as a guide in implementing the adopted budget. The adopted budget deals with summaries and totals and often is not in sufficient detail to be used as a working plan.

BUDGET REVIEW AND ADOPTION

During the budget process, the budget requests pass through several reviews and hearings. During this time budget proposals can be revised. The budget finally must be adopted by the governing body.

Budget Reviews and Explanations

The individual who determines the needs, sets the objectives, plans the programs, sets priorities, listens to public interests, and finally makes them all into a budget proposal according to the rules is the individual that knows what is involved, who can anticipate the best results, and who, perhaps, will help interpret the budget plan to others, either in the written supportive information or in personal discussions, or both. Although it is the administrator who is responsible for preparation of the budget and its presentation, it is usually prepared by technical staff members, except in autonomous agencies such as a recreation commission. The individual that prepares any part of a budget must then provide sound explanations and convincing reasons that will withstand the competition of all other programs plus critical questioning from management, administrator, policy board and public. If it has good public support, chances are good it will please the policy board and others. This is one reason so much emphasis is placed on involving the public in surveys, planning, determining of needs and priorities. Problems, differences of opinion, opposition, support, wants, and desires are simple to deal with in the planning stages but become more complex as they progress towards legislative action and deadlines.

The first reviews in the recreation budgetary process are informal and generally at the program unit level with the program leader discussing needs and program ideas with participants, parents, interested citizens, advisory council members, co-workers, and volunteers; getting ideas; and testing ideas and how much interest and support there is for changes and new programs. There may not be any written program or budget figures at this point. The unit director may or may not be present.

The unit director reviews the proposals and presentations of the different program leaders. He compiles the programs and budget proposals for the entire unit which he then reviews with the unit staff for the purpose of informing them, coordinating ideas, strengthening weaknesses, and correcting omissions. The unit director may also wish to review the completed unit budget with the unit advisory council.

The area supervisor reviews the unit director's needs, programs, and proposals. It is here that supportive information begins to take on importance. From this point the responsibilities for explaining programs and budget needs are passed progressively from one line officer to another along the organization structure and get farther from the place of origin. At this point, also, the unit program budget begins direct competition with other unit budgets, explanations, and supportive information. The supervisor will ask questions and try to get a complete understanding of the proposals, and maybe add, revise or delete.

The division head reviews and discusses the proposals and recommendations with the area supervisors. He may include unit directors and supportive staff for training and to provide information that may have been overlooked in the prior review. At this point, the unit budget and programs become a part of a division and are in competition with other divisions. Changes may be made here.

The agency executive reviews the proposals to date with the division heads who may also include area supervisors. A more critical review is made at this point. Usually changes are made and budget proposals revised. It has become competitive with programs and budgets of the entire agency. Until this point the process has been entirely within and under the control of the agency. Changes are relatively simple. The agency executive discusses the agency proposals with the agency board, if there is one.

The fiscal officer and/or administrator reviews agency proposals with executive (and division heads) in complete detail. At this point, total estimated revenues and estimated expenditures are analyzed and budget policies are formulated by the administrator. The recreation agency budget at this point is still the director's proposal (not the administrator's or council's) and he should fight hard for its approval. If estimated expenditures are greater than income, the administrator has the choice of increasing revenue (taxes, charges) or curtailing expenditures, or a little of both. The law requires the budget to be balanced. If he curtails expenditures, he may set policies such as "hold the line" or "no new programs" or "pay increases only." The fiscal officer will adjust all budgets to conform to the policy by himself or in consultation with the executive, or refer the budget back to the executive to adjust the budget to a specified total. The cooperative approach provides a better opportunity for fair discussion. The other two approaches tend to be arbitrary and provide little opportunity for further informing the decision maker and no opportunity for negotiating important exceptions. Some executives feel the budget cutter would be less apt to cut money if he also had to decide what programs to cut. This is an argument for presenting only realistic and essential amounts in budget (no padding).

During the preparation stage of the budget making process, budget information is not publicized. When the administrator presents his budget recommendations to the policy board, he makes copies available to reporters and news media, agency heads, key staff members, and the public. The members of the policy board are first to receive final budget recommendations of the administrator.

The policy board reviews the budget proposals with the administrator, fiscal officer, and agency heads. At this point, the total government budget has been made up. Estimated expenditures are balanced out with estimated revenues and all money is allocated by the administrator for a use. The agency budget has become the administrator's budget recommendation. Now, the recreation executive does everything he can to support this budget. (To try to restore, without his approval, cuts the administrator had made, as many are temped to do, would be insubordination and serious violation of conduct.)

This review may or may not be open for public comments and questioning. Usually, policy board members like to be briefed and become familiar with as many aspects of the budget as possible before holding a public hearing. Usually, the public is permitted to sit in on policy board briefings.

The procedure is for the administrator, his fiscal representative, or agency executives to present the highlights of their programs and fiscal needs (changes, new programs, new costs, outstanding features, what makes up increases, where decreases are, and why) and to be open to questioning. Answers should be brief, direct, to the point, courteous, with the speaker calm, confident, pleasant, as if carrying on a normal conversation. It is acceptable procedure for the executive to have an assistant or technician answer questions he may not know well. Also, if statistics and additional information on a subject are needed, provide it as soon as possible through the administrator, or by a specified time. The administrator may choose to answer questions.

Public Hearings

Public hearings on the budget are reviews by the public. They are usually conducted in the legislative chambers, or large assembly room, by representatives of the people (council, policy board, or committee of policy board) with the chairman (mayor) presiding and chief administrator, agency heads, and key staff present to provide information and answer questions.

The headings and main features of the budget are well publicized in advance. Copies of the budget are made available at the office of administrator (or fiscal officer) for the public. Usually, names are recorded of those receiving copies. Agencies inform people directly they know are interested in attending the hearings. Sometimes citizens ask to be informed. Both pros and cons attend. Some may be organized for or against a matter.

Budgets may be presented by agencies or the public may be given an opportunity to speak on, or ask questions about, any phase of the budget they wish. Unless a major controversial subject is involved such as raising taxes or there are organized community efforts concerning a subject, too few people attend public budget hearings. Some speak against items in the budget they do not believe in, others speak for funding, or increased funding, of a special project and others speak generally for or against the budget or phases of it. Some ask questions for clarification. Sometimes public discussions are heated, sarcastic, emotional, offensive, dull, exciting, helpful, complimentary. Executives and staff in a calm, courteous, pleasant, confident manner answer questions concisely and briefly. They should avoid bringing in points not under discussion.

Adoption of the Budget

After the administrator makes his recommendation the budget is the responsibility of the policy board. The members review it critically, seek clarification and further information from the administrator, inspect areas and facilities, and in their own ways satisfy themselves that the budget properly reflects their feelings. They may amend it, adopt it, or take any action within their authority. It should be approved or adopted in advance of the beginning of the fiscal year to which it applies.

If the policy board fails to adopt the budget, legal approval is provided in other ways. For instance, in some jurisdictions, if policy board fails to adopt it by a specified date, the budget becomes legally approved in the form it was presented by the administrator. It is very seldom that a legislative body fails to adopt a budget.

The budget should be adopted in a form, such as totals only, to provide management with as much flexibility as possible to make minor adjustments for unanticipated situations. Controls are handled by procedures and systems of approvals, allotments and reviews.

Implementation

Promptly after adoption, the recreation agency makes any necessary modifications of its programs, objectives, and plans necessitated by any amendments that were made to the budget or work programs and informs staff and citizens affected. The agency also submits monthly or quarterly allotments as may be required for fiscal management. The finance and accounting units set up proper accounts (revenue and expenditure) and inform the agencies involved.

The program personnel present program plans and needs for the year along with program calendar or schedule of main events from which are made the quarterly (or monthly) allotments, personnel, requisitioning, and work schedules. Appropriate financial controls are then established as needed within the agency and central services (data processing, finance, personnel, purchasing, and stores).

ALLOCATION AND MANAGEMENT OF APPROPRIATIONS

The final major step in the budgeting process is the management of funds and the accomplishment of the programs planned by the agency and authorized by the policy board upon adoption of the agency budget. The budget, in effect, authorizes the executive to proceed with all programs. It is now the obligation and responsibility of the executive to perform the functions in the best way possible and to see that the funds are used for the purposes intended and within the totals allowed. In order to keep up to date on progress and maintain general jurisdiction over expenditures, he sets up a system of reporting, allotments, inspections and controls.

Quarterly Allotments

The quarterly allotment is a means of scheduling the work programs monthly or quarterly and assigning funds to carry them out. It is a plan for assuring funds for the various work programs for the year. The division of funds may not be equal by quarters, depending on seasonal needs. It requires good advance planning on the part of supervision and is a means of evaluating the progress of the work performed in the separate work programs. The administrator receives a copy of monthly or quarterly expenditure statements from the fiscal officer and a performance report from the program supervisor. This provides him with the information to analyze status of performance, revenue, and expenditures. This is usually followed by an allotment review with the person in charge of the work program. Adjustments may be made if expenditures are heavier than estimated. Unspent and unneeded balances are transferred to a contingency fund which may be used for emergencies or other needed programs, but it requires the administrator's approval to spend money from the contingency fund.

Budgetary Controls

Every monetary transaction (collection or expenditure) should pass through at least two individuals in different areas of responsibility. Only a minimum number of signatures should be authorized to sign official papers such as requisitions, vouchers, contracts, time sheets, and payrolls. The budget after adoption and accounts are set up becomes the guideline for execution of programs and control of expenditures.

Long range master plan, the budget, the work programs and allotment plan, personnel merit system, procedure for purchasing, budget totals and ceilings on contracts, data processing controlled accounts, accrual accounting systems, weekly reporting, amounts that can be spent without advertising and bidding, contracting with lowest responsible bidder, concurrent and postaudits, payment by check, pre-numbered receipts, and financial statements are means of budgetary control which almost every government uses and adopts to accommodate its own specific need.

Accumulated Savings

Since budgets are estimates which are made in advance, conditions, changes of interest, unexpected vacancies, good bidding, deferred starts, efficient management and similar reasons may result in accumulation of savings. Except as otherwise controlled, these funds may be spent for other needed purposes, allowed to revert back to the general fund at the end of the year, or be transferred, with approval of the administrator, to accounts where additional funds are needed for other authorized projects. It is well to get consent of administrator before funds, even savings, are used for purposes not included in the approved budget. To save money and present a sound recommendation to use it for improved services helps credibility considerably. Care should be taken, however, not to commit savings to start a program that will depend on similar budget savings in expenditures or new appropriations (additional funds) the next budget year.

Financial Statement

Local conditions and kinds of information required determine largely the kinds of accounts and records that are kept. Basically, they include appropriations, encumbrances, expenditures, uncommitted balances, statements of revenues and a balance sheet for each fund and account. Summary information of these types is used by the executive and administrator to evaluate progress, determine costs, and control expenditures. They separate revenues, expenditures, special funds, capital projects or other division and provide information on a continuing basis. Mechanical record keeping equipment can provide statements at any time, usually daily or weekly. Manually prepared statements are usually made less often, weekly or monthly.

Most attention is given to control of operational expenditures. They are accounted for by character and object classification under the general categories of personal services, contractual services, fixed charges, materials and supplies, equipment, maintenance, capital improvements and various subdivisions.

One of the greatest problems of control is the lapse of time between the time requisitions are authorized, purchase orders or contracts are committed, deliveries are completed, net costs (including discounts) are determined, payments are made and transactions are processed in the form of a statement. This may vary from a few days to several months and emphasizes the importance of maintaining information on encumbrances as well as actual expenditures. Most agencies supplement central accounting by maintaining simple records, uncompleted requisitions file, pending purchase orders file, payments on contracts, and status of larger transactions and authorizations.

SUMMARY PROCEDURE FOR BUDGET PREPARATION

— Budgeting is a continuous process.

— Make notes of public and staff requests and budget needs discovered during the year that should be considered at budget time.

— Keep administrator and fiscal officer informed of unusual budget needs and problems developing so they may review them to their satisfaction or take alternate action before the rush of normal budget reviews.

— Involve public in determining recreation needs as well as the budget process at every opportunity.

— Inform staff and public of the budget schedule (calendar) and procedures. Invite them to make their needs known.

— Ask staff for their budget requests and justifications.

— Review requests with staff.

— Prepare budget proposals.

— Obtain estimated costs, pictures, specifications and other supportive information.

— Review budget proposals with board or advisory board, if there is one.

— Submit final budget document to administrator or the designated fiscal officer.

— Review budget with administrator (fiscal officer or committee of policy board). Supporting staff may attend. Budget proposals may be changed at this point.

— Administrator presents total budget recommendations (including revenues) to policy board.

— Policy board reviews, holds public hearings, makes amendments, if it wishes; then adopts and returns budget documents to administrator (agency heads and key staff may be involved).

— Administrator and agency heads execute the budget as adopted.

PROJECTING REVENUES AND EXPENSES

Many problems develop in urbanized areas because of inadequate planning. In the past few years cities have been faced with growing difficulties in fiscal matters because of inadequate planning. Past trends, comparisons, balances on hand, forecasting ahead a few months at a time and old patterns of figuring income and expenses continued to be used in preparation of operating budgets and determining capital expenditures. In fact, financial problems of some cities reached crisis proportions before the real seriousness of the situations were realized. The crisis might have been avoided if longer range financial forecasts had been made.

A few cities have hired consultants or set up committees of local experts in planning, accounting, taxation, assessments, research, fiscal administration, politics, business, education, and best resources possible to study, report, and recommend solutions concerning the growing fiscal problems. Most of them found that new sources of revenue were hard to find. State and local politicians were reluctant to permit or enact payroll taxes or local income taxes. Costs for schools and other human services (welfare, health, recreation) were increasing rapidly, but more startling was the fact that annual rates for essential government services were increasing at a much greater percentage than potential income. There was strong resistance generally to further increase in taxes and only minimal opportunities for new sources of income, and several cities were already curtailing expenses to balance their budgets. Some governments had reached their legal debt limit for borrowing, including the federal government but it has the authority and did continue to raise its own debt limit as needs arose to borrow money to finance deficit spending which included large amounts for grants-in-aid to states and localities. Some cities were finding it difficult or impossible to provide local matching funds for the state and federal grant-in-aid projects. On January 1, 1972, the federal general revenue sharing program, which involved direct grants to states and in turn to localities on a per capita basis formula, eased the financial strain a bit. It gave localities more time and resources to do financial planning and establish priorities.

There is definite need for long-term financial projections, both revenue and expense, in order to provide effective fiscal management. At the federal level, multi-year budget presentations are required. This method provides some flexibility for planning and adjustment. At this point, states and localities have not incorporated long-term projections in their operating budgets. Many have projected long range capital improvements needs, usually for five years, plus longer range master plans, but few localities include financial planning for the same periods.

Planning commissions traditionally have been very responsive and effective in physical planning. It appears that they will now give more attention to fiscal planning, perhaps in conjunction with fiscal experts, which may be included as staff to forecast such items as salaries, sources and amounts of public income, changes in tax base, economic conditions, state and federal aid, and other fiscal items.

NEW APPROACH TO FORECASTING

It is predicted that localities will be developing new approaches to fiscal planning and projections. The New Haven expenditure model is a new approach developed by Claudia Devita Scott.

> The New Haven expenditure model developed by the author represents a new approach to forecasting city expenditures. It provides a mechanism for projecting current and capital expenditures

for all departments in the city's budget annually over a five-year period.

The projections which the model makes are based on the values of a number of aspects or variables which have an important impact on future expenditure levels. The variables are of three kinds.

- Population variables which are projections of the size, age and racial composition of the population of the city.
- Salary variables which are projections of the levels or rates of increase for individuals in the various salary and wage classes.
- Service variables which are projections of the way in which the level of service or manner in which services are provided will change, given some assumed change in the demand for services by the residents of the city.

Unlike other expenditure forecasting techniques, the New Haven model has a fairly flexible structure. Each particular class of expenditures can be projected according to various explicit assumptions regarding the demand for and supply of services. Every projection made by the model is associated with specific statements concerning the values of the major variables. The variables are supplied to the model by city planners and other officials, the persons best qualified to predict because they have greatest access to the pertinent facts. Even in instances where a high degree of confidence cannot be attached to a particular projection, the ability to determine and compare the effects of a variety of different assumptions can be very useful. The author finds that, through experimentation, the user quickly learns about the sensitivity of the model's projections as different assumptions are made about changes in population, salaries and service levels.

Unlike other forecasting models in existence, this model makes explicit statements concerning the level of services which will be provided over the period of projections. Moreover, each service is treated independently. Thus the model can examine the impact of a decision to expand or contract particular services in some period. The model requires separate information inputs for each year over which projections are being made. Unlike techniques based on the extrapolation of previous trends, the projections devised here are more independent in character. The model also can be used as a device for examining the future cost of providing current levels of city services. More interestingly, it may deal simultaneously with a wide range of different projections—some services expanded, some contracted, and others at their present level—for any given year. Then the mix may be altered to check new projections. The capacity to spell out the anticipated results of many different options makes this approach to budgeting particularly useful to a local decision maker.[5]

Questions for Discussion

1. What is the purpose of the budget? How is it used after it is adopted?
2. What is the purpose of a budget calendar?
3. What are the steps in the budget process?
4. What is the difference between a work program and a work unit?
5. Describe the different types of budgets.
6. What guidelines are used in preparing a recreation budget?
7. What is the role of the chief administrator in budget administration? The policy board? The citizen?
8. What is included in supportive information?
9. How are expenditures controlled?
10. Distinguish between concurrent audit and postaudit.

Short Problems

1. List sources of revenue, other than taxes, that you would recommend for a public recreation agency and establish rules, security measures, collection and accounting procedures pertaining to them.
2. Outline a procedure including safeguards and administrative controls for budget expenditures, from initiation of request for purchase through postaudit.

References

1. Lynn S. Rodney, *Administration of Public Recreation* (New York: The Ronald Press Company, 1964), p. 245.
2. *Operating Budget,* City of Richmond, Va., 1974.
3. A.E. Beck, *Public Budgeting* (New York: Harper and Row, 1929), pp. 201–203.
4. Rodney, *Administration of Public Recreation,* pp. 256–58.
5. Claudia Devita Scott, *Forecasting Local Government Spending* (Washington, D.C.: The Urban Institute, 1972), pp. 4–5.

Selected Readings

Hinriches, J., and G. Taylor, *Program Budgeting and Benefit Cost Analysis.* Englewood Cliffs, N.J.: Prentice-Hall, Inc., 1969.

Hjelte, George, and Jay S. Shivers, *Public Administration of Recreational Services,* pp. 341–359. Philadelphia: Lea and Febiger, 1972.

International City Managers' Association, *Planning and Budgeting in Municipal Management.* Chicago: The Association, 1965.

Moak, Lennox L., and Albert M. Millhouse, *Concepts and Practices of Local Government Finance,* pp. 65–118. Chicago: Municipal Finance Officer Association, 1975.

Powers, Stanley Piazza, F. Gerald Brown, and David S. Arnold, eds., *Developing the Municipal Organization,* pp. 147–159. Washington, D.C.: International City Management Association, 1974.

Rodney, Lynn S., *Administration of Public Recreation,* pp. 244–283. New York: The Ronald Press Company, 1964.

CHAPTER 15

Planning for Recreation Areas and Facilities

Community planning involves consideration of all matters that relate to the physical form and character of the community, its structures and relationships, patterns of land use, aesthetics, forecast for future, distribution of population, and related physical services. Community planning, like the functions of government it serves, is a continuing process and is affected by every movement, new development, or change in the area. Planning is performed by a separate planning agency which is responsible for total needs of a locality and an operating agency which is responsible for the specific agency needs and usually is performed by its staff or consultant.

Planning in the United States has developed as a municipal function since 1900. Model plans, the basis of current enabling legislation, were developed by 1935. They basically provided for the establishment of a separate, semi-dependent planning commission with technical staff outside the regular administrative jurisdiction.[1]

The format of the planning organization and the selection of its personnel varies from city to city. In recent years some cities, although leaving the planning commission in the status of a semi-independent body, have placed the technical staff under the jurisdiction of the city administrator [2] to be in a better position to involve and assist the administrative staff with the growing problems of urban and urbanizing communities. Small communities may use planning consultants, regional planners, and their professional staff to perform planning duties. Larger agencies may have their own planning and engineering department.

RECREATION PLANNING

Planning for the immediate and long range needs of population, including recreation, is a function interrelated with other functions in the community, both public and private. Planning for recreation is a total community concern. It relates to schools, streets, utilities, safety, urban renewal public housing, commercial recreation, and private interests, as well as the total population. Planning involves research and provides standards, planning principles, guidelines, and information to help direct energies and resources toward predetermined objectives.

Every recreation executive and his administrative and supervisory personnel are recreation planners and use very much the same guides and standards as the full-time planning technician and professional planning consultant, but the recreation executive and staff are in a better position to do practical (functional) recreation planning. Usually, a better job of planning is done when planners, recreationists and the public plan together as a team. Each has experiences to offer that, generally, the others do not have.

Suitable recreation facilities properly planned, located, developed, and maintained are essential to an effective public recreation program. This chapter deals with the planning for recreation, implementation of plans, involvement of citizens, standards and guidelines, site selection and development, methods of acquiring land, design, and maintenance. There are three types of plans: the master plan, the five-year plan, and the one-year plan.

THE MASTER PLAN

The master plan is a tool (document) for guiding individual, corporate, and government decisions which affect the future physical growth and development of a locality, usually projected for a period of 25 years—a generation. It deals with matters involving population trends, land uses, community facilities, traffic ways, utilities, slum clearance, urban renewal, public housing, redevelopment, monuments, beautification, open space, parks, and recreation areas. The master plan coordinates needs, preserves space, and reduces duplication and chances of error.

Planners consider that adequate and diversified recreational opportunities provide economic advantages since they improve general living environment and social conditions.

To serve most effectively, public recreation facilities must be strategically located, imaginatively designed, adequately supplied, and well maintained if they are to contribute to the appearance and overall vitality of the locality.

Each type of area or facility has a specialized function to perform in meeting the varied recreational needs of the entire community. A recreation plan is based on assumptions, principles, standards, experiences and studies which are helpful in determining the location, size and type of proposed recreation facilities needed in relation to future population, trends, land use, and other community needs.

A recreation master plan projects for 25 years all of the physical needs for program, maintenance, land acquisition, development, expansion, and other facilities, and coordinates all with the overall master plan. It is a general plan subject to updating, adjustments, and addition or deletion as time progresses, and needs become clearer, or change.

IMPLEMENTATION OF PLANS

The master plan is only a long range plan. It must be implemented by action and appropriations. Usually, this is done by two types of short range plans; the five-year plan and the one-year plan. Some communities have a three-year plan.

The Five-Year Plan

The five-year plan is composed of most needed projects taken from the master plan and based on information, facts, experience, proposed projects, and priorities to serve needs of the foreseeable future. The five-year plan becomes the five-year capital budget proposal. As time progresses, it may be that unforeseen needs have developed since the master plan was prepared. If so, they are added and the master plan is amended to provide for them.

The five-year capital budget is prepared in detail to coincide with the five-year plan. Priorities and estimated costs are prepared for each separate year. Locations, particularly for the first two years, become rather definitive.

Each budget year, the programs of the five-year plan (the capital budget) advance a year. The first year group then becomes the "one-year plan." Projects from the master plan are selected and added as the fifth year of the five-year plan. Estimates, information, and priorities are updated and it becomes the new five-year plan. Some projects may extend over two or more years.

The One-Year Plan

The one-year plan is the "immediate plan," and is the capital budget proposed for the budget year. Exact locations are selected (but plans for land acquisition are not yet revealed), working drawings are in progress or completed, cost estimates are updated, best methods of financing are recommended, and estimated yearly costs of operation and maintenance are included.

The five-year capital budget then follows the procedure of reviews established by operating budget except where there is a local planning commission an extra step may be added before it is presented to the legislative body namely, review by the planning commission and possible public hearings. Changes may be recommended at this point.

The Planning Process

The planning process depends upon the government and administrative structure in the local community. The master plan may be prepared by a professional planning consultant, a local or area planning commission staff, or a combination. It may be a total plan including all aspects and agencies; it may be in the form of a series of plans on separate subjects such as traffic ways, utility, and community facility; it may be a single service plan such as recreation, or portion of a single service plan such as a neighborhood, or a single program facility such as swimming pools, or a single facility such as a park. In any event, it is coordinated with and incorporated in the total community master plan.

The master plan projects immediate, short range and long range needs and recommends priorities. In order to do this and make sound forecasts, the planners obtain complete information on past experiences and make up-to-date factual studies that indicate trends and numbers. Perhaps, the most difficult projections are what people are going to do, where they will be, and when they will be there. Few localities have all of the skills and resources on their own planning staffs, therefore, they seek outside planning consultant firms, or employ specialized personnel or consultants to supplement their staff resources.

In order to deal with the interrelated problems and needs of total communities and metropolitan areas, master planners need specialists trained and experienced in many fields such as zoning, safety (police and fire protection, sanitation), transportation, housing, recreation, education, public administration, civil engineering, landscape architecture, environmental problems, conservation, law, sociology, economics, financing, and urban planning.

Whatever method, or combination of methods, is used in arriving at a completed master plan, the local planning staff, the respective agency executive, the technicians responsible for executing the plan, and the citizens who will be affected or involved in carrying out an effective plan must have a guiding role in its preparation.

The preparation of a total master plan is generally directed by the local planners or the administrator with agency heads cooperating. The preparation of the separate unit (recreation) plan may be directed by the agency executive or his designated representative.

The planner (meaning whoever is preparing the plan) consults with agency executive, local planning commission, appropriate community leaders, and citizen groups; holds discussions or group meetings with local people involved, and prepares recommendations. Then he reviews the preliminary draft with the agency executive, planning staff, and sometimes key citizens to get reactions, suggestions for refinement or rephrasing statements for better local understanding and acceptance. Sometimes a consultant states a thought in a way that could be misunderstood or is not clear; or the planner may have omitted consideration of an element important to the community.

Copies of the proposal are then prepared (holding the type for possible changes) and presented to the planning commission and/or chief administrator with the planner discussing recommendations and answering questions. Agency heads, members of policy board, and key citizen contacts may, or may not, be present.

Copies of the proposed master plan are publicized and made available to the public. The planning staff or commission holds public hearings on the proposal at convenient sites in the community. Everyone is encouraged to attend and express views or make suggestions. Frequently, excellent suggestions for improvement are made and accepted.

When all hearings are completed and accepted changes are incorporated, the master plan proposal is put in ordinance form and presented to the legislative body for adoption. The planner usually makes the presentation and answers questions. The legislative body, in accordance with customary procedures on ordinances, holds public hearings at either regular or special meetings. The legislative body must amend or adopt the proposed master plan in order to make it effective. States may vary in procedures in dealing with the master plan. In Virginia, for example, upon approval by the legislative body there is an implicit agreement that the governing body will stand by the plan in the event of a conflict in land development with the community's needs. Upon adoption by the legislative body, it becomes law and is administered by the planning staff or commission and respective agencies involved in regulatory matters such as subdivision regulations, applications for building permits, and land uses which are in conflict with the master plan. The master plan becomes the immediate and future guide for agency proposals for capital improvements and, in turn, the capital budgets.

STEPS IN PLANNING TO MEET COMMUNITY NEEDS

Much of the recreation executive's time is spent in planning. Effective planning may determine the quality, quantity and future status of the program. Space must be acquired and made available when needed and the program and staff must be ready. This means the executive must anticipate the future including the nature, interests, and distribution of the population; trends in leisure time pursuits; and public support for service not yet available. He must have an attractive program as a basis for planning the facility followed by plans for budget and staffing.

Briefly, the steps in planning would be:

1. Determine program and facility needs, as outlined later in this chapter, being sure to involve the citizens as much as possible and to keep the administrator informed.
2. Prepare long range plans and objectives based on the needs of the people, keeping in mind the policies and concept of the agency, the 15 planning guides, outlined later in this chapter, and the program services to be provided in the plan.
3. Mobilize available resources and support. Determine how facilities will be paid for such as sale of bonds, donation, tax revenue, and grants-in-aid. Bonding plus cash paydown from current revenues is a popular method of financing capital improvement programs.
4. Select architect or consultant. Sometimes an architect, landscape architect, or consultant's services are needed for feasibility and other studies to provide information needed to determine sites.
5. Select and acquire sites.
6. Implement plans.
7. Maintain and operate.

DETERMINING NEEDS: INVOLVING THE CITIZENS

Before 1900, little consideration was given to acquisition of land for recreation and the preservation of open space except around city halls and courthouses. There were few city-wide plans. The few parks and play areas were largely gifts or separate purchases because of a special interest of an individual. Consequently, park and recreation areas were not always located to serve the greatest needs. There was limited involvement on the part of planners and neighborhood people. In more recent years, as vacant lots and desirable open spaces, including park and play areas, were converted to thoroughfares and other public uses, the need for planning and citizen involvement in recreation and other human services became essential elements of neighborhood and community development.

The general requirements for open space and recreation areas are incorporated in the general community master plan along with schools, streets, libraries and other land uses. Since the people pay the costs and receive the services, it is natural in a democratic society that they want to be involved in determining greatest needs and priorities of services. Local recreation planning and citizen involvement may be done on neighborhood, community, city-wide, or regional basis.

Neighborhood Involvement

The neighborhood is considered by planners and recreationists as the basic unit for social and physical planning. It may be defined as a homogenous grouping of people with similar interests and social, religious, economic and cultural background who tend to develop a feeling of loyalty and identification with others of the area. The neighborhood may be bounded by natural or artificial barriers. However, since the latter part of the 1960's forced busing of school children, the elimination of the neighborhood school concept, and other federally regulated guidelines and laws, some neighborhoods have lost much of their human interest, loyalty, social, religious and cultural identity definition.

The neighborhood is also considered to be a residential area varying from one-half to one mile square with 2,000 to 10,000 * population [3] and served by an elementary school and playground.

Playground and center advisory councils and youth councils composed of interested neighborhood citizens and youth (organized by recreation staff) serve to interpret neighborhood recreation needs. They are in a good position to know and advise the staff concerning physical needs for recreation at the neighborhood level. Other recreation interest groups including P-TA's, church groups, civic associations, women's and men's clubs, Community Action Program advisory councils, school counselors, private recreation agency staffs, and community leaders are good sources of neighborhood information also.

The neighborhood, being rather a complete identifiable area with 2,000 to 10,000 population, is almost an ideal unit for recreation planning and standards if facilities can be placed on a suitable space near the center. Facilities are then within walking and bicycling distances of the people they serve and may include playlot, playground, neighborhood center, and neighborhood park. Recommendations, not administration decisions, are made at this level.

Community Involvement

The term community sometimes refers to a district as a part of a city and sometimes refers to an entire city. It is defined as a large identifiable area, mainly residential, composed of a natural grouping of several neighborhoods somewhat interrelated. It usually has a population of 20,000 to 40,000 and is served by high school facilities and a major recreation complex (pool, tournament area, center, large park, special facilities) in addition to the elementary schools and neighborhood recreation areas. It may be bounded by streams, railroads, highways, major thoroughfares and rugged topography.

It is likely that the recreation organization structure will conform to the community structure. If so, an area recreation supervisor would be the contact for involving the citizens with area interests. Two representatives (1 male, 1 female) from each of the neighborhood recreation councils plus five or six citizens at large such as the recreation chairman from high school P-TA, member of athletic league, garden club, children's theatre, choral society, tennis association, and church sports league make a good working committee providing the individuals are really interested. Some communities do not form committees so that staff makes the contacts with citizens and groups. The committee and staff would be involved in long range planning, implementation of plans for programs, attractive areas, and facilities (including special facilities) for the community and in coordinating planning with public and private agencies.

Recommendations, only, are made at this level to the administrative staff.

City-Wide Involvement

Many recreation agencies have official or advisory boards on which citizens are involved in policy and decision making. In a smaller community the board may be sufficient contact for community recreation planning, depending on scope of the program. In larger communities more citizens are involved on city-wide program committees such as senior citizen councils, youth councils, programs for the handicapped (advisory), booster clubs, sports commissions, special activities, and special interest groups all of which have interest in present and future programs and facilities. They support the official board and often appear at planning commission hearings and policy board meetings to support their interests. Some of their most effective work is participation on surveys and personal contacts by letter, telephone, or in person with decision makers.

Most decisions are made at the city-wide level by the agency head, who applies policy; the chief administrator, who makes administrative decisions and recommends policy; the planning commission which regulates, makes decisions, and recommends policy; and the policy board (legislative body) which makes policy, makes agreements, commits the government, and appropriates funds for implementation.

Regional Involvement

Citizen participation plays a major role in regional boards, commissions, authorities and committees, such as regional governments, regional park authority, regional planning commission, study committees, special project programs, and others funded, sometimes, partially by state and federal grants. Citizens may be appointed to regional policy boards and advisory committees by local governments. Study committees and project advisory groups may be appointed in several ways—by legislative bodies, policy boards, or administrative personnel.

Sometimes government procedures require conformity to regional plans and regional approval of grant-in-aid projects, environmental impact studies, and similar matters that affect the region and involve citizen appointments.

More and more, local matters, that may involve people outside the local political jurisdiction, are reviewed, approved, rejected or modified by procedures at the regional and state levels. Trends lead towards more surveys, planning, jurisdiction, approval, and government at the regional level.

Recreation Surveys

A recreation survey, as used in recreation planning, consists of obtaining and researching total or specific information about a subject. They may be conducted by private consultants, staff, citizen groups (volunteers), and joint efforts.

Private consultants are employed in three ways: (1) under contract for a fixed amount for a complete job as specified in signed agreement, (2) at a daily rate or hourly rate, or (3) on a cost-plus basis. Transportation expenses, printing, reproduction, clerical, and other extra costs may, or may not, be added. To prevent overspending, a maximum limit that can be spent is specified in the contract.

The private consultant method is popular when money is available. It provides additional experience and knowledge and permits agency executive and staff to continue their normal functions. When a serious community controversy is involved, it provides a better opportunity for unbiased recommendations and community acceptance.

Staff, either alone or in combination with other agencies, is involved in survey work, evaluations, and research continuously as one of their normal functions. Sometimes, staff are relieved of their normal functions temporarily to make special studies and surveys. This method keeps costs lower but often lacks skills and prestige for major jobs.

Citizen groups (volunteered or sponsored) very often sponsor or conduct with their membership surveys in which the group is especially interested and provides the agency with pertinent information and support. The usefulness of this method depends largely upon expertise, leadership and sincerity of the group. It is particularly useful for community involvement and support on single issue matters.

Joint efforts, involving the leadership and expertise of professional staff plus resources and support of citizens, make an outstanding combination. However, the professional leadership must be strong to obtain maximum results. In this method, the staff singularly, or preferably with a small steering committee of citizens, decides on objectives, methods of obtaining required information, and how it is to be compiled, summarized, evaluated, and presented. They obtain additional interested volunteers, if needed, and orient them well before making contacts for information.

One method of obtaining good coverage of the area to be surveyed is to ask appropriate organizations to send two representatives (allowing for one male and one female from mixed groups). It is desirable to have representation from all groups and ages, if applicable. This method can be used in any size community for a long range or short range program.

After the survey is completed and summarized the same group of volunteers and staff along with executive staff, if possible, make recommendations and set priorities, if appropriate.

This method of establishing capital improvement and program needs has the advantage of involving the staff that must execute plans and the public for which services are to be developed. It helps both to understand and support them. Problems can be dealt with during the stages of planning with much greater understanding. It tends to coordinate public and private agency planning and prevents duplication of effort.

STANDARDS AND GUIDELINES

Space standards, which have been developed within the last 50 years, are the chief guidelines for recreation area planning. They are used to set quality and adequacy of a facility or service. Again, because of the wide range of varying situations in recreation, standards are considered minimum and subject to modification with different local situations. In fact, it is a common practice in some localities to use the standards recommended by the National Recreation and Park Association as a minimum base to form specific standards for their respective communities by making adjustments based on use experience in the locality, potential users, unusually small or large numbers of private and semi-private sources, extended use by lighting or shelter covering, and other unusual local situations.

Standard may be defined as a criterion, guide, or model which has been established by authority, law, use experience, or general agreement. In recreation and planning, standards are usually prepared and adopted by national professional organizations and sometimes endorsed by federal and state government agencies.

Common Space Standards

The need for recreation space and facility standards has been evident since the turn of the nineteenth century, but there was not much experi-

Space Standards by Classification and Population Ratio
(Recommended by the National Recreation and Park Association[5])

Classification	Acres per 1000 people	Size range	Population served	Service area
Playlots	—	2500 sq. ft. to 1 acre	500–2500	Sub-neighborhood
Vest pocket parks	—	2500 sq. ft. to 1 acre	500–2500	Sub-neighborhood
Neighborhood parks	2.5	Min. 5 acres up to 20 acres	2000–10,000	¼ to ½ mi.
District parks	2.5	20–100 acres	10,000–50,000	½ to 3 mi.
Large urban parks	5.0	100 + acres	One for each 50,000	Within ½ hr. driving time
Regional parks	20.0	250 + acres	Serves entire pop. in smaller communities	Within 1 hour driving time

ence on which to base recommendations except from public schools. In the 1920's, one acre of land per 100 city population [4] was the recommended space standard for urban parks and recreation outdoor areas which continues to be the widely accepted minimum standard. Smaller communities, new developments, and renewals should have one acre per 50 population. Natural areas, reservations, forest preserves, regional parks, parkways, street medians, special areas, zoos and golf courses are not included in the base space standard of one acre per 100 population. Therefore, a minimum of 20 acres per 1000 populations should be added for these items to the one acre per 100 population standard. Recreation areas should be well distributed throughout residential communities. In older built up cities where needs are greatest, it is very costly and impractical to acquire and demolish high value property and to change street and neighborhood patterns to meet the one acre per 100 population standard. Considerable improvements have been made in low value areas through public housing and urban renewal projects. New and expanding communities are able to meet or even surpass the standard.

STANDARDS FOR SPECIAL FACILITIES
(RECOMMENDED BY THE NATIONAL RECREATION AND PARK ASSOCIATION [6])

FACILITY (OUTDOOR)	STANDARD/1000 PEOPLE
Baseball diamonds	1 per 6000
Softball diamonds (and/or youth diamonds)	1 per 3000
Tennis courts	1 per 2000 (in units of 4)
Basketball courts	1 per 500
Swimming pools (25 yard)	1 per 10,000
Swimming pools (50 yard)	1 per 20,000
Skating rinks (artificial)	1 per 30,000
Neighborhood centers	1 per 10,000
Community centers	1 per 25,000
Outdoor theatres (non-commercial)	1 per 20,000
Shooting ranges	1 per 50,000
Golf course (18 hole)	1 per 25,000

The 10 acre per 1000 population standard is applied by recreationists to provide 2.5 acres for neighborhood uses (about half for active recreation uses), 2.5 acres for community or area uses, and 5 acres for larger parks and open space.

Other standards [7] communities use are:

1 gymnasium	per 10,000 population or less
1 auditorium	per 20,000 population or less

1 swimming pool (indoor)	per 50,000 population or less
1 game room (active)	per 10,000 population or less
1 game room (quiet)	per 10,000 population or less
1 arts and crafts room	per 10,000 population or less
1 multiple use room (large)	per 10,000 population or less
1 club or activities room	per 4,000 population or less
1 social room	per 10,000 population or less
1 group camp [8]	per 25,000 population or less
1 football field	per 10,000 population or less
1 soccer field	per 10,000 population or less
1 handball court [9]	per 10,000 population or less
1 shuffleboard court [10]	per 1,500 population or less

Standards are important planning aids, but they need to be guided by agency policy, goals, objectives, philosophy and principles. Today's plans will become tomorrow's activities and responsibilities, therefore, greatest of care should be exercised in forecasting needs and in planning.

Recreation Planning Principles

Recreation planning principles provide major guidelines for physical planning. They give general direction as to type, location, balance, scope, procedure, relationship and uses in planning areas and facilities. They represent a general truth or fact, such as a recreation facility should be conveniently accesible to persons it serves.

The following guidelines concern physical planning for recreation areas and facilities.

1. Evaluate present and future unmet needs by relating them to existing public facilities, scope of services to be rendered, master plan, and accepted standards.
2. Evaluate present and future facilities to avoid unnecessary duplication and provide orderly coordinated community development.
3. Provide opportunities for everyone, all groups and ages including senior citizens and the handicapped.
4. Provide a balance in facilities to serve the varied interests of the population; indoor, outdoor, and special facilities as may be required by the community and in line with policy.
5. Involve the public in order to better determine needs and maintain public support.
6. Plan joint uses, including acquisition. Very often multiple services (schools, clinics, fire stations, libraries) may be planned advantageously at a site.

7. Locate facilities centrally in the population area to serve more conveniently and attract a greater participation.
8. Select a suitable site. The entire site should be usable, properly shaped, properly located with good drainage, free of safety and health hazards including harmful snakes, insects and obnoxious odors.
9. The selected site should be readily accessible to public transportation, driving, walking and bicycling.
10. Make the facility adaptable to changing population and uses.
11. Stress the economy of improvement, maintenance, and supervision. Utilize natural features. Avoid costly grading, drainage, utility construction, maintenance.
12. Consider convenience of public using the facility, transportation, parking, restrooms, and entrances.
13. Acquire open space well in advance of neighborhood development in order to obtain suitable sites at a fair rate.
14. Consider aesthetics, appeal, and environmental factors, as well as functional efficiency.
15. Permanence in use of land for recreation purposes is a high priority. There is a trend to divert open space for other public uses (highways, schools, parking, fire stations, utility lines). Care should be taken to minimize these opportunities in planning, acquiring, developing, and gaining public support.

ARCHITECTURAL AND CONSULTANT SERVICES

The master plan is only a plan, a guide. It has to be implemented with other action—an action plan for facilities and budget. One of the first requirements of construction is a working plan and accompanying specifications which are detailed written instructions how the work is to be performed and what materials are to be used. Very few agencies have the skills and resources to prepare plans for structures. If the structures are constructed by a contractor, and most of them are, law requires bids to be made. Written plans and specifications, therefore, must be provided for bidding. For a major recreation structure, preparation of the plans may take several months. Sometimes a contractor will volunteer to draw the plans and construct small facilities. Even if this is legal, one should be careful that all safety and health requirements are met. Use of a competent professional architect is recommended.

Usually, credentials of three or more architects experienced in preparing plans for the type of recreation facility proposed (center, swimming pool) are reviewed in detail and one selected that has most favorable experience and meets the requirements of the project. It is helpful if the architect is experienced and knowledgeable in recreation construction.

Sometimes, the landscaping design and planting is awarded under a separate contract from the structure. If the agency has competent landscape architects and horticulturists, the agency does its own landscaping. Generally, it is best to award one contract to avoid divided responsibility. Sometimes, the planning and supervision of construction is performed by another agency of government such as public works.

It is the recreation executive's responsibility to see that the design is functional, the materials appropriate and proper, and the completed project and grounds attractive in appearance and satisfactory all the way.

The Contract

A written contract drawn by the agency attorney should specify the fee and method of payment in complete detail as well as what is expected of the architect. It should include deadlines, services to be provided on preliminary drawings, agency and community contacts, working drawings, specifications, detailed drawings, extras, advertising and taking of bids, preparation of contracts; preparation of change orders and certificates of payments; inspections and supervision on the job, and generally look out for the agency's interest. Architects usually have available standard contract forms.

It is well to designate who will be the architect's contact with the agency and to include a statement to the effect that the "structure must be designed within funds available. If it is necessary to revise plans to reduce costs within funds available the architect agrees to make the necessary revision without extra charge." This has become advisable because some persons tend to overdesign a facility and staff tend to want more than was provided for in the appropriation. Not knowing the final bid the architect proceeds to include the additions in the drawings which sometimes inflate the costs beyond the funds available and the contract cannot be let until adjustments are made to reduce costs. The law requires that funds must be available before a public expenditure can be authorized. It may be advisable to provide flexibility in instances where funds are limited by planning for alternate bids with allowances made for deductions in event bids are too high. This means that plans are drawn so certain features can be deducted without rebidding or changing drawings.

At least 5 percent of estimated cost should be reserved for contingencies. This is not included in the totals allowed the architect for construction and gives the agency a little buffer which always seems to be needed for unforeseen circumstances.

SITE SELECTION, ACQUISITION, AND DEVELOPMENT

The four most important ingredients of a recreation program are money, staff, people and space. People, money, and staff must have space in order to function. People can use space without money or staff; therefore, it appears space is the most important and is becoming more important each year. With land almost impossible to obtain in developed neighborhoods and in open fields before subdivisions move in (and there is rapid acceleration of costs as improvements are needed), it behooves the recreationist and the public to put more effort into planning, wise selection and use of land available, and preservation or acquisition of land for projected future use well in advance of need. Surplus government property and open spaces created through urban renewal projects are two opportunities that can make space available in built up areas.

Site Selection

The selection of sites for parks and recreation uses in the past has been a hit or miss situation. Often, it was a donation of land formerly used for other purposes, abandoned property, tax delinquent property, hillsides, swamps, residues, waste lands, odd parcels too small for other purposes, dumps, and land-fill disposal areas, none of which were selected for location and suitability for recreation purposes and most of which required high cost maintenance returning very low benefits to the tax-paying citizen. The locations, shapes, sizes, topography and opportunities for recreation were minimal.

Unfortunately most of better suited sites are developed and area begins to have problems of congestion and lack of free open space, before sufficient public interest can be aroused to support appropriations for public acquisition. Strong effort should be exerted to approach as near an ideal situation as possible in new areas added in the future.

Factors to consider in selecting a site are:

1. The purposes for which it will be used.
2. Distribution of population, future trends.
3. Relationship to existing facilities in the area (public and private).
4. Centrally located in the area of people it is to serve. Neighborhood facilities should be within walking distance of most users.

5. The entire site should be usable at reasonable costs for improvements, proper shape, adequate size, good drainage, usable topography, and free of safety and health hazards.
6. Located at or near public transportation, needed utilities (water, sewerage, electricity).
7. Interesting usable natural features, if possible.
8. Sometimes zoning regulations do not permit all of the present and future uses intended. Neighborhood and community facilities are usually planned in residential areas. Commercial type facilities, amusement parks, and rides are not permitted in some residential areas.
9. Trees for shade or maybe a buffer strip to screen the area from adjoining properties.
10. Possibilities of dual uses, particularly with schools.
11. Financing and costs of improvements and continuing maintenance.

Methods of Acquiring Property

Acquisition of public open space for recreation and park use should be done well in advance of need. Public acquisition of land is a slow process, especially when relocation and condemnation are involved. Since it may take several months to purchase, obtain possession of land, and prepare working drawings for realistic estimates and bidding, it is well to plan funds for acquisition and drawing of plans the first year and construction of facilities the second year—a two-year program.

The law requires a stated purpose for acquiring public property. It may be general such as "for general government purposes" or the legislation may specify a specific purpose such as "for a public playground." The space must be used for the stated purpose which usually is routine unless public opposition develops.

In the planning stages, locations for purchase are referred to in a general way such as a circle on a map. It is usually not advisable to reveal in advance that the government is planning to purchase an exact site lest speculators become involved or owners raise the price. Sometimes governments obtain options to preserve the status of negotiations while government goes through budget and legal procedures.

In acquiring property, it is customary for the government to obtain from at least two qualified impartial appraisers the fair market value of the subject property. In acquiring occupied property the government is required to pay moving and relocation costs, putting the occupant in substantially equal or better facilities without cost to him.

Usually, the agency lawyer and real estate specialist on staff handle government purchases. Generally, commissions to realtors are not legal. The legislative body, of course, must finally approve any commitment or purchase on the part of the government.

Public property may be acquired by one of the following methods.

Direct purchase of property from the owner or owners is the most common method. It is one of the simpler procedures and less costly than condemnation. This involves the owner and the government negotiating and completing an agreement.

It is difficult (illegal in some states) to purchase land on an installment basis, because the incumbent administration cannot legally make a commitment or expenditure binding on a future administration unless, of course, it provides the money to go with it such as a construction project.

Condemnation is a direct purchase of property from the owner through the right of eminent domain when the owner and government cannot come to an agreement. The price is fixed by the court. In some places the condemnation procedure is used to clear title to land when the recorded owner cannot be located and title cannot be cleared otherwise.

Right of eminent domain is the legal power of any government to acquire property for public purposes through due process of law with just compensation to the owner. This right is provided through state statutes based on the premise that property may be acquired by a government for the common good of all the people it serves.[11] The price fixed by the courts must be paid by the government involved.

Excess purchase is the acquisition of more land than is actually required for a specific project, especially one that increases the value of surrounding land. When improvement is completed, the land is sold and the difference in price is used for the improvements to the land. This has the advantage of regulating use of the property. There is some question as to the constitutionality of this method since public condemnation and purchase of property is only for essential public use. If this method is widely used, it could very well result in crippling legal acquisitions.

Transfer or exchange of property permanently between government agencies is quite advantageous to recreation and park agencies. Often transfer of abandoned or unused portions of larger parcels relieves the existing owner of maintenance and upkeep and provides a favorable site for recreation, particularly in older sections. Examples are government surplus property, river fronts, flood areas, land-filled disposal areas, storage yards and warehouses, abandoned schools, firehouses, water sheds and easements. Sometimes agencies or private owners will exchange properties for better suited property, if approached.

Tax delinquent property, particularly in older sections, sometimes makes good usable recreation spaces. However, the agency may have to pay the cost of back taxes in order to clear the records. Sometimes it can be a paper transfer with approval of the legislative body. Before investing money in improvements, one should check carefully to see that title is cleared and what are the rights and chances of the owner paying the back taxes plus penalties and reclaiming the property. In times of low property values, it might be advisable to go through condemnation proceedings on favorable long term use properties and clear the title. This would mean a fair market value would have to be paid, but this may prove advantageous in the long run.

Subdivision dedications of a certain percentage of space for recreation and park use are required of land developers and subdividers, particularly in suburban communities. This land may be maintained by the owner as in an apartment complex, deeded to an association of owners who have purchased homes in the development, or deeded to the local government which then manages the park and recreation area. In instances of dedication to government, the public body must officially accept the dedication and responsibility. Property acquired in this manner may not be sold without the written consent of every homeowner in the development. Care should be taken that the percentage of land dedicated is suitable and usable for public purposes and not wasteland. Sometimes the percentage is paid in cash and the funds used to acquire nearby space or to add to nearby public area.

Gifts and bequests are a very satisfactory way of obtaining property. The governing body accepts the gift, and the deed is properly recorded. Very often the gift is for a specific purpose, such as a park, and the deed provides a reversionary condition that property reverts to the donor or heirs if use for the purpose given is discontinued or it is used for other purposes. This is usually an advantage to recreation but care should be taken that there are not restrictive conditions that are unacceptable for public property in perpetuity.

Bequests should be encouraged. Often there are public minded individuals who are pleased to consider bequeathing, for public use in perpetuity, property for a memorial park or playground. They need to be contacted and informed.

A *lease agreement* is a way of acquiring land, sometimes indefinitely, with other government agencies, such as federal, state, regional authorities, county governments, school districts and airports; also private property such as industrial woodlands, railroad holdings, and flood plains.

Use of vacant lots and temporary uses of facilities have proven insecure unless there is a definite use period and written agreement. Many pieces of vacant property, without lease agreement, have been improved by community or public groups only to find they have made them salable and are soon required to vacate.

In a few places, *lease-purchases* are possible. This method provides agreement to buy a total parcel for a specified total amount. The land and payments are divided (usually equally) over a specified time. The owner agrees to sell a section at a time and gives option to buy and lease the remainder until the total is paid. The lease is subject to cancellation or renegotiation any year that public funds are not appropriated. This method is used when a large parcel is needed and the annual appropriation is small.

In some places, land may be used more or less permanently without purchase by negotiating *easements.* Scenic and open space easements provide that the owners will keep property in a natural state, such as lookouts and along trails. The public views but does not use the property. In other easements the public may have a right to cross the property. And in still other easements, or permits, there may be specified use of the property such as flood-control lands, wooded areas, historical sites, and hiking trails. Another type of easement is the joint use of an existing easement such as a utility line right-of-way.

There is a movement, not too widespread at this time, to give owners of strategically located, undeveloped land a reduced tax rate on the undeveloped land as an incentive to keep it as open space.

FACTORS IN THE DESIGN OF AREAS

The design affects the appeal, use, safety, supervision and maintenance of a recreation area. Poor design will increase indefinitely costs for each of the above. A good functional designer will more than pay his cost in the long run in savings to the agency. Unfortunately, some decision makers do not see this until construction is completed and the facility is put in use.

There are many examples of poor design to avoid such as construction of a large surfaced area like tennis courts or parking lot without means of carrying fast water runoff when it rains; it will wash out the side where it drains. Another example is a swimming pool constructed in poorly drained soil without provisions for adequate drainage; floors and walls will crack. If a retaining wall is built without weep holes and reinforcements, hydrostatic pressure will topple it over.

The better designs are made when the experienced recreation designer (landscape architect or engineer) *and* the experienced recreationist (or executive) work as a design team to make it both appealing and functional. Among the factors they will consider are:

1. The uses to be made of the area: scope of program (usually all categories); ages to be served (usually the entire family); per-

manent structures; year-round or seasonal; provision for parking; and special features (pool, track, amphitheatre).

2. Entrances: One main entrance is desirable in the direction which the most people come with other accesses conveniently located for facility use and people.
3. Buffer strip, plantings, landscaping, trees to screen less attractive features from adjoining property owners.
4. Plan noisy and objectional activities in interior, if possible.
5. Compatibility with the neighborhood.
6. Safety: Fence from street active areas such as playground, tot lot, wading pool, outdoor swimming, swing and horseshoe areas, baseball and softball backstops; place bicycle racks at entrance; and place soft materials (sand, pine bark) under swings and equipment.
7. Preservation of natural and interesting features.
8. Grading and drainage.
9. Location of permanent structures. They are placed, if possible, near border for easy access, conservation of space and flexibility in use of open area.
10. Layout of area: Areas needing greatest supervision and equipment are located near activity building and supervision (tot lot, small children's area and equipment). Small children's area should be isolated, if possible, so larger children will not have good reasons to cross through it. Play equipment and apparatus for larger children are also near supervision close to the entrance. Other distinct areas are:
    - — Game areas including open grass area and surfaced area for dancing and active game and informal games.
    - — Courts area such as volleyball, basketball, paddle tennis, badminton, shuffleboard, tennis, horseshoes. If space permits, there should be more than one of each. Tennis courts provide best service and economy in units of four or more.
    - — Quiet or passive area for story telling, crafts, dramatics, puppetry, and senior citizens.
    - — Sports area baseball, softball, track, football, soccer, rugby, field hockey types, with seating; swimming pool. Beauty, attractive equipment, landscaping, appropriate planting.
11. Surfacing: Different activities require a variety of surfacing. Good well maintained turf is most frequently used for children's areas, ring games, croquet, bowling on green, athletic fields, golf courses,

stadiums, and grass tennis courts. Courts and areas heavily used require surfaces of clay, asphalt, concrete, cork, and commercial materials.

12. Lighting: Many places consider lighting standard equipment on playgrounds and athletic facilities. It extends the usefulness of areas about 50 percent, mostly for adults who work during the day. Sometimes facilities are used all night by the use of coin activated meters. Usually, in residential areas neighbors complain if lights are allowed after 10:00 p.m. For control purposes, it is well to have centrally controlled light switches in building.
13. Location of drinking fountains near the shelter, backstops of baseball diamonds, battery of tennis courts, and swimming.
14. Multiple uses of areas, such as baseball and football which are used at different seasons; football and track at different hours of the day. Multiple use of the same facility which is used at the same period of the day or during the same season creates conflict, tension, and behavior problems. It is far better to have separate facilities when they are needed at the same time.
15. Facilities should be oriented with the sun to the best advantage of participants and spectators.
16. Economy of space arrangement, ease of supervision, minimum maintenance, durable, safe equipment.

FACTORS IN THE DESIGN OF STRUCTURES

In order to provide recreation activities throughout the year and in summer during inclement weather, it is necessary to have indoor facilities. In the warmer climates, indoor facilities are not so important, except for protection during inclement weather.

The recreation building may serve general purposes such as a community center, youth center, senior center, or school or it may serve special functions from a picnic shelter in a park to a stadium or coliseum. Although recreation activities are conducted in schools, libraries, health buildings, courthouses, and other public buildings, the separate facilities designed for recreation purposes provide the greatest services.

There is no standard recreation structure and there is no standard community. The recreation center is planned to fit the community purposes and resources. A recreation building, in effect, compacts the activities of the playground indoors. They have many features in common. The design of the building can best be accomplished by a competent architect, trained and experienced in design and functions of the specific type of structure in close consultation with the recreation executive responsible for operating the facility. They will consider the following factors in preparing plans for a comprehensive community building, for example:

1. Local policies, guidelines, building regulations, environmental impact, availability of utilities needed, programs and objectives.
2. The uses to be made of the facility: Scope of the program; ages to be served; special features (pool, gym, kitchen); number of people to be accommodated at one time; multiple use of rooms; use of only portions of the building at times; heating cut-offs; use gym or pool without using rest of building; the relationship of rooms to outside facilities: gym and pool near athletic field and convenient to dressing rooms; activities rooms and craft room near playground.
3. Financing: Amount of money available for construction, supervision, and maintenance.
4. Rooms needed and arrangement: At least 5 activity rooms of different sizes from a committee room for 15 persons to a meeting room for 100; one room should be adaptable for music groups, a craft room with large storage and clean out sink; a game room (for pool, ping pong, table games); a multipurpose room, with good acoustics, for games, socials, portable stage, large storage (for chairs, games tables, portable stage, games equipment); a dark room; a woodwork shop (used also for stage props) and other specialized rooms if desired; kitchen with outside entrance and access to a large room and a smaller room, perhaps a library; office next to entrance, overlooking as many rooms as possible, with central light switch controls, closet, and entrance to interior central supply storage room; central supply room; rest rooms near office (rest rooms are trouble spots); lounge and waiting space near entrance; gymnasium, storage space, dressing rooms with lockers, showers and toilets; space for vending machines or snack bar; drinking fountains; furnace room with outside entrance; janitor room; large central storage space.
5. Provisions for later expansion.
6. Auditoriums often are not justified when public schools can be used.
7. Halls and offsets reduced to a minimum.

It may be that the above building is too comprehensive for one neighborhood, or too costly. All of the features are seldom provided in one building. Some communities prefer to spread facilities around the community, perhaps using school gymnasium, swimming pool and auditorium to supplement a community center of two clubrooms, a craft room, a multipurpose room, kitchen, and supporting facilities.

The comprehensive center is more of a community wide facility. Actually, the smaller neighborhood center supplemented by specialized school facilities is the more economical way to provide indoor recreation for a neighborhood and is convenient for more people.

Construction should be of durable fireproof material; masonry exterior, washable walls interior; in toilets glazed tile, translucent glass, recessed lighting and plumbing fixtures in so far as possible, pipes put in pipe chase (corridor between walls), minimum of protrusions, push button valves, masonry partitions. Skylights are vandal problems and should be avoided. Windows should be vandal and burglary resistant using metal frames, bars, heavy hardware cloth, grilles or height; drain pipes encased; exterior flood lighted; minimum of recessed and sheltered areas to tempt vandals; concrete drip pad all around building to reduce hand maintenance of grass and weeds.

MAINTENANCE

Physical maintenance of recreation properties and program management are carefully coordinated for best results. The quality of maintenance contributes to the quality of behavior and quality of program. Unmarked athletic fields, sand and glass on tennis courts, broken windows, dirty facilities and many similar items greatly affect quality of program and conduct. Most agencies prefer maintenance to be coordinated and performed by their own personnel. Sometimes it is performed by another agency which has other primary responsibilities. In such instances, the performance schedule and work habits tend to be geared to policies and practices of their primary duties, and recreation services are neglected or poorly timed.

Usually, maintenance is divided two ways, namely, routine maintenance (unskilled and semi-skilled) and general maintenance (skilled type).

Routine Maintenance

Routine maintenance, indoor and outdoor, consists of janitor, custodial, caretaker, security, and cleaning types of services which are performed daily by persons assigned to the site or itinerant workers or crews which perform complete service on a scheduled basis or specialized work such as mowing grass or maintaining and marking athletic fields.

Indoor duties include sweeping, cleaning, dusting, waxing, polishing; care of heating, electrical, and air conditioning systems; disposal of trash; making minor repairs; inspecting for safety; maintaining supplies in washrooms; maintaining furniture in orderly manner; and handling or reporting emergencies.

Outdoor duties include inspection of area and facilities for safety, repairs; remove barricades, broken or unsafe equipment; collection and disposal of refuse; handraking places around home plate, pitchers box and bases on ball diamonds; care and marking of athletic areas; sweeping or washing sand, glass, trash from surfaced areas; cleaning sandbox; arranging equipment for programs; making minor repairs to area, turf, plumbing, fencing, program facilities; watering fields, lawns and shrubbery; control of weeds and growth along fences; mowing and care of lawn; fertilizing, pruning, and care of plants and shrubbery.

Maintenance work is performed, if at all possible, at times when it does not interfere with program or public use. Janitor services, cleaning, painting, and repairs are often scheduled at night or when facility is not in use. Sometimes, maintenance of fields, beaches, and swimming pools may be performed early in the mornings before public is scheduled to use them. If it is necessary to close a facility for maintenance, program is re-scheduled, if possible, and participants are advised in advance in an appropriate manner.

Heavy vehicles create depressions in lawns and playing fields, especially when they are wet, and should not be permitted on them, except in case of dire emergency.

Automatic sprinkler systems are used for irrigation where watering is required for lawns and plants regularly. Hand watering is usually costly and time consuming.

Inspections for breakage and safety are made daily before opening by maintenance staff and before scheduled use by program staff.

General Maintenance

General maintenance consists of special work that the routine maintenance personnel are not prepared to do or that requires special skills and equipment. It includes the skilled trades and major maintenance. It may be performed by contract, by other agencies, or by agency personnel. When an agency has enough work to keep a technician and equipment in use full time, he provides service as needed when employed on the agency staff. Agencies that have need for technicians only part time tend to perform the work by contract or by other agencies.

Needs for general maintenance are determined by periodic inspections, emergency requests, and weekly supervisor's reports. The general maintenance crews may perform certain duties on regular schedule such as grass maintenance every 10 days. They perform at least annually trimming trees (before opening of outdoor season); reconditioning athletic areas, play equipment, lawn areas, painting lines or surfaced areas; inspection and reconditioning power mowers and similar motor equipment; repairing and painting park benches and tables, fireplaces, and similar items; inspection repairs and painting, as needed, all wood structures, outdoor equipment, fencing, metal roofs, gutters and down spouts, barricades, signs, markers; and repair, replace or recondition roadways, walkways, and other surfaced areas.

Most places require plumbing and electrical work to be performed by licensed personnel.

One of the most frustrating duties of maintenance men is the unscheduled unanticipated extras they perform with men, materials, and equipment for special occasions, program events, postponements, rescheduling, extra scheduling and odd hours, often with little advanced notice. Even though procedures call for advanced scheduling there are emergencies and uncontrollable situations that develop.

Central Shops and Warehouse

Every agency, large or small, needs a central shop and warehouse for maintenance where indoor and outdoor facilities and equipment can be made or repaired. A small agency may have a consolidated shop. A large agency may have several specialized shops at one location or decentralized shops located in the districts. Services performed include carpentry and cabinet work, painting, plumbing, electrical, forge and machine work, metal, welding, fencing, mechanical, and automotive services. Some agencies may perform some of these services by contract and perform others themselves.

Shops and warehouse are closely related and are usually located together.

Questions for Discussion

1. Why is planning for public recreation necessary?
2. What is a master plan? A neighborhood? A community?
3. How is city planning related to recreation?
4. How does the recreation executive determine the recreation needs of a neighborhood?
5. Define the term standard. What common standards are used in recreation planning?
6. Define the term principle. What principles would you use in planning a total municipal recreation service?
7. How should citizens be involved in planning?
8. What are the basic steps in planning to meet community needs?
9. What would you consider and how would you select an architect?

10. What factors would you consider in selecting a recreation site?
11. Describe the methods by which land may be acquired for recreation purposes.
12. What is meant by condemnation? Right of eminent domain?
13. What basic factors would you consider in designing a functional recreation site plan?
14. Describe what should be included in a neighborhood recreation center plan and what is the best arrangement of the rooms?
15. What is included in routine maintenance? In general maintenance?

Short Problems

1. Make a recreation survey of a neighborhood to determine the unmet needs. From the information obtained, make and justify recommendations for program improvements in order of priority.
2. Prepare a comprehensive site plan for a neighborhood playground to accommodate interests of the entire family.
3. Prepare the floor plan of a neighborhood indoor recreation center that will provide opportunities for the entire family.
4. Prepare a balanced five-year plan complete with project estimates and justifications for annual expenditures of $300,000 in improvements.

References

1. *The Techniques of Municipal Administration*, 4th ed. (Chicago: The International City Managers' Association, 1958), p. 309.
2. Richmond, Virginia.
3. *The National Park Recreation and Open Space Standards* (Arlington, Va.; The National Recreation and Park Association, 1971), p. 13.
4. L. H. Weir, *Parks A Manual of Municipal and County Parks* (New York: A.S. Barnes and Company, 1928), I, 49.
5. *NRPA—Open Space, Standards*, p. 12
6. *NRPA—Open Space Standards*, p. 13
7. Indoor space standards from *Standards, Playgrounds, Playfields, Recreation Buildings, Indoor Recreation Facilities* (New York: National Recreation Association, undated), p. 9.
8. *The National Park Recreation and Open Space Standards*, p. 39.

9. *Ibid,* p. 38.
10. *Recreation Standards,* Richmond, Va.
11. Lynn S. Rodney, *Administration of Public Recreation* (New York: The Ronald Press Company, 1964), p. 305.

Selected Readings

American Association for Health, Physical Education, and Recreation, *Planning Areas and Facilities for Health, Physical Education, and Recreation* (rev. ed.). Chicago: The Athletic Institute, 1966.

Babcock, Richard F., *The Zoning Game Municipal Practices and Policies.* Madison, Wisc.: The University of Wisconsin Press, 1966.

Buechner, Robert D., ed., *National Park Recreation and Open Space Standards.* Washington, D.C.: National Recreation and Park Association, 1970.

Bureau of Outdoor Recreation, *Outdoor Recreation Space Standards.* Washington, D.C., U.S. Government Printing Office, 1964.

Goodman, William I., and E. C. Freund, *Principles and Practices of Urban Planning.* Washington, D.C.: International City Managers' Association, 1968.

Hjelte, George, and Jay S. Shivers, *Public Administration of Recreational Services,* pp. 360–425. Philadelphia: Lea and Febiger, 1972.

Kraus, Richard G., and Joseph E. Curtis, *Creative Administration in Recreation and Parks,* pp. 117–145. St. Louis: The C.V. Mosby Company, 1973.

Rabinowitz, Francine A., *City Politics and Planning.* New York: Atherton Press, 1969.

Rodney, Lynn S., *Administration of Public Recreation,* pp. 284–326. New York: The Ronald Press Company, 1964.

CHAPTER 16

Evaluating the Programs and Services

Evaluating is a continuous administrative process. It is used often in conjunction with planning and research and is a major factor in controlling, making judgments, improvements, budgeting, and almost every process of management and operations. It involves every member of the staff in two ways—in judging and in being judged as to quality and quantity of performance. It relates to such matters as more efficient operations, more effective programming, better procedures for achievement, conservation of time, strengthening of weaknesses, determining needs, efficiency of equipment, records, reporting, and even revisions of aims and objectives of the agency to serve better the recreation needs of the community.

Perfection in recreation and its related aspects may be impossible to attain, but perfection is the final goal towards which all performances are aimed and in terms of which they tend to be measured. Realistically, of course, goals are often set at some point of the scale below perfection and sometimes objectives are set a little lower but not always. Both are expected to change through the process of evaluation and progress. The closer quality of performance comes to the ideal situation or perfection, the more effective the performance or the program is said to be. Usually, the closer a participant or a group comes to perfection, the more competitive, challenging, or stimulating efforts become. This may be exemplified in the instance of a championship winner as compared to a novice. The champion could be a reason for raising the guidelines for evaluations. It may be a reason for changing the goal.

Situations and circumstances in recreation are constantly changing in one way or another, therefore, evaluations are being made continually and new goals and objectives are being determined. When a goal is raised, the system of evaluation related to that goal will tend to be affected by it because an important guideline has changed.

In instances where there is no criterion by which to evaluate a situation at a given time, such as periods of vacancies in personnel or faulty equipment, the situation is judged by what it should be. This is often the situation when establishing new programs or expanding existing ones. But in these instances a person trained and experienced in the situation can draw on experiences and knowledge from situations closely related to the one under consideration and make a fairly accurate evaluation.

Definitions

The terms evaluation and research are sometimes used interchangeably and are closely related processes. *Evaluation* is an objective judgment of value or worth. It often is based on comparative information. *Research* is a systematic study or search for knowledge. Both are especially useful elements of the planning process.

Approaches to Evaluation

Knowledge of the purposes and processes of recreation management is a prerequisite for evaluation and research. Principles must be applied systematically and with considerable judgment to all administrative problems if the process of evaluation is to be effective in helping the decision maker improve the end products with greater efficiency, economy and satisfaction to the participant. Since evaluation involves all staff and all progressive activities of the recreation service, it naturally involves a range of approaches and applications to both tangible and intangible situations.

Evaluations are made at all levels of the agency; for example, the custodian evaluates the results of materials he uses in cleaning and building maintenance; the grounds keeper, the effects of the various chemicals to control weeds; the painter, the best paint for different situations; the recreationists, methods of presenting affective programs; the supervisor, effectiveness of staff; the executive, efficiency of total operations.

At each level, persons make evaluations for their own purposes at the site and formulate recommendations to pass on to other decision makers. Supervisors, of course, also receive recommendations and use them or pass them on with their own. The process of evaluation therefore involves research to obtain information, evaluation (judgment) to determine its worth or usefulness, recording to preserve it in usable form, reporting (or communication) to get it to decision maker, salesmanship (or diplomacy) to call attention to it and its merits, appraisal (or evaluation) by the decision maker, adaption and inclusion in the administrative process.

Among the methods of recreation evaluation are scientific method or problem solving, qualitative, quantitative, use of standards and guidelines, attendance or participation, and research.

SCIENTIFIC METHOD

The scientific method is borrowed from private industry and is applied to production operations based on standards of human capabilities and correlation of facts so as to simplify procedures in order to get production with least effort. The scientific method is the careful examination of procedures, analyzing each component part, comparing with similar experiences and results, and discovering measurable facts from which decisions can be made. Recreation involves so many intangibles including differences in human characteristics that no basic set of standards or norms have been established that can be applied universally. The scientific method as applied to recreation where factual knowledge is not always measurable or complete, often must be based on logic, experiences, and deductions from information that is available.

QUALITATIVE METHODS

Efficient recreation administration depends on different forms of measurements to assist in improving efficiency of operations and conducting of its many services for greater satisfaction of the public. One method may not apply well in all circumstances. For instance, quantitative methods may show the popularity of a program but they do not show its quality. Qualitative evaluation is hardly possible in terms of fixed tangible measurements because of the differences in human factors. It is dependent more on such factors as relationship of values, objectives, clearly defined purposes, degree of accomplishment, and analysis of performance and results in terms of purposes. These factors cannot be measured by a look at reports and records alone. Records are helpful in indicating interest, regularity of attendance, or ideas to check out but qualitative evaluation requires personal contact, close observations of all facets of program in operations, reactions of people involved and performance in relation to guidelines. The conclusions should be recorded for use of any staff member which may be involved later with any aspects of the situation.

Normally evaluations are made immediately after the termination of a program because the clean-up, storage and follow-up activities may be involved in the purpose of the evaluation. If such evaluation concerns quality of instructional program, the follow-up activities may not be involved. In such instances, it would be well to make program evaluations while activities are in operation so contacts and observations can be used to assist in making final judgments.

In the process of making qualitative evaluations, records are used to define purposes, objectives and guidelines; for recording accumulation of incidents, actions, observations, impressions, strong points, weaknesses, omissions, additions, progress and similar information utilized in evaluation. Too often, qualitative evaluations of programs are neglected, are made without all pertinent information that could be obtained, or made from a single observation. A single observation, of course, is all that is necessary to recognize a bad situation that needs immediate action but, even then, follow-up observations are essential on continuing programs.

At a base unit level in recreation, daily assignments vary considerably and are generally more changeable day by day than at the supervisory or administrative levels, therefore, the foreman has more contacts and follow-up observations. In fact, he may be in constant contact with staff at a center or field unit and in the best position to make qualitative evaluations. Supervisors and administrators usually have much less frequent contacts with personnel and are, therefore, often dependent upon views of subordinates.

Qualitative evaluation may have to be made sometimes almost entirely by the observations and judgments of the problem solver. In other situations they may be made by comparisons to measures established by the agency or problem solver. Others may be value judgments made by the use of criteria and experiences of others and the resulting satisfactions or dissatisfactions of persons involved. All of the processes may involve observations and counseling of staff and participants.

QUANTITATIVE METHODS

Quantitative evaluation of recreation programs are made from records such as enrollment, attendance, frequency of meetings, frequency of participation, number of group activities conducted, receipts collected, hours of operation and completed projects. It deals in measurable units such as actual figures and percentages. The total attendance and participation of spectators is the most commonly used method for comparison of like operations, progress, publicity, making qualitative evaluations and determining unit costs.

The collection of accurate quantitative figures for many recreation programs is a management problem that has not yet been completely solved. Judgment estimates are used in arriving at attendance figures for such activities as informal use of areas, parks, mass activities, playgrounds, spectators at free events, beaches and most free-use outdoor spaces. In such instances, the figures reported depends upon the judgment of the individual, his integrity and sincerity. Sometimes estimates are made by the combined opinions of several staff members, but usually they are the judgment of one person who is responsible for the management of the site. Under estimated or over estimated figures greatly affect cost accounting, budgeting, and management decisions, therefore, great care should be taken in obtaining accurate figures. Estimated figures should be used with caution. Inflated or under estimated figures help no one in the long run.

It is impractical, very costly, and time consuming to register or try to count everyone that attends an activity or uses an open recreation area that does not have controlled entrances. Most areas are not enclosed; therefore, the public may enter at several points, and counting is impractical.

Fairly accurate figures may be obtained where admission charges are made; at small playgrounds and enclosed facilities with controlled entrances; by use of meters, counters, turnstiles and tickets; and of organized groups, where there is registration and roll call. Where seating is provided estimates are made of the proportion of the total seats occupied plus count of anyone not seated.

The National Recreation Association in the late 1930's prepared a method of estimating attendance on playgrounds that was widely used and continues to be used by many recreation agencies today which is as follows:

1. Actual counts are made of the peak playground attendance during morning, afternoon and evening sessions.
2. These counts are multiplied to get totals as follows:
   — morning session, peak count multiplied by 2;
   — afternoon session, peak count multiplied by 2.5;
   — evening session, peak count multiplied by 1.5;
   — organized groups, actual count.
3. Adding of the totals gives the total attendance for the day.

This method is recommended only for supervised playgrounds where a varied program of activities is conducted. It provides for those that attend and leave before the count and those that arrive after the count. Where possible actual counts should be used. Even if numbers are lower, actual counts provide accurate, defensible figures and credibility for the agency.

The use of total attendance in evaluation of program at recreation facilities may be of minimum value except for publicity and some management functions such as planning and parking. When estimated figures are used, they should be identified as such.

Forms used by the department for reporting should be designed to reflect maximum opportunities for accurate counts even if it takes a little more staff time. Sometimes volunteers take great pride in making such counts and they can be used effectively under guidance.

Figures are usually recorded on forms each day and reported weekly. These figures are then consolidated monthly and annually for supervisory and administrative purposes such as evaluation, counseling, planning and reporting. Quantitative evaluations often are related to standards and guidelines.

USE OF STANDARDS AND GUIDELINES

Every executive uses standards and guidelines as a gauge and a means of determining degree of excellence in making evaluations, judgments, justifications, and decisions. Some standards apply better to some recreation interests than others. Every recreation department should adopt or establish its own set of standards and guidelines that apply best to its particular situation. These should be put in writing and given wide distribution. Too often, no standards are provided which results in uncertainty, confusion and inefficiency.

Standards are used for such items as planning, selection and performance of staff, programming, construction of areas and facilities, determining efficiency, costs and budgeting.

Application of Standards

National standards are based on national data such as costs or large population concentrations and may need to be adjusted slightly to apply realistically to local situations. Some standards established for congested urban conditions may not apply in the same way to small communities and rural areas without some adjustments. Local conditions in recreation are so varied that standards have not yet been established for many situations. Therefore, some government units make no effort to establish realistic standards of service. Consequently and unfortunately, supervision, program effectiveness and general agency efficiency are performed and evaluated by personal opinion and a few agency goals and objectives.

A staff performs better when it has guidelines, such as goals, policies, standards of efficiency, rules and procedures to use as a guide. For example, efforts, thoughts, and energies used and lost in trying to figure out what to do in every separate situation or in waiting for the boss to set guidelines for individual situation not only lowers effectiveness of production but also impedes development of initiative. Fortunately, where there are not agency-wide guidelines, there are individuals with strong initiative who develop their own standards and guidelines which may result in better programs. Several things may then happen: jealousy may develop among other staff in the same title position or the person is promoted or takes a better job elsewhere, leaving the agency where it was initially because the replacement may not have the strong initiative needed. Also, in this example, the program opportunities provided throughout the agency would be operated by different guidelines and standards of service. It is well, therefore, to have strong initiative at the administrative level as well as staff levels to provide written guidelines for uniform general application throughout the agency. Only when agency-wide guidelines are uniformly applied to all similar segments can performances be compared or critical examination of the total program be a valid means for program evaluation.

Standards and guidelines are used in four ways: general administration, standards of service, standards of efficiency, and standards of achievement.

General Administrative Guidelines

General administrative guidelines relate to more or less constant intangible items for guidance looking to the future. They are general and designed to fit every situation. They include agency concept or general purpose, goals or directions, attainable objectives, policies or plans of action, rule or regulation of conduct, and procedure or manner of action. These guides apply uniformly throughout the agency and take precedence over all other guidelines. They are used as general guides by all individuals in decision making, conduct and program service matters. Usually, interpretation of these items is included in orientation, staff meetings, manuals of operation and supervision. When there is uncertainty concerning appropriate application in specific instances, supervision is requested to assist in determining proper application. Sometimes, in an unusual situation, a constant guideline cannot be made to apply effectively. In such instances, the staff calls the matter to the attention of supervision for consideration of appropriate adjustment in the guideline or for approval of an exception.

Standards of Service

Standards of service guidelines apply to planning of programs to carry out phases of administrative guidelines. They include specific program goals; criteria for determining quality such as number in group, how often service is provided, and other items relating to level of service; determination of measurable work units; most effective work load, criteria for determining quantity such as numbers receiving service and number of programs provided; amount of space to be provided such as acres of land needed and spacing in the community; how often trees are to be trimmed or grass cut; amount of equipment needed; and scope of program.

Standards of Efficiency

This group of standards involves the programs in operation and are more extensive and varied than other groupings. They include standards for evaluating efficiency of performance of personnel, equipment, facilities, money and administration. They include measurable units of work being performed in terms of objectives; cost of operation per work unit based on cost accounting records; alternate methods of performing work; time it takes to perform a unit of work; progress towards achieving proposed objectives; quality of work; and general status of progress in comparison to costs and the amount of work to be performed. The unit of work in recreation is usually class-hour or participant-session.

The supervisor and the administrative staff use information available at this point to make improvements, to counsel staff, to strengthen weaknesses, change emphasis, or even terminate services that do not meet standards or cannot be made to meet acceptable standards.

Standards of Achievement

Guidelines for standards of achievement are usually the "general guidelines" of the agency plus applicable ones from the above groupings of standards of service and efficiency. They are related, at this point, to the completed performance in terms of work accomplished as compared to objectives, goals, and purposes and the units of work produced from funds expended. Standards are used as a measurement of achievement which in turn is used as a means of evaluation and control. It is also a source of information for reporting and planning.

The administrator, budget director, taxpayer and participant are interested in results, therefore, standards of achievement are significant tools in the functions of management.

Specific standards are discussed in respective chapters on the subject. A good source of information is the National Recreation and Park Association publication, *Evaluation and Self Study of Public Recreation and Park Agencies.*[1]

ATTENDANCE AND PARTICIPATION

One of the first questions asked when professionals inquire about recreation programs is "What is the attendance?" This is followed by the questions "How many different individuals are served?" and "How much is the budget?" Unfortunately, the answers to these questions do not indicate quality, satisfaction or results, only that a certain number of people were present. They do not tell how long participants were present, whether they did anything, or what the distribution was by ages, sex, or specific activity. Nor do they indicate whether an individual was a liability or an asset. Attendance records are useful in making local comparisons and determining progress or trends, but because of differences in local situations and methods of taking counts they may not provide an accurate means of figuring unit costs or comparisons with other communities unless they have the same method of counting.

Methods of Taking Counts

Due to the wide variety of situations in recreation there are several methods of taking attendance counts:

1. Actual count of individuals is the best method. This method was discussed earlier in this chapter under "Quantitative Methods."
2. National Recreation Association formula (also discussed earlier) used for summer playgrounds only.
3. Double count method involves taking an actual count twice during a summer playground morning, afternoon and evening session and using both counts. This method is a little more conservative than the National Recreation Association formula and more time consuming, too.
4. Registration and issuance of membership cards. This method is good for counting organized groups, small units, and participants in special programs such as dancing, drama, crafts and other classes.
5. Admissions and tickets are used where charges are made or tickets are distributed to regulate numbers.

The record of attendance is the only measurement and record of performance for some recreation programs. The total count at any particular time will indicate the percentage of total population of the community that is being served. Until recently recreation executives considered they did well if the recreation agency served three percent of the total population in a day. A recent check in urban areas which conducted broad programs indicated this figure should be six percent. This, of course, varies with local conditions such as number of private, semiprivate, and commercial facilities, summer resort, and similar factors.

Where attendance is estimated, the method used should be checked with actual counts periodically to see if it continues to be reasonably accurate or needs adjusting to the local situation.

REPORTING AND MAINTAINING RECORDS

Reporting, and its related activities of record keeping and filing, is an important function of the public recreation agency. In fact, it may well be considered the life line of the agency. Reporting tells the recreation story, needs, and accomplishments to the supervisor, the executive, decision makers, and the public. It is a major factor in obtaining funds, gaining support, and finding out what needs to be done and has been done. Reports are used in public relations, evaluations, planning, and every phase of management and decision making.

Records and record keeping are close companions to reporting. Records are essential as the factual uniform basis upon which reports are made, and the work performed. Records serve as references for staff, administration, and public as a basis for action. Certain records are required to be kept by law, but most records are maintained at the discretion of the agency and are determined by the needs of the local recreation agency and the requirements of the administration.

Reports are usually based on records, or information based on action before it becomes records. A report is commonly used to give an account of a matter. In recreation, it may be a summary of several accounts or reports. Reports may be classified in three ways, namely, administrative, special, and annual.

Administrative Reports

Administrative reports make up the largest group. Their purpose is to give management and decision makers a running account by units of operations and programs for which the agency is responsible, usually in a prescribed form so they can be consolidated at the various levels (area, district) and finally summarized in a single report often accompanied by recommendations. Routine management type reports may be made daily, weekly, or monthly and used for evaluation of progress and administrative guidance, reference for making special reports, or accumulation of information for making annual reports, preparation of budget, planning, and future references (records). (See Appendix J for an example of such a form.)

Reports, even though vital to management, can be burdensome, voluminous, and time consuming when one considers the time of preparation, reading, consolidating, typing and filing; therefore only essential information pertinent to the subject should be included. Most field people do not like paper work and preparation of reports and tend to neglect this phase, or become upset with it; therefore, the simpler the process is, the better the production is, usually.

Daily or weekly reports are required, usually, from the person in charge of each separate recreation facility, special activity or place of recreation. Reporting is not only essential to functions of management but, if performed in the proper spirit, is beneficial to the one making it because it provides an opportunity for self evaluation and review of operations with which one is involved.

The monthly report is the most valuable report for administrative purposes. It is a summary report of highlights of daily and weekly reports and generally goes to the executive and sometimes chief administrator and policy board where it is used for making decisions and important judgments which may determine the course of administrative action affecting the entire agency operations. The content of the report will vary with local conditions and administrative needs. In a small community, the executive and chief administrator have more personal contacts with staff and public. In a large community the administrator is greatly dependent upon reporting for background for judgments. Careful choice of words, phrases, tables, and pictures is important. Often, words mean something different to the politician and chief administrator than they do to the recreationist. The reporter, therefore, should use common terms the receiver understands rather than use of technical recreation terms not universally understood by laymen.

The monthly reports should include such items as total attendance of all operations broken down by work programs, special facilities and special events, and sometimes comparative figures for previous month or same month the preceding year; average daily attendance; highlights of the month; changes made; changes in staff; major program or facility improvements; action of policy, advisory board, or major community involvement; special accomplishments; plans for coming month and matters and problems that may involve executive, chief administrator, policy board, major public concern, or controversy.

Special Reports

It is not practical to include details or information on every subject in the routine reports. Although routine administrative reports may include all of the information needed for general administrative purposes, there are times when the reports are not sufficient or in proper form such as when more specific information is needed to answer a public complaint, inquiry, or management matter. It may involve a detailed investigation, a study, research and compilation of records in a specific way, summary of findings, and recommendation with justification. It usually involves an in-depth review of a single subject such as the need for more tennis courts, report on an incident involving loss of life or property, alleged misconduct of staff member, or alleged failure to provide services or facilities when desired. Such reports are essential to higher management decision making or human relations and usually have a short deadline. It usually involves review and compilation of information from routine records, consultation with staff, inspection of site, and perhaps research of information not locally available which then involves a contact with professional or technical sources and other localities. The report is presented promptly and may be followed by a personal contact for answering further questions.

Annual Reports

Every recreation agency needs an annual report. Heads of government agencies are usually required by charter or other legislation to submit an annual report of activities of the agency to the chief administrator where they are consolidated with other agency reports and published for general information of the public. Sometimes, reports are published in the local newspaper in a supplement or special section. Sometimes the department report is published separately and distributed to board members, key and interested staff members, administrator and agency heads, local and state libraries, and news media. Copies are always available for interested citizens upon request. Usually, the general public is not particularly interested in long reports with a lot of narrative. Reports, therefore, should be attractive, easy to read, and use simple tables, graphs, and pictures that tell a story, and with a minimum of narrative.

From the administrative angle, the annual report is an indispensable, convenient source of reference, is informative to those who are interested in agency activities, and is invaluable as a time saver in answering inquiries particularly those from other cities, applicants and students.

The content of the annual report is largely composed of summaries and highlights of information submitted in the reports of staff during the year. An attractive cover with name of agency, official symbol (or seal), year the report covers, and activity pictures adds appeal. The report should contain the following:

1. Letter of transmittal in instances where a policy board reports to chief administrator or legislative body.
2. Names of members of policy board (or advisory board), executive and administrative staff, and may include name of mayor and chief administrator.
3. Table of contents and list of tables.
4. A brief statement of functions of the agency.
5. Organization chart showing agency structure.

6. Financial statements of revenue and expenditures by major divisions or work programs, special funds, and capital improvement projects.
7. Personnel information showing numbers and changes during the year.
8. Summary of program features, showing attendance and spectators by major locations or work programs.
9. Listing and brief statements of accomplishments and changes.
10. Capital improvements completed.
11. Listing of areas and recreation locations by types with addresses and major service features.
12. Statements of major problems and unmet needs.
13. Recommendations.

The approach throughout should be positive. Complaining, blaming, or negative attitudes should be avoided. The report should be clear, concise and dignified looking but should not include expensive frills and extras. It is a featured report and should be distributed as soon as possible after the close of the fiscal year, within 30 days is recommended for best results. It is well to have an exchange of annual reports between cities.

Record Keeping

A record is a written account of a situation, event, or happening. It is a preserved report filed for retrieval when needed. Record keeping can be expensive and voluminous. Space around city hall and central office areas are usually expensive, therefore, only records that serve a useful purpose should be kept. It is not unusual for larger departments to have a special record room and trained staff to handle record keeping duties. In small agencies, the executive's secretary usually has that responsibility along with many others.

In most communities, certain phases of record keeping are done by other agencies such as engineering records, drawings, and specifications are kept by public works department; fiscal matters and property inventory by finance officer; legal records by the law department; personnel records by personnel agency; and acquisition records by purchasing agent. Every recreation agency, however, must maintain routine administrative records needed for daily operations, including program, inventory, staff, purchases, revenue, meetings and recreation functions.

Agency-wide records are usually kept in the central office. Those pertaining to an area field operation or special facility, like golf course, and needed for daily references are kept in the respective field office. Data processing handles many items.

Records are usually classified according to functions or subjects which relate closely to major departments such as administration, legal, personnel, properties (public works), fiscal services (finance), and agency programs (recreation). However, not every agency may have need for every type.

Administration. Records at this level have to do with administrative services and policy-making functions. They include records, minutes, reports, and actions of policy or advisory boards, and committees; policies; standards; rules and regulations; publicity; procedures; administrative instructions; official studies and reports; staff development (conferences and institutes); staff directory; plans; and correspondence.

Legal Records. These records would include a copy of charter, state code, local ordinances, legal opinions, court decisions, agreements and contracts, leases and rental agreements, easements, and all legal matters.

Personnel Actions. Every agency needs a complete record of each staff member's employment history. This includes application for employment, date of employment, pay record, copy of signed deduction forms, schedule of assignments, efficiency ratings, time reports, promotions, sick leave, vacations, disciplinary actions, commendations, accident and injury leave, military leave, in-service training, extra allowances such as vehicle, and workmen's liability cases.

Since volunteers give much service, the names and accumulated records of junior and volunteer program leaders and record of accomplishments should be maintained.

Lists of members of boards, advisory councils and committees with addresses, phone number assignments and evaluations should also be recorded.

Properties. All agency properties should be listed showing location, size, assessed valuation, improvements on it, method and date of acquisition, and any changes and disposals, if any. Blueprints and pictures of all buildings and facilities; layout plans showing size, arrangement, change in grade, permanent improvements, and costs; as well as a complete inventory of equipment, tools, supplies, and estimated worth are also essential records.

Business and Fiscal Matters. The fiscal records are maintained by the fiscal officer or data processing with copies to the agency. They include accounting records (revenue and expenditures), sources, amounts, and disposition; daily or weekly statements; income contracts such as concessions, bids, lease agreements and related material; budgets, appropriations, expenditures, incumbrances, and balances; requisitions, purchase orders, deliveries, vouchers, payrolls, insurance policies, and all financial transactions.

AGENCY PROGRAM. Recreation involves such a variety of conditions that it has a large number of records to assist in carrying out its program functions. They include daily, weekly, and seasonal attendance records; enrollments in classes and special activities; rosters of clubs, teams, classes, and officials; permits issued; consultation services; calendar of events; activity schedules; accidents and injuries; community contacts; donations; amount of income by facilities; winners in agency events.

FORMS

The number of reports required is rather large. Multiply the number of reports by the number of people reporting and we can see how much time is spent handling reports, therefore, time saved in preparation of reports means considerable saving in time and money. The use of forms provides uniformity of information, simplifies reporting and record keeping, and reduces cost. Forms for services provided by other departments are prepared by them and are fairly well standardized for use by all agencies. There are recreation forms for every purpose. Consequently much effort is expended in filling out, processing and filing such forms. However, it is better than writing reports in longhand without a form.

A few of the forms used in recreation programs are daily, weekly, monthly attendance reports; accidents and property damage; registration; doctor's certification; use permit; application blank; parent's permission form; team roster blank; individual contract form, transfers, and releases; receipt blanks; entry forms; report forms; score sheets; schedule blanks; pick-up order for store; supervisor's report forms; inspection report form; community contact form; requisition for supplies; mileage report, swimming report; and golf course report form.

It is well to keep the number of forms to a minimum, to one, if possible. Some suggestions for designing forms are:

1. Use standard sizes for easy handling such as 8½ × 11 inches. Odd sizes get lost, are hard to file and sometimes difficult to find.
2. Put all information on a single sheet, if possible. Use both sides, if necessary. Even if carbon copy is necessary, it is easier to distribute and file one sheet than two.

3. Assign a color to each major division; then print forms with copies of different colors to match the color of the agency. It is well to have an identification such as color or marking for easy identification of letterhead and memo pads.
4. Design form, if possible, to use "check-offs" or a minimum of writing.
5. Make them simple and easy to fill in as well as easy to tabulate.
6. Provide only for essential information needed and used.

RESEARCH IN RECREATION

Research in recreation is a fertile field for action. The recreation needs of people are so great, the response to opportunities is so good, and often resources including staff are so limited or involved in other phases of recreation that recreation professionals have not taken time to do in-depth research or find answers to questions that need to be answered soon. In the past, most of the research in recreation by public recreation agencies has been in the form of statistics, surveys, studies, questionnaires, observations and experiences. Useful information has been borrowed from related fields. Recreation is so broad in scope it can adapt similar research and findings from older professional fields and private enterprise. Currently, much of the research in recreation is being done by students in educational institutions, naturalists, conservationists, economists, and sociologists.

Recreation involves many intangibles for which no norm has been established, but recreation has now reached the stage of progress where research of the more specialized and scientific nature is needed.

Most recreation agencies conduct research in various forms in connection with phases of their operations and benefit from it, but the problem is it is not recorded or published so it can be shared with others. It would be well if such research information could be made available for general use. Although some state and federal planning grant funds are available for research, few communities have participated in use of them.

Only a few public recreation agencies have planned research programs that would qualify under the generally accepted definition that research is "an organized search for knowledge." [2] The research that takes place is in connection with daily work programs or incidents in planning, evaluation, analysis of statistics or specific studies of information resulting from program and staff experiences most of which take a minimum amount of time. Executives, politicians, decision makers, and even the public are program oriented. Budget funds are channeled into program with less concern for maintenance and still less concern for a planned research program. Supervised programs supplemented by use of facilities by self-directed groups are well attended and leave a good impression on politicians and others that observe them. To spend money on research for programs that are going well and many times overcrowded is unheard-of and decision makers channel funds to more programs. Research, therefore, is left behind or attached to or done in conjunction with something else.

The lack of specialized and scientific research is not because of lack of capabilities but lack of staff time, understanding, and support of the decision makers. The desire for "an organized search for knowledge" is not yet strong enough to overcome the lack of knowledge and understanding of the values of research by many decision makers.

Research is often motivated by need for knowledge to save money or make money. For those who think in these terms, the time is past due to find ways of stretching the budget dollar, to find how things can be done better with less effort, and to discover ways of providing satisfactory services with do-it-yourself projects.

Questions for Discussion

1. How is evaluation used in the recreation agency?
2. What methods of evaluating are used in recreation? Explain each.
3. What standards and guidelines are used in recreation?
4. What methods of taking attendance counts are used? Which in your opinion is the best?
5. What are the different methods of reporting? Which is the most effective?
6. What types of reporting are used? Explain the strong points of each.
7. What would you recommend as a model format for the annual report?
8. How are records used in a recreation agency? What would you consider essential records to keep?
9. What forms would you recommend for a recreation agency?
10. What is the value of research in a recreation agency?

Short Problems

1. Using a recreation center or playground site of your choice, evaluate its program in terms of balance of program, efficiency of staff, effectiveness of program in the neighborhood, and attaining its objectives.
2. Design the basic program form or forms to handle the essential reporting of a recreation center or playground.

3. Develop an outline of a specific research program in recreation and follow it through to conclusion.

References

1. Betty Van der Smissen, *Evaluation and Self Study of Public Recreation and Park Agencies* (Arlington, Va.: National Recreation and Park Association, 1972).
2. Richard G. Kraus and Joseph E. Curtis, *Creative Administration in Recreation and Parks* (St. Louis: The C.V. Mosby Company, 1973), p. 189.

Selected Readings

Bureau of Outdoor Recreation, *Outdoor Recreation Research: A Reference Catalogue.* Washington, D.C.: U.S. Government Printing Office, 1971.

Hatry, Harry P., and Diana R. Dunn, *Measuring the Effectiveness of Local Government Services: Recreation.* Washington, D.C.: The Urban Institute, 1971.

Hjelte, George, and Jay S. Shivers, *Public Administration of Recreational Services,* pp. 489–499. Philadelphia: Lea and Febiger, 1972.

Kaufman, Herbert, *Administrative Feedback.* Washington, D.C.: The Brookings Institution, 1973. *A research study and appraisal of administrative feedback in nine federal agencies.*

Kraus, Richard G., and Joseph E. Curtis, *Creative Administration in Recreation and Parks,* pp. 189–203. St. Louis: The C.V. Mosby Company, 1973.

Lopex, Felix M., Jr., *Evaluating Employee Performance,* pp. 143–238. Chicago: Public Personnel Association, 1968.

Miller, David W., and Martin K. Starr, *Executive Decisions and Operations Research.* Englewood Cliffs, N.J.: Prentice-Hall, Inc., 1967.

Otto, Calvin P., and Rollin O. Glaser, *The Management of Training, A Handbook for Training and Development Personnel,* pp. 152–165. Reading, Mass.: Addison-Wesley Publishing Company, 1970.

Rowland, Virgil K., *Evaluating and Improving Managerial Performance.* New York: McGraw-Hill Book Company, 1970.

Van der Smissen, Betty, *Evaluation and Self-Study of Public Recreation and Park Agencies.* Arlington, Va.: National Recreation and Park Association, 1972. *A guide with standards and evaluative criteria.*

CHAPTER 17

Office Management

Every agency, whether it has one or a thousand employees, needs to have a base of operations. A one-man department needs only minimum facilities because all the internal duties and functions rest with one person and perhaps a part-time secretary and volunteers. There will be, however, need for filing, reporting, contacts, and communications with the public and other agencies. When the one-man department becomes a two-man department supplemented by more volunteers, general principles and functions of office management apply.

To effectively control the collection, processing, storage, retrieval, and distribution of information is the responsibility of administrative office management.

Recent Trends in Office Operations

Although the traditional office services of collecting information, preparing forms and reports, typing, filing and record keeping continue, the methods of performing them have moved towards mechanization, greater speed, more highly trained personnel, greater capabilities, added functions, specialization, team work and interdependency, motivation of group interaction, need for more information, and better communications.[1] The computer, copier, calculating machine, cash register, bookkeeping machine, data processing, dictating machines, intercoms and other mechanical devices have revolutionized many phases of office work and brought with them new specialists, new systems and procedures and new problems.

State and federal aid, each with special requirements and procedures, plus expanded scope of many local recreation programs have brought about increased paper work; deadlines to meet; application forms to fill in; reports to make; increased bookkeeping and record keeping; and better accountability, audits, and purchasing procedures. Broader programs and responsibilities, volumes of work, and increased emphasis on efficiency have brought about needs for specialists such as space technician, office machine operator, file clerk, public information officer, research analyst, accountant and others.

The variety of responsibilities; use of specialists; emphasis on effective results, deadlines and need for setting priorities; new problems; and need for better information, best use of machines and technicians, and staff interaction have developed the need for office management and coordination. The above developments have brought changes in staff organization to include office management, specialists and changes of titles and duties. Smaller departments with limited staff and resources have made changes commensurate with their local needs and resources. Some have use of specialized staff and equipment from other agencies or have shared personnel and costs with them in order to obtain services of a specialist. Not all smaller agencies, of course, are able to make all changes indicated here, however.

The Agency Executive and the Office

The agency head cannot personally keep in touch directly with all operations for which he is responsible nor can he involve himself in many details or commit a large percentage of time indefinitely to any one subject. But it is essential that he obtain pertinent information for sound direction and decision making. In a large organization volumes of information, records and reports are received and need to be read and processed. The top official usually delegates the smaller but important responsibilities with commensurate authority to act to an office administrator, line officers, staff officers, specialists, and technicians who screen and handle direct all matters they can. Those matters needing the attention of the executive are summarized and forwarded to him with recommendations accompanied by drafts of letters for signature.

The secretary and specialists handle contacts, details, and routine matters, referring only the essential items to the office manager or executive for handling and decision making. Very often, the small matters take more time than big ones. The executive and office personnel must clear matters promptly lest they hold up or greatly cripple production (services). In screening calls and appointments, it is not that the executive or administrative staff does not want to receive everyone that wants to talk to them in person or by telephone; it is a matter of discretion and priority in the use of time to get the work done and to clear items most essential to agency operations. The office manager is obliged to use his time with staff and agency functions, with the public, and with the recreation executive and other agencies.

The main administrative responsibility of the central office is to clear all the elements of management, make decisions, make assignments, provide necessary authority, and to provide essential resources (including future needs) for operation of all agency functions that lead towards accomplishing agency objectives.

FUNCTIONS OF THE OFFICE

Functions of a recreation agency are so varied there can be no standard set of functions for any single locality. In a one-man department, the office is a contact point, meeting, and storage place. In larger agencies, the office is the base of operations, management and control center.

The office, often under the direct supervision of the executive, particularly in small agencies, is at the apex of the organization pyramid. It is the nerve center, the information center and terminal exchange for communications within and without the agency. It is the collection, storage, and distribution center. It provides for the coordination of information, plans, and resources; program analysis and efficiency experts; the expediters and promoters, management of paperwork and people; and perhaps most importantly, it is the provider of services to the general public and to the agency staff.

Much of office work is of the essential daily routine nature. All office work is a service to the public and to staff, or is a coordinating, expediting and facilitating function. A tremendous amount of paper work and factual information is required to carry out these housekeeping functions. Such functions involve collecting of information, record keeping, report writing, duplicating, channeling materials, and disseminating information which is performed largely by secretarial, clerical personnel, and machines. In addition, the administrative and technical staff are involved in analyzing, evaluating, and projecting programs in terms of goals and predetermined objectives. Management then becomes involved in planning, setting priorities, coordinating, implementing, communicating, and promoting, which, in turn, involve office staff functions. This chapter deals with services of the general office staff rather than the specialists.

The functions of office management relate to physical facilities, the office staff, and services performed in the office including communications and management of facts and information. (See Fig. 17-1.)

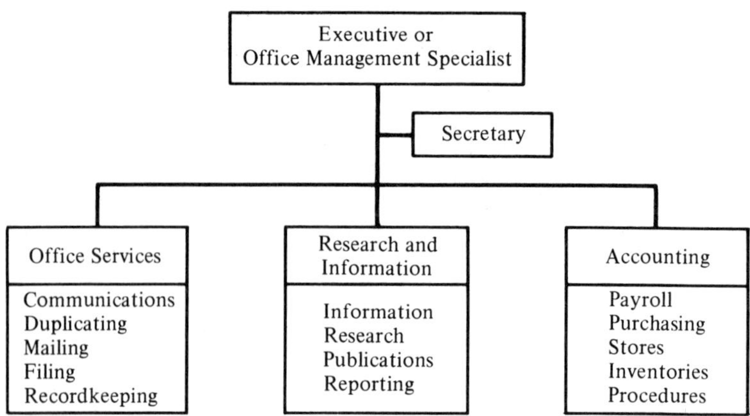

FIGURE 17-1. Sample form of office organization.

Physical Facilities

In consultation with staff and users of space in the office, the office manager plans, designs and arranges office spaces, equipment, and furnishings. He acquires necessary items to implement the plan; marks objects acquired and maintains accurate inventory; handles complaints, changes, maintenance, and housekeeping items; manages scheduling, and uses of service rooms and facilities; formulates rules and procedures for their use; purchases supplies; and is responsible for supply room. He is also responsible for petty cash as well as the office staff.

Office Staff

The office manager determines the needs, plans, and establishes an effective staff organization; makes position analysis and prepares job specifications; selects, orients, and develops necessary staff; handles staff matters and problems; makes studies for improvement of practices, procedures and performance; prepares manual of procedures; and establishes work criteria for performance. The office manager works closely with the executive and performs many tasks at his direction.

Work Performed in the Central Office

The office management staff is responsible for a variety of functions. These include the following.

Regular Office Hours

One of the first responsibilities of staff is to maintain regular business hours, usually 8:30 A.M. to 5:00 P.M. It is well to have field forces that come to the central office each day to be present at the same hours in the event the executive needs a conference or someone wants to make an appointment. Office hours should be posted at entrance.

Personnel Services

This includes requisitioning and referring eligible lists to appointing unit; checking and handling all personnel transactions; placing names on payroll, checking time sheets with payroll, checking payroll deductions, verifying and certifying payroll, checking pay checks received against time sheets and distributing them to responsible person in accordance with procedure; maintaining permanent personal file on each individual including application, employment record, deduction schedule, annual evaluation reports, any disciplinary actions, raises, promotions, demotions, transfers, letters of commendation, vacation record, sick leave record, compensatory time, and termination. Although some of the records and information may be handled by mechanical equipment, transactions and figures must be checked, verified, and processed by staff.

Budget

Generally the accounting and recording, statements, auditing and many fiscal items will be handled by mechanical equipment or by another agency. If not, it will be handled by the agency central office. It would include accounting for receipts and expenditures of regular, special, capital improvements projects, grant funds, gifts, and other accounts, and providing daily or weekly, monthly and yearly figures in accordance with procedures. It prepares and controls allotments and special information reports. It makes contacts with other agencies on fiscal matters. It verifies all fiscal transactions and is the source of control of all agency expenditures and property inventories.

Purchasing

All requisitions for personnel, services, and material things are authorized by the central office. Purchase orders are held until approved delivery slips are received and checked against the purchase order. While it is the responsibility of the field force to see that all deliveries of material and services rendered are satisfactory and conform to the purchase orders, it is the responsibility of the central office staff to see that all paper work checks out, vouchers are certified for payment and copies filed.

Petty cash is handled and accounted for by one person in the central office. Staff which presents signed receipts may be reimbursed for expenditures for cash items, usually not to exceed $10.00. The paid receipts are then submitted with a summary statement to the fiscal officer for reimbursement to the agency petty cash fund.

Contracts, warehouse delivery slips, professional services, and other forms of expenditures are processed in the same manner as regular vouchers by office staff. Copies of expenditure transactions are filed and kept for 12 months and then sold for waste paper or disposed of in an appropriate way as provided by agency rules.

Correspondence

All correspondence is expected to be answered promptly, within 48 hours, if possible. Promptness is an essential quality of a good administrator. Sometimes, correspondence concerns matters requiring considerable investigating, reports from other agencies, referrals to other people in which instances the correspondence should be acknowledged perhaps by the secretary, and the writer advised about the status of his letter and when he might expect an answer. It is all right to channel the letter to someone else who is better able to provide information. Copies of correspondence are provided to those concerned for information. A rule in correspondence and reporting is to identify, date, and sign each.

Incoming mail is opened, except that marked "personal," read, sorted and sometimes logged by the secretary or designated office staff. Routine matters are handled by the secretary or channeled to the proper persons for handling. Other matters are placed on the appropriate desk in order of importance and urgency. Sometimes the staff will prepare draft of correspondence and have it ready for signature at time the mail is read. Outgoing mail is picked up in time to meet the mailing schedule. It will help the office staff if a time can be set for dictation, lunch period, and making appointments. Dictating machines add flexibility and save time. They are a good investment.

Since few field workers have secretaries, their work is performed by the central office staff. They should make appointment or allow extra time for processing work and pick up.

Filing

This is a form of record keeping, but it generally refers to correspondence, reports, and matters in current use at some stage of completion that can be made available promptly when needed. Field forces seldom have places to file and store materials, therefore, they use central office for filing items of importance.

Filing in recreation is usually done alphabetically or by subjects.

The numerical system is used, but generally in larger systems that have skilled filing personnel. File material should not be removed from office unless properly recorded and checked off when returned.

Once a year, files should be purged of inactive materials. Those needed for future reference are transferred to record room or inactive storage and unneeded materials sold for waste paper or discarded.

Special Services

The reference library provides professional books, magazines, federal, state and local laws, federal and state grant guidelines, local and state maps, directories, policies, administrative directives, operational manuals, personnel rules, budget, city charter, city and state codes, city and county ordinances, master plan, regional and state recreation and open space plans, and other pertinent information. A system of checking out material is provided.

The professional staff is expected to keep up to date on latest developments and ideas. Many do not have a personal reference library. It is good investment for management to provide opportunities for research of information and self development. It is expected that the professional will take advantage of it.

Service to the public is the reason for the existence of a public recreation department. Every staff member should be glad to have the public visit the operations. It is the only contact with agency staff that some have. Some come to complain, others to compliment and to seek more information about the recreation programs and services. Prompt and courteous handling of their interests is important to the image and well being of the agency. If appropriate attention and satisfactory service are not given, chances are very good it will be followed up in a less satisfactory way to higher offices or to news media which means investigation and reports. Contacts with people usually are welcomed by recreation people and they generally end the contact by making a friend and an ambassador of good will for the department. This is the desired objective.

Expediter service is a popular service provided by the central staff in response to daily requests from field personnel such as "Write a requisition, I'll pick it up in five minutes," or "Can I get a pick-up order number" or "Will you check and see if the purchase order has come through on five tons of sand," or "I have a flat tire out here five miles from nowhere, what should I do?" These are common requests for office assistance, and although they take time, they should be handled as expeditiously as possible. It is an important service because it helps keep production units in operation and it helps the field unit to know it has a contact for help when it needs it.

One special service of staff concerning *information* is the special assignments and studies requiring special information and research, then preparation of a report. This can be done by office staff and does not take supervision out of production except to review the final draft. This may involve correlation with existing laws, orders, and practices, as well as making surveys or contacts with key people and drafting changes in procedures, rules and regulations.

OFFICE SPACE: LOCATION AND ARRANGEMENT

The fundamental reason for an office is to provide services to the public and to the agency. In order to provide these services, the staff, space, information, materials, and ready access (transportation and parking) are needed. Space, location, and arrangement depend on space and resources available, scope of services, number and kinds of staff, equipment, and functions of the office.

Location Of Office

Recreation agencies, among the last agencies to be added to government, are usually housed in whatever office space can be made available. Therefore, very little opportunity is provided for planning and arranging. Sometimes offices are in more than one building, in basements, attics, schools, city halls, recreation centers, park houses, renovated buildings with inadequate storage, working space, filing, parking, and conveniences.

Administrative offices should be grouped together, centrally located, convenient and easily accessible to public, staff, other government agencies, and separate from program activities. Offices need to be convenient to chief administrator and other government offices to expedite the growing numbers of interrelated matters at all levels of government. A great deal of time is saved by this arrangement. When the general supervisory or administrative offices are located in combination with activity facilities, the program staff and public tend to by-pass the appropriate program people and take up their matters with the higher level administrative offices. This creates a constant problem, particularly with the public.

Staff members usually like a separate building for administrative offices. This plan is good if the offices are well arranged and convenient to the chief administrator, the other government offices, and the public. If a separate building is constructed, it is well to consider also supply and material storage in conjunction with it.

Other factors to be considered in locating office are convenience to transportation and parking; available space that meets the requirements;

cost of making it available and usable; appearance and adaptability to needs; comfort factors; and good physical arrangement.

Centralized or Decentralized Location

Office work is generally centralized in small and medium agencies. In some medium and large organizations it is decentralized. Each has advantages.

In centralized location, offices are usually at city hall or nearby and convenient for administrative and public contacts. It is easier to expedite matters and for the executive to keep in close contact with management problems. Field forces understand office problems better. There is more work to be performed, therefore, more opportunity to obtain full-time specialists. Vacancies, peak work loads, and emergencies can be handled more efficiently. Central office is more adaptable and flexible to changing needs. Opportunities for staff development and in-service training are usually greater in central offices. Cost of operation and maintenance of a single office, staff, specialized equipment needed and janitor service is usually more economical. Office practices, procedures, and work rules may be applied more uniformly and effectively. Staff, information, and resources of the total agency are readily available when needed. There tends to be greater unity and understanding of the total office operations.

In decentralized locations, staff services are nearer the production phases and to an area of population. The staff can spend full time on a unit function and become more adept in a single phase of operation. Files and records that are used continuously are convenient and personnel that need them can become more familiar with them. Adjustments, corrections, and revisions of records can be made promptly. Time may be saved in transportation to and from central office.

A combination of centralized and decentralized offices is very practical and almost essential in areas of specialized field facilities (stadium, coliseum, theatres, camps) where records are needed daily. In these instances the permanent records and general services are maintained at central offices and specialized services and records are maintained at the decentralized office, with or without a copy to the central office. In this kind of situation, the office manager and staff of the central office may serve as consultants and advisors to the field office personnel.

Space Needs

Space needs vary depending on number of staff, amount of equipment, and services to be rendered. Small departments may need only two or three rooms, a large department may need an entire floor of city hall.

Space needs may be affected slightly by the number of staff entitled to private offices and where they are located. Factors to consider in assignment of private offices are disturbing noises and need for quietness, need for private or confidential discussions, prestige, and lack of conference room.

Types of space needs will vary with situations but may include any or all of the following: reception room or lounge, private office spaces, multiple use offices, small conference room for interviews or private talks, board room with cloak closet or large meeting room, library and reference room (could be with other room), central file and record room, office supply room, space or room for mimeograph and copying equipment, staff lounge with provision for coffee and/or refreshments, water cooler, restrooms. It is well to have a low rent but secure place for dead storage of old files and records that are no longer used regularly but must be retained. If office is to be a separate building, add utility room, janitor supply or maintenance room, and parking space.

Physical Arrangements

The office arrangement has a serious effect upon efficiency of clerical workers that spend day after day in the offices and upon organization relationships. The receptionist and offices that have frequent outside contacts are placed convenient to the public. Offices with frequent routine interrelations adjoin each other. The office manager and staff that frequently contact the executive, or handle administrative contacts in his absence adjoin the executive office, or reception room, or are conveniently near. Other offices are arranged for convenience to public, other staff, and easy flow of work (paper, materials) through and between departments in a straight line, preferably from desk to desk.[2] The conference rooms are convenient and near the people who use them. The central file and record room, water cooler, and duplicating room are located conveniently to clerical personnel who use them most. The board room, staff lounge, and restrooms may be slightly removed from the usual flow of traffic. Individual offices and secretary should be adjoining. Other considerations are entrances and exits, traffic lanes, power and telephone outlets recessed in walls or floors where needed, light switches, window space, support columns, barriers, and partitions.

MANAGEMENT PERSONNEL

There is a difference in office management in public and private business. Private business emphasizes such office functions as research, accounting, efficiency studies, and collecting statistics. Government agency offices usually do not stress these items but emphasize clerical and technical services to the agency.[3]

Office management is a staff function that gives services to the administrator and to management on the one hand and to line personnel and field forces on the other. Field forces usually are not provided separate clerical and office personnel. The office work for the entire agency, except specialized functions like a stadium, is performed for everyone at the central office. Agency field personnel are usually far-flung and mobile, performing rather specific assignments with few public contacts. Office services and paper work can be performed best centrally located by skilled technicians, trained office personnel, and modern equipment. The office personnel, therefore, perform and relieve the field personnel of many routine and time consuming tasks such as filing, record keeping, making reports, and managing paper work.

Office services may be provided in three ways, namely, those performed by other government agencies, specialist staff, and secretarial and clerical staff.

Other Government Agencies

In this age of specialization and equipment, many agency staff services are provided by other government agencies which have expert technical skills and highly specialized equipment. Such services include personnel recruiting and services, accounting and auditing, legal, retirement, social security, data processing, record keeping, cost accounting, purchasing, engineering, and a degree of planning. These services are coordinated by the agency specialists and clerical usually in central office. In some instances, these services are on a reimbursable basis. With increased interest in cost accounting and actual costs, trends are towards reimbursing other government agencies for work performed. Even the federal government makes charges for services rendered in some instances such as inspections for grant programs.

Specialist Staff Services

Small agencies spend their budgets largely on program personnel and field workers. Usually, they do not have funds for staff specialists in the office. Medium and larger agencies may add specialists as they expand, depending on the need of the agency and whether the service is available through the administrator's office, or another department. These specialists may be attached to the administrative division, a separate department of business administration, or technical division, but their services are available to agency personnel. They may include specialists in public relations and information, research, program analysis, planning, drafting, landscape architect, government liaison, purchasing, and personnel services.

Secretarial and Clerical Staff

In smaller agencies secretarial and clerical services may be performed by another agency, the executive secretary, or one or more persons under the supervision of the executive. In medium and larger agencies the services may be performed by a central group under a chief clerk, office manager, administrative assistant, or an assistant executive, depending on size and organization structure. This is a very important and responsible unit. It handles the daily services and controls paper work for the entire agency. The personnel in this unit, in addition to the office administrator, may include secretaries (in central pool), stenographers, typists, clerks, accountants, if necessary, trainees, interns, and similar positions. It generally does not include individual staff secretaries but does give services to personnel who do not have clerical help assigned to them individually.

The purpose of office staff is to perform the important but time-consuming detail office work thus permitting the highly paid professional and technical staff members to pursue full-time their skilled functions, for which they are trained.

BASIC OFFICE EQUIPMENT

The purpose of equipment is to make it possible for an employee to do more and better work with less effort and sometiems to provide a better means of performing repetitive, time-consuming, and monotonous work. Naturally, the kind and amount of equipment provided depends on quality and quantity of work to be accomplished plus amount of funds available for purchase and maintenance. Economics plays an important part in decision making. If a job can be performed quicker, better, at less cost and effort by a machine than by a person, decisions favor the machine. Displacing personnel with machines may cause a morale problem unless the staff is used in other jobs. On the other hand, spending large amounts for labor annually when work could be performed cheaper by a combination of labor and machines becomes a serious management problem. Continuous use of obsolete and inefficient equipment also is a morale and image problem that may adversely affect production. The convenience, comfort, contentment, and general attitude of the employee is a consideration.

Types of Equipment and Furnishings

Office equipment is being improved constantly. If new improved models will increase production at less cost than the difference in purchase price and exchange for better equipment the decision is obvious. Then, too, new equipment has a morale benefit.

In equipping and arranging an office, planners generally recommend that consulting experts be obtained to advise on matters important to the staff that are confined to a space all day and to the visiting public. These matters include most effective colors, lighting equipment, air circulation, ventilation, temperature controls, floor covering, desk arrangements, communication services, elimination of distracting sounds and movements,[4] and proper space requirements.

Desks, furniture, and furnishings come in all shapes, sizes and colors. Office furnishings should be selected on the basis of individual requirements, convenience, comfort, use and harmony with office environment. Metal desks are preferred to wood desks in most instances. Wood furniture often gets jagged and rough edges which snag clothes, and sometimes come unglued.

Basic office equipment, carried to an extreme, would be a table, two chairs, and a file cabinet. However, equipment for average recreation offices includes desks, chairs, tables, clothes rack, files, typewriter, bookcase, adding machine, calculator, communication equipment (dictating machine, intercom, telephone), floor covering, mimeograph machine, copier, safe or vault, paper cutter, paper punch, stapler, scissors, pencil sharpener, clock, desk or other lamp, letter trays, postal scales, wastebaskets, and postage meter or a central government mailing service.

Some departments may add more sophisticated equipment such as computers, motorized filing equpiment, punch card machines, tabulating machines, and addressing machines.

Today's executive is obliged to look at operations in two ways, one is from the point of view of the employer and the other is from the point of view of the employee. Equipment is one big factor that is important from the employee's point of view. It affects his attitude, prestige, proficiency, and physical and mental well being as well as production efficiency. These factors are worthy of careful consideration.

ELECTRONIC DATA PROCESSING

The electronic data processing system (EDP) is a procedure for manipulating data to obtain desired information. It has had a tremendous impact on management in recent years. Although the electronic computer has been used to some degree for many years, its acceptance, capabiilties, and general use by private and public organizations has increased since 1960. Since then, technological improvements have been made so rapidly the operating technicians and users have had difficulty keeping up to date with the advancements. There was more that could be done by computer than could be programmed by users and technicians in the initial stages.

Usually, the public agency first uses the computer for information storage, mathematical problems, data tabulation, and repeat items such as handling payrolls, budgets, accounting, personnel and purchasing records, and inventory control. These are high priority management functions that are generally performed for all agencies of a government jurisdiction by central general service units. Since 1970, technicians and computer time have become available to the various agencies for more extended uses which appear limited only by the capacity of the human mind to direct its activities.

In discussions with a sampling of professionals, consultants, administrators, managers, users, and auditors in the various fields related to the use of electronic data processing, the authors have found that they consider the computer essential to the efficient management of a modern agency of any size. The users of computers emphasized six points:

1. The computer is a tremendous aid in solving complicated problems using a combination of information that is impossible or impractical to obtain otherwise.
2. Better judgments and decision making result.
3. The computer performs at fantastic speed.
4. Computers require skilled technicians to operate them effectively.
5. There must be careful direction of purpose and programming from the using agency.
6. There must be a team effort.

The using agency must provide adequate and meaningful programming information and the EDP technician must adequately communicate the information to the machine in the language it understands. Good management practices apply to the administration of electronic data processing operations as well as other functions.

There is much to be said about EDP, but because of space it is not practical in a book of this nature to discuss all aspects of data processing. We will, however, present the highlights that may assist the recreation executive in visualizing the capabilities, potential uses, relationships, and cautions inherent in the use of the computer.

Capabilities of the Computer

Computers can perform accurately all mathematical functions from simple addition through algebra and calculus. Laird states:

> Present day computers are of two general types—analog and digital. The analog computer is a glorified calculator since it measures on a continuous scale like a slide rule. . . . The numerical controls of the analog computer form the basis for automated factory machinery, such as punch presses and lathes, by permitting instructions to be fed to the machine in the form of coded tapes to which the machine will respond. . . .
>
> The digital computer counts specifically, responding only to signals and never varying or responding in degrees. . . . Digital computers can control complicated accounting and record analyzing systems. One of the chief differences between analog and digital computers is the unique ability of the digital computer to store information in its memory.[5]

The computer basically is a simple machine that can perform complicated problems. Stokes states:

> Computers owe their position of influence to their ability to add, subtract, multiply and divide at bewildering speed. For example, they can design a transformer in 20 seconds. Calculations that require months of clerical time can be performed in a few seconds.[6]

Computers can perform much of the tedious and time-consuming office work, research, record keeping, fact finding, and reporting. Lundell and Bride state that "we have moved from man performance of one operation at a time to computer performing thousands of operations per second."[7] The computer makes it possible for management to consider several kinds of analyses at the same time in the decision-making process. This gives the decision maker an opportunity to consider all related facts in making judgments.

Computers can accumulate, store, and retrieve instantly information that management and professionals can use for planning, evaluating, and measuring efficiency against standards or previous records, and making future determinations. They are especially valuable in handling complicated mathematical and information processes where many variables and sources are involved.

Computers base their solutions on the accumulated facts programmed into them. Hjelte and Shivers state:

> An automatic computer is able to ingest and retain programmed information, perform whatever is required in terms of comparing, offering alternatives, selecting best choices, and the like on the information that is necessary in problem solving, and produces solutions. The information for the machine is simply encoded symbols, a series of ciphers or marks arranged on a magnetic spool that, when activated, becomes meaningful to the human user. The computer does not understand, that is, it has no knowldege of what any symbol means. The machine works only with logic or mathematical consistency of data inputs. Men program or organize the machine to accept and store certain marked materials so that at some later time they may be utilized as instructions that the machine is programmed to receive and act on.[8]

Computers can be made to build on information previously programmed and can be adjusted to the changing needs of recreation. They can merge information from various separate specialized units and work programs of the agency as a basis for management to make better decisions for the benefit of the whole. "The machine is nothing more or less than an extension of human capabilities subject to human control." [9] The capabilities of the computer are limited mainly by the initiative, resourcefulness, understanding, desires, and ability of management to use it, and they extend greatly available information and human resources with a minimum of human effort.

Potential Uses of the Computer for Recreation

Data processing actually includes many manually operated office machines, cash registers, and copiers, particularly in some of the smaller offices. As magnificient as the computer is, it needs supporting equipment like the key punch machine and the equipment to receive, record, and transmit communications. The users need telephones, dictating machines, copiers, terminal receiving screens, electric typewriters, and similar items. Much checking, filling in of figures, or adjusting of information is done in the agency offices, although the large and difficult jobs are performed in the computer center.

The computer can perform various kinds of staff skills, some of which were not available to the recreation executive before. The larger the agency, of course, the greater the need for a multiplicity of services. In the one-man departments and in the hundreds of departments which are limited to small clerical staffs, the research, clerical, filing, bookkeeping, and record keeping services as well as written and verbal communications are performed by one or two persons. In these kinds of situations, there is limited staff time for performing the bare essentials in researching information for problem solving, yet their problems are no less real. The use of computer time for any size agency not only could save time but also could provide information in depth from a variety of sources at the same time. If instructed to do so, the computer could compare, match, choose, combine, merge, reject, and communicate or store the information requested. In doing so, it may perform hundreds of calculations in a split second in order to arrive at the best answer.

Computer services may be decentralized and have "remote" units at distant terminal sending and receiving points, if needed. Central or in-house systems, either owner-operated or leased, are in greater use today. The owner-controlled ones are the most popular because then priorities can be determined, confidential information can be better maintained, and the machine can be made available when needed.

So often laymen think of the computer in terms of a machine to perform mathematical problems and the usual routine bookkeeping, accounting, and record keeping functions. The modern executive is obliged to consider the computer as a relatively untapped mechanical resource that can perform any request, both mathematical and logical, that can be programmed into it by man.

Suggested computer uses, by no means all inclusive, in the several elements of the administrative processes are:

1. Personnel
- Time sheets, payroll, and leave records.
- Individual personnel rating and evaluation records.
- Personnel position inventory and control.
- Health and accident records.
- Amount of turnover, absences, average time lost.
- Authorized payroll deductions—pension, social security, etc.

2. Finance and budgeting
- Daily and continuous budget accounting.
- Forecasting revenues from each source—concessions, fees and charges, rentals.
- Forecasting expenditures by work programs, by facilities separately or grouped.
- Accumulative information for budget preparation.
- Supplies and materials daily inventory.
- Cost accounting on each vehicle, facility, program, or other unit.
- Property inventory.
- Daily audit of fiscal records.

3. Planning
   - Land use data by SMSA or census district, geographic area, or as needed.
   - Inventory of vacant land and open spaces—size, characteristics.
   - Population distribution by any breakdown desired.
   - Population densities; existing public, semi-public, and private recreation facilities and resources.
   - Origin and destination information.
   - Forecasting uses.
   - Forecasting deficiencies as measured against standards.
   - Space analysis and projecting deficiencies.
   - Bid analysis.
   - Cost analysis.
   - Construction cost accounting.
   - Contract progress and forecasting completion schedules.
   - Separate force and other accounting as may be desired.
4. Organizing
   - Matching of likenesses—skills, functions, services.
   - Analyzing goals and projecting work loads.
   - Personnel rating and qualifications.
   - Matching personnel skills with job requirements.
   - Providing information on the most efficient staff grouping.
   - Determining supportive and supplemental services.
5. Directing
   - Providing status reports periodically or on call—budget, revenue, expenditures, employment, vacancies, accomplishments, special funds, new programs.
   - Storing information for instant retrieval.
   - Progress towards objectives; forecasting schedule of accomplishments—deficiencies and strong points.
   - Combining information from many sources for administrative decisions.
6. Programming
   - Inventory of recreation activities which the agency proposes to provide showing maximum enrollment.
   - Inventory of recreation sites' maximum capacity.
   - Processing of applications for the uses of facilities and enrollment in classes.
   - Matching staff and participant interests, skills, abilities.
   - Preventing enrollments and facilities from exceeding their capacities.

- — Forecasting participation and projecting deficiencies.
- — Determining effectiveness of activities.
- — Participation by age, sex, area, facility, activity, or any desired grouping.
- — Staff-participant ratio.
- — Activity costs.
- — Forecasting the benefits and effects of activities.

7. Evaluating and researching
   - — Analyzing progress in terms of objectives.
   - — Analyzing results in terms of costs and benefits.
   - — Evaluating use of supplies and materials.
   - — Appraising employee effectiveness.
   - — Determining the most efficient methods, procedures, and groupings.
   - — Determining effective staff-participant ratio.
   - — Most effective methods of determining attendance at open areas and for informal activities.
   - — Effects of professional leadership on the participant.
   - — Benefits of group leadership as compared to informal activities.
   - — Best basis for organizing advisory committees.

We wish to emphasize that the above listings are but a few of the many possibilities as compared to the total capabilities of the electronic computer.

Planning for the Computer

Although the electronic computer is a machine with almost unlimited capabilities, it requires human planning for the physical environment, programs, and instructions. There should be a master plan for physical layout, development, and future expansion as well as a master plan for services, accompanied by cost estimates and a computer time schedule to ensure maximum use of equipment. The size and capabilities of the computer that fills the particular needs best should be selected. The computer, files, and all processing equipment require security protection to safeguard the information as well as the sensitive equipment. Air conditioning, dehumidification, and automatic heating should provide rather uniform room conditions. The data processing center and equipment, of course, should be protected from natural disasters such as fire, wind, flood, and power failure.

In developing the master plan for services the machine should be planned for full-time use. Special staff, security, equipment, and unproductive time of personnel, as well as equipment, are costly and should be kept productive. There will be prime time, priorities, availability, and peak load periods to consider.

There are many types of computer services and many ways of performing the desired services. It is very essential initially to design the system that will best serve the agency's needs because future adjustments are built around the base plan, even though services may be added or subtracted as needs arise.

In planning for the computer, the agency staff should be oriented to the computer system and trained in procedures, uses, and relationships that will best fill the agency needs. Computer services are not static. They should be evaluated and improved as are other services and contracts.

OFFICE PUBLIC RELATIONS

Although every public employee is involved in public relations to a degree, the office staff, being at the headquarters operations, are almost in constant contact with the public in one way or another including office contact, telephone, written communications, and sometimes news media. These contacts, for many, are the only contacts the public has with agency personnel. It is in the best interest of the agency to make them good ones.

Office Contacts

First, the general appearance of the approach and inside of the office gives the first impression to a visitor. The approach to the office should be clean, well maintained, orderly arranged, dignified, and attractive in keeping with what is expected inside. A recreation and parks office would be expected to have attractive plants, flowers or symbolic recreation features at the entrance. Inside, the same general condition is emphasized. Walls have appropriate pictures, no gaudy calendars or extras, well placed plant stands with plants, or an aquarium, or recreation art and craft items, comfortable matching furniture, and a coat rack. Desk tops should be orderly with only current materials showing.

Acknowledge visitors promptly in a normal friendly voice and handle their matters. Invite them to wait if the person they wish to see is occupied but can see them soon. Provide them with something to occupy their time, if possible, then resume work or follow the rules for the occasion. Show them to their destination as soon as the way is clear. Introduce them if they are not acquainted, offer any courtesies and return to the work routine.

It is well for office management to decide with office staff on the most appropriate rules that will achieve the objectives of the office and allow as much individual freedom of expression and comfort as possible. The few rules may include such items as no chewing of gum or tobacco; eat in lounge rather than at the desk; avoid loud talk, hilarious laughter and other distracting noises and actions. Avoid cluttering. Keep tops of desks, files, bookcases, and windowsills orderly and free from inappropriate items. Be prompt. Do not be late for appointments. And, of course, be courteous at all times.

Rules in reference to personal matters can be very touchy and can best be framed in a general way with staff input. Situations that need adjustment may be handled on an individual basis.

Telephone

The telephone should be dealt with as though the person on the other end of the line were present. Answer the telephone promptly in a friendly, courteous, and dignified manner such as "Mr. James' office, Maria Gonnet speaking. May I help you?" This saves time, orients the caller, hopefully puts him at ease, and expresses friendly willingness to help. If there are loud or undesirable noises in the background, they should be quieted before picking up the receiver. The telephone easily picks up the noises which are not only distracting but tend to give a bad impression to outsiders.

Every telephone should have someone assigned to answer it or see that it is answered providing there is another person available. In a one-person office, arrangements may be made for persons in adjoining office to answer it; to connect it to an answering service; or post a time of return, or another number to call, and close the office. Sometimes, field forces will arrange to work in the office and answer the telephone while the secretary is out for lunch.

General courtesy in handling telephone calls is to let the caller know promptly what the situation is if the call cannot be completed at the time. It is not unusual for the intended receiver to be in a meeting or conference at his desk. It is discourteous to interrupt him. The receptionist then asks if she can help, or if anyone else can help, or would the caller mind having the call transferred to another office, or would he like to leave a message or have the call returned. A note is made, usually on a form for the purpose, and given to the intended receiver when he is free, containing the necessary information as to date, time, name of caller, telephone number, the message, and signature of person taking the call.

The telephone company has programs on how to answer telephones and handle different situations in the recommended manner. It is a free service and very effective in helping to establish proper telephone answering techniques.

Written Communications

It is rare that official letters are written by hand, therefore, the typewriter is used by agency for communicating directly with more people than any other method. It, therefore, is an important contribution to the agency's image and public relations. A letter may be the only contact many people, far and near, have with the agency. It should be a good one.

The person that uses the typewriter has the responsibility for seeing that the machine is functioning properly and other circumstances are in order to assure quality work which means that:

1. The typewriter keys are clean and even. Dirty keys make the completed work look smudged; bent and worn keys give typed communications an uneven distorted look.
2. The ribbon, carbon paper, and paper of such quality letters will be clear and distinct.
3. The typist, of course, uses correct spelling, sentence structure, punctuation, and good form.
4. Each communication is identified, dated, and signed.
5. There are no smudge spots, cigarette burns, sticky stains, or any other smears on the paper.
6. Eraser marks and corrections should not show. With improved methods of making corrections, this is no longer a problem.
7. Material is well centered and distributed on the typewritten page.
8. Legible carbon copies should be made for information of others and for record.

Sometimes the office copy is used for court cases and for providing correct information. Use of copier and carbon copies of letters are an excellent way to keep people informed that are involved in a matter. Signing with the first name and adding a hand written note adds a personal touch and is used sometimes on correspondence between friends and close acquaintences. Personal notes, however, should not be written on strictly official letters, documents and most letters. This defeats some of the reasons for typing and provides no copy for files.

It is well to include frequently used typewriters and office equipment in an annual maintenance contract. This usually provides regular and prompt services and keeps equipment in good condition as compared to the old methods of letting equipment break down before calling the repairman.

DISPOSAL OF RECORDS

Two of the big problems of central offices are the lack of space and accumulation of files and records many of which are never needed. It is costly to handle a paper transaction with all its carbon copies from the time it is written until it is discarded several years later. Unneeded copies and material should be discarded before they are filed.

It is not necessary for several government agencies to maintain duplicate carbon copy records indefinitely. Many carbon copies are for information only. After the copy of a communication has served its purpose it should be discarded. A practical rule, if there is no central file, is for the agency to file the original and other agencies dispose of the carbon copies unless copies are required by law. If it is necessary to review the matter later, the original can be borrowed or duplicated.

Public law requires that certain records be maintained indefinitely such as finance and property. Other records must be held for different periods of time such as 10 years, 5 years and 3 years. It is a good policy to review the files annually and dispose of all unnecessary paper.

The law does not concern many papers and subjects in the file and some cities have formed a permanent evaluating committee of ranking officials such as fiscal officer, auditor, personnel director, purchasing agent, and legal advisor to decide on kinds of files and records that must be held and for what period of time. After that time, records are discarded. If an agency has any doubt, it contacts the committee for interpretation. It works well.

Questions for Discussion

1. What is the best way for the recreation executive to use his time in the office?
2. What are the functions of the central office?
3. What factors are to be considered in determining the location of an office?
4. What physical arrangements would you recommend in an office?
5. What office services are usually performed by other agencies of government?
6. What office services are performed by specialists? By secretarial and clerical staff?
7. What equipment and furnishings would you purchase for a new comprehensive recreation office?

8. What spaces would you recommend for a comprehensive office for a medium-size city?
9. What are the advantages and disadvantages of a central office as compared to the decentralized offices?
10. What are the duties of a good secretary? A good receptionist?
11. How does the central office relate to good public relations?
12. How would you go about disposing of unneeded office records?

Short Problems

1. Draw a floor plan for a comprehensive recreation office arrangement and list by rooms the basic equipment and furnishings for it.
2. Prepare a staff organization plan for a well managed comprehensive recreation office showing titles and responsibilities of each position.
3. Prepare a complete set of policies, rules, regulations and other guidelines a good recreation executive uses in managing the affairs of the central office.

References

1. John J. W. Neuner, B. Lewis Keeling, and Norman F. Kallans, *Administrative Office Management,* 6th ed. (Cincinnati, Ohio: South-Western Publishing Co., 1972), pp. 1–2.
2. *The Technique of Municipal Administration,* 4th ed. (Chicago: The International City Managers' Association, 1958), p. 286.
3. *Ibid,* p. 285.
4. George Hjelte and Jay S. Shivers, *Public Administration of Recreational Services* (Philadelphia: Lea and Febiger, 1972), pp. 235–36.
5. Eleanor S. Laird, *Data Processing Secretary's Complete Handbook* (West Nyack, N.Y.: Parker Publishing Company, Inc., 1973), p. 24.
6. Paul M. Stokes, *A Total Systems Approach to Management Control* (New York: American Management Association, 1968), p. 16.
7. E. Drake Lundell, Jr., and Edward J. Bride, *Computer Use: An Executive's Guide* (Boston: Allyn and Bacon, Inc., 1973), p. 1.
8. Hjelte and Shivers, *Public Administration of Recreational Services,* p. 279.
9. *Ibid.,* p. 283.

Selected Readings

Bassett, Ernest D., and David G. Goodman, *Business Filing and Records Control* (4th ed.). Cincinnati: South-Western Publishing Co., 1974. *Filing systems, procedures, and records management.*

Brooks, Philip C., *Public Records Management* (rev. ed.). Chicago: Public Administration Services, 1961.

Hjelte, George, and Jay S. Shivers, *Public Administration of Recreational Services*, pp. 225–314. Philadelphia: Lea and Febiger, 1972.

Littlefield, Cleatice L., and Frank Rochel, *Office and Administrative Management: Systems Analysis, Data Processing, and Office Services* (2nd ed.). Englewood Cliffs, N.J.: Prentice-Hall, Inc., 1963.

Neuner, John J. W., B. Lewis Keeling, and Norman F. Kallans, *Administrative Office Management.* Cincinnati: South-Western Publishing Co., 1972. *The information management concept, organizing and planning office services.*

Public Administration Service and International City Managers Association, *Automated Data Processing in Municipal Government.* Chicago: Public Administration Service, 1966.

Starr, Martin K., *Production Management: Systems and Synthesis.* Englewood Cliffs, N.J.: Prentice-Hall, Inc., 1964.

Stokes, Paul M., *A Total Systems Approach to Management Control*, pp. 131–139. New York: American Management Association, 1968. *The use of machines for controlling and decision making.*

CHAPTER 18

Public Relations

Providing recreation opportunities and services are the primary functions of the recreation agency. In order to do this, it provides ideas, areas, facilities, equipment, leadership, and program in a variety of ways. It relies upon public interest and finances for participation and support. It has many audiences of varying interests, ages, responses, capabilities, and needs which change and expand. In order to accomplish its purpose, it must participate in a continuous two-way voluntary free communication system; one way to listen to needs, interests, complaints, suggestions and support from the public to help the staff determine the best kinds of programs; and the other way to inform the public of its services and programs, to interpret its objectives, to promote interest and participation, and to enlighten, motivate, and challenge.

Public relations, to some degree, is a duty of every member of the agency staff with the final authority resting with the executive as it is with other functions of the agency. Until recently, the full responsibility of handling public relations rested with the executive. Public relations is still one of the executive's major responsibilities, but executives of larger departments no longer have time to assume new, complicated duties of management and, in addition, maintain the expertise required to handle the now highly specialized and competitive field of public relations. There is a strong tendency for executives to employ a public relations specialist or assign a staff member to assume some of the functions. In smaller communities the recreation program makes good news; therefore, if good rapport is maintained with representatives of the news media a very effective public information program can be provided with agency cooperation and a minimum of staff effort. After all, public relations involves a cooperative relationship and the news reporter makes a good member of the team.

In the early stages, public relations often was thought of as publicity and publicity was thought of as news stories and advertising. In a way, this was a logical relationship because *publicity* means information intended to promote interest and *advertising* means attracting public attention so as to create interest or opportunity for sales. Publicity and advertising represent only two aspects (press-agentry, propaganda, persuasion) of public relations. Publicity is usually free, and sometimes unwanted when things are wrong; advertising is usually purchased.

Over the past four decades, public relations has expanded its scope considerably and has become an essential function of most private businesses and a growing number of public agencies.[1] Private businesses may employ a public relations firm to perform their work but laws generally do not permit public agencies to use tax money for advertising or promoting themselves, except in a few instances which are authorized by their respective charters or by special state legislations.

Public relations may be used in several ways. Businesses use it successfully with relationships in advertising, promotional activities, and to develop goodwill among its customers and in the community. Professional organizations and institutions use it successfully to inform memberships and the public about their programs and objectives. Public agencies are using it for all of these plus added emphasis on public involvement. Some public relations programs are focused on particular segments of the public; others, on the total population. Public services, being supported by public funds, are almost obliged to develop public relations information and goodwill programs that will reach the total population, for support, even though, in some agencies, their services are geared only to a special segment.

DEFINITION

The term *public relations*, perhaps because of its variety of uses, may be defined in different ways. A popular definition among professionals is that it is the activities and techniques used in behalf of an organization, institution, or individual to establish for them public understanding, favorable attitudes and responses of people. The International City Managers' Association suggests that public relations is "the sum total of all the contacts, attitudes, impressions, and opinions that constitute the relationships between the public and its government."[2] In public recreation, the definition needs to be broad to include interests of the public, the governing bodies, and the agency.

A public relations campaign is a continuous extensive effort to create and maintain a mental environment conducive to the acceptance of a product, an idea, or ideology, or a personality, individual or corporate.[3]

Objectives and Purposes

The main objective of a public relations program in government is to improve and maintain good interrelationships between the different segments of the government and the public. It accomplishes this purpose by developing favorable attitudes of confidence, respect, goodwill, cooperation, and approval towards the government and simultaneously promotes among government officials and staff similar attitudes of respect, cooperation, confidence, understanding, and leadership.

The purposes of a public relations program in a public recreation agency involve the following:

1. Informs the public of ordinances, regulations, policies, objectives, and practices and gives interpretation.
2. Informs the public where areas, facilities, and recreation opportunities are, when they are available for use, and what activities are conducted at each location.
3. Arouses attention and creates interest of the public to participate.
4. Reports to the public on status of programs, progress, accomplishments, services rendered, improvements made, and plans for the future.
5. Emphasizes efficiency, competence, quality, adequacy, promptness and effectiveness in all of its programs and services including maintenance.
6. Interprets the services, benefits, and importance of recreation in general, and the recreation agency in particular, to life in the community.
7. Prepares the public for proposed changes, additions, deletions, different procedures, expansions, and recommendations, and seeks approval and support.
8. Promotes community (groups and individuals) involvement and enlists individuals to give volunteer services.
9. Encourages agency staff to participate in community affairs and services.
10. Supports joint sponsorship of community programs where feasible and permissible.
11. Supports uses of lay committees and advisory councils and use of lay citizens on studies, surveys, and official boards.

12. Deals realistically in facts and good practices, taking into consideration the interests both of the public and of the agency.
13. Maintains a spirit of cooperation and helpfulness in a friendly, courteous, pleasant manner.

IMPORTANCE OF GOOD PUBLIC RELATIONS IN RECREATION

Recreation executives consider public relations to be among the most important functions of the agency. Even though a full-time or a part-time specialist may assume major responsibility for public relations, the policy board members, the chief administrator, his administrative staff, program supervisors, recreation professionals and the public either have a direct responsibility for public relation matters or supply factual materials.

The community which recreation serves is composed of a number of publics which have diverse interests, reactions, and responses. Although they live in the same general community, their interests are stimulated in different ways by different methods. Their response to a general approach may be minimal, but they may respond well to a specialized approach. Too often citizens tend to rely on hearsay and their imaginations which are formed from bits of information. Most people tend not to attend or participate or even inquire about activities until they know something about them. A public relations program needs to be developed to reach the several different publics in the community, to provide them up-to-date information about the opportunities available, stimulate their interest, and motivate them to participate in community and recreation affairs for their mutual benefit. Even for those who are not motivated to participate, it is well for them to be informed in a manner they understand including convenient ways for making contacts should they wish further information. This reduces the opportunity, and sometimes the desire, to deal in rumors and half truths and at the same time helps their prestige "to be in the know."

Recreation is subject to many changes to fit the needs of the community with various programs for the different seasons, such as football in fall and swimming in summer, free time periods such as holiday programs and summer playgrounds for youngsters out of school, and irregular schedules such as tournaments and programs for shift workers. In recreation, nothing is more exasperating than after a build up and anticipation of an exciting period at the recreation area to get there and find it closed or the schedule changed.

Recreation deals with so many kinds of situations that need to be explained to the taxpayer in order to maintain his good will such as the reasons for charging for some recreation activities, why programs are provided for adults, why the city provides a stadium or an auditorium, why more convenient places for riding mini-bikes are not provided, and many more situations where lack of information and differences of opinion and interests are involved. Recreation programs are based on the wide variety of interests of the people and accordingly are just as different. Persons with one kind of recreation need often do not understand why people with other kinds of needs are given public service. Nor do they understand the reasons for having public recreation at all. The public relations function is to foster a better understanding.

In this discussion, the word "why" has been rather prominent. The answer to "why" is an important element in the current public relations programs, perhaps, because the publicity type information programs of former years gave "why" the least consideration. Also, in several instances the reasons for "why" keep changing. For instance, a few years ago programs were mainly for children during the summer months. Now programs are for the entire family the year round and seven days a week. People want to know why things are done or not done. The public relations program interprets to the public the changing needs, changing values, reasons for expansion, and philosophy of recreation. People are accustomed to a planned public relations program in other matters and respond well to a similar approach in recreation.

The community expects so much of recreation which touches the lives of so many people in a positive way. When something goes wrong, such as the delay of a contractor in completing the community gym on time because of a 90 day strike out-of-state, it has a tremendous impact on the community. The public relations program, anticipating this well in advance, reduces the shock by preparing the people for it, keeps them informed, and presents the alternate plan for the interim.

Public relations tries to prevent development of suspicion, false impression, and misunderstanding by presenting facts in advance and adding information as it develops. It also serves as a sounding board for public opinion, interests, and support concerning activities of the agency.

Positive Values Emphasized

In early stages, the by-products of recreation were emphasized such as crime prevention, keeping children off the street, and reducing accidents. In more recent years, emphasis is placed on the positive values of recreation such as dveloping boys and girls for the future, emphasizing growth and development, education for leisure, training for citizenship, practicing the principles of democracy, keeping mentally and physically fit, attracting business and industry, and contributing to the making of a better community in which to live.

Effective Timing

The proper timing of communications and distribution of information is almost as important as the information itself. Timing, of course, depends on the nature of the information, its objectives, the procedure it has to follow, and delays in reaching the intended receivers. The choice of method of communication also may be involved. Cancellations, postponements, emergency closings, and changes of any kind on short notice that would affect individuals adversely should be communicated to them with brief explanations as soon as practical. It is well also to include the rescheduled time and other information, if possible. The receiver will want to know why the change and how it will be resolved.

Emergencies, disasters, loss of life and property, serious injuries, and emotional matters should be communicated as soon as information is available, then investigated promptly, and new pertinent information reported, except matters of liability which may be referred to a legal department.

Announcements of future events are made one week to three months in advance (sometimes longer), usually less than a month for routine program activities and meetings. A program calendar may be prepared for a full year. Busy people, community-wide and special events, and activities that require considerable time for planning will need a month's notice. Items like workshops, institutes and other city-wide events involving general staff and/or outsiders require 60 to 90 days. Timing of advanced information on events is often in proportion to the frequency of the events with a minimum of one week. For instance, on the annual budget the astute executive will begin to educate the policy board, administrator, and key citizens (including organizations) a year in advance. Sometimes this is initiated at the budget hearings the previous year.

Preparations for referendum campaign begin usually six months prior to election day with intensification of activities building to a climax the day before the vote.

In communities where there are morning, evening, and weekly newspapers, timing will be an important consideration to reach the right audience desired.

Timing to coincide with related national, state, and local events of wide interest, such as announcement of a revised state open space plan, provides excellent opportunities for a followup feature on plans for a new park. A drowning in the river might be the opportunity to arouse interest in proper swimming facilities.

PLANNED PUBLIC INFORMATION PROGRAM

A public recreation program is only as good as the public thinks it is. No matter how attractive a program is or how well it conforms to good planning and national standards, unless the general public knows about it and is satisfied, much effort is wasted and support may be expected to be minimal. This is not to imply that the executive should build an empire for himself. It does mean, however, he should maintain a good image for the agency, provide the most opportunities possible from the resources available to him, and devise a balanced plan for informing the public. That will include all of the agency activities and the most effective means of informing the various publics about them. Emphasis is on what the public needs and wants. By satisfying the public, the agency lifts its own presige. When the public is involved in the process, its prestige and importance is lifted further. Good information and proper timing are major ingredients in a good public relations program.

Steps in Formulating a Public Information Program

Although local conditions vary, such as size, scope of program, and resources, the following steps are suggested as basic:

1. Identify the different needs of the public for information. The needs were outlined earlier in the chapter under "purposes."
2. Determine the sources of available communications most convenient for them that will serve their needs. The sources will be discussed later in this chapter.
3. Determine when the information is needed by the public and the media. Public contacts (individuals, groups, and participants) are asked for this information.
4. Make arrangements with media and staff to provide information; perhaps at a joint meeting, if several are involved.
5. Establish objectives and procedures in consultation with staff and representatives of public involved.
6. Prepare the plan, review it with staff for possible improvements, make necessary revision, and give it wide distribution.
7. Review effectiveness of plan periodically; make adjustments and improvements.

The total public relations programs involves five principal groupings of resources which include visual, audio, reading, and experiencing as follows:

1. News media, which usually make contacts with large areas—city, state, national—include television, radio, newspapers, house organs, and magazines.
2. Community-wide opportunities, which are limited in area but closer to active users, include attractive posters, mobile programs, motion picture shorts, exhibits and demonstrations, staff participation in community activities (membership, recreation causes), speaking engagements and slide talks, fillers in pay envelopes or monthly bills, floats and parades of children, training conferences and institutes.
3. Citizen involvement includes memberships on boards, commissions, advisory councils, committees, task forces, and special studies; citizens' speaker's bureau; sponsoring sports banquets, citizen suggestions, and volunteer workers.
4. Agency activities include distribution of brochures, leaflets, reports, annual report; newsletters; informative letterheads, envelopes, and postage meters; bulletin boards; personal contacts (home visits, sick visits, congratulatory notes); holiday celebrations; special events; tours and open house; sponsoring community events (hobby shows, cultural events, concerts); recreation week and special days; cooperation with other agencies.
5. Other includes referendum campaigns, and assisting community organizations in annual outings, centennials, and special programs.

Each medium listed above is used in some way by most recreation agencies. Often they just occur without planning such as a visit from a reporter, distinguished guest, a complaint, an observation, or someone reports something. Unplanned information is like unplanned programs; it is often ineffective, spotty and incomplete.

Planning Information Programs

In formulating informational programs the planner considers the total needs of the public, the mutual interests of the public and agency, the total resources and programs of the agency, the type and length of the message to be delivered, the best timing, the appropriate medium, and the proper procedures and *makes a specific staff person responsible* for each specific situation.

Usually line officers are responsible for routine, in-house activities (housekeeping and conduct) and information on programs for which they are individually responsible. They are also responsible for informing higher officials or information specialist about big events and unusual situations they do not feel they can handle well themselves. The routine items include daily program schedules, cancellations, postponements, game winners, scores, announcements, meetings, and community involvements relating to the programs. Arrangements are usually made with radio or television to receive calls and announce at a specified time last minute postponements of sports events because of rain. This is a big item in urban areas with several hundred teams.

Specific staff is assigned responsibility for handling exhibits, demonstrations, and special features.

Program staff are responsible for major events. There must be cooperation at every level of government in order for a public relations program to be most successful.

All matters involving policy, the executive, the chief administrator, legislative body, or public controversy should clear through the executive's office. Information, announcements and items involving more than one major unit often are in the form of joint communication with joint signatures with all concerned receiving a copy.

Training Staff in Public Relations

Public relations is so important and involved that it is well to provide special training in the subject at different levels of staff. The caretaker of the animals, janitor, and custodian have many contacts with the public and should be trained on matters helpful in their positions. Most employees like to know better ways of handling telephone contacts, complaints, writing letters, dealing with people, and procedures. Demonstrations, discussions, supervised practice, lectures, slides and movies are effective methods. It is well to have citizens participate as instructors.

PLANNING WITH NEWS MEDIA

The news media as related to recreation consist of newspapers, television, radio, house organs, and professional publications. Although their characteristics and policies may be quite different, their procedures for handling news and people are similar. Although television and radio are very popular the newspaper has wide appeal.

House organs and professional publications generally are involved with specialized news for a limited yet important audience.

News reporting requires some skill especially the feel for what makes a good news item, special feature, or human interest story. Recreation is a good source of news and the news media respond well to friendly and helpful relationships.

Some tips in dealing with the news media include:

1. Learn the policies and desires of the media. Their policies and emphasis are different, therefore, information is directed differently.
2. Learn deadlines and lead times.
3. Cultivate acquaintances with the editor and reporters.
4. Inform media personnel about the plans, objectives and practices of the agency. Show interest in providing information with least effort to them.
5. Cooperate by volunteering information, giving tips on news leads you may observe.
6. Be fair, impartial, and factual. Release news when it happens while it is still news.
7. Use names often in stories. Names add interest.
8. Provide all media a copy of monthly calendar and give adequate notice of coming events.
9. Prepare information stories or fact sheets. Contact media or reporter in advance, review briefly the facts; they may send a reporter.
10. Format for preparing information for news media.
    — Identify agency, phone number, name of writer at top of page in upper left corner.
    — State time and date it is to be released in upper right corner.
    — Double space, leave good margin.
    — Be brief but factual; avoid editorializing.
    — The first (lead) paragraph should include all pertinent information (who, what, when, where, how and why).
    — Use simple words and easily understood sentences.
    — Attach charts, graphs and pictures, if appropriate, or suggest time and place for good pictures.
    — Use originals only; practice a degree of exclusiveness.
    — Mail or deliver in person information direct to editor or reporter.
11. A schedule of dates of story releases for major events, like a national tournament that generates a series of news stories and features, should be provided to the news media in advance. This will help the editor assign personnel, photographers, and space.

Newspapers

The local newspaper is considered by most recreation agencies as the most effective outlet for printed information. It is inexpensive, available area-wide, can provide sustained coverage, and its staff knows the feelings of the people. Before an article is printed, it is usually well reviewed and has the stamp of approval of the editor which tends to add prestige. The advantages of the printed media are that it can be read at any time convenient to the reader, articles can be cut out and used for personal interests indefinitely (scrapbook, reference, proof), and are aimed at many different publics at the same time such as news, sports, woman's page, youth section, senior citizens, recreation calendar, editorials, pictures, letters to editor, or feature articles. Usually, the leadership of the community read the local newspaper and are interested in items involving people and activities of government. The recreation executive obtains from news media impressions, reactions of citizen and citizen groups, the political situation, status of related programs in the community, and a great deal of information that is helpful in planning and carrying out his administrative functions. After all the news media are the main outlets for feeling of the public. The masses tend first to contact the newspaper to tell the news, to complain, or promote their favorite interests.

Newspapers may run daily or weekly recreation columns, calendars, or announcement sections. Some carry columns written by playground participants. However, none should replace regular features.

Regular news includes daily happenings such as policy announcements, opening of new facilities, new programs, key staff appointments, adoption of budget, and changes in schedules.

Sports news is vital to the recreation program. Contacts and good relations with the sports editor are essential to learn policy, procedure, form, and deadlines for carrying results of league games, league standings, contests, tournaments, schedules, and human interest stories.

Special features deal with human interests, unusual accomplishments, unique hobby, state or national recognition, outstanding service, and exceptional leadership. This may be in news section, woman's page, youth page, sports page, senior citizen's page, Sunday feature section, or picture section. It deals in depth with interesting subjects and is a valuable method.

Editorials are stimulated by outstanding accomplishment (or poor results), letters to the editor, suggestion and material from the agency, a community controversy or good will interest of the newspaper.

Newspapers sometimes sponsor or co-sponsor community recreation events such as a pushmobile contest, sports events, holiday celebrations, backyard contests, and roller skates derby. If there is more than one local newspaper, similar opportunities should be provided each paper so as to be impartial in all respects.

Magazines

Magazines and house organs provide good contacts with local, state, and national audiences for announcements, plans, problems, and accomplishment types of feature articles most of which are geared to specialized interests, such as conservation, rehabilitation, government, industry, professions, youth, senior citizens, travel, sports and hobbies. The articles are usually longer than a newspaper article but guidelines for preparation are similar. Pictures and good feature articles in a national or professional publication about activities of the local department add considerable prestige and enthusiasm to the local program.

Television and Radio

Television is a popular medium, especially for women and children in the home. It has the advantage over radio in that it provides both for visual and audio. The radio has the advantage of being able to be taken everywhere (car and portable) and, therefore, is available constantly. It is very effective for announcements, sudden changes of schedules, and contacts with men and youth. There are more television and radio stations than newspapers in most communities, therefore, they have to share the listening public, and competition is greater. Both television and radio are required to provide a percentage of time for free public-service programming which may be used for recreation interests such as announcements, interviews and talks, panel discussions, on the spot movies of events, and agency programs, perhaps on a weekly or monthly basis.

Some communities have educational and cable television stations which are involved in providing programs for education and services to the community and are not so much dependent on advertising commercials for support. Both have good potential for the recreation community.

USING COMMUNITY RESOURCES

Good public relations are dependent largely on the exposure the agency has with the individuals and organizations in the community. The contacts may be made within the department by the use of facilities or participation in department-sponsored programs. They may be made outside the department indirectly through various media or by staff involvement, community involvement, and mobile programs.

Mobile Programs

The increase in mobile recreation programs provides an excellent opportunity for the staff to meet citizens that never visit the playground or center. An appropriately marked mobile unit, attractive and well maintained, plus effective leadership and program provide excellent opportunity for attracting and serving more people. This often is a way of interesting volunteer leadership.

Exhibits and Demonstrations

Exhibits are designed to present a special message and usually show work already accomplished in words, finished products, attractively arranged to display what the agency does. Exhibits are presented at fairs, windows of banks, hotel lobby, department stores, city hall, community centers, schools and similar places. They may include art, photography, nature, hobbies, and other skills.

Demonstrations are live exhibits showing a recreation activity in progress. Such a demonstration held in a downtown store window, shopping mall, or court yard at noon hour attracts much attention. Demonstrations of skills such as sketching, folk dancing, fly casting, handcraft or any small group activity accompanied by appropriate music, attractive posters, or comment by the leader provide very effective contacts.

Motion picture and slide talks are very effective. Many recreation agencies have prepared their own, or have access to audiovisual materials. Some have coordinated background music and comments with color slides. With automatic focus cameras, almost anyone can prepare a good picture presentation.

A motion picture requires much more skill than slides. It is recommended that only skilled or professionals attempt to make a feature program with movies. They are effective because they show action but are costly in comparison to other media and are usually soon outdated. They are more effective with sports activities where movement is an important factor.

Posters and Window Cards

Attractive posters and window cards, sometimes with photographs and art work performed at the agency, are designed to be placed in public places and store windows in the community. They are especially effective in announcing events of local interest. Since they are a public service of good will, business places usually like to cooperate. One caution is to be sure posters are removed when the event they announce is over.

Floats, Parades of Children

Almost every community has a public parade of some kind during the year. This is a happy festive occasion with which to be identified and it is good for the agency to enter a float or group. These projects add extra incentive and action to the program during several weeks of preparation and plenty of fun and talk afterwards. It is a natural activity for recreation agencies but requires considerable work and some cost. Groups that often participate in parades are baton twirlers, bands, dancing or other costumed groups, decorated bicycles, clowns, decorated cars and equipment all with attractive agency signs.

Employee Involvement

It is just about as important for administrative and supervisory recreation personnel to be involved in community contacts as it is to be involved in agency programs. A person who deals with public service programs adds greatly to his success when he identifies with good community interests and contacts involving the participants with whom he works. It is well to speak at P-TA's, civic associations, to help with a community outing, and support *good* community projects related to recreation. His role in the community is leader of good recreation movements and leisure time services to people. Like the business and professional people who are community minded and give of their talents so the good recreation professional is expected to do likewise and be a leader in his field in the community.

Training Conferences, Workshops, and Institutes

A training conference geared to persons in the community who do volunteer work involving leisure time activities such as youth leaders, church workers, recreation volunteers and members of the agency staff, especially new members, does much to develop understanding between public services and the citizens. The sessions might be held three mornings and might include a dutch treat lunch if they preferred to stay all day. The important factor is that instructors and enrollees are both from the agency and the community.

Other Ideas

Some localities insert printed fillers about recreation in pay envelopes and utility bills. Some play a midget football game at half time of regular football games. Department stores include the major recreation events in their Sunday newspaper advertisements. Motion picture shorts and announcements are shown at neighborhood movies. Key and influential personalities are used in programs such as crowning the queen, presenting awards, and pitching the first ball at season's opening game.

INVOLVING THE CITIZEN

One of the most essential elements of a good public relations program is the successful involvement of the citizens in meaningful ways to learn citizen interest and concerns, to seek their advice, share their talents and services, and, in turn for them to interpret to the community the agency's plans, programs, objectives, and other matters of interest. Since the citizen both pays the bills and receives the service, it is logical that he should be involved in planning, objective evaluations of programs, and assisting with the services. He does that by serving on boards and committees, helping to promote activities, sponsoring events, and volunteering his services.

Citizen Boards and Committees

Recreation has been a leader in involving citizens in partnership activities. Its national, state, and local professional organizations include lay memberships. Many local departments have policy or advisory boards and their program activities are often assisted by citizen committees. (The organization of advisory groups was discussed in Chapter 5.) Citizen boards which are involved in public relations are:

Policy boards and commissions, which are authoritative boards, have power to set policies, interpret programs and services, keep the public and officials informed of the status, progress of recreation services, and provide programs that will serve the needs of the public. The citizens contact this type of board as well as the executive.

Advisory boards, appointed by the legislative body and ex-officio agencies, are advisory only but, with proper leadership, have almost as much influence with administration and council as authoritative boards. They serve as a sounding board for the citizens and interpret needs and recommend policy to the executive or legislative body.

Task forces and special studies are often performed by citizen groups under direction of the executive or a specialist representative. They are ad hoc committees usually with representatives of the authoritative or advisory board and other departments included in the membership. They may make studies of facilities, program needs, adequacy of certain types of areas or facilities, or where emphasis should be added.

Neighborhood or playground recreation councils are at the playground or recreation center level and are vital to the center director in interpreting neighborhood needs, facilitating recreation planning and community cooperation, recommending policy matters, supporting the recreation program and personnel, raising funds, helping to alleviate problems, and serving as volunteer workers.

Citizen Speakers Bureau

In some places the recreation board provides a speakers bureau; however, frequently the board members are too busy or are not strong in public speaking. Sometimes a speakers bureau composed of staff, board members, interested and informed lay citizens is organized. They attend meetings, speak on recreation, and support the program and community activities. It is designed to be an effective partnership in support of community and department recreation interests. The agency audio-visual material and resources are available to them.

Sponsoring Events

The staff and resources of most recreation agencies are supplemented considerably by community-sponsored activities directed by the recreation agency or the use of its facilities. Such sponsorships include athletic teams, tournaments, contests, sports, banquets, youth programs, special events, awards, trips, and uniforms.

Volunteer Workers

There are many services in a public recreation system that can be performed well by lay individuals. In fact, some individuals share special talents that the agency does not have and could not afford to buy. They share musical, dramatic, dance, art, hobbies, fund raising, and other talents; serve as leaders, hosts, hostesses, and officials; and perform related services that not only supplement staff services but also are excellent promoters and community relations people.

AGENCY PUBLIC RELATIONS ACTIVITIES

The most important public relations activity an agency can perform is a well managed department with excellent recreation services which are generally satisfying to the users. This would include attractively designed and well maintained offices, buildings, facilities, and equipment; areas, buildings, and mobile equipment appropriately identified or signed; entrances and signs well lighted; and personnel prompt, courteous, efficient, considerate, appropriately dressed, proper in deportment and neat in appearance. Every employee in a public department comes in contact with the public and is involved to varying degrees in public relations. Some specific activities include the following:

Brochures and Leaflets

These items are prepared for specific purposes to carry a message to the reader or serve as a reference concerning activities of the agency. Often they inform the public where the agency facilities are and what programs are conducted at them and the time. They are attractively designed with photographs and art work and of convenient size to carry in the pocket or handbag. They may be distributed in school home rooms, on the playgrounds, at recreation offices and buildings, at community meetings, the libraries, and large industries. Some may be mailed to key people, but mailing is expensive. Leaflets may be distributed at the location or distributed to homes in the neighborhood by participants.

Newsletters or Bulletins

Weekly or monthly newsletters present a status report of accomplishments and events to come in the immediate future. Children may take them to their parents. On the city level they may be available for pickup at office or council meetings. A few may be mailed to officials and other key persons.

Speeches

The executive and program staff are obliged to make talks at community and neighborhood meetings to keep citizens informed, answer questions, learn their needs, receive suggestions, and perhaps win their support or approval. If it is a prepared speech, it would be well to have an extra copy for their records or for the local reporter.

Bulletin Boards

Bulletin boards are an excellent inexpensive way of communicating information to the interested public that attends or passes an area frequently, at least once a week. They are attractively located in prominent positions at offices, city hall, recreation locations and other places of assembly or along pedestrian traffic lanes. Those located out of doors should be protected from the weather and be vandal resistant with plastic framed front. They are used for posting such items as announcements, program schedules, hours of operation, team standings, messages, rules and changes. They should be checked daily, obsolete material removed, and kept up-to-date.

Personal Contacts

Visits in the home to visit the sick, to follow up accidents to participants or members of their families, to inquire about an absentee or to discuss a problem important to a participant and the family, and similar matters do much to spread good feelings and goodwill in the community. Sometimes a note or telephone call will be effective to inquire about a participant or to congratulate an individual or family on a worthy accomplishment.

Open Houses and Tours of Facilities

The open house and tour is a form of exhibit but it is an excellent way of stimulating participant and community interest and at the same time providing an occasion to show officials, parents and families, citizens and news media the accomplishments and opportunities at the facility. It is a good way to generate publicity, identify officials and key people with the program, and broaden interest in the program.

Recreation Week and Special Days

This type of occasion is used to take advantage of state or national publicity, to emphasize special objectives, and stimulate interest. It is a kind of agency-wide open house where an effort is made to show all activities and programs possible, broaden participation, and involve the communities in planning and participation. Regular activities throughout the agency are demonstrated at a specified time and special programs such as tournaments, outings, performing arts, swimming meets, folk festivals, square dancing and items of mass participation and entertainment value may be scheduled. Large numbers participating at the same time are impressive and generate interest.

Special Events

Special events, built around a theme such as a festival or neighborhood fair, unite in one program a cross-section of activities at a location. Its purpose is to stimulate activity, expand interests, demonstrate accomplishment, involve the community, and attract public interest in the program at a particular location and at the same time is sort of an accounting of what has been going on at the recreation center.

Sponsoring Events in the Community

In order to reach more people in the community sometimes programs are taken where people are, such as the courthouse square, city hall mall, state capitol grounds, the park, school auditorium, civic center, or shopping center mall. Such programs may include a concert, community sing, folk festival, square dance demonstration, choral presentation, hobby show, flower show, puppet show, nature display or hand craft exhibit.

OTHER PUBLIC RELATIONS ACTIVITIES

Other public relations activities include conducting holiday celebrations such as July 4th, Halloween, and Christmas events; opening and closing programs; dedication ceremonies for new facilities; preparing for referendum campaigns; joint sponsorships of community programs; special slogans, announcements, information on letterheads, envelopes and postage meters; and educational programs.

Questions for Discussion

1. What are the objectives of a public relations program?
2. What do you consider are the main elements of a good public relations program?
3. How does the recreation executive relate to a good public relations program? the staff? the community?
4. How would you go about planning a good public relations program?
5. What, in your opinion, are the ten most effective resources to use in a public relations program?
6. What would you include in a training program for agency public relations?
7. What advice would you give a staff member who is expected to use the news media regularly?
8. How does an education type public relation program differ from news reporting?
9. How are facilities and maintenance personnel involved in a good public relations program? The office staff?
10. What do you consider are the advantages in use of the different news media? How is each used best?

Short Problems

1. Outline a good public relations plan for a medium-size public recreation department.
2. Prepare a step-by-step procedure and use it in evaluating the public relations program of an existing public recreation department. Outline practical ways it can be improved.
3. Outline a complete plan for handling public information for a state basketball tournament to be conducted at the city arena from the inception of the idea through any follow-up proposal.

References

1. Scott M. Cutlip and Allen H. Center, *Effective Public Relations,* 4th ed. (Englewood Cliffs, N.J.: Prentice-Hall, Inc., 1971), p. 1.
2. *The Technique of Municipal Administration* (Chicago: The International City Managers' Association, 1958), p. 380.
3. L. Roy Blumenthal, *The Practice of Public Relations* (New York: The Macmillan Co., 1972), p. 2.

Selected Readings

Albers, Henry H., *Principles of Management: A Modern Approach* (4th ed.), pp. 369–414. New York: John Wiley and Sons, Inc., 1974. *Discussion of the specifics of handling information and communication.*

American Management Association, *Measuring and Evaluating Public Relations Activities.* New York: The Association, 1968.

Anderson, Desmond L., ed., *Municipal Public Relations.* Chicago: International City Managers' Association, 1966.

Bloomenthal, Howard, *Promoting Your Cause.* New York: Funk and Wagnalls, 1971. *Aspects of communicating, selecting, and using the appropriate media.*

Cutlip, Scott M., and Allen H. Center, *Effective Public Relations* (4th ed.), pp. 186–657. Englewood Cliffs, N.J.: Prentice-Hall, Inc., 1971. *The process of fact finding, feedback, planning, action, evaluation, and other aspects of public relations.*

Hjelte, George, and Jay S. Shivers, *Public Administration of Recreation Services,* pp. 467–489. Philadelphia: Lea and Febiger, 1972.

Weiner, Richard, *Professional's Guide to Public Relations Services.* Englewood Cliffs, N.J.: Prentice-Hall, Inc., 1968.

Appendices

Recreation Enabling Law of North Carolina*

ARTICLE 18
Parks and Recreation

§ **160A-350. Short title.** - This Article shall be known and may be cited as the "Recreation Enabling Law."

§ **160A-351. Declaration of State Policy.** - The lack of adequate recreational programs and facilities is a menace to the morals, happiness, and welfare of the people of this State. Making available recreational opportunities for citizens of all ages is a subject of general interest and concern, and a function requiring appropriate action by both State and local government. The General Assembly therefore declares that the public good and the general welfare of the citizens of this State require adequate recreation programs, that the creation, establishment, and operation of parks and recreation programs is a proper governmental function, and that it is the policy of North Carolina to forever encourage, foster, and provide these facilities and programs for all its citizens.

§ **160A-352. Recreation defined.** - "Recreation" means activities that are diversionary in character and aid in promoting entertainment, pleasure, relaxation, instruction, and other physical, mental and cultural development and leisure time experiences.

§ **160A-353. Powers.** - In addition to any other powers it may possess to provide for the general welfare of its citizens, each county and city in this State shall have authority to:

* (North Carolina General Statutes, Ch. 160A, Art. 18). Reprinted by permission of the North Carolina Department of Natural and Economic Resources, Recreation Division.

(1) establish and conduct a system of supervised recreation;

(2) set apart lands and buildings for parks, playgrounds, recreational centers, and other recreational programs and facilities;

(3) acquire real property, including water and air rights, for parks and recreation programs and facilities by gift, grant, purchase, lease, exercise of the power of eminent domain, or any other lawful method;

(4) provide, acquire, construct, equip, operate, and maintain parks, playgrounds, recreation centers, and recreation facilities, including all buildings, structures, and equipment necessary or useful in connection therewith;

(5) appropriate funds to carry out the provision of this Article;

(6) accept any gift, grant, lease, loan, bequest, or devise of real or personal property for parks and recreation programs. Devises, bequest, and gifts may be accepted and held subject to such terms and conditions as may be imposed by the grantor or trustor, except that no county or city may accept or administer any terms that require it to discriminate among its citizens on the basis of race, sex, or religion.

§ 160A-354. Administration of parks and recreation programs. - A city or county may operate a parks and recreation system as a line department, or it may create a parks and recreation commission and vest in it authority to operate the parks and recreation system.

§ 160A-355. Joint parks and recreation systems. - Any two or more units of local government may cooperate in establishing parks and recreation systems as authorized in Article 20, Part 1, of this Chapter.

Enacted by 1971 General Assembly
Effective January 1, 1972

A Charter Example (with Advisory Board)

Chapter 16

DEPARTMENT OF RECREATION AND PARKS *

Sec. 16.01. Department of recreation and parks. There shall be a department of recreation and parks which shall consist of the director of recreation and parks and such other officers and employees organized into such bureaus, divisions and other units as may be provided by ordinance or by the orders of the director consistent therewith.

Sec. 16.02. Functions. The department of recreation and parks shall be responsible for: (a) Organizing and conducting recreation programs for all age groups in various parts of the city; (b) operating and maintaining all public parks, grounds, playfields and playgrounds of the city both within and without its boundaries except those under the jurisdiction of the school board; (c) operating and maintaining all city cemeteries; (d) operating and maintaining nurseries for flowers, vines, shrubs and trees for use in the public parks, grounds, streets and ways of the city; (e) planting and care of all flowers, vines, shrubs and trees in the public parks, grounds, streets and ways of the city; (f) operating and maintaining all buildings, museums, gardens, monuments, lakes, swimming pools, rest rooms, restaurants, refreshment stands and other facilities and establishments situated in the public parks and grounds under the jurisdiction of the department; (g) promoting, sponsoring and managing public concerts, entertainments and other recreational activities;

* Richmond City Charter.

and (h) such other powers and duties as may be assigned to the department by ordinance. The department of recreation and parks shall be permitted to utilize grounds and buildings under the jurisdiction of the school board at such hours and on such days as they are not in use for other educational purposes, subject to such reasonable rules and regulations as the school board may establish, and provided, that the department of recreation and parks shall be responsible for any damage or extra expense arising from its use of the school grounds and buildings. When authorized by the council and upon such terms and conditions as it may provide, the department of recreation may lease concessions and other facilities in the public parks and grounds under its jurisdiction, fix and collect charges for the admission to concerts, entertainments and other recreational activities sponsored by it, and sell or exchange the surplus products of the city nurseries. The repair and maintenance of all buildings, drives and walks in parks and grounds under the jurisdiction of the department may, when so directed by the city manager, be performed by the department of public works.

Sec. 16.03. Director of recreation and parks—Qualifications. The head of the department of recreation and parks shall be the director of recreation and parks. He shall be a person trained and experienced in recreation activities, with experience in the administration of public recreation or parks.

Sec. 16.04. Same—Powers and duties. The director of recreation and parks shall have general management and control of the several bureaus, divisions and other units of the department. He shall appoint and remove, subject to the provisions of chapter 9 of this Charter, all officers and employees of the department, and he shall have the power to make rules and regulations consistent with this Charter and the ordinances of the city for the conduct of its business.

Sec. 16.05. Rules and regulations. The council shall have power to adopt by ordinance all needful rules and regulations relating to the use of public grounds, parks, playfields, playgrounds and cemeteries, whether within or without the city, and for the preservation of order, safety and decency therein. For the purpose of enforcing such rules and regulations all such public grounds, parks, playfields, playgrounds, and cemeteries shall be under the police jurisdiction of the city. Any member of the police force of the city, or park employee appointed as a special policeman, shall have power to make arrests for violations of any such rule or regulation.

Sec. 16.06. Advisory board of recreation and parks. There shall be an advisory board of recreation and parks consisting of nine members of whom one shall be a member of the school board, appointed by the school board, and one a member of the city planning commission, appointed by the city planning commission, for terms of two years from the first Tuesday in September 1948 and every two years thereafter, but in no case shall a member so appointed continue to be a member of the advisory board of recreation and parks after the expiration of his term as a member of the school board or the city planning commission, as the case may be; and of whom seven shall be appointed by the council for terms of three years; provided, that the members of the advisory board previously appointed by the council and in office at the effective date of this section shall continue to serve as members of the board for the terms for which they were appointed; and provided, that of the additional members appointed by the council two shall be appointed for terms of one year and two shall be appointed for terms of two years from the first Tuesday in September following their appointment. Vacancies shall be filled by the authority making the appointment, for the unexpired portion of the term. The advisory board of recreation and parks shall choose annually one of its own number to be chairman for a term of one year and until his successor is chosen and qualified. An employee of the department of recreation and parks shall be assigned by the director of recreation and parks to act as secretary of the board. It shall hold such regular meetings as it may determine. Special meetings may be held at any time on the call of the director of recreation and parks. The advisory board of recreation and parks shall advise with the director of recreation and parks on all matters submitted by him for their consideration. The members of the advisory board of recreation and parks shall serve without compensation.

An Ordinance or Resolution to Create a Recreation Commission*

WHEREAS, by virtue of Article 18 of Chapter 160A of the General Statutes of North Carolina, the lack of adequate recreation programs and facilities has been declared as a matter of public policy to be a menace to the morals, happiness and welfare of the people in this State; and

WHEREAS, in its considered judgment, the governing body of ______ believes that adequate recreation programs and facilities can best be advanced by placing the recreation system under the supervision and direction of a Recreation Commission as authorized by Section 160A-354 of the General Statutes:

NOW THEREFORE, BE IT ORDAINED OR RESOLVED by the governing body of __________:

SECTION 1. That there is hereby created a commission to be known as the Recreation Commission of __________.

SECTION 2. The Recreation Commission shall be appointed by the governing body of the unit and shall consist of ______ members. The governing body shall appoint ______ members for a term of one year; ______members for a term of two years and ______ members for a term of three years. Upon the expiration of their original terms of office each succeeding term shall be for three years and until their successors qualify for office. Vacancies in the board or commission shall be filled for the unexpired term by appointment of the governing body of the unit. The members shall serve without compensation.

* Reprinted by permission of the North Carolina Department of Natural and Economic Resources, Park/Recreation Planning/Consulting Section.

SECTION 3. The Recreation Commission shall appoint from its membership a chairman and such other officers as it may deem necessary for the orderly procedure of its business and may adopt by-laws, rules and regulations governing its procedure not inconsistent with the provisions of the State laws. The Recreation Commission shall, from time to time, make rules and regulations governing the operation and conduct of the recreation facilities operated by the Recreation Commission. The Recreation Commission shall hold regular meetings at such times and places as it may designate.

SECTION 4. The Recreation Commission shall provide, maintain, operate and supervise the public parks, and playground, athletic fields, and recreation centers and other recreation facilities owned or controlled by the governing body of ____________ or leased or loaned to the Recreation Commission by the owners thereof. The Recreation Commission shall have complete supervision of the facilities and activities provided and conducted on or in connection with the parks, playgrounds, athletic fields and recreation centers provided, and shall have the power to conduct any form of recreation or cultural activity.

SECTION 5. The Recreation Commission may accept any grant, gift, bequest or donation of any personal property offered or made for recreation purposes and, with the approval of the governing body may accept any grant, gift, or devise of real estate. Any gift, bequest of money or other personal property, grant or devise of real estate shall be held, used and finally disposed of in accordance with the terms or conditions under which such grant, gift or devise is made and accepted. The Recreation Commission shall have no authority to enter into any contract or incur any obligation binding the governing body of ____________ other than current obligation(s) or contracts to be fully executed within the current fiscal year and all within the budget appropriations made by the governing body of ____________.

SECTION 6. The Recreation Commission shall have power to appoint and designate a director of recreation who possesses the necessary foundation training and who demonstrates by actual work his ability to organize and direct a community recreation system. Such other trained persons as may be necessary in the maintenance of an operation of the recreation facilities and system may be employed.

SECTION 7. Funds appropriated by the governing body of ____________ and budgeted to the Recreation Commission shall be disbursed by the fiscal disbursing officer of the governing body of ____________ upon vouchers issued by the Recreation Commission and within the budget appropriations made. Funds received by the Recreation Commission from sources other than budget appropriations shall be deposited by the governing body of ________ to the credit and for the use of the Recreation Commission and disbursed as budget funds are disbursed, except that funds received by gift, bequest or otherwise shall be disbursed in accordance with the terms of such gift or bequest.

SECTION 8. The Recreation Commission shall make full and complete reports to the governing body at such times as may be requested and at such other times as to the governing body may seem proper. The fiscal year of the Commission shall conform to that of the governing body of __________.

SECTION 9. Such powers as are now provided by statute of the State of North Carolina or by the Ordinance or Resolution of the governing body of __________ relating to the development and operation of recreation systems, parks and playgrounds are hereby vested in the Recreation Commission to be exercised by its subject to all restrictions contained in such powers and ordinances or resolutions.

SECTION 10. All ordinances and/or resolutions of the governing body of __________ in conflict herewith are hereby repealed.

SECTION 11. That this ordinance or resolution shall be in full force and effect ______ days after its passage.

Adopted this the ______ day of __________, 19___

____

Chairman, (governing body)

Suggested Recreation By-Laws*

This is suggested as one plan of operation for organized recreation committees, community development groups, for communities or organizations. Each individual group shall incorporate some of its own adaptations, or delete some of these, to have the best operational by-laws with which to suit their particular purposes.

BY-LAWS

ARTICLE I. Name

The recreation committee created by *(name of community or organization)* on *(date)* shall be known as the *(name of committee)* Committee.

ARTICLE II. Recreation Activities

For this purpose, recreation includes those areas which fall within the following general classification of recreation activities: The arts, drama, crafts, athletics, sports and games, dance, hobbies, music, nature and outing, reading, writing, social recreation, special community events and special events, recreation travel, and volunteer services.

ARTICLE III. Powers and Duties

1. Establish, promote and/or conduct a system of recreation for the community.

* Reprinted by permission of the North Carolina Department of Natural and Economic Resources, Park/Recreation Planning/Consulting Section.

2. Acquire land and water areas, structures and accept any other grant, gift, bequest or donation, and any personal or real properties offered or made available for recreation purposes.
3. Set policies as to controls and operation of these and all other recreation facilities which are owned or controlled by the named group.
4. Establish rules and regulations, in accordance with policy, concerning the conduct, management and operation of the recreation areas, facilities, personnel and program.

ARTICLE IV. Appointment of Committee

Each member of the Committee shall be appointed by the governing body of the unit, which may request recommendations from the Recreation Committee after it becomes operational.

ARTICLE V. Length of Appointment

Each member shall be appointed for a (3) year term. Initial appointments shall be arranged so that approximately one-third of the terms shall expire each year except that the representative from the governing body of the unit shall serve on the Recreation Committee concurrent with his term of office on the governing body.

ARTICLE VI. Meetings

Regular meetings of the Committee shall be held on *(day)* of each *(month)* in the *(place)*.

The chairman, or in his absence the vice-chairman, may call a special meeting of the Committee at any time by giving to each member 24 hours notice of the meeting. Special meetings shall be scheduled upon request by four or more appointed members. A quorum of the Committee shall be in attendance before action of an official nature can be taken. A quorum is at least 1 more than the number absent.

ARTICLE VII. Officers

There shall be a Chairman, Vice-Chairman and Secretary of the Committee. An annual election of the officers shall be held by the Committee members and shall occur at the regular monthly business meeting in *(month)*. In the event an office becomes vacant, a replacement to this office shall be elected from the Committee membership at the next official meeting.

ARTICLE VIII. Duties

1. Chairman—shall preside at all meetings, sign all official papers, appoint committees, call special meetings when he deems it advisable and perform all such duties as usually devolve upon a chairman, except when such duties are properly delegated.

2. Vice-Chairman—shall serve in the absence of the Chairman. When both the Chairman and Vice-Chairman are absent a temporary Chairman shall be elected by those members who are present.

3. Secretary—shall keep the official records of the Committee, handle the correspondence of the Committee as directed, and keep accurate minutes of each meeting.

ARTICLE IX. Term

The business year of the Committee shall run from *(date)* through *(date).*

ARTICLE X. Order of Business

The order of business at the meetings of the Committee shall be as follows: Roll call, read minutes of last meeting, report of Chairman, report of Committees, unfinished business, new business, adjournment.

ARTICLE XI. Amendments

All amendments of these by-laws must be proposed in writing at least 30 days prior to being acted upon in a regular meeting of the Committee. They will have immediate application if they are approved.

Prepared by:
North Carolina Recreation Commission
Mansion Park Building
Raleigh, North Carolina 27601
March, 1964

A Suggested Guide for the Center Advisory Council of a Department of Recreation and Parks

Every unit of Recreation (center or playground) should have an advisory group to work with the unit director in planning and developing a program that will best fill the needs of the community. Since the director and the council must work together closely, the director should select the members, explain the functions of the organization in relation to the community and the operation of the program, and assist the group in carrying out its functions.

Advisory councils become helpful only when they clearly understand what they are supposed to do, and when they accept their responsibilities willingly and enthusiastically. They function in an advisory capacity and have *no legal status*. Care should be taken to make sure this point is clearly understood.

Six or seven local people, preferably participants or prospective participants who are genuinely interested in developing a broad community recreation program for all age groups, usually make a good council. Members do not have to be "key people" and should not be selected because of certain political or organization associations. Real interest in recreation is the main requirement. The natural or potential leadership ability of a person is also a good quality. A person should be selected on the basis of what he is as a person, what his interests are rather than because of the fact that he belongs to an organization that is interested in a field related to Recreation.

An individual who is genuinely interested in developing a good program in his community can be more helpful than an influential person who has many other interests and who probably will be too busy to visit the programs, attend meetings, and learn the true interest and recreation needs of his community. Although members who are congenial should be selected, one should not let personal friendships determine decisions. High officials and people in important positions do not always make good council members.

Councils should consist of both men and women from the following age interests:

1. Youth (1 Man; 1 Woman)
2. Young Married Couples (1 Man; 1 Woman)
3. Middle-Aged (1 Man; 1 Woman)
4. Elderly People (1 Man or Woman)

Six or seven persons selected from the above age interests make a very workable council that will be rather broad in its views, experiences and interests. In selecting council members, one should keep in mind general responsibilities of the council as well as specific duties of committee chairmen because of the job they have to do.

An advisory council group is the "go-between" between the leisure-time interests of the community and the directors of the program; their duties are purely advisory in nature.

General Responsibilities of a Recreation Advisory Council

1. Carry on the business interests of the council;
2. Evaluate leisure-time needs of the community;
3. Cooperate in making studies or surveys that are of interest to the program;
4. Interpret needs to program directors;
5. Assist in determining local program policies;
6. Inform community concerning nature and objectives of the program;
7. Assist in matters related to the best interests of good leadership, especially voluntary and club leaders;
8. Assist in matters related to good physical facilities, equipment, and supplies;
9. Cooperate with directors in other factors which affect the efficient operation of the program;
10. Coordinate program with future community planning;
11. Assist director in the solution of various problems to the best interest of the community.

It is recommended that:

(*a*) The council elect officers and organize as a recognized group;

(*b*) The council hold regular meetings (monthly) and be subject to call meetings when special problems arise;

(*c*) Major problems be worked out jointly by council and recreation director;

(*d*) The council break down its membership into committee chairmen of Program, Facilities, Publicity, Finance, Special Events, and such other responsibilities as deemed advisable. This plan expedites the handling of many trivial matters not of interest to the entire council, minimizes confusion and affords a committeeman the opportunity of directing his interest in one phase of the program. All members of the council, of course, should be interested in the work of all committees, but each person has a particular "job" to do as chairman and he may enlarge his committee by selecting "outside" people to help him. For instance, the committee chairman may do all the work himself (as a committee of one) or he may select others in the community to help him. The persons he selects would be a part of his committee, but would not necessarily become council members. The chairman, who is officially a member of the council, would handle all matters pertaining to his committee in council meetings;

(*e*) Qualities and responsibilities of committee chairmen be kept in mind when selecting original council members.

Some essential general qualities of council members

They should be:

1. Interested in developing a community-wide program for all age groups
2. Community-minded
3. Unselfish and impartial
4. Congenial
5. Enthusiastic
6. Imaginative
7. Cooperative
8. Well-informed in community leisure-time needs

9. Tactful
10. Practical
11. Able to plan ahead
12. Potential leaders

Some special qualities of committee chairmen (to be considered in addition to general qualities of council members)

1. *Chairman of Program Committee should be:*
   (*a*) Interested in programs for all age groups
   (*b*) Well informed on program aims and objectives
   (*c*) Informed on community needs, interests, resources, possible leadership
   (*d*) Alert
   (*e*) Social minded
   (*f*) Community leader
   (*g*) An organizer
   (*h*) Informed as to different methods of presenting activities
   (*i*) Adaptable to changing situations
2. *Chairman of Facilities and Equipment Committee should be:*
   (*a*) Informed on equipment needs for all age groups
   (*b*) Able to obtain use of community facilities and equipment for recreation use
   (*c*) Familiar with best help and safety principles
   (*d*) Able to develop community interests and feeling of responsibility
   (*e*) Informed on proper construction and use of facilities
3. *Chairman of Finance Committee should be:*
   (*a*) Apt in financing matters
   (*b*) Businesslike
   (*c*) Systematic
   (*d*) Able to keep records and prepare reports
   (*e*) Able to raise special funds, if needed
4. *Chairman of Publicity Committee should be:*

(*a*) Sincere
(*b*) Well informed as to leisure-time program (needs, objectives, plans, etc.)
(*c*) Capable of reporting news and planning exhibits (not limited to newspaper stories)
(*d*) Alert and active
(*e*) A practical promoter
(*f*) Able to interpret the program to the community in many different ways

5. *Chairman of Committee on Special Events should be:*
(*a*) A practical promoter
(*b*) Able to interpret program objectives to the community through special features
(*c*) Informed on community needs, interests and resources
(*d*) An organizer
(*e*) Well informed on program objectives

Members are selected for a period of one year. They may be reelected.

The director's relationship to the council

The director selects the council members, explains the organization, responsibilities, and working relations of council, explains program objectives to them, assists them in organizing and assists in all matters related to a good organization. After it is organized, she works closely with it in matters of interest to the operation of an efficient program. She is an ex-officio member (by virtue of her office) and attends council meetings, but does not hold office and does not vote. She cooperates with the group as a whole, and with committees and committee chairmen in the best interest of a broad program. She keeps the council informed concerning the interests, etc., and other factors of importance to them. She is the intermediary between the council and the playground or center.

A Suggested Agreement for School-Community Cooperation*

CITY AND/OR COUNTY

This AGREEMENT, made and entered into this (*day*) of (*month*), 19 (*year*), by and between the Governing Body of (*County or City*), North Carolina, hereinafter called "Governing Body," and the Board of Education of (*County or City*), State of North Carolina, hereinafter called "Board."

WITNESSETH:

WHEREAS, the official agencies of the Governing Body and the Board are mutually interested in an adequate program of community recreation under the auspices of the Governing Body Recreation Commission, and

WHEREAS, said official agencies are authorized to enter into agreements with each other, and to do any and all things necessary or convenient to aid and cooperate in the cultivation of citizenship by providing for adequate programs of community recreation, and

WHEREAS, in the interest of providing the best service with the least possible expenditure of public funds, full cooperation between the Governing Body and the Board is necessary.

NOW, THEREFORE, in consideration of these premises, said Gov-

* Prepared for you by the Recreation Division, Department of Natural and Economic Resources under the auspices of the Governor of North Carolina and the State Department of Public Instruction.

erning Body and said Board do now agree to cooperate with each other in carrying out the above purposes, and to that end do agree as follows:

(1) The Board will make available to the Governing Body for community recreation activities all school areas and facilities which are suitable for community recreation activities, these areas are to be recommended by the Director of Recreation of the Governing Body, subject to the approval of the Governing Body Recreation Commission and the Board.

(2) The Governing Body will make available to the Board for school events, activities and/or programs Governing Body recreation facilities which are suitable for said events, activities and/or programs, the facilities to be selected by the Superintendent of Schools, subject to the approval of the Governing Body Director of Recreation.

(3) It is hereby agreed that a schedule of dates for the use of the Board's school facilities will be worked out in advance by the Governing Body Recreation Director and that this schedule will be arranged so as to avoid conflict between school and recreation use; that in the scheduling of said facilities, school events and programs shall have first priority and recreation programs, established by the Recreation Department, shall have second priority and other events by other groups or agencies shall have third priority unless scheduled by the Recreation Department when they shall have second priority along with other recreation events.

(4) It is further agreed that a schedule of dates for the use of the Governing Body facilities will be worked out in advance by the Board and that this schedule will be arranged as to avoid conflict between recreation and school use; that in the scheduling of said facilities, recreation department activities shall have first priority and school events and programs shall have second priority and any other events by other groups or agencies shall have third priority, unless scheduled by the recreation department when they shall have second priority.

(5) The Governing Body through its Department of Recreation agrees to provide adequate personnel to supervise the recreation activities which take place after school hours and during holiday and vacation periods at the selected areas and facilities.

(6) It is understood and agreed that the personnel employed by the Governing Body in its Recreation Department shall be under the supervision of the Governing Body Recreation Department and further that the school principals shall be consulted in the planning and administering of a recreation program to be conducted by the Recreation Department of the Governing Body on or in the facilities which are normally under the jurisdiction of said principals.

(7) It is recognized that school properties and facilities are intended primarily for school purposes and for the benefit of children of school age. It is therefore agreed that, in planning programs and scheduling activities on school grounds and in school facilities, the recreation needs and opportunities of such children will be well considered and the program and property adequately protected.

(8) It is further agreed that in the event of any dispute or difference arising as a result of the recreation program being conducted on the Governing Body facilities jointly used and selected as above outlined, or as to joint use of Board facilities, then, in that event, said dispute or difference shall be settled and arbitrated by appealing to the respective department heads of the Governing Body and Board in accordance with established procedures, and to the Board and the Recreation Commission if needed.

(9) It is further agreed that the Governing Body Recreation Department will furnish and supply all expendable materials necessary for carrying on a Community Recreation Program for all ages, in or on the facilities under its supervision.

(10) It is further agreed that the Governing Body may install sprinkler systems, turfing, lighting, play equipment, fencing and additional equipment for recreation, not in conflict with school use, on areas selected by the Director of Recreation, subject to the written approval by the Superintendent of Schools and the Board. Any installations of equipment or construction on said premises, for community recreation purposes shall then be at the Governing Body's cost or proportionally shared by the Governing Body and Board, as the respective annual budget appropriations of Governing Body and Board permit.

(11) It is further agreed that plans and specifications for the placement of all equipment, facilities and permanent improvements upon school premises and the type, design and construction thereof, shall be approved by the Board prior to any installation thereof.

(12) It is further agreed that the cost of maintaining said improved areas shall be borne proportionately by the Governing Body and the Board as determined by the relative use of said areas, and further that the Governing Body and Board agree to maintain such areas in good condition during the periods of their respective responsibility.

(13) It is further agreed that any permanent improvements or equipment installed or erected on school premises by the Governing Body shall remain the property of the Governing Body and may be removed if use of area is terminated.

(14) It is further understood and agreed that either party to this agreement may at any time terminate this agreement upon giving in writing, to the other party, three months notice of its intention to terminate same.

In the event any or all Governing Body improved school premises be required for exclusive use by the Board, the Governing Body shall be reimbursed for actual cost in installation of any permanent improvements where it will not be practical to remove such or where they must be removed for exclusive use by the Board.

(15) It is further agreed this Agreement nullifies and voids any previous agreements between the Board and Governing Body Recreation Commission as apply to ____________ School; ____________ School; ____________ School; ____________ School; and ____________ Stadium; ____________; ____________; ____________; ____________; ____________.

IN WITNESS WHEREOF, and pursuant to the authority granted by duly recorded resolutions, the parties hereto have caused this Agreement to be executed on their behalf.

Governing Body of ____________
(County or City)

By ____________________
Mayor; Chairman, County Commissioners; or other Head.

ATTEST:

____
Clerk (City, County, or other)

____________ Board of Education
County or City

By ____________________
Chairman of the Board

ATTEST:

____
Secretary of the Board

3/73

A Suggested Agreement for a Joint Parks and Recreation Commission*

AN AGREEMENT BETWEEN LOCAL UNITS OF GOVERNMENT CREATING A JOINT PARKS AND RECREATION COMMISSION TO BE KNOWN AS THE ______________ — ______________ PARKS AND RECREATION COMMISSION.

THIS AGREEMENT, made this ______ day of ____________, 19__, between ______________ and ______________, the "Participating Units," creating a Joint Parks and Recreation Commission.

WITNESSETH

In consideration of the mutual convenants herein set out and pursuant to G.S. 160A-355 and G.S. 160A-462, General Statutes of North Carolina, ______________ and ______________ mutually agree as follows:

1. *Creation of ______________ — ______________ Parks and Recreation Commission*
   There is hereby established a Joint Parks and Recreation Commission, to be known as the "______________ — ______________ Parks and Recreation Commission."
2. *Purpose*
   The Commission shall provide, maintain, promote, administer, and conduct recreation and cultural programs, activities, opportunities and services, and shall acquire, operate, supervise, use, maintain,

* Reprinted by permission of the North Carolina Department of Natural and Economic Resources, Park/Recreation Planning/Consulting Section.

develop and provide recreation areas and facilities for the benefit, enjoyment and use of citizens of ____________ and ____________. Any recreation area or facility owned, leased or used by a Participating Unit or the Commission will be under the supervision, direction and administration of the Commission.

3. *Duration*

The duration of this agreement shall be for the Fiscal Year beginning July 1, 19__, and ending June 30, 19__. Written notice of intent to withdraw from the Commission and terminate this Agreement shall be made by a Participating Unit to the Commission and all Participating Units before January 1, 19__. Failure of both or either Participating Unit to give notice of intent to withdraw and terminate will automatically extend this Agreement unto and through Fiscal Year beginning July 1, 19__ and ending June 30, 19__.

4. *Composition, Organization, Nature, Powers and Duties*

A. *Commission Membership and Compensation*

The Governing Body of each Participating Unit will, by July 1 of each year, appoint members to the Commission. One-half of the 12-member Commission shall be appointed by each Governing Body. Each Governing Body shall initially appoint two members to a one-year term, two members to a two-year term, and two members to a three-year term. Following initial appointments all terms will be for three years. No appointed members shall serve more than two consecutive three-year terms. Vacancies on the Commission will be filled in the same manner as the initial appointment for remainder of unexpired term.

Members of the Commission shall serve without compensation but will be reimbursed for travel and other expenses necessarily incurred while engaged in the performance of their duties for the Commission. The Commission may set a limit on the amount the members may be reimbursed.

B. *Organization, Officers, Records*

At the Commission's organization meeting held in July of each year, the Commission shall elect a Chairman, Vice-Chairman and Secretary, and shall adopt rules as it sees fit for the transaction of its business. These officers will have the usual duties and responsibilities associated with the office. The Treasurer of the Commission shall be appointed by the Commission and shall be the Treasurer, Accountant, Finance Director or similar officer of one of the Participating Units. The Commission shall hold regular monthly meetings and all meetings shall be open to the public. The Commission shall keep minutes of its meetings, and the records shall be public records.

C. *Powers and Duties*

The Commission shall provide, maintain, operate and supervise the public parks, playgrounds, athletic fields, recreation centers and other recreation facilities owned or controlled by the Participating Units or leased or loaned to the Commission by the owners thereof. The Commission shall have the powers of G.S. 160A-353 (1), (2), (3), (4), (6). The Commission shall make rules and regulations governing the operation and conduct of the recreation facilities operated by the Commission.

The Commission may accept any grant, gift, bequest, or donation of any personal property offered or made for recreation purposes; and, with the approval of the Participating Unit in which the area or facility is located may accept any grant, gift, or devise of real estate, as provided in G.S. 160A-353 (3).

The Commission shall have no authority to enter into any contract or incur any obligation binding the Participating Units other than current obligation(s) or contracts to be fully executed within the Fiscal Year beginning July 1, 19__ and ending June 30, 19__.

D. *Reports*

The Commission shall make full and complete reports to the Participating Units monthly and at such times as may be requested.

5. *Personnel*

A. The Commission shall appoint a Director of Recreation and such other persons as may be necessary, or

B. *(One of the Participating Units)* shall appoint the Director of Recreation and such other persons as may be necessary, or

C. All Participating Units shall jointly appoint the Director of Recreation and such other persons as necessary.

6. *Financing*

The Commission shall by March of each year, prepare and submit a budget to the Participating Units. Each Participating Unit will review the budget and notify the Commission by June 30 the amount they will appropriate for use by the Commission for the Fiscal Year beginning July 1. G.S. 160A-462 (b).

The Commission will be financed from (1) funds appropriated by the Participating Units and budgeted to the Commission and (2) such other funds as herein provided.

All funds shall be disbursed by the Treasurer of the Commission upon vouchers issued by the Commission and within the budget appropriations made. All vouchers will be signed by the Commission Chairman and the Treasurer.

Funds received by the Commission from sources other than budget appropriations (fees, charges, rentals, concession profits, admissions, etc.) shall be deposited to the credit and for the use of the Commission and disbursed as budget funds are disbursed, except that funds received by gift, bequest or otherwise shall be disbursed in accordance with the terms of such gift or bequest.

Any funds unexpended during current Fiscal Year will be rebudgeted as an item in the next budget.

7. *Ownership and Disposition of Real Property*

   A. *Title to Real Property*

      Title to all real property presently owned by the Governing Bodies of each Participating Units will remain with the Governing Body. Real property acquired by either of the Participating Units will become and remain the property of the acquiring Participating Unit. All park and recreation property owned by a Participating Unit will be under the control, operation and supervision of the Commission.

      Properties which the Commission received by gifts, purchase or otherwise shall be held by the Participating Units jointly as tenants in common.

   B. *Disposition of Real Property*

      Disposition of real and personal property owned by the Commission or held jointly as tenants in common will be disposed of by negotiation between Participating Units of the Commission. If the Participating Units fail to agree on the manner of disposition of the property, each Participating Unit will name one citizen to a binding arbitration committee and the members of the committee will select enough additional committee members so that the committee membership constitutes an odd number of members. The committee will have the power and authority to determine the manner of disposition of the real property.

8. *Amendments and Modifications*

   This agreement may be amended by action of a majority of the Governing Bodies of the Participating Units and repealed by action of any one of the Participating Units.

9. *Addition of Withdrawal of Participating Units*

   Any additional Participating Unit may be included in this agreement by adopting this agreement and with the majority vote of the Participating Units. Such additional Participating Units shall be a party of this agreement and so governed by the terms set out herein.

10. *Effective Date*
    This agreement shall become effective when duly executed by the parties hereto.

IN WITNESS THEREOF, that the local Units of government whose endorsement appears hereafter has caused this instrument to be executed by the authorized officers of that local unit of government and attested by its Clerk and its corporate seal attached.

ATTEST: CITY OF

____________________ BY ____________________

(*Seal*) *Authorized Officer*

Adopted on ____________________, by the ____________________
of ____________________.

ATTEST: CITY OF

____________________ BY ____________________

(*Seal*) *Authorized Officer*

Adopted on ____________________, by the ____________________
of ____________________.

Suggested Job Specifications

Director of Recreation and Parks

Function. Is the chief executive of a department. Manages both park and recreation functions, including planning, development, coordination and direction of comprehensive recreation programs; operation, maintenance and development of parks, recreation areas, and facilities and exercises considerable independent professional judgment in directing affairs of the agency.

Supervision. Is responsible to city manager and responsible for bureau chiefs, administrative assistant and secretary.

Examples of Duties (not inclusive).

— Plans, organizes and directs recreation and park services, consistent with general laws, policies, and guidelines.
— Establishes procedures, guidelines, rules and regulations for agency.
— Prepares and justifies budget; controls agency expenditures.
— Interviews, appoints, develops staff and determines management policies.
— Directs planning, acquisition, improvement and maintenance of all properties under jurisdiction of the department.

— Makes surveys and determines future needs for progams, areas, and facilities.

— Interprets and promotes department services and policies.

— Establishes procedures and system for reporting and record keeping.

REQUIRED KNOWLEDGE, ABILITIES, AND SKILLS.

— Thorough knowledge of theory, philosophy and principles of public recreation and park administration and organization.

— Extensive knowledge of methods and procedures involved in budget preparation and control; municipal personnel rules and procedures; and general business management.

— Ability to deal tactfully and effectively with the public, present ideas clearly and concisely both orally and in writing.

NECESSARY TRAINING AND EXPERIENCE.

— Graduation from an accredited college with major in recreation and master's degree in administration, recreation or park management.

— Seven years of experience in recreation, four years of which must be in supervisory or administrative capacity.

SPECIAL REQUIREMENTS.

— Valid vehicle operator's license.

— Registration or certification as a professional by a recognized unit of APRS.

ADMINISTRATIVE ASSISTANT

FUNCTION. Under administrative direction, assists the executive in the business and office management of the agency. Is responsible for management of fiscal matters, budgeting, personnel, purchasing, inventories, legal matters, records and similar staff administrative services.

SUPERVISION. Responsible to the executive. Responsible for secretary, accountant, payroll clerks, other office personnel as may be assigned.

EXAMPLES OF DUTIES (illustrative only).

— Serves as chief budget, personnel, and properties officer for the agency and advises agency staff on general management matters.

— Directs office personnel, budget and business procedures.
— Assists executive by relieving him of administrative details.
— Assists in establishment of management procedures.
— Evaluates forms, reporting, procedures, record keeping, purchasing, utilization of material and human resources and makes recommendations.
— May represent the department in dealing with other governmental agencies and the general public.
— May act for executive in his absence.

REQUIRED KNOWLEDGE, ABILITIES, AND SKILLS.

— Thorough knowledge of principles and practices of public administration, particularly as related to finance and accounting systems, modern office methods, personnel management, budgeting.
— Ability to deal tactfully with people; to plan, organize, and direct comprehensive administrative functions and programs; to prepare relatively complex clerical and financial reports; to present ideas and recommendations effectively, both orally and in writing; to maintain harmonious and effective working relationships with staff and general public.

NECESSARY TRAINING AND EXPERIENCE. Graduation from college with specialization in public administration, business administration, accounting, or acceptable related fields and three years of acceptable experience in responsible administration, local government and/or business management.

SPECIAL REQUIREMENTS. Knowledge and skills in use of modern office equipment.

SUPERINTENDENT OF RECREATION

FUNCTION. Under administrative supervision, has charge of and is responsible for planning, organizing, promoting, developing, and coordinating the programs and functions of a public recreation agency and does related work as may be required.

SUPERVISION. Responsible to the executive or administrator. Responsible directly for work program division heads and secretary.

EXAMPLES OF DUTIES (illustrative only).

— Plans and directs a broad varied program of public recreation activities for all age groups and interests.

— Selects, employs (subject to personnel policies of the jurisdiction), develops and manages professional, technical, volunteer, and other personnel for the successful operation of the agency services.

— Prepares, justifies and administers agency budget.

— Reviews and evaluates the progress and effectiveness of public recreation programs; brings about needed revisions and improvements.

— Directs the public relations program; maintains records; makes reports; coordinates work of department with other agency programs.

Required Knowledge, Abilities, and Skills.

— Thorough knowledge of the philosophy and objectives of public recreation; purposes and benefits of various components of a comprehensive recreation program.

— Extensive knowledge of the organization, operation, methods, and procedures used in management of public recreation and budget preparation, personnel practices, and general business management.

— Exceptional ability to motivate, train, and supervise subordinates; to deal tactfully and effectively with staff and public; to plan, interpret and promote successfully services of the agency; to maintain records and make reports; to present ideas and recommendations clearly and concisely both orally and in writing.

Necessary Training and Experience.

— Graduation from college or university of recognized standing with major in recreation and five years of successful experience in professional recreation work, three years of which shall have been in supervisory or administrative capacity.

— Graduate study leading to a master's degree in recreation or administration may be substituted for experience on the basis of one year of education for one year of the required experience, with a maximum substitution for two years of experience.

Special Requirements.

— Valid state vehicle operator's license.

— Registration or certification as a professional recreationist.

Superintendent of Parks

Function. Under administrative direction, has charge of and is responsible for planning, development, management, coordination, and direction of maintenance and construction of all properties, areas, landscaping, and plants under the jurisdication of the department; and does related work as may be assigned.

Examples of Work (not inclusive).

- Selects, employs (subject to general personnel policies of the jurisdiction), develops and manages professional, technical, skilled and other personnel for the successful operation of functions of the agency.
- Works with peers, consultants, and architects in the development of plans and facilities in the department.
- Plans, coordinates and directs the activities of the arborist, agronomist, horticulturist and physical facility maintenance, security and development of properties.
- Prepares, justifies and administers the budget for parks.
- May represent the director at park related meetings.
- Makes speeches; maintains records; makes reports.

Required Knowledge, Abilities, and Skills.

- Thorough knowledge of municipal park and recreation area maintenance and development practices.
- Extensive knowledge of methods and practices involved in personnel management, budget preparation, park and recreation administration and business management.
- Working knowledge in the fields of arboriculture, horticulture, agronomy, engineering, landscape architecture.
- Ability to deal tactfully and effectively with associates, employees, public and to present ideas and recommendations clearly and concisely both orally and in writing.

Necessary Training and Experience.

- Baccalaureate degree in park management, landscape architecture, agricultural or civil engineering or closely related fields with seven years of experience in park management or one of above listed (or closely allied) fields, three of which must have been in a supervisory or administrative capacity.

— Graduate study in a pertinent field may be substituted for experience with a maximum of two years.

Special Requirements.

— Valid state vehicle operator's license.
— Registration or certification as recognized by the profession.

District Recreation Supervisor

Function. Under direction, is responsible for all recreation staff, programs, and services for a district or large geographic area; and does related work as may be required.

Supervision. Is responsible to recreation superintendent. Is responsible for key recreation professionals, specialists, and program facility managers.

Examples of Duties (not inclusive).

— Interviews, selects, employs, develops and recommends all staff actions involving the programs in the assigned district.
— Inspects recreation sites; evaulates programs, facilities and staff performance; makes recommendations for revisions and improvements; makes requests for needed repairs.
— Investigates complaints; takes appropriate action.
— Makes talks; attends community meetings; interprets program policies and practices; confers with school and other public agencies in matters relating to public recreation programs.
— Makes recommendations; prepares district budget; prepares news articles and other public relations items; maintains records and makes reports.

Required Knowledge, Abilities, and Skills.

— Thorough knowledge of philosophy, objectives, methods, techniques of equipping and organizing a comprehensive recreation program.
— Thorough knowledge of group work and leadership techniques as applicable to a broad and varied program for all age groups.

— Knowledge of recreation administration, management and coordination, principles, and techniques.

— Ability to organize, integrate, manage and evaluate varied recreation programs on area wide basis.

— Ability to attract, orient, train, motivate and supervise professionals and volunteers in effective recreation activities.

— Ability to develop and maintain effective working relationships with associates, staff, volunteers, and public.

— Ability to present ideas and recommendations effectively both orally and in writing.

Required Training and Experience. Baccalaureate degree with specialization in recreation and four years of successful recreation group leadership experience, two years of which must be in a supervisory capacity.

Special Requirements.

— Valid state vehicle operator's license.

— Registration or certification as a recreation professional as recognized by the profession.

Recreation Supervisor (General)

Function. Under direction, is responsible for a comprehensive agency-, district-, or area-wide recreation program; does related work as may be assigned.

Supervision. In smaller organizations is responsible to agency executive. In larger organizations may be responsible to superintendent or district recreation supervisor. Is responsible for three to eight playgrounds or center directors, activity specialists, or facility managers.

Examples of Duties (illustrative only).

— Plans, organizes, and supervises operation of a comprehensive recreation service as a major function of the agency or geographical area.

— Selects, orients and develops staff; evaluates performance, effectiveness of program and operational practices; makes recommendations for revisions and improvements.

— Plans program plan; recommends and allocates area program budget.

- Coordinates recreation services with those in related agency services and with community and other agencies.
- Investigates complaints and acts upon requests, suggestions, and recommendations concerning recreation services.
- Researches and introduces new recreation program activities, materials, facilities and equipment to administration, staff, and participants.
- Orders, stores and provides materials and resources for programs of the area subject to administrative approval.

REQUIRED KNOWLEDGE, ABILITIES, AND SKILLS.

- Thorough knowledge of the philosophy, objectives, methods and techniques of public recreation programming and group work.
- Professional skill in planning, organizing and administering a major public recreation function utilizing all available community resources.
- Ability to inspire, motivate, train, evaluate, and develop professional and non-professional recreation leaders; ability to develop and maintain effective relationships with associates, volunteers, participants and the public.

REQUIRED TRAINING AND EXPERIENCE. Baccalaureate degree with specialization in recreation and three years of successful experience in recreation leadership or acceptable closely related field, one year of which must be at supervisory level.

SPECIAL REQUIREMENTS.

- Valid state vehicle operator's license.
- Registration or certification as a professional recreationist.

RECREATION CENTER DIRECTOR

FUNCTION. Under supervision, is responsible for the direction of a comprehensive recreation program at a single location which may be a general or specialized facility and/or area or combination of these; and does related work as required.

SUPERVISION. Is responsible to executive in small agency; a district or general supervisor in a larger agency. Is responsible for all the staff at the assigned location.

Examples of Duties (illustrative only).

- — Plans, initiates, organizes, and directs an extensive and diversified recreation program at a recreation facility and grounds.
- — Assigns duties, trains, evaluates, supervises staff—professionals, para-professionals, volunteers—full-time, part-time and seasonal.
- — Relates agency objectives, regulations, policies, services and guidelines to programs of the center.
- — Evaluates program, participation, attendance, effectiveness of personnel, needs, problems, and takes or recommends appropriate action.
- — Relates to the community; determines needs, recommends and justifies operational and improvement budget for the center. Works with advisory committee.
- — Schedules and supervises use of facilities; maintains records and submits reports.

Required Knowledge, Abilities, and Skills.

- — Thorough knowledge of the theory and philosophy of recreation and its application to individual and group behavior.
- — Professional ability to plan, organize and administer comprehensive recreation programs for a neighborhood or major location.
- — Ability to direct the operation and programming of a complex center; to develop and maintain effective relationship with associates, staff, volunteers, participants, and public.

Training and Experience. Baccalaureate degree with major in recreation and two years of acceptable full time group leadership or supervisory experience.

Special Requirements. Registration or certification as a professional recreationist.

Recreation Group Worker (Senior Recreation Leader)

Function. Under supervision, is responsible for the organization, promotion, and professional leadership of a variety of recreation activities.

SUPERVISION. Is responsible to a center director, recreation supervisor, district supervisor, or special facilities manager. Is responsible for specialists, para-professionals, volunteers and participants.

EXAMPLES OF DUTIES (illustrative only).

— May be in charge of program at a recreation area or facility.
— Plans, organizes, leads and conducts diversified recreation groups activities such as arts, crafts, dance, drama, music, nature, sports and games, special features, and events.
— Consults with individuals, groups, and community leaders to determine their recreation needs and interests; conducts studies and makes evaluations.
— Organizes, promotes and directs contests, tournaments, entertainments, socials, exhibits and special features.
— Organizes, leads and serves as advisor to clubs and special interest groups.
— Supervises assigned functional areas of the location; makes rules for safety and welfare of users and staff.
— Schedules use of facility; maintains records and makes reports.
— May work with an advisory committee for the location.

REQUIRED KNOWLEDGE, ABILITIES, AND SKILLS.

— Thorough knowledge of philosophy, objectives, methods and techniques of recreation; purposes, uses and benefits of the various components of the recreation program for the different age groups.
— Knowledge of techniques of planning, organizing, motivating, promoting, and evaluating recreation programs.
— Ability to supervise, evaluate, and develop staff, volunteers, and participants; to inspire confidence and enthusiasm and maintain effective relationships with associates, participants and public.
— Professional skills in leadership of several types of recreational activities.

TRAINING AND EXPERIENCE. Baccalaureate degree with specialization in recreation leadership.

SPECIAL REQUIREMENTS. Registration or certification as a professional recreationist.

Suggested Recreation Program Activities (by Classifications)

ART

Art classes
  Charcoal, china painting, drawing, finger painting, pastels, pen and ink, water color
Art exhibits
Sculpturing
  Wood, stone, snow
Sketching

CRAFTS

Basketry
  Broom grass, hickory splints, honeysuckle vines, oak splints, pine needles (long), raffia, reed, willow
Bead craft
  Indian seed beads, wood beads
Block printing
  Linoleum, potato, soap, wood
Boat craft
Book binding
Carving
  Bone, ivory, plastic foam, soap, wood
Ceramics
Christmas cards
Clay modeling and molding
Cookery
  Cake decorating, outdoor cooking
Card craft
Cork craft
Craft exhibits
Crayoning
Decorating
  Fabric, home, interior
Designing
Dyeing and coloring
  Tie and dye
Handmade games
Kite making
Lapidary
Leather craft
Macramé
Map making
Marionettes
Masks
Metal craft
  Art metal, copper foil, copper enameling, etching, jewelry making

Model craft
  Airplane models, car models, railroad models, ship models
Nature craft
  Corn husks, leaves, mounting, pine cones, pine needles, stone, walnuts
Needle craft
  Crocheting, embroidery (needle, liquid), hook rugs, knitting, millinery, quilting, sewing, tapestries
Paper craft
  Cardboard, paper bag craft
Papier-maché
Photography
Plaster of Paris
Plastics
Poster making
Pottery
Push mobile
Rug making
Sand craft
Scrapbook
Shell craft
Silk screening
Spatter printing
Stagecraft
Stenciling
Tin can craft
Toy making
Weaving (cord, rope)
Woodwork
  Antique refinishing, birdhouse building, cabinet making, chair caneing, furniture refinishing, games, rustic furniture, wood burning

DANCE

Acrobatic
American
  Round, social (ballroom), square, tap
Ballet
Clog
Creative
Folk
Interpretive

DRAMA

Amateur programs
Barn dances
Carnivals
Ceremonials
Charades
Chautauqua
Children's theatre
Choral speech
Creative dramatics
Drama appreciation
Dramatic games
Dramatic stunts
Dramatizations
Family dramatics
Fashion shows
Festivals
Grand opera
Impersonations
Informal dramatizations
Little theatre group
Making scenery
Marionettes
Minstrel shows
Mock trials
Monologue
Musical dramas and comedy

One act plays
Pageants
Pantomimes
Peep shows
Play production
Play reading
Play writing
Puppetry
Shadowgraphs
Shadow plays
Skits
Stagecraft
Story reading
Story telling
Stunts
Tableaux
Theatre in the round
Three act plays
Traveling theatre
Vaudeville acts
Water ballet
Water pageant

MUSIC AND RHYTHM

Acappella choirs
Action songs
Amateur programs
Band
Band competition
Barbershop quartets
Cantatas
Choral groups
Christmas caroling
Community sings
Drum and bugle corps
Fife and drum corps
Folk songs
Folk festival
Glee clubs
Harmonica bands
Kazoo bands
Mandolin and guitar groups
Musical games
Music appreciation clubs
Music study clubs
Old fiddlers contest
Opera groups
Operettas
Orchestras
Quartets
Singing games
Song festival
Rhythm bands
Symphony orchestras
Whistling groups
Ukulele groups

NATURE AND OUTINGS

Astronomy
Beach parties
Bee culture
Birdhouse building
Bird walks
Boating and canoeing
Camping
  Day, overnight, group, family
Caring for pets
Center aquarium
Coasting
Cookery
Clam bakes
Collecting
  Flowers, insects, leaves, minerals, shells, stones
Dog obedience
Entomology

Exploring or excursions
Fishing and fishing clubs
Flower shows
Flower pressing
Fruit raising
Gardening
Garden show
Hiking, hiking clubs
Hobbies
Horticulture
Hunting, hunting clubs
Indian lore
Marshmallow roast
Mounting specimens
Nature crafts
Nature games
Nature museums
Nature poetry
Nature study (animals, birds, etc.)
Nature trails
Ornithology
Pet shows
Photography
Picnicking
Pigeon clubs
Playground zoos
Snow tracking
Trailing
Traveling zoo, museum
Treasure hunts
Tree clubs
Wiener roasts
Woodcraft
Zoology

SPORTS AND GAMES

Archery
Apparatus work
Athletic tests
Banquet for players
Baseball
Basketball
Bicycling
Bicycle polo
Billiards
Boating and canoeing
Bobsledding
Boccie
Bowling
Bowling on the green
Box hockey
Cage ball
Calisthenics
Captain ball
Chess, checkers
Clock golf
Crew racing
Cricket
Croquet
Cross country running
Curling
Deck tennis
Diving
Dodge ball
Dog sledding
End ball
Fencing
Field events
  Discus throwing, javelin throwing, jumping, pole vautling, shot put, etc.
Field hockey
Figure skating
Fly casting
Football
Games
  Story and song, skill and competition, social and party
Goal-hi
Golf

Gymnastics
Handball
Hopscotch
Horseback riding
Horsemanship
Horseshoes
Ice hockey
Ice sailing
Ice skating
Jogging
Judo
Junior Olympics
Karate
Kickball
Kite flying
Lacrosse
Lariat throwing
Lifesaving
Longball
Marbles
Model boat sailing
Newcomb
O'Leary
Paddle tennis
Ping Pong
Pistol shooting
Polo
Pool
Progressive games party
Pyramid building
Quoits
Rifle shooting
Roller skating
Roller skate hockey
Rope jumping
Roque
Sailing
Scooter racing
Scuba diving
Shuffleboard
Skiing
Ski-jumping
Soccer
Softball
Speedball
Squash
Surfing
Swimming
Tennis
Tether ball
Tobogganing
Top spinning
Touch football
Track events
Trampolene
Trap shooting
Tumbling
Volleyball
Water polo
Water skiing
Wrestling

EDUCATIONAL ACTIVITIES

Book reviews, book clubs
Charm schools
Creative writing
Debating
Excursions
Foreign language study
Forums
Listening groups
Lectures
Poetry club
Reading
Story and play writing
Traffic schools

SERVICE ACTIVITIES

Board and committee work
Camp counselors (junior)
Clerical volunteers
Club leaders
Costumes workers
Entertainers (sharing talents)
Hosts and hostesses
Judges and officials
Junior leaders
Master of ceremonies
News reporters
Library helpers
Visiting the sick
Volunteer leaders

SPECIAL EVENTS

Amateur circus
Anniversary programs
Arctic carnival
Arts and crafts exhibits
Bicycle rodeo
Christmas pageant
Dance review
Doll show
Exposition
Fairyland program
Fun night
Halloween program
Harvest festival
Hobby show
Holiday program
Neighborhood fair
Open house
Pageant
Play day
Playground radio
Science fair
Talent and variety show
Vehicle show
Water pageant
Winter carnival
World's fair

MISCELLANEOUS ACTIVITIES

Birthday parties
Block parties
Bridge and social card games
Candy pull
Children's village
Coin collecting
Corn roast
Easter egg hunt
Family reunion
Father and son dinner
Hobbies, collecting, etc.
Magic programs
Mother and daughter dinner
Socials
Treasure hunts
Visit to parks, museums, etc.

APPENDIX J

Examples of Forms

ATTENDANCE FORM Page 1

DEPARTMENT OF RECREATION AND PARKS

WEEKLY REPORT

Week Ending ____________ 19 ________________ Center

Daily Attendance	*Sun*		*Mon*			*Tues*			*Wed*			*Thurs*			*Fri*			*Sat*			*Weekly Total*
	Aft.	Eve.	A.M.	Aft.	Eve.	A.M.	Aft.	Eve.	A.M.	Aft.	Eve.	A.M.	Aft.	Eve.	A.M.	Aft.	Eve.	A.M.	Aft.	Eve.	
Boys																					
Girls																					
Men (over 16)																					
Women (over 16)																					
Total Participation																					
Spectators																					
Total Attendance																					
Weather*																					

Organized Groups	*DIFFERENT INDIVIDUALS PARTICIPATING*				*SPECIAL FACILITIES REPORT*			
	Boys	*Girls*	*Adults*	*Total*	*FACILITY*	*Participants*	*Spectators*	*Total*
Total Enrollment					Badminton Courts			
Sports and Games					Baseball Diamonds			
Dramatics					Basketball Courts			
Arts and Crafts					Football Fields			
Music and Rhythm					Hockey Fields			
Nature					Horseshoe Courts			
					Softball Diamonds			
					Tennis Courts			
					Volleyball Courts			
					Gymnasiums			
					Picnic Areas			
TOTAL					TOTAL			

*F – Fair; T – Threatening; R – Rain; S – Snow; W – Wet grounds; H – Hot; C – Cold.

ATTENDANCE FORM

Page 2

SPECIAL FEATURES HELD DURING WEEK

Event	*Day*	*Hour*	*Participants Spectators*	*Total*

SPECIAL FEATURES PLANNED FOR NEXT WEEK

Event	*Day*	*Hour*	*No. Taking Part*	*Directed By*

NEIGHBORHOOD VISITS AND COMMUNITY CONTACTS

Nature Of Contact	*Made By Whom*	*Purpose And Results*

SUPERVISORS' VISITS

Name	*Date*	*Time Arrival*	*Time Departure*	*Purpose Of Visit And Help Received*

Number of Volunteer Leaders: Junior ______ Junior Assistants ______ Adults ______

Number Major Accidents: ______________ Number Minor Accidents: ______________

Number Registered This Week: Boys __________ Girls _________ Adults ___________

Number Advisory Council Meetings: ________________________ List Topics Discussed:

____

____

____

Repairs Needed: ____

____

____

____

Comments: ____

____

____

____

Signed: ______________________________

DETAILED PERSONNEL SCHEDULE
BUDGET – FISCAL YEAR 1975-76

Page ______

______ (Spending Unit) ______ (Department Or Agency)

		ACTUAL 1973-74			ESTIMATED 1974-75			PROPOSED 1975-76			ANALYSIS 1975-76	
(1) *Classification*	(2) *Pay Range*	(3) *No.*	(4) *Man-Years of Performance*	(5) *Total Salary Costs*	(6) *No.*	(7) *Man-Years of Performance*	(8) *Total Salary Costs*	(9) *No.*	(10) *Man-Years of Performance*	(11) *Total Salary Costs*	(12) *Step Increase*	(13) *Man-Years Increase (Decrease)*

DETAILED EXPENSE SCHEDULE
BUDGET – FISCAL YEAR 1975-76

Page ________

________ (Spending Unit)

________ (Department Or Agency)

Object Code Object of Expenditure Item And Quantity	*Actual Expenditure Fiscal 1972-73*	*Actual Expenditure Fiscal 1973-74*	*Budget Fiscal 1974-75*	REVISED ESTIMATE 1974-75			*Requested Fiscal 1975-76*	*Explanation*
				Six Months Actual	*Six Months Estimate*	*Total*		
1	2	3	4	5	6	7	8	9

DESCRIPTION OF SERVICE IMPROVEMENT
BUDGET – FISCAL YEAR ________

Page ______

____
(Spending Unit)

____
(Work Program Number And Title)

____
(Department Or Agency)

Purpose And Justification		
Expenditures By Character And Object	*Budget Year*	*Second Year*
1000 Personal Services	$	$
3000 Supplies and Materials		
2500 Maintenance of Equipment and Structures		
4100 Rents and Utilities		
6100 Replacement of Equipment		
6280 Additional Equipment		
Other (Specify)		
Total Cost	$	$

CHARACTER AND OBJECT SUMMARY
BUDGET - FISCAL YEAR 1975-76

Page ______

______ (Spending Unit)

______ (Department Or Agency)

Description	*Expenditures*		
	Actual Fiscal Yr. 1973-74	*Estimate Fiscal Yr. 1974-75*	*Budget Fiscal Yr. 1975-76*
General Fund			
Expenditures By Character And Object			
Man-Years of Employment			
1000 Personal Services			
2100 Communications and Transportation			
2300 Printing, Binding, and Publications			
2500 Maintenance of Equipment and Structure			
3000 Supplies and Materials			
4100 Rents and Utilities			
4200 Insurance			
5000 Interest, Pensions, Grants			
6100 Equipment, Furniture, Tools			
6150 Automotive Equipment			
6180 Replacement of Equipment			
6270 Trees and Shrubs			
6290 Sundry Charges			
6300 Land			
Total			

EXPENDITURE SUMMARY
BUDGET – FISCAL YEAR 1975-76

Page ______

______ (Spending Unit) ______ (Department Or Agency)

Description	*Expenditures*		
	Actual Fiscal Yr. 1973-74	*Estimate Fiscal Yr. 1974-75*	*Budget Fiscal Yr. 1975-76*
General Fund			
Annual Appropriation.	$	$	$
Additional Appropriation.			
Change of Appropriation by Transfer:			
Total *General Fund* Appropriation.	$	$	$
Less: Unexpended Balance.			
Net Total *General Fund* Expenditures.	$	$	$
Expenditures By Spending Units			

CAPITAL IMPROVEMENT PROGRAM 1974-1979

Page ______

Project Class:		*Project No. & Title:*						
PROJECT ESTIMATE		*Estimated Total Cost*	*Prior Authorizations*	*Budget Year 1974-1975*	*Fiscal Years*			
					1975-1976	*1976-77*	*1977-78*	*1978-79*
PRIMARY PROJECT COST								
ANCILLARY PROJECTS								
TOTAL PROJECT COST								

Project Description

Project Justification

Programming Of Project By Years

Relationship To Other Projects

Improvement Project History

Effects On Operating Budget

Land Requirements And Relationship To Master Plan

CAPITAL IMPROVEMENT PROGRAM
PROJECT CALCULATION AND WORK SHEET*

Page ______

Project Class:	*Project No. and Title*						
	Estimated Total Cost	*Prior Authorizations*	*Budget Year*	*Fiscal Years*			
1. *Land:*							
1. Appraisal Fees							
2. Demolition Cost							
3. Purchase Price							
Total							
2. *Architectural And Engineering:*							
1. Consultant Study							
2. Architectural Fee							
3. Engineering and Testing							
Total							
3. *Construction:*							
1. Building/Facility							
2. Built-in Equipment							
3. Site Work							
Total							
4. *Equipment and Furniture:*							
1. Equipment – Not in Contract							
2. Furniture							
3. Carpets, Blinds, Etc.							
Total							
5. *City And Off-site Costs:*							
1. Clerk of Works, Engineering, Inspection							
2. Off-Site Improvements							
3. Utilities							
4. Landscaping							
5. Miscellaneous							
Total							
6. *Contingency:*							
1. Contingency							
Total Primary Project Cost							
Financial Assistance:							
Federal Government							
State Government							
Gift or Bequest							
Total							
Net Cost:							

**Reprinted by permission of the City of Richmond, Virginia.*

Index